A NATION OF CHANGE AND NOVELTY

A NATION OF CHANGE AND NOVELTY

Radical politics, religion and literature in seventeenth-century England

'England, that Nation of Change and Novelty'

– La Nuche, a 'Spanish courtesan' in *The Rovers: Or, The Banished Cavaliers,* by Aphra Behn

CHRISTOPHER HILL

London and New York

First published 1990 by Routledge
11 New Fetter Lane, London EC4P 4EE

Simultaneously published in the USA and Canada
by Routledge
a division of Routledge, Chapman and Hall, Inc.
29 West 35th Street, New York, NY 10001

Typeset in 10/12 pt Baskerville by
Colset Private Limited, Singapore
Printed in Great Britain by
T. J. Press (Padstow) Ltd, Padstow, Cornwall

British Library Cataloguing in Publication Data

Hill, Christopher *1912–*
A nation of change and novelty: Radical politics,
religion and literature in seventeenth-century England.
1. England, 1603–1714
I. Title
942.06

ISBN 0-415-04833-8

Library of Congress Cataloging in Publication Data

Also available

Dedicated to the memory of Tim Curtis

CONTENTS

Preface   ix
Acknowledgements   xi

1 INTRODUCTION   1

2 THE PLACE OF THE SEVENTEENTH-
  CENTURY REVOLUTION IN ENGLISH
  HISTORY   6

3 POLITICAL DISCOURSE IN EARLY
  SEVENTEETH-CENTURY ENGLAND   24

4 ARCHBISHOP LAUD'S PLACE IN
  ENGLISH HISTORY   56

5 THE WORD 'REVOLUTION'   82

6 GOVERNMENTS AND PUBLIC
  RELATIONS: REFORMATION TO
  'GLORIOUS' REVOLUTION   102

7 GERRARD WINSTANLEY AND FREEDOM   114

8 SEVENTEENTH-CENTURY ENGLISH
  RADICALS AND IRELAND   133

9 ABOLISHING THE RANTERS   152
    Postscript 1   191
    Postscript 2   193

10 LITERATURE AND THE ENGLISH
   REVOLUTION   195

vii

CONTENTS

11 THE RESTORATION AND LITERATURE   218

12 HISTORY AND THE PRESENT   244

Index   258

PREFACE

I have been talking and writing about the English Revolution for fifty years now. The pieces in this volume sum up some conclusions which I have arrived at over this period. They deal with the Revolution itself, and with historical writing about the Revolution. Historical fashions change with political fashions; it is difficult for historians to avoid writing either contemporary history or autobiography: some do not even try. I have tried; but the reader will no doubt detect beams in my eye where I have spotted motes in others'.

In writing these essays I have incurred many debts. I was invited to give lectures at the Folger Library, Washington, at the Centre for Seventeenth-century Studies, Durham, at Le Moyne College, New York State, at King Alfred's College, Winchester, at St Patrick's College, Maynooth, to the South Place Ethical Society at Conway Hall. I benefited by the subsequent lively discussions, and am especially grateful for generous hospitality to Barbara Mowat and Lena Orlin of the Folger Library, to Roger Richardson at Winchester, to Bill Shaw at Le Moyne, to Professors Corish and Canny whilst I was at Maynooth, and to Nicholas Hyman of Conway Hall. Hugh Stretton, Wilfrid Prest and other members of the Adelaide History Department made a term which Bridget and I spent teaching there a most enjoyable experience, as did Margaret Jacob and other friends at Eugene Lang College, the New School for Social Research, New York.

I have tried to acknowledge in footnotes specific debts when I am aware of them. I am particularly grateful to Frank McGregor and Barry Reay for help with Chapter 9, to Margot Heinemann for help with Chapters 10 and 11; and to the late Leslie Morton for guidance on Chapter 8. I owe much to the kindness of Penelope Corfield, Valerie Drake, Dena Goldberg, Ann Hughes, Willie Lamont, Michael Roberts, Sir Keith Thomas, Michael Wilding, David Zaret and to students of my graduate seminar at the New School for Social Research. Sue Roe was a tower of strength and a haven of refuge. My greatest indebtedness, as always, is to Bridget. I can never find words to say it adequately, but she knows best that but for her nothing would get done.

The book is dedicated to the memory of Tim Curtis, late Deputy Director of the Lancashire Polytechnic, in inadequate acknowledgement of my debt to him over many years. His combination of wit with wisdom, the bravura of his style and the common sense which underlay his epigrams – all these made discussion with him perennially exciting. His death at the age of forty is a terrible loss. He had published little, not even his splendid thesis on crime in Elizabethan England from which I quote on p. 19, though I hope this may soon appear. He dedicated his superb energies and political skills to promoting the welfare of the Lancashire Polytechnic, with great success; and there he will be long remembered. I count myself fortunate to have known him so well. I was honoured by being invited to deliver the first Tim Curtis Memorial Lecture in Preston in December 1988: the first chapter in this book is the text of the lecture I gave.

I have observed the usual conventions. Seventeenth-century spelling, capitalization and punctuation have been modernized except in titles of books. Dates are in the Old Style, but the year is taken as beginning on 1 January. Place of publication of all books quoted is London unless otherwise stated.

ACKNOWLEDGEMENTS

Earlier versions of some of the pieces in this volume were originally published elsewhere. I am grateful for permission to include them here. 'Political discourse in early seventeenth-century England' appeared in a Festschrift for Ivan Roots, *Politics and People in Revolutionary England*, edited by C. Jones, M. Newitt and S. Roberts, Oxford, Blackwell, 1986. 'The word ''Revolution'' ' was published in *For Veronica Wedgwood, These: Studies in Seventeenth-Century History*, edited by R. Ollard and P. Tudor-Craig, Collins, 1986. 'The place of the seventeenth-century Revolution in English history' was delivered as the first Tim Curtis Memorial Lecture at the Lancashire Polytechnic, Preston, on 6 December 1988. 'Archbishop Laud's place in English history' was a paper given to a Folger Shakespeare Library seminar in October 1985. Chapter 7 was a paper given to a conference at King Alfred's College, Winchester, in the summer of 1984. The conference papers were printed in *Freedom and the English Revolution: Essays in History and Literature*, edited by R.C. Richardson and G.M. Ridden, Manchester University Press, 1986. Chapter 8 was a paper read before the Irish Conference of Historians at Maynooth in June 1983. These papers were printed as *Radicals, Rebels and Establishments*, edited by P.J. Corish, Appletree Press, Belfast, 1985. Chapter 10, a paper given at a Conference held at the Centre for Seventeenth-century Studies in Durham, July 1985, was printed in *The Seventeenth Century*, January 1986, I, no. 1. 'Abolishing the Ranters' is expanded from a review in *History Workshop Journal*, 1987, 24, of Colin Davis, *Fear, Myth and History: the Ranters and the Historians*, Cambridge University Press, 1986. 'History and the Present' was a Conway Memorial Lecture given at Conway Hall on 26 April 1989 and separately published by the South Place Ethical Society. I have incorporated a few sentences from an article in *The Guardian* of 15 July 1989. Chapter 11, delivered at a forum on 'Salvation and Damnation in the Religion and Literature of the 17th century' at Le Moyne College, New York State in October 1985, is due to be published in *Praise Disjoined: Changing Patterns of Salvation in Seventeenth Century Literature*, edited by W.P. Shaw, New York, 1990.

1

Introduction

> Before you study the history, study the historian. . . . The serious historian is the one who recognizes the historically conditioned character of all values, not the one who claims for his own values an objectivity beyond history.
>
> E.H. Carr, *What is History?*, 1961, pp. 38, 78

Carr's advice is wise. My prepossessions will no doubt become clear to the reader; but it may be fair to start by stating some of the considerations that were in my mind during the years in which these essays were written.

First, I remain convinced that the seventeenth-century English Revolution was a decisive event in the history of England and of Europe, comparable in world significance with the French and Russian Revolutions. When I was young the with-it thing was to discover (or invent) a revolution: the Tudor revolution in government, industrial revolutions in the sixteenth and even thirteenth centuries. Today, quite the other way, it is smart for forward youths that would appear to abolish revolutions, not to invent them. The English Revolution, the French Revolution, the Industrial Revolution have all been whisked away: the Russian Revolution is no doubt on somebody's hit list. Now we should not take these fashions too seriously: they go in cycles, and it is no doubt my age that makes me a little sceptical of latter-day 'revisionist' historians who try to convince us that there was no revolution in seventeenth-century England, or that if there was it had no long-term causes or consequences. Their case has lost some of its freshness and fervour these days. I think the enterprise was ill-conceived, but it had some useful results. We have all learnt a great deal from Conrad Russell and John Morrill. But their work, with all its merits, seems to me to demonstrate

1

that if you concentrate narrowly on a short period of history, it is possible to suffer a loss of perspective. Events are more likely to seem determined by chance or by the accidents of personality. From this I would conclude that it is important to stand back from the trees and look at the wood as a whole: which I have tried to do in my Chapters 2 and 4.

It also made me more than ever aware of the dangers of dwelling exclusively on state papers or debates in parliament for our understanding of what is going on in English society. A speech in the House of Commons is arguing a case; so are most state papers. Their object is to convince, not to convey abstract truth to the historian. They take for granted many things which now escape us; their mode of expression is governed by convention, but also by anxiety not to offend. They will depict some things in a more favourable light than they do in their private diaries. They no more give us an 'objective' view of early seventeenth-century society than Jacobean dramatists do in their plays. The latter were writing to entertain but they had to be plausible. Falstaff is no doubt a caricature, but he caricatures persons whom the audience would recognize. The fact that so many plays deal not with England but with countries far away in time and space, or both, made it safer for the playwright to comment on English events and institutions. 'To disguise the King as a Roman . . . would not necessarily provide adequate cover', writes Professor Dena Goldberg in a wise study of Webster's plays; and he instances Ben Jonson's *Sejanus*. But he gives examples where Webster and others were able to get away with highly critical comments on their society. 'It may be that most of the weeping over the fall of great men towards the end of the play represents nothing but the efforts of prudent writers to get a subversive play past the censor'.[1]

England before 1640 was no doubt a highly inefficient police state by modern standards. But it was a society in which censorship prevailed, and in which incorrect thoughts about religion or politics could bring very unpleasant consequences. In such a society silence by no means implies assent. In attempting to understand it we must get below official and public discourse. Stress on the importance of public political documents helps those who wish to deny that there was an English Revolution, or that it had any causes. There was a

---

1. D. Goldberg, *Between Worlds: A Study of the Plays of John Webster*, Waterloo, Canada, 1988, pp. 152–3, 146.

great deal of discontent and rebelliousness in the society, which the literature, plays especially, helps us to understand. And there is much literary evidence from the years of liberty after 1640 which aids us in estimating the state of opinion before that date.

Such considerations underlie my Chapter 3, in which I suggest that we should not take public speech at face value: what is said in private is more likely to represent the real views of the speaker. In Chapter 5 I try to illustrate the importance of considering words in the context in which they are used.

History is not, cannot be, value-free. Innocent-sounding phrases like 'pre-industrial', 'early modern', 'backward economies', are heavily loaded with ideology. They *assume* that all societies go through the same sequence of economic development, and are to be evaluated according to the progress they have made on this inevitable and desirable path. This overestimation of the economic and under-estimation of the political and ideological wouldn't do much harm if it was restricted to historians: but it influences policies of the great industrialized powers today, of the World Bank and those considering 'aid' for the Third World. They know what will be best for Third World countries in their struggle to catch up with the developed 'West'. If the inhabitants of a Third World country do not agree, that shows how backward they still unfortunately remain: they must be forced to become free, to be 'modernized'.[2]

As an example of the importance of comparative history I instance the failure of the peasantry in the English Revolution to win the security of land tenure which French peasants won in and because of the French Revolution (Chapter 2). How do we explain the relative lack of violence and terror in the English Revolution by contrast with the French and Russian Revolutions? It will hardly do just to say that we are nicer than Frenchmen and Russians. Was it due to the absence of foreign intervention? Violence in Ireland and the colonies contrasts sharply with relative tolerance at home. Or was it due to belief that Christ's kingdom was coming on earth in the last of the great religious revolutions? But Christianity has led to violence and terror elsewhere and in other periods.

This connects with the question, why has England no national patriotic holiday? The United States celebrates 4 July; France has its

---

2. Cf. p. 20 below. See P. Dockès and B. Rosier, *L'Histoire Ambiguë: Croissance et développement en question*, Paris, 1988, pp. 246–50. See also Ch. 12 below.

Bastille Day, the USSR 7 November. The only comparable anniversary in England is 5 November, when king and parliament were preserved from 'Guy Fawkes' treason'. At the time of the Popish Plot, celebration of 5 November came to be an occasion of popular solidarity, together with Queen Elizabeth's Day, 17 November. I suspect that both may have been popular celebrations rather than ones favoured by governments, just as the London populace showed its joy at the return of Prince Charles *unmarried* from his trip to Spain in 1623 by lighting bonfires everywhere in the streets, spontaneously: a far better show than when bonfires were *ordered* for his original landing in Spain. Bonfires proliferated, again unordered, when Charles I accepted the Petition of Right. Already the Protestant state and parliament are more popular than the person of the monarch.[3] But in England the word 'popular' came to mean 'vulgar', and by the nineteenth century blatant anti-catholicism, having lost its political significance, was becoming embarrassing. Guy Fawkes' Day became a festive non-political occasion; the left in England lost one of its patriotic traditions.

A more general point arises from my first chapter. In postwar Germany historians have been wrestling with the Nazi inheritance.[4] Should we not come to terms with our imperial history starting with the history of Anglo-Irish relations? What about the responsibility of the English and the Americans for slavery and its consequent racialism? The British Empire achieved many good things, but its strength and prosperity owed much to slavery and the slave trade. Whom but ourselves can we blame for atrocities which have poisoned the atmosphere of the world for four centuries? Alas: we haven't even got round to sufficient sense of responsibility and guilt to look for someone else to pass the buck on to. Post-imperial societies should think of these things more than they do; and it is impossible to think of them seriously without thinking historically. But they are not D.Phil. subjects.[5]

So the pieces in this volume may be more contentious than they appear. I am putting forward my own views, sometimes in conscious opposition to the views of other historians. But I hope I have remembered Laurence Sterne's dictum that 'heat is in proportion to

---

3. See pp. 45–6 below. For Dryden, Queen Elizabeth's Day was 'the feast the factious rabble keep', J. Dryden, *Poetical Works*, 1886, p. 254.
4. Geoff Eley, 'Nazism, politics and public memory: thoughts on the West German *Historikerstreit*', *Past and Present*, 1988, 121, *passim*. See p. 246 below.
5. See pp. 246–7 below.

the want of true knowledge'.[6] No historian, and no type of history, has a monopoly of truth: the writing of history is a co-operative, cumulative task, to which we all have to contribute to the best of our ability.

6. Laurence Sterne, *The Life and Opinions of Tristram Shandy, Gentleman*, World's Classics, p. 239.

2

The place of the seventeenth-century Revolution in English history

> Ignorance of remote causes disposeth men to attribute all events to the causes immediate and instrumental: for these are all the causes they perceive.
>
> Thomas Hobbes, *Leviathan* (1651), ed. C.B. Macpherson, Penguin, p. 166

I

My aim is to try to understand how and why England, a second-class power during the Middle Ages, became top nation in the eighteenth century and the first world industrial power; and why in the sixteenth and seventeenth centuries England did not go the way of the rest of Europe towards absolutism. I think they are two versions of the same question.

In the sixteenth century England seemed to have missed out. Whilst on the continent absolute monarchies – France, Spain, Austria, Portugal – were strengthening their military might, England, as the strongest power in an island, did not need an army to defend its frontiers. Gunpowder, whose use dates from the fifteenth century, made possible a state monopoly of force within the country, and a reduction of private armies; but no English standing army was created to replace them. An army is not useful only for repelling an enemy from your frontiers; it is even more useful for collecting taxation internally. A government with a standing army can tax very nearly as it wishes. The government decides what it wants, and in the last resort the army enforces collection. On the continent absolutism seemed the up-and-coming thing.

In England there was no standing army, no internal police force, and consequently no bureaucracy such as in continental countries

6

collected the taxes which paid for war. England's defence depended on the navy; its main overseas interest was in trading. This was just at a time when, as Bacon observed, the mariner's compass and gunpowder had opened up the world to European trade and European domination. In England Henry VII and Henry VIII reduced the power of the nobility; the gangs of retainers who used to terrorize the countryside added to the surplus of agricultural labourers created by the population explosion of the sixteenth century. There was no lack of personnel who could be employed in the mercantile marine. Noble castles were destroyed, order of sorts was established. In England there was relative internal peace, at a time when religious and international wars were tearing other European countries apart. Because of the government's weakness, England was one of the least-taxed countries in Europe: the gentry were very lightly assessed – hardly surprisingly, since they assessed themselves.

In the sixteenth century the English gentry came to take an increasing interest in sheep farming, in the expanding cloth trade, and in developing English exports. On the continent, younger sons of the landed class found careers in the army, or in the growing bureaucracy. In England, with no army or significant bureaucracy, younger sons had to make their careers elsewhere. They became sea-dogs, pirates; they explored and colonized America; they colonized Ireland in a particularly brutal manner; some actually took part in trade themselves. Or they might take service in continental armies, where there was always employment for them.[1]

In early seventeenth-century parliaments a third of the members of the House of Commons held investments in overseas trading companies. Even more interesting, more than half of these invested in trading companies *after* becoming MPs. Parliament acted as a sort of recruiting ground for business investment from the gentry.[2] In continental absolute monarchies merchants were buying their way into the bureaucracy, purchasing offices rather than re-investing their money in trade or industry. In England offices were not on sale to the same

---

1. See Joan Thirsk, 'Younger sons in the seventeenth century', *History*, 1969, 182, *passim*; N.P. Canny, *The Elizabethan Conquest of Ireland: A Pattern Established, 1565-76*, Hassocks, Sussex, 1976; George Marteen states the case eloquently in Aphra Behn's *The Younger Brother*, Act I, sc. i (posthumously published 1696).
2. T.K. Rabb, *Enterprise and Empire: Merchant and Gentry Investment in the Expansion of England, 1575-1630*, Harvard University Press, 1967, pp. 93-4 and *passim*. There might be other reasons: the Puritan John Preston invested in the East India Co. 'the willinger because estates there were invisible', and so safe from arbitrary taxation (T. Ball, *Life of the Renowned Dr Preston*, 1885, pp. 94-5: first published 1628).

extent; trade and piracy were more speculative but – for the fortunate few – more profitable investments. The nearest England got to a bureaucracy was in the machinery of the church – subordinated to the crown from Henry VIII's reign. The Court of Ecclesiastical Commission was an instrument of government, bishops were royal civil servants, under Laud, ministers of state. In Charles I's reign, and again under his eldest son, bishops were royal agents for the subordination of Scotland. There is at least a partial reason here for Puritanism among the gentry, who resented the independent power of the church's bureaucratic machinery.

But though England prospered economically in the sixteenth century, it slipped behind as a state power, just when Spain and France were building up massive armies. Spain and Portugal seized much of America and parts of south-east Asia to establish world empires; from 1580 to 1640 Spain annexed Portugal and its overseas possessions. Merchants of the tiny Dutch republic were also grabbing a share of world trade and plunder. Henry VII and – for a short time – Henry VIII at the beginning of his reign envisaged the possibility of state-supported western exploration; but this was submerged by Henry VIII's ruinous French wars. These were paid for by the nationalization and immediate privatization of church property which might have financed either the establishment of absolute monarchy or (as radical Protestants urged) a programme of social reform.[3] England's merchants did not get the support from their state that Spanish, Portuguese and Dutch merchants enjoyed. Elizabeth's war against Spain was fought by sea-dogs rather than by the navy. In 1588 England was lucky to defeat the Spanish Armada. The royal navy was small; merchant vessels did most of the fighting.[4] Similarly colonization of Ireland was the achievement of private enterprise rather than of the state.[5] The East India Company, the Virginia Company, the Massachusetts Bay Company, the Providence Island Company, all had to fend for themselves in their respective zones.

In 1618 the Thirty Years War broke out, the first European war involving all the major powers. A Catholic victory at one time seemed probable: England's turn would come next if Protestants on the

3. J.J. Scarisbrick, *Henry VIII*, 1968, pp. 21, 123–5, 453–6, 507–26.
4. W.T. MacCaffrey, *Queen Elizabeth and the Making of Policy, 1572–1588*, Princeton University Press, 1981, p. 336.
5. Karen Ordahl Kuppermann, 'Errand into the Indies: Puritan colonization from Providence through the Western Design', *William and Mary Quarterly*, 1988, 3rd series, 45, pp. 81–2, 97–8; Canny, *Elizabethan Conquest*, op. cit., *passim*. See Ch. 8 below.

continent were defeated. The gentry whose forebears had plundered the monasteries were as reluctant to envisage the restoration of catholicism as were more disinterestedly pious Protestants. But before this threat England was powerless because its government had no money. James tried hard to make a virtue out of necessity by mediating, but neither side took him seriously.

There was an economic problem too. The Thirty Years War caused English merchants to lose markets for their main export, cloth, in north Germany and the Baltic lands, cold countries needing heavy English cloth. The way forward for England's clothing industry, informed commentators agreed, was by developing the 'new draperies', lighter cloths which could be sold to Mediterranean countries. But this called for protection of English merchants against Turkish, North African and other pirates who swarmed all over the Mediterranean and indeed were taking English ships in the Channel and slaves from southern English coasts. The governments of James and Charles were not able to give the necessary protection. In other ways too they failed to come up to expectations. After James had signed peace with Spain in 1604 English merchants were left to their own fate when they ran into trouble in the Spanish West Indies. Ralegh was executed in 1618 as a sign of James's determination not to permit the commercial and colonial aspirations of sea-dogs and merchants to upset his design for an alliance with Spain. The profitable contraband trade to Trinidad and Tobago had to be abandoned when it threatened to hamper negotiations for a Spanish marriage for Prince Charles.[6] In the 1630s Charles I ordered English merchants to stay out of the Mediterranean because he could not protect them there. The road out of the depression of the twenties and thirties for the English clothing industry seemed to be blocked by the government's weakness.

The final straw came in the late 1630s when war broke out between England and Scotland – a seventh-rate power if we class England as second or third rate. A Scottish army invaded the north of England, and the government could not drive them out. Financial collapse forced the king to summon parliament after eleven years' intermission. The Venetian ambassador in November 1641 told his government that England had become a country useless to all the world

6. Joyce Lorimer, 'The English contraband tobacco trade from Trinidad and Guiana, 1590–1617', in K.R. Andrews, N.P. Canny and P.E.H. Hair (eds) *The Westward Enterprise: English Activities in Ireland, the Atlantic and America, 1480–1650*, Liverpool University Press, 1978, pp. 142–4, 150.

and consequently of no consideration.[7] Simultaneously Ireland revolted against English rule and exploitation. Those who had been offended by these feeble policies, feeble because of lack of finance, included Protestants, patriots and merchants: the three interests which coalesced against Charles in the 1640s.

Yet to forward-looking Englishmen the opportunities seemed great. Spain's seizure of the Portuguese empire had overtaxed her naval strength; and she was fully occupied with the Thirty Years War. Her empire seemed wide open to naval attack. But a Revolution was necessary before England possessed a government committed to aggressive commercial imperialist policies, and able to raise adequate taxes to implement them. Crown and parliament made many attempts to agree on financial reorganization – in 1610, in the 1620s, in the Long Parliament: they broke down every time. Charles I's ship money in the 1630s was based on a reassessment, but since this was unilaterally imposed it was unacceptable to those whom parliament represented. No agreement could be reached in 1640–1.

In the 1620s there had been quarrels over the objects of the war which parliament was being asked to finance: in effect the Commons were demanding control of foreign policy. The crown was unable to improve revenue from its lands; instead it sold them, squandering capital. It lived from hand to mouth, allowing its civil servants to pay themselves by corruption.[8] It was only after the Revolution of the 1640s that this situation changed. The Long Parliament declared taxation levied without consent of parliament illegal. Taxes particularly obnoxious to the monied men were abolished – monopolies, forced loans, arbitrary fines, impositions – and were replaced by taxes imposed by parliament. The assessment, a land tax ironically based on the reassessment for ship money, lasted right through to the eighteenth century; the excise, a value added tax imitated from the Dutch, lasted even longer. These taxes fell more heavily on the landed class and the poor than on the middling sort which had hitherto borne the main financial burden.

---

7. *Calendar of State Papers, Venetian, 1640-2*, pp. 77–8.
8. Derek Hirst appropriately quotes Keynes as saying that in such a society corruption is the most efficient form of taxation (*Authority and Conflict in England, 1603-1658*, 1986, p. 124; cf. pp. 172–4).

II

As a result of this financial reorganization the English state suddenly had far greater financial resources at its disposal than ever before. It was able to indulge in a quite new foreign policy and a quite new economic policy. In 1651 the Navigation Act was passed, declaring the whole British empire a closed trading area, in which only English merchants were entitled to trade, and to take the profits of trade. Foreigners were excluded unless they had special licences, for which they had to pay and which as time went on became fewer and fewer.

English merchants had wanted a Navigation Act for a very long time, indeed since the late fourteenth century. The idea had been seriously canvassed in the 1620s as a way out of the economic problems created by the Thirty Years War and the collapse of markets in northern Europe. As early as March 1642 the Long Parliament was discussing a Navigation Act.[9] But the effectiveness of an act shutting foreign merchants out of the British empire would depend on sea power. The Dutch were virtually monopolizing trade with English colonies, and they had a powerful navy; their republic was run by and for merchants. Before 1640 no English government would have been capable of taking them on. Between 1652 and 1673 the Dutch were forced in three wars to accept the exclusion of their merchants from the British empire. In the middle fifties, after the financial reorganization and the passing of the Navigation Act, Admiral Robert Blake's fleet swept the Mediterranean, cleared it of pirates, and made it a safe area for English merchants to trade in. Oliver Cromwell's Western Design of 1655 – the first use of English state power for transatlantic conquest – led to the establishment of much more secure bases in the West Indies, which guaranteed the safety of English merchants and colonizers in Central and North America.[10] Cromwell in 1657 annexed Dunkirk, and suppressed piracy in the English Channel. Portugal had liberated its empire from Spain in 1640, and in 1654 Cromwell signed a treaty presaging a long period of alliance, in which the English navy secured Portugal and its colonies from reconquest by Spain. Among other things this alliance transformed the drinking habits of the English upper classes. In 1634 James Howell observed that Portugal

9. V.F. Snow and A.S. Young (eds), *The Private Journals of the Long Parliament, 7 March to 1 June 1642*, Yale University Press, 1987, pp. 51–2.
10. For the economic importance of the conquest of Jamaica see Nuala Zahedieh, 'Trade, plunder, and economic development in early English Jamaica, 1655–1689', *Economic History Review*, 1986, 2nd series, 39, pp. 205–22.

produced no wines worth importing;[11] a century later port was the wine on which patriotic English gentlemen got drunk. French claret and Spanish canary were out. From the later seventeenth century English trade not only to America and the West Indies but also to the East Indies and Africa was monopolized by English merchants.

So the state in the 1650s, on the basis of this financial reorganization, took over from private enterprise. In Ireland colonization had for the two preceding generations been mainly left to private individuals; it was, said Elizabeth's Lord Deputy Sir Henry Sidney, 'no subject's enterprise: a prince's purse and power must do it'.[12] But no prince before the 1640s had a full enough purse, still less sufficient military power. An act of parliament of 1642 proposed to finance the reconquest of Ireland by a public subscription raised on the security of lands to be confiscated from the Irish. All this changed when the republican state took over. With the extremely brutal conquest by Cromwell, the transplantation of large numbers of Irish men and women, Ireland became a colony to be exploited by Protestant Englishmen. This again was something the old régime had not been able to accomplish.

These policies continued after Charles II was restored to the throne. In 1660 it was parliament which revised the rate of customs – before 1640 a royal prerogative.[13] The king's marriage to Catherine of Braganza has been described as virtually a condition of the restoration. It confirmed the vital Anglo-Portuguese alliance, and brought Bombay (England's first possession in India) and Tangier (the former pirate base in the Mediterranean) as well as consolidating English trading privileges in the vast Portuguese empire. Henceforth wars for markets were conducted by the state: the plunder raids of Elizabethan sea-dogs, the privateering of the Providence Island Company, gave place to state-sponsored colonial wars.[14]

The importance of the slave trade was shown by the close links of the *Royal* African Company with the crown. Parliament was always extremely generous to the navy, but was invariably suspicious of attempts by any government to build up an army – even by William III,

---

11. James Howell, *Familiar Letters, or Epistolae Ho-Elianae*, Temple Classics, II, p. 198.
12. Canny, *Elizabethan Conquest*, op. cit., p. 90; cf. p. 36 below.
13. R. Hutton, *The Restoration: A Political and Religious History of England and Wales, 1658–1667*, Oxford University Press, 1985, p. 148; cf. pp. 218, 234, 258, 263, 279–80.
14. Carole Shammas, 'English commercial development and American colonization, 1560–1620', in Andrews et al., op. cit., p. 170; Ian K. Steele, *The English Atlantic, 1675–1740: An Exploration of Communication and Community*, New York, 1986, *passim*.

the king they had chosen themselves – because of the threat to parliamentary control that an army would constitute. In the early eighteenth century the power of merchants over the English state was great enough for the navy to be used to suppress piracy even by English freebooters.[15] The navy has always been the senior service. Even in the worst periods of repression, England has never known military rule since the seventeenth century.

In France the financial power of the state was hampered by the absence of a long-term public debt. Samuel Pepys had it explained to him in the late 1660s that a bank was incompatible with monarchy because it would give too much power to merchants. The Dutch republic had a bank: England did not. After 1688 England was no longer a monarchy in the sense that France was,[16] and the Bank of England was established to crown parliament's financial power. Henceforth England enjoyed the economic advantages of a republic with the social advantages, for the propertied class, of a monarchy. Governments seem to have had a limitless capacity to borrow from that section of the citizens which was enriching itself equally consistently. Trade expansion was to a considerable extent self-financing; revenue from customs and excise was increasing all the time and paid for the navy. None of this would have been possible without the financial reorganization and the change in the orientation of policy made possible by the Revolution. Before 1640, without a bureaucracy or an army, the government could collect taxes only through the gentry and their subordinate parish élites: the 1630s had shown the impossibility of taxation without their consent for more than a limited period. Those who assessed and collected and paid the taxes enjoyed a virtual veto which, after the Revolution, was institutionalized as parliamentary control of taxation; no taxes could, for long, be collected without this representation.

At the beginning of the century England was a corn-*importing* country, which suffered widespread starvation in bad years like 1597 and 1623.[17] By the end of the century corn production had increased so much that England *exported* corn in normal times; even in bad years like the 1690s, when there was starvation in France and Scotland, there was none in England. A main reason for this was the abolition of

15. R.C. Ritchie, *Captain Kidd and the War against the Pirates*, Harvard University Press, 1986, Ch. 6.
16. See pp. 54–5 below.
17. A.B. Appleby, *Famine in Tudor and Stuart England*, Liverpool University Press, 1978, pp. 141–54.

wardship and feudal tenures. Feudal tenures originated when all big landowners were tenants-in-chief of the crown, holding their lands in return for rendering military service in time of war. This had long ceased to be a military reality, since landowners no longer turned up on the battlefield with their tenants; they paid for wars through taxation. But one survival of the tenure was wardship. If a tenant-in-chief died leaving a minor as his heir, who could not lead his tenants into battle, the crown resumed the lands which he held. Life expectancy was short in the seventeenth century, and it was rare for any big landed family to go for three generations without a minority. When the heir was a minor, his land was at mercy. It might be handed over to some impecunious courtier, some hanger-on of a favourite. During the minority the guardian was free to cut down timber on the estate, to plough up lands or not plough them up according to his own estimated gain; not with any view to long-term profitability. Such 'wicked guardians' 'defaced instead of cultivating their seats, and made every heir a new planter'.[18]

Abolition of feudal tenures had the effect of freeing big landowners from frequent but irregular death duties, heavy enough to disrupt long-term agricultural investment. Production could now be planned; this is the basis of English agricultural prosperity in the late seventeenth and eighteenth centuries, the 'agricultural revolution'. Landowners who could raise the necessary capital invested heavily in agriculture. Agriculture prospered, and England became self-sufficient in food. The link between monied and landed interests was strengthened. H.J. Perkin saw this as 'the decisive change in English history, which made it different from the continent'.[19] Historians who think nothing changed between the early seventeenth and early eighteenth centuries appear to miss this point, among many others.

Abolition of feudal tenures established absolute ownership for the gentry, but lesser men remained dependent on their lords and could be evicted when the latter so willed. Agitation in the forties and fifties to win equal security of tenure, equal property rights, for copyholders, although supported by Levellers and other radicals, was defeated. When the abolition of feudal tenures was confirmed by act of parliament in 1660 copyholders were specifically excluded. Big landowners won both absolute ownership of their land and a free hand to evict

18. Lucy Hutchinson, *Memoirs of the Life of Colonel Hutchinson*, J. Sutherland ed., Oxford University Press, 1973, p. 16.
19. C.G.A. Clay, *Economic Expansion and Social Change: England, 1500–1700*, Cambridge University Press, 1984, I, pp. 123–4; Appleby, *Famine*, op. cit., pp. 159–61; Perkin, 'The social causes of the British industrial revolution', *RHS Transactions*, 1968, p. 135.

tenants whenever convenient for them in the interests of enclosure, consolidation or reorganization of their estates.[20] As his friend Moses Wall put it to Milton in May 1659, copyholders 'care not to improve their land by cost upon it, not knowing how soon themselves or theirs may be outed it' or from their houses.[21] By the eighteenth century the yeomanry who had figured so prominently in the parliamentary armies had all but ceased to exist. We may contrast the security of tenure which French peasants won during and because of the French Revolution.

Agriculture became what Edward Thompson called England's greatest capitalist industry: aristocratic and court privileges, landlords' rights over rivers and so on, which were to delay capitalist advance in pre-revolutionary France and elsewhere, were minimal in England. The change was made at the expense of the poor and led to greater differentiation in the countryside between landlords on the one hand and those on the other who were ceasing to be yeomen tenant farmers and were becoming agricultural labourers. State power was now in the hands of men who put capital accumulation and growth above social welfare. Legislation or case law redefined traditional customs to the disadvantage of the poor – such as gleaning, rights to cut turfs and to collect wood and furze for fuel, and fruits and berries as food. New and fierce laws protected landlords' game. Statutes against depopulating enclosure were repealed. There had been many pamphlets attacking enclosure in the 1640s and 1650s; they ceased after 1660. Expropriated tenants joined the pool of wage labour.

The dates of all these events are interesting. The Navigation Act was passed in 1651, the second year of the republic. Abolition of feudal tenures had been under discussion since at least the early seventeenth century. There was bargaining between crown and parliament over it in 1610, but this broke down because agreement could not be reached on the compensation to be given to the king. It was discussed again in the Long Parliament in April 1642.[22] When the civil war had been won, one of the first things parliament did was to abolish feudal tenures (1645). Eleven years later, when it looked as though the

20. A memorandum submitted to the Council concerning the Midlands Revolt of 1607 had argued that open-field agriculture was incapable of feeding England's rapidly growing population (W. Cunningham, *Growth of the English Industry and Commerce in Modern Times*, Cambridge University Press, 1907, I, pp. 898–9).
21. John Milton, *Complete Prose Works*, D.M. Wolfe ed., Yale University Press, 1953–82, VII, p. 511.
22. Snow and Young, *Private Journals*, op. cit., pp. 202, 206.

Revolution was going to stabilize under a Cromwellian dynasty, parliament passed an Act confirming the abolition. Then the House of Cromwell collapsed, and in April 1660 the Commons received a declaration from Charles II announcing the terms on which he proposed to return to the throne of his fathers. The House agreed to accept him; and the first business they turned to after acceptance was to set up a committee to prepare a bill reconfirming the abolition of feudal tenures – such was the importance they attached to it. [23]

III

The restoration of 1660 established liberty for landlords, but – to quote Moses Wall again – copyholders were 'far more enslaved to the lord of the manor than the rest of the nation is to the King'. [24] England was a freer country than France or Spain, but we must always ask, Freedom for whom to do what? In the later seventeenth century emigration and transportation of homeless vagabonds, together with a declining birth rate, solved the problem of relative over-population of which people had been conscious in the first half of the century. Vagabondage diminished and was replaced by a shortage of 'hands' for industry. The obverse of emergent capitalist agriculture was proletarianization and land hunger. [25]

The Navigation Act created a closed imperial economy in which English merchants were able to buy cheap in order to sell dear at home or abroad. The colonial area was expanding steadily all the time. Sir Josiah Child, who knew about these things, said 'None can deny that the Act of Navigation has and does occasion building and employing three times the number of ships and seamen that otherwise we should do. [26] The grammar is odd, but his meaning is clear. Under the Act there developed a vast re-export trade to Europe in colonial products, new processing industries, sugar and tobacco, and a stimulus to home industries to produce goods for the colonies – again within a closed monopoly market. Industrial development as well as plunder-trade and the agricultural revolution contributed significantly to the accumulation of capital which prepared for the Industrial Revolution.

23. [W. Cobbett] *Parliamentary History of England, 1660–1688*, 1808, IV, p. 30.
24. Milton, *Complete Prose Works*, op. cit., VII, p. 511.
25. David Levine, *Reproducing Families: The Political Economy of English Population History*, Cambridge University Press, 1987, pp. 82–93.
26. J. Child, *New Discourses on Trade*, 1751, pp. 87, xxi. First published 1672.

Merchants' wealth derived very largely from employing slaves in the colonies, and from the slave trade. Charles Davenant in the late seventeenth century said that 'the labour of a slave in the plantations is worth six times as much as the labour of an Englishman at home'.[27] Six times: it is quite a large figure if you think about it. In the early eighteenth century England had got a near-monopoly of the lucrative slave trade, thus realizing the ambitions of John Hawkins under Elizabeth. The charitable Society for the Propagation of the Gospel owned slaves in the West Indies, and would not allow them to be instructed in the principles of Christianity lest they should get ideas above their station.

IV

Before 1660 England had been culturally dependent on Italy, France and Spain. No Englishman had any serious reputation on the continent, with the possible exception of Sir Thomas More. Milton in his *Defences of the People of England* in the fifties was the first Englishman to address Europe. 'I had expected nothing of such quality from an Englishman', wrote a surprised Vossius in 1651.[28] In the scientific revolution especially England lagged behind Italy and France. Bacon was a prophet with little honour in his own country before the 1640s. Charles Webster has demonstrated that scientists were favoured by 'the new men' who came to power in the forties and fifties. 'There was a marked elevation of science and medicine in the public esteem and an acceleration of the pace of scientific development.' This survived the restoration, and was institutionalized in the Royal Society. Margaret Jacob adds that

> the road from the Scientific Revolution to the Industrial Revolution . . . is more straightforward than we may have imagined . . . The culmination of the Scientific Revolution is unthinkable without Newton, Newton is unthinkable without the English Revolution. From being a scientific backwater, England became the centre of the Scientific Revolution.

She speaks of 'the alliance forged . . . between the new science and the landed and commercial élite whose interest prospered in the late

27. C. Davenant, *Discourses on the Public Revenues and on the Trade of England*, 1698, in *Political and Commercial Works*, 1771, II, pp. 17–47 and *Reflections upon the Constitution and Management of the Trade to Africa*, 1709, ibid., V.
28. See my *Milton and the English Revolution*, 1977, p. 182.

17th century'. This alliance was unique to England among European monarchies, and created an intellectual climate which facilitated the Industrial Revolution. Newton got his knighthood; and in the eighteenth century 'man of science' was part of the definition of a gentleman.[29]

Professor Eisenstein suggested that the free press in England and the Netherlands was the only guarantee of the survival of science in the seventeenth century. Galileo was persecuted in Italy, Descartes left France for the Netherlands where he could publish more comfortably, Newton congratulated himself on being born an Englishman. If England had followed continental absolutisms, the emergence of modern science might have been very much delayed.[30] But Charles II wisely became patron of the Royal Society, the gentry flocked in, and their utilitarian interests pushed science in practical directions. The ideas of the European Enlightenment are the ideas of the English Revolution – of Levellers, Hobbes, Harrington, Milton, Boyle, Locke, Newton. Eighteenth-century European intellectuals had to read English, as sixteenth-century Englishmen had to read French and Italian. At a different level, *Paradise Lost*, *The Pilgrim's Progress*, *Gulliver's Travels* and *Robinson Crusoe*, all became part of world popular literature.

V

Nobody in 1640 intended any of these things. The Revolution was not planned, not willed. Some historians think there can have been no revolution if it was not planned, just as all strikes are made by wicked agitators. But parliament did not make the Revolution; no one advocated it. In the 1640s defenders of parliament's cause had to make do with sixteenth-century Calvinist theories of revolt led by the lesser magistrate, or with the rights of freeborn Englishmen against the Norman Yoke. In the course of struggle theories of popular sovereignty and the rights of man were evolved, which later revolutionaries drew upon. But there was no Bolshevik party in England in

29. Webster, *The Great Instauration: Science, Medicine and Reform, 1626–1660*, 1975, p. 84 and *passim*; M.C. Jacob, *The Cultural Meaning of the Scientific Revolution*, New York, 1988, pp. 7, 25–6, 86, 92–3, 123, 130, 145, 182, 245, and *passim*. Margaret Jacob's thesis is illustrated, apparently independently, in an interesting article by Robert Unwin, 'Cabinets of curiosities', *The Historian*, 1988, 19.
30. Elizabeth Eisenstein, *The Printing Press as an Agent of Change: Communications and Cultural Transformations in Early-Modern Europe*, Cambridge University Press, 1979, Ch. 8.

1640. For that matter, neither the French nor the Russian Revolutions were willed in advance by anyone. By 1917 the Bolsheviks, building on English and French experience, were able to take advantage of a revolutionary situation; but they did not *make* the Revolution. A revolutionary situation developed when the Tsarist state collapsed, just as the English state collapsed in 1640; and the Bolsheviks were prepared to take advantage of it. Great revolutions are not made by conspiratorial minorities.

When the late Tim Curtis in a memorable phrase called the Elizabethan government 'a beleaguered garrison', he was referring, I think, not only to the hostility of the victims of inflation, enclosure and eviction. He also meant that many of the gentry on whom the government had to rely to keep the Many-Headed Monster under control themselves had ideas very different from those of the queen. The Leicester-Walsingham faction in the Council spoke for those who wanted a closer alliance with the republican Netherlands against Spain, for sea-dogs who wanted an aggressive commercial foreign policy in search of trade and plunder. Ralegh said that the gentry were 'the garrison of good order throughout the realm',[31] and in the absence of a standing army they were all the government had got. But their position was ambiguous. Some agreed with Strafford, that the monarch was the keystone of the social arch, any shaking of which might threaten the collapse of all order. Others came ultimately to feel, like Oliver Cromwell, that there was 'no fear' of such an outcome.[32] They could weather the storm, put themselves at the head of the foes of the old order and yet retain control for 'the garrison of good order'. Such men thought that the gentry who controlled local government should also direct the policies of the centre, using state power for novel purposes. We may note as a matter of interest that many of the peers who supported parliament during the civil war had previously been advocates of a forward commercial policy; John Pym was Treasurer of the Providence Island Company; most of the navy and many English ports supported parliament.[33] But Oliver Cromwell was probably more interested in establishing the kingdom of God on earth than in making the world safe for capitalism. MPs wanted to get

---

31. W. Ralegh, *Seat of Government*, in T. Birch (ed.) *Works*, 1751, II, p. 320.
32. To Colonel Robert Hammond, 25 November 1648, W.C. Abbott (ed.) *Writings and Speeches of Oliver Cromwell*, Harvard University Press, 1937–47, I, pp. 698–9.
33. The great Puritan preacher John Preston, advocate of a forward foreign policy in the 1620s, seems to have wanted to enlist the help of pirates (*Fourteen Godly and Learned Treatises*, 3rd edn, 1633, p. 259; *The Churches Marriage*, 1638, p. 39).

back to the days of Good Queen Bess, idealized as a time of consensus.

Some historians these days tend to emphasize industrialization, 'modernization', as the decisive turning-point in West European and indeed world history. I think that England's take-off into industrial revolution was made possible by the political liberation achieved in the seventeenth century. It is a little ironical that one of the few things that the Russians and Chinese agree on today is that modern history begins in 1640, whereas many Anglo-American historians date the modern world not from the seventeenth-century struggles for liberty but from the economic transformations of the eighteenth and early nineteenth centuries.

Present-day controversies among historians about seventeenth-century England stem from attempts to prove that nothing significant happened then. I am arguing, on the contrary, that the seventeenth century was a crucial turning-point in the evolution of England from a monarchy which structurally had much in common with the great absolutisms of the continent – though far weaker – into a state in which power resided with a parliament representative of the propertied classes. State power was then used ruthlessly to foster economic growth, not only by exploiting the English and Irish lower classes but even more by plunder-trade with America, Africa and Asia, and especially by the slave trade. Not for nothing was political economy born in late seventeenth-century England.

I reject the view that all the changes I have emphasized would have happened anyway, without revolution. Some argue that the ideas – financial reorganization, the Navigation Act, abolition of feudal tenures – were not novel, which is true; that the Revolution was just an unfortunate accident, which temporarily interrupted trade, and that 1660 restored 'normality'. I think this is quite wrong. First, pre-revolutionary governments lacked the financial resources to pay for the vast navies which were needed to enforce the new commercial and colonial policy. They could not have raised the money without the agreement of the taxpayers, and could not have won this agreement without a massive fiscal reconstruction such as the Revolution brought about. But even if they could have raised the taxes they would not have had the will or the desire to forward a commercial imperial policy. When there were quarrels between the Dutch and English East India Companies in James I's reign, the king had representatives of the two companies brought before him and tried to negotiate between them. Although the Dutch Company was establishing a monopoly in the East Indies, James did not see it as his job to protect the English Company's interests against them, as any post-1649 government would have done, and as the Dutch government was doing. James thought such sordid trading matters were not the concern of kings. The massacre of Amboyna (1623) was not avenged until the Commonwealth's Dutch war of thirty years later. Charles I intended to use the fleet which ship money would pay for in order to give 'assistance to the King of Spain' rather than against the Spanish empire.[34] The *ideas* had been about for a long time – of a Navigation Act since the four-teenth century, of abolishing feudal tenures since at least the early seven-teenth century; but a revolution was necessary to put them into effect.

1660 did not – could not – restore 1640. There was far greater con-tinuity between the 1650s and 1660s than between the 1630s and the restoration period. When Charles II came back, England had been ruled for nearly twenty years without king or House of Lords, without bishops, without a Privy Council. The instruments of Charles I's personal government – Star Chamber, Court of High Commission, Court of Wards – were not restored; censorship and the church were brought under parliament's control. In the 1640s and 1650s the clergy had ceased to be taxed by their own Convocation: acceptance of this after 1663 marked an end to the medieval and Laudian concept of the clergy as a separate estate of the realm.[35] By the early eighteenth cen-tury Convocation itself, which in 1640 had been strong enough to defy parliament, had become a superfluous institution.

In the 1620s and 1630s almost the only theorists to support absolutism had been clergymen, and in the thirties Archbishop Laud and his bishops had a great share in the government of England. After 1660 bishops never again played a significant part in government. The first open opposition to James II in 1688 came from the Seven Bishops, who refused to read his Declaration of Indulgence from pulpits. The church had ceased to be the instrument of an indepen-dent monarchy and had chosen subservience to parliament. 1688 simply confirmed all of this. Revolution had happened in 1640 because Charles I could no longer rule in the old way.[36] Charles II

34. Patricia Haskell, 'Ship Money in Hampshire', in J. Webb, N. Yates and S. Peacock (eds) *Hampshire Studies presented to Dorothy Dymond*, Portsmouth, 1981, p. 75; cf. p. 100.
35. C.B. Macpherson, *The Political Theory of Possessive Individualism: Hobbes to Locke*, Oxford University Press, 1962, pp. 300–1. Cf. Ch. 4 below.
36. One of the best ways of grasping that there was unease, an awareness of impending crisis in pre-1640 England, is to look beyond parliamentary debates and government pronouncements at English literature of the early seventeenth century. See Ch. 10 below.

announced that he did not intend to go on his travels again; James II, more foolish, travelled. Both tried to pack their Parliaments; neither tried, as their father had done, to abolish them altogether.

My argument may seem to be based too exclusively on what did in fact happen in England, not on what contemporaries expected to happen. So perhaps it is worth citing a few relatively disinterested contemporary observers. In June 1640, scenting trouble ahead in England, King Philip IV of Spain told two emissaries leaving for London that it is of the highest importance 'that we do not lose that King [Charles I], for, should that country become a republic, I have no doubts that I will lose my province of Flanders'.[37] Cardinal Mazarin agreed with this assessment. In January 1646 he drafted instructions for the French ambassador about to take up his post in London. 'It would be far less harmful for us', he made Louis XIV say, 'to see the King of Great Britain re-established in his former authority, even if we were certain that he would be our enemy, than to have a republic formed in England and Scotland, even if we were uncertain whether it would be friend or enemy'. The main reason he gave was that in a republic taxes – being voted by the taxpayers – would be collected without difficulty and in any quantity necessary. Witness the Dutch, who pay fifty times as much a year for wars as they did when they were subjected to Spanish rule; witness too parliament's ability to pay its civil war armies. So we must do all we can to prevent a republic in England. England's object, French envoys reported from London in 1665, is to control the seas so as to seize all the trade of the world. As the French ambassador had explained earlier, the English government 'has a monarchical appearance, and there is a king; but it is far from being a monarchy'.[38]

Such views on the superiority of a republic became commonplace in later seventeenth-century England. Henry Neville, Harringtonian and republican, in a dialogue which he wrote about 1681, made his English gentleman explain that where sovereignty 'resides in the people [by which he means the propertied people] . . . the government is much more powerful than aristocracy'. The noble Venetian

37. A.J. Loomie, 'Alonso de Cárdenas and the Long Parliament, 1640–1648', *English Historical Review*, 1982, 97, p. 292. In fact Spain lost only Dunkirk, and that only temporarily. But she had to recognize the independence of the Dutch republic – a far more significant defeat.

38. J. Jusserand (ed.) *Recueil des Instructions données aux Ambassadeurs et Ministres de France*, I, *1648–1665*, Paris, 1929, pp. 35–8, 356; cf. *ibid.*, p. 85: virtues of a republic (1649); p. 123: incorruptibility of republican officials.

replied that when the Venetian constitution was drafted 'we did not then much dream of the consequences, else without doubt we must have made a popular government'. The English gentleman later listed the powers which he thought the king should not be allowed to exercise – control of foreign policy, of the armed forces, of taxation, and of the appointment of ministers: all of which seemed in 1681 to be endangering the compromise settlement of 1660 which 1688 was to reconfirm.[39] If there was to be a vigorous commercial and colonial policy, the government must be controlled by the taxpayers: on this Philip IV, Mazarin, and the republican Neville saw eye to eye.

So my argument is that England was the country of the first political revolution (adjusted in 1688); that this produced governments able to concentrate single-mindedly on economic growth. Their policies led to England becoming the country of the first Industrial Revolution, and the first world empire. The three processes are, I think, indissolubly connected. England's seventeenth-century Revolution is a decisive event not only in English but in world history. 'Such dispensations as these', Marchamont Nedham persuasively argued, 'cannot be looked upon, by the most envious eye or profane heart, as the birth and product of any fore-laid contrivements of men, biassed with corrupt and carnal interest'.[40]

39. H. Neville, *Plato Redivivus*, in C. Robbins (ed.) *Two English Republican Tracts*, Cambridge University Press, 1969, pp. 92–3, 185–6.
40. M. Nedham, *A True State of the Case of the Commonwealth*, February 1653–4, p. 2. Oliver Cromwell said something similar a year later: see his *Writings and Speeches*, op. cit., III, p. 591, quoted on p. 92.

I am greatly indebted to M.A. Barg's *Popular Classes in the English Bourgeois Revolution*, Moscow, 1967 (in Russian) for my understanding of the significance of the abolition of feudal tenures. For the English Revolution in general, see the most useful *Conflict in Early Stuart England: Studies in Religion and Politics, 1603–1642*, ed. R. Cust and A. Hughes, 1989, *passim*.

3

Political discourse in early seventeenth-century England

Dependence on a single kind of source or even on limited kinds of sources is bound to lead to a partial history.

Susan Staves, 'Where is history but in texts? Reading the history of marriage' in J.M. Wallace (ed.) *The Golden and the Brazen World: Papers in Literature and History, 1650–1800,* California University Press, 1985, p. 131[1]

A common political language . . . is . . . not a sign that all assumptions are shared.

Derek Hirst, 'Revisionism revised: the place of principle', *Past and Present,* 1981, 92, p. 83

Critics of scholasticism in seventeenth-century England emphasized strongly that things are more important than the words which describe them. Words must be related to actions if we are to understand them. The point needs stressing in relation to current controversies about seventeenth-century English history, since it is easy for inexperienced historians, or historians approaching the seventeenth from the sixteenth century, or those who limit themselves to political and administrative matters, to take parliamentary discourse at its face value; and to believe that because the gentry spoke of themselves as 'the county community', therefore nobody else in the county mattered. This is to fall for what Marx called 'the illusion of the epoch'.

In every society subject to censorship we should be wary of resting on the surface of what politicians say. Kremlinologists understand this, even if their interpretations are sometimes a little fanciful. Every Conservative MP today knows that a special language of codes and

1. See this valuable article *passim* for examples of the distinction between official discourse and what was actually thought.

symbols must be used if the leader is to be criticized: she cannot be attacked directly. Anyone who during the Second World War was in the army – that last survival of the hierarchical society – knows what venom and contempt could be put into the correctly deferential words 'Yes – sir!' The printed page cannot convey the different significances which context and emphasis may give to accepted forms of discourse. I want to discuss some confusions which historians risk falling into by failing to allow for seventeenth-century conventions of political discourse.

Members of parliament constantly professed boundless respect for the king, and horror at any suggestion of opposition to the government. Even in 1643, after parliament had been fighting the king for a year, Henry Marten was sent to the Tower for suggesting that the kingdom might be more important than the royal family.[2] If we look only at official sources – parliamentary debates, state papers – the case for believing that the civil war happened by accident seems strong. But formal documents are not the only evidence available. Side by side with Sir Simonds D'Ewes's subserviently monarchical speeches in the House of Commons, his hope in 1625 that 'the affection of prince and people would be settled in a firm concord and correspondence',[3] we have his diary, which he wrote in cypher 'that I might write more freely, as of the public occurrents, so of mine own private occasions'. With this safeguard D'Ewes referred to James I's sin of sodomy, his 'base and cowardly nature', for which he was 'laughed at by the vulgar'. God justly punished James's 'self-conceit of his wisdom in the carriage of his Spanish match'.[4]

When Prince Charles left for Spain D'Ewes prayed that 'God would preserve him from damned apostasy.' James 'showed small policy in giving credence to base informers against his lower House of Commons'. D'Ewes recorded portents which reminded him of 'Richard II's time'. 'God forbid the like consequents as succeeded them.' (But earlier riots of the unemployed in Wiltshire had 'raised a rumour of a hoped-for rebellion'.) After describing public dissatisfaction with the king's reasons for the dissolution of parliament in 1622, D'Ewes continued with heavy irony: 'To-day also went his worthy Majesty out of town towards his pleasure, leaving all his good

---

2. S.R. Gardiner, *History of the Great Civil War, 1642–9*, 1901, I, p. 202.
3. J.O. Halliwell (ed.) *The Autobiography and Correspondence of Sir Simonds D'Ewes*, London, 1845, I, p. 279; cf. p. 241.
4. E. Bourcier (ed.) *The Diary of Sir Simonds D'Ewes, 1622–4*, Paris, n.d. ?1974, pp. 55, 92–3, 113, 135.

subjects much perplexed.' D'Ewes's conclusion was 'to pray . . . and to arm myself for preparation against worser times should come, which without God's admirable and infinite mercy towards us, we could not but shortly expect'. He thought that Thomas Scott's illegal but vastly popular *Vox Populi* (1620) was 'generally approved of not only by the meaner sort that were zealous for the cause of religion but also by all men of judgement'.[5]

D'Ewes was a convinced Puritan. Can he really have respected a king guilty of the sin of sodomy? Or one capable of 'damned apostasy'? The contrast between D'Ewes's public speeches and his private words gives food for thought. Drummond of Hawthornden is another example. When James came to Scotland in 1617 Drummond published *Forth Feasting: A Panegyric to the Kings most Excellent Majesty*, whose extravagance in praise startled his biographer, David Masson. Drummond left unpublished *The Five Senses*, an extremely critical poem about James in which he prayed, with much detail, that:

> Thou wilt be pleased, great God, to save
> My sovereign from a Ganymede,
> Whose whorish breath hath power to lead
> His excellence which way it list.[6]

Prynne, Burton and Bastwick, the three most inveterate opponents of the Laudian régime, who in 1637 were condemned to severe corporal penalties and perpetual imprisonment, never failed to express their reverence for and confidence in the king.

Another example is John Preston, whose court sermons use Aesopian language to press home political recommendations – in this case a change of foreign policy – without actually saying so. The Bible showed that God had stirred up rebels against wicked princes: Preston quoted Mordecai to Esther: 'If thou holdest thy tongue at this time, deliverance shall appear to the Jews from another place, but thou and thy house shall perish.' God 'doth not need princes', said Preston in a Cambridge sermon.[7]

5. ibid., pp. 58–60, 65, 121, 130; cf. pp. 85, 145, 158; Halliwell (ed.) D'Ewes, *Autobiography*, op. cit., I, p. 159.
6. D. Masson, *Drummond of Hawthornden: the Story of his Life and Writings*, 1873, pp. 55–9; W.C. Ward (ed.) *The Poems of William Drummond of Hawthornden*, 1894, II, pp. 185–7.
7. John Preston, *A Sermon of Spirituall Life and Death*, 1630, p. 27; *Life Eternall*, 4th edn, 1634, sermon 7, p. 126; cf. *A Sermon . . . preached before the Commons-House*, July 1625, printed with *The Saints Qualification*, 2nd edn, 1634, pp. 261–2. See my *Puritanism and Revolution*, Panther edn,. 'The political sermons of John Preston', esp. pp. 245–50, 259–60.

Even better documented is Fulke Greville, a lifelong aspirant to royal office, who ultimately became Chancellor of the Exchequer. His public persona throughout his life was that of devoted servant to Elizabeth, James I and Charles I. But in his *Life of Sidney* and his poems and plays, all written long before his death in 1628, Greville deals with problems which did not surface till after 1640. He warns continually of the dangers of the drift towards absolutism, arguing consistently for parliamentary control over taxation and for a forward commercial-colonial policy in alliance with the Dutch. Assuming that absolutism corrupts, his interest is in analysing those who sell themselves to power, those who sit on the fence (especially prelates), and those who try inadequately to maintain their integrity (presumably Greville himself). Well before the Laudian ascendancy he had profound contempt for most churchmen.[8]

It may well be that compilers of parliamentary diaries – aware that their papers might be seized – omitted direct attacks on the king. We find few remarks like Rudyerd's in 1624: 'let us not lay all the blame on the King. . . . We have had our own heats'; or Sir William Herbert's, apropos of a financial grant: 'the people would be satisfied', it 'being given to the war, and not to the King'. The Venetian ambassador was amazed at some of the direct attacks on James in the Commons in 1610. We need not believe his story that one member called the king a traitor and was defended by the House; but certainly men were already distinguishing between the king and the commonwealth. The French ambassador was talking of a general insurrection.[9] Why did James I make such a song and dance about monarchy being the divinest thing on earth? Surely because men were now denying what Henry VIII and Elizabeth had never needed to emphasize.

In Somerset in 1626 Hugh Pyne, a lawyer recently dismissed from his position as chairman of Quarter Sessions, was alleged to have said that the king 'was no fitter to be a King than Hick Wright, which Hick Wright is Mr Pyne's shepherd and a natural fool'. Pyne added that 'the King was script and governed by a company of upstarts'. While still in jail for this offence Pyne was elected as burgess for Weymouth

---

8. See pp. 150–1 below.
9. Christopher Thompson (ed.) *The Holles Account of Proceedings in the House of Commons in 1624*, Orsett, 1985, pp. 29, 49; E.R. Foster (ed.) *Proceedings in Parliament, 1610*, Yale University Press, 1966, I, p. xii; II, p. 142; cf. pp. 241, 332.

in 1628.[10] Alexander Gil, Milton's schoolmaster, was exceptionally foolish to describe King James and Prince Charles *in writing* as 'the old fool and the young one', and to say that drinking the health of Felton, the assassin of Buckingham, was common in London and elsewhere.[11]

John Selden was a trained lawyer and parliamentary politician, whose propaganda services Charles I used. Selden's cool sceptical intelligence is revealed in his *Table Talk*, probably to be dated from the 1640s. However, it is unlikely that the jovial irreverence with which Selden treated sacred cows had been acquired only after 1640.

A king is a thing men have made for their own sakes, for quietness' sake. Just as in a family one man is appointed to buy the meat. . . . A king that claims privileges in his own country because they have them in another, is just as a cook that claims fees in one lord's house because they are allowed in another. If the master of the house will yield them, well and good. . . . The king's oath is not security enough for our property, for he swears to govern according to law; now the judges they interpret the law, and what judges can be made to do we know.[12]

Who was 'the master of the house'?

It was easier to express such sentiments after 1640. But good Calvinists could hardly at any time have disagreed with what John Harington was free to say in January 1641-2. The king can do no wrong, but 'all kings, even the best that ever were, . . . are extremely full of infirmities and commit innumerable sins. It is needless to cite examples of that that is so common and apparent.' The meaning of the phrase 'the king can do no wrong' is 'to preserve the affections of all the English to their prince', since they will 'lay the blame wholly upon the councillors of the king'.[13]

Long before the civil war many had accepted the merely conventional nature of the king's incapacity of doing wrong. Buchanan in 1570, writing of earlier Scottish aristocrats, said 'lest they should . . . appear to be violators of their oath and fidelity promised to the King,

10. Quoted in Richard Cust, *The Forced Loan and English Politics, 1626-1628*, Oxford University Press, 1987, pp. 192-3; G. Roberts (ed.) *Diary of Walter Yonge*, Camden Society, 1848, pp. 110-14. For other examples of personal opposition to the king see C. Thompson, *Holles Account*, op. cit., p. 72; Thompson (ed.) *Sir Nathaniel Rich's Diary of Proceedings in the House of Commons in 1624*, Orsett, 1985, pp. 16-17, 25, 33; Cust, *Forced Loan*, op. cit., p. 330.
11. My *Milton and the English Revolution*, p. 28.
12. Selden, *Table Talk*, 1847, pp. 97-8, 103-4.
13. Margaret F. Stieg (ed.) *The Diary of John Harington MP, 1646-53*, Somerset Record Society, 1972, p. 103.

they proclaimed [that they] were not against him but against his wicked councillors.'[14] Dutch sixteenth-century rebels professed loyalty to their king whilst attacking his ministers: so did French Huguenots, D'Avila records in 'Mr Hamden's *vade mecum*'; so too did Czech rebels in 1618.[15] In *The Birth of Merlin*, a play probably dating from James's reign, King Aurelius denounces his natural councillors as traitors, and allies with Saxon invaders to revenge himself on them. Clearly he must be opposed. But how can such opposition be justified? The answer anticipates the Parliamentarian position in the civil war: we must

> with all the speed we can
> Preserve the person of the King and kingdom

against the

> traitorous Saxons . . .
> That with advantage thus have won the King.[16]

Sir Roger Chomley in *Sir Thomas More* said

> his majesty
> Is not informed of this base abuse . . .;
> For if he were, I know his gracious wisdom
> Would soon redress it.[17]

Pym's method of criticizing Charles I was to attack Roger Manwaring for going about 'to infuse into his Majesty that which was most unfit for his royal breast – an absolute power not bounded by law'. On the kindest interpretation this suggested that the 'king's mental abilities were those of a child'.[18] MPs regularly used 'the king can do no wrong' in this sense, not that his actions were above criticism (as some councillors argued) but that where wrong was done it must be attributed to ministers. During the civil war this came to mean that the king had somehow been kidnapped by evil councillors

14. H.R. Trevor-Roper, 'George Buchanan and the ancient Scottish constitution', *English Historical Review*, suppl. no. 3, 1966, p. 43.
15. J.L. Motley, *The Rise of the Dutch Republic*, 1892, II, pp. 178-9, 240-2, 358, 566; H.C. D'Avila, *The History of the Civil Wars of France*, 2nd imp., 1678, p. 271; Geoffrey Parker, *Europe in Crisis, 1590-1648*, Brighton, 1980, p. 159. In Marlowe's *The Massacre at Paris*, the Guises called the Huguenots 'Puritans'. So did Richard Bancroft.
16. In C.F. Tucker Brooke (ed.) *The Shakespeare Apocrypha*, Oxford University Press, 1967, p. 372; cf. p. 390. The play was not published until 1662, but it is most improbable that such a passage would have been interpolated then.
17. V. Gabrieli and G. Melchiori (eds) *The Book of Sir Thomas More*, Bari, 1981, p. 121.
18. J.P. Sommerville, *Politics and Ideology in England, 1603-1640*, 1986, p. 139.

who were fraudently issuing orders in his name. Somewhere along the line the doctrine that the king is literally incapable of wrong-doing had been replaced by the later constitutional doctrine.

'Since princes must see and hear with other eyes and ears', said Sir Francis Seymour in 1625, 'how happy is that king who reposeth his counsel upon men of worthiness, and how unhappy he who resteth upon one or two, and they such as know better how to flatter and beg of him than how to give him good counsel'. He cited Elizabeth as an example of a sovereign who was 'happy' in this respect. 'If his Majesty's honour be in question', said Sir Robert Phelips pointedly, 'and he in such necessity, they who have brought him to this strait have dishonoured the king'.[19] It is worth pondering the logic of Sir John Strangeways's remark: 'By how much we extol the goodness of the King, by so much we must think worse of those who counsel these courses'.[20] Already Nicholas Fuller in 1610 and Coke in 1628 interpreted the maxim to mean that in certain circumstances the king could not legally do what he wanted to do. 'Nothing that is against the good of the King and his people' could be part of the prerogative, Coke declared: 'the common law hath so admeasured the King's prerogative as he cannot prejudice any man in his inheritance', including his person. In 1628 Attorney-General Heath declared 'it cannot be imagined of the King that he will at any time or in any case do injustice to his subjects. It is a maxim of our law that the King can do no wrong'.[21] If the property rights of subjects and their personal liberty are always to be respected, the doctrine that the king can do no wrong falls far short of meaning what it appears to mean.

Ralegh in his best-selling *History of the World* drew very sharply the traditional distinction between the King and his evil councillors, but did not leave it at that. Since the Norman Conquest, he suggested, the 'only motives of mischances that ever came to the kings of this land' resulted from 'the defence of others in wrong-doing'.[22] Eliot possessed and carefully annotated a manuscript copy of *The Prerogative of Parliaments*: it seems to have influenced his tactics in 1626. MPs never forgot

19. S.R. Gardiner (ed.) *Debates in the House of Commons in 1625*, Camden Society, 1873, pp. 78, 109; cf. p. 81: 'the malice of his ministers'.
20. R.C. Johnson and M.J. Cole (eds) *Commons Debates, 1628*, Yale University Press, 1977, III, p. 196; cf. p. 212: Wentworth.
21. Foster, *1610 Parliament*, op. cit., I, p. 187; S.D. White, *Sir Edward Coke and 'The Grievances of the Commonwealth,' 1621–28*, North Carolina University Press, 1979, pp. 122, 232, 241, 247.
22. W. Ralegh, *The History of the World*, Edinburgh, 1820, VI, p. 35; *Works*, 1751, I, pp. 175–6; cf. pp. 200–2, 208–9, 211–13, 216–17, 233–5, 240–8.

the threat to property posed by unparliamentary taxation. The chief subject of the law is property, declared Thomas Hedley in 1610. Liberty and property were the same thing: the liberties of Englishmen meant the property rights of well-to-do Englishmen. Many were the MPs, including Coke, who echoed Fuller's remarks of 1610: the common law 'do measure the king's prerogative, as it shall not tend to take away or prejudice the inheritance of the subject'.[23] This issue would not go away, because the crown's ever-increasing financial problems continually forced it to seek for new sources of revenue. Conflict over taxation was a fact of life, only secondarily of constitutional theory. It also seemed to many MPs a religious issue. God's law, the Ten Commandments, defended property. Almost the only theoretical defenders of arbitrary taxation were the high-flying 'Arminians'. Selden said 'of our property, I never heard it denied but in the pulpit'.[24]

That blaming 'evil councillors' was often a fiction is apparent. In a private letter to Sir Ralph Winwood, John Pory asked in 1610 'with what cords we shall bind Samson's hands, that is to say his Majesty's prerogative?'[25] Pym in 1621 was much praised for 'a neat speech', in which 'he laboured to show that the King's piety, clemency, justice, bounty, facility, peaceable disposition and other his natural virtues were by the adverse party perverted and turned to a quite contrary course'. Would not this line of argument lead men to ask how 'the adverse party' had won such powerful positions in the king's confidence? 'Adversary politics' was not an invention of the 1640s. Pym filled in a delicate pause in negotiations about the Petition of Right by raising the question of Manwaring. 'Great is the love and piety of his Majesty to his subjects, and *therefore* [my italics] it may be easily judged, his abhorring this man that would draw him from justice and piety'.[26] Can his tongue really have been entirely out of his cheek when he said that? How did he feel when Charles made Manwaring a bishop?

'Even in 1628', Sir Geoffrey Elton insists, 'the opposition leadership carefully avoided any proposals which could be read as an invasion

23. Foster, *1610 Parliament*, op. cit., II, p. 187; W. Notestein, F.H. Relf and H. Simpson (eds) *Commons Debates in 1621*, Yale University Press, 1935, IV, p. 79.
24. Johnson and Cole, *Commons Debates, 1628*, op. cit., III, p. 96.
25. Foster, *1610 Parliament*, op. cit., II, p. 284.
26. N.E. McClure (ed.) *The Letters of John Chamberlain*, American Philosophical Soc., Philadelphia, 1939, II, p. 412; Johnson and Cole, *Commons Debates, 1628*, op. cit., IV, p. 103.

of prerogative rights'.[27] Indeed. They were wise to do so. But verbal caution should not be equated with acquiescence. The wholly conventional nature of the distinction between the king and his advisers was assumed on all sides. 'I know we have a good king', said William Coriton, 'and this is the advice of his wicked ministers, but there is nothing can be more dishonourable unto him' than 'thus to oppress his subjects'. 'We have law enough', said one MP, 'and if we get the King on our side we have power'.[28] Sir Edward Coke, even more flatly, stated: 'The King's answer is very gracious, but what is the law?' 'What we agree upon the King must grant'.[29] Sir Edward Phelips spoke of 'the original contract between king and people', and Sir Nathaniel Rich noted that some said 'this House hath no good opinion of a monarchical government. 'Tis false', he added.[30]

It would be tedious and unprofitable to recite the many occasions on which in 1628 MPs expressed abhorrence of blaming the king for anything, whilst savaging his ministers. Secretary Coke felt he 'must speak plain' on the king's behalf against the endeavour 'to sever the act of the customers from his Majesty's command'.[31] Lord Cary openly expressed fear 'that the King's heart stands not so well affected', whereupon the Speaker took him up. But how were they to recover their 'liberties and privileges which have been seized upon by some of the King's ministers?' 'The hearts of the people [are] possessed with fears and jealousy', reported a sub-committee. 'If we have those enemies at home', cried Eliot, 'how can we strive with those that are abroad?' Edward Kirton thought that 'the enemies of the kingdom' were advising the king. When Sir Giles Eastcourt logically complained that 'we go about to tax the King's judgment in taxing this man [Buckingham] thus', Eliot had him called to the bar.[32]

The king called the bluff of the Commons in 1628 by ordering them to cease distinguishing between him and his ministers. 'It is not vox

27. Elton, *Studies in Tudor and Stuart Politics and Government*, 1974, II, p. 160.
28. Johnson and Cole, *Commons Debates, 1628*, op. cit., I, pp. 196, 193, 211; IV, p. 183; Sir Thomas Crewe, *Proceedings and Debates of the House of Commons in 1628*, 1707, p. 75.
29. Johnson and Cole, *Commons Debates, 1628*, op. cit., III, p. 272; cf. ibid., p. 95: 'the kings contended for it [the prerogative] before Magna Carta, and could never prevail'.
30. ibid., II, pp. 61, 436. Sir Roger Owen and Sir Edwin Sandys had argued in 1614 that all kings had originally been elected, on conditions (*Commons Journals*, I, p. 493).
31. Johnson and Cole, *Commons Debates, 1628*, op. cit., III, pp. 94, 212, 273, 282; IV, pp. 115-6, 139. Cf. Foster, *1610 Parliament*, op. cit., I, pp. 109-10; Crewe, *1628 Proceedings*, op. cit., pp. 35-6, 122.
32. Johnson and Cole, *Commons Debates, 1628*, op. cit., III, pp. 212, 238, 272, 553, 560, 569-70; IV, pp. 64, 123-4, 247.

regis', cried Coke. 'It is not King Charles that advised himself',
added Phelips, 'but King Charles advised by others'.[33] Desperate
attempts were made to contradict the king without contradicting him,
in order to recover 'liberties and privileges which have been seized
upon by some of the king's ministers', by 'the enemies of the
kingdom'. The only way out was suggested by Coke. 'We must name
the Duke [of Buckingham] lest the aspersion lie on his Majesty.' 'It is
certain the King has the same ends that we have', Pym explained.
'How far particular persons do mislead him let us show.' 'We know
the King cannot have knowledge himself of these things', Wentworth
agreed; it was 'a lewd and hateful speech' when Auditor Sawyer
pleaded the king's command for actions questioned in the House.[34] In
1624 Cranfield's defence against his impeachment had shielded the
king by blaming other ministers; it led directly to attacks on them in
the Commons. Bacon was wiser: he did not defend himself at all, but
submitted to the king's mercy. The more councillors covered up in
order to defend the king, the more vulnerable they were themselves.
This was a lesson the Commons did not forget.

In 1640, when Lord Keeper Finch pleaded the king's commands in
defence of his actions, William Strode was 'much troubled'. He
hoped 'no more of that kind will be spoken of his Majesty'.[35] It was
not long before Charles's attempted arrest of the Five Members was
described as a 'traitorous design against *the King* and Parliament' [my
italics]. Pretences were collapsing. A clause deleted from the Grand
Remonstrance at the instance of the moderates declared roundly that
'the King has not bread to put in his head . . . but by the bounty of his
people.' 'If this King will join with us', said Pym, 'we shall set him up
on as great grounds of honour and greatness in that all the world shall
not be able to move him.' Does the unusual phrase, 'this king' imply
the possibility of another king? Chillingworth in December 1641 was
speculating about whether MPs would have a right to protest against
legislation to depose the king.[36]

---

33. ibid., IV, pp. 115, 139.
34. My *People and Ideas in 17th-Century England*, Brighton, 1986, pp. 27-8, 33, 42-4;
Johnson and Cole, *Commons Debates, 1628*, op. cit., III, pp. 212, 238, 272, 278-82, 553,
560, 569-70, 584; IV, pp. 49, 64, 115-16, 123-4, 139, 191-6, 211, 244-8, 258, 292-5.
35. A.H.A. Hamilton (ed.) *Notebook of Sir J. Northcote*, 1877, pp. 94-6.
36. W.H. Coates (ed.) *The Journal of Sir Simonds D'Ewes, from the first recess of the Long
Parliament to the withdrawal of King Charles from London*, Yale University Press, 1942,
pp. 394, 185-6; W. Notestein (ed.) *The Journal of Sir Simonds D'Ewes, from the beginning of
the Long Parliament to the opening of the Trial of the Earl of Strafford*, Yale University Press,
1923, pp. 233-4.

Sir Thomas Barrington had no doubt that in 1628 it was the king, not his ministers, who had been pressurized. 'Princes', he told his wife, 'should in policy have some time and way left to evade when the point of honour is in competition; if they acknowledge their actions past illegal and their ministers confess it and plead ignorance', we should leave it at that – as had been done in the Petition of Right.[37]

So we might perhaps have another look at the high road to civil war. If this phrase means that there were any conscious revolutionary plotters in the House of Commons before 1640, any long-term programme of opposition aiming at subordinating the king to parliament, we can agree that there was no high road. But high roads run in two directions. Men may not have looked forward to revolution. But they did look backwards and acquire ideas and techniques from earlier conflicts between crown and Commons, and slowly built up a body of wisdom on the subject. It seems to me difficult to deny continuity here, just as the publication and sale in 1640–1 of reprints, imitations and echoes of the Marprelate Tracts shows that men remembered Martin Marprelate after fifty years of official silence. (And, we may add, republication under the Laudian censorship of Cowell's *Interpreter*, suppressed in 1610 in response to parliamentary pressure, shows a long memory too.)[38]

It was an age of precedents. In 1621 the House of Commons appealed to the Apology of 1604 which, Conrad Russell tells us, 'was one of the things which annoyed James most. For, just as the Commons could not sign on his dotted line, he could not sign on theirs'.[39] Precisely: it was long-term causes like this which made revolution ultimately the only outcome. In the same parliament it was recalled that no one should speak to the king about what is done in committee until it has been reported and the House has decided. In 1628, after looking up the debates of 1610, 1614 and 1621, the Commons were united in claiming a right to adjourn themselves, not to be adjourned by the king. In the same parliament Sir Robert Phelips recalled that when 'money was

37. A. Searle (ed.) *Barrington Letters, 1628–32*, Camden Society 4th series, 28, 1983, p. 59.
38. C. Hibbard, *Charles I and the Popish Plot*, North Carolina University Press, 1983, p. 128.
39. C. Russell, *Parliaments and English Politics, 1621–1629*, Oxford University Press, 1979, p. 139. Hexter produces overwhelming evidence for continuity between 1604 and 1621 (J.H. Hexter, *Reappraisals in History: New Views on History and Society in Early Modern Europe*, Chicago University Press, 2nd. edn, 1977, p. 210; 'The Apology', in R. Ollard and P. Tudor-Craig (eds) *For Veronica Wedgwood, These: Studies in Seventeenth-Century History*, 1986, pp. 38–43); cf. C. Thompson, *The Debate on Freedom of Speech in the House of Commons in February 1621*, Orsett, 1985, pp. 4, 9–10, 20, and my *People and Ideas*, op. cit., pp. 29–31.

demanded of us', in 1621, 'we would not give, till somewhat was done' to remedy grievances. The fact that impositions were more than once opposed *nem. con.* in 1610 was not forgotten. 'Let no man think liberty and sovereignty incompatible', said Hedley in his great speech in that parliament.[40] The idea was not forgotten, though not often as felicitously expressed.

In 1624 effective Commons' control over royal expenditure was secured by naming treasurers in the act for supply;[41] Sir Miles Fleetwood advocated the same procedure in November 1640 – as a means of persuading the City to advance money to the bankrupt government.[42] The practice of deputing reluctant Privy Councillors to carry unwelcome messages to the king was regularly repeated. It was said in 1621 that 'the lower house of Parliament being the supreme court may as well make precedents as follow precedents, for everything must have a beginning, and so had they theirs'. Whether or not the observation was recalled in the 1640s, the principle was acted upon. Lord Chancellor Ellesmere, on the other hand, thought that in cases where there is no authority or precedent, the king alone should decide; otherwise he would be no more than a Doge of Venice.[43]

James and Charles seem to have believed in the high road. In 1617 James wanted an Anglo-Spanish alliance in order to check 'a growing disposition to make popular states and alliances to the disadvantage of monarchy'. Charles too. When he dissolved parliament in 1629 he said of the ringleaders of the Commons that they 'pretend indeed our service; but their drift was to break . . . through all respects and ligaments of government, and to erect an universal over-swaying power to themselves, which belongs only to Us, not to them'.[44] Certain family and regional groups seem also to have had some conception of a high road. The Puritan Barrington family, for instance, was

40. Johnson and Cole, *Commons Debates, 1628*, op. cit., IV, pp. 14–15, 447; Foster, *1610 Parliament*, op. cit., II, p. 191; cf. pp. 91–2, 165, 267, 411.
41. The act insolently made the grant of subsidies conditional on James reversing his foreign policy.
42. Notestein (ed.) D'Ewes, *Journal*, 1923, op. cit., pp. 33–4.
43. Notestein et al., *1621 Debates*, op cit., VI, p. 347; D.H. Willson, *The Privy Councillors in the House of Commons, 1604-1629*, Minnesota University Press, 1940, p. 311; Sir W. Holdsworth, *The History of English Law*, V, 1924, p. 433.
44. S.L. Adams, 'Foreign policy and the parliaments of 1621 and 1624', in K. Sharpe (ed.) *Faction and Parliament: Essays on Early Stuart History*, Oxford University Press, 1978, p. 141; J. Rushworth, *Historical Collections* (1659-1701), I, Appendix, p. 8. Buckingham thought that those who sought his impeachment aimed to eliminate 'free monarchy' (ibid., I, p. 356).

with its dependants fairly consistently opposed to the court from at least 1604 onwards. There is a similarly identifiable group in Wiltshire.[45] Richard Cust points out that opposition to the forced loan of 1626 'often provided the best indication of ultimate political allegiance prior to the civil war, especially amongst those who had no aspirations for royal office. This is a measure of the extent to which the later lines were already drawn'.[46]

Lord Chancellor Ellesmere indeed had seen a high road to civil war opening up as early as 1610. 'The popular state', he wrote, 'hath swelled more and more'. He accused the Commons of 'a new invented and supposed privilege and liberty'. 'Some particular persons . . . used very audacious and contemptuous speeches against the King's prerogative . . . This hath passed with applause of many others there, and with little or no reprehension at all'.[47]

Ellesmere saw aggression only from the Commons. Chamberlain, writing to Sir Ralph Winwood in the same year, thought that the aggression came from the crown. 'If the practice should follow the positions, we are not like to leave our successors that freedom we received from our forefathers'.[48] The practice did not follow the positions, on either side. The positions had been taken up not because of the wicked ambition of leaders of the Commons or the petulant ignorance of a foreign king, but because continuing inflation was undermining royal finance. That is why the 'undertaking' of 1614 turned the House of Commons against those who had appeared to be its leaders and spokesmen in the preceding parliament: the conflicts were not between 'ins' and 'outs' but reflected slowly diverging interests between which mediation became impossible.[49] 'The most popular men', wrote Arthur Wilson, 'as soon as they wore the court livery, lost the love of the people; but those that suffered for them, were the more beloved and admired by them.'[50] This does not fit very easily into the picture of a House of Commons whose members' main wish was to co-operate with the government.

In 1626 the Venetian ambassador reported that the kingdom was

---

45. Searle, *Barrington Letters*, op. cit., pp. 7-9, 13, 40, 179; Roberts, *Diary of Walter Yonge*, op. cit., pp. xxviii–xxxii.
46. Cust, *Forced Loan*, op. cit., p. 335; cf. p. 337.
47. Foster, *1610 Parliament*, op. cit., I, pp. 276-8; cf. pp. 278-83.
48. McClure, *Chamberlain Letters*, op. cit., I, p 301.
49. Cf. Willson, *Privy Councillors*, op. cit., p. 144.
50. A. Wilson, *The History of Great Britain*, 1653, p. 192; Willson, *Privy Councillors*, op. cit., pp. 70-9, 158, 203, 212; cf. Thompson, *Holles Account*, op. cit., p. 59 - against court papists.

divided into two: the king, Buckingham and a few lucky individuals against the rest of the country.[51] Rejection of 'courtiers' in elections, even when they had the king's backing, would seem to support this. In the elections of 1624 and 1625 the word 'royalist' was used disparagingly of court candidates.[52] In 1628 Joseph Mede referred to opponents of the court as 'patriots' – a phrase which anticipates the French Revolution.[53] But there was no more a continuous 'court' interest than there was a continuing opposition in parliament. There was much disaffection among the courtiers and government servants. The diarist Robert Bowyer was secretary to Lord Buckhurst and clerk to the House of Lords; but his sympathies were with the Puritans.[54] Many courtiers opposed dissolutions of parliament. It is as naive to think that divisions within parliament were stirred up by dissident courtiers as to think that agitators cause strikes. We should assume rather that divisions in parliament, court and privy council reflected divisions in the country.

So we should be prepared to use evidence from outside the House of Commons to assess the nuances of what was said there in highly stylized and conventional language. It is important in such matters not to try to be wiser than S.R. Gardiner, Wallace Notestein, and R.H. Tawney, who were not only great historians of parliamentary politics but were also soaked in the literature and culture of the times they studied. Fortunately literary historians can help us here, notably Margot Heinemann, Jonathan Dollimore, Simon Shepherd, David Norbrook and Martin Butler.[55]

From about the beginning of the century dramatists clearly assume that courts and courtiers are corrupt. Wicked favourites deceive and abuse their masters, sometimes ultimately attempting to supplant them. The nature and duties of kingship were under continual dis-

---

51. Willson, *Privy Councillors*, op. cit., pp. 189, 200; R.E. Ruigh, *The Parliament of 1624: Politics and Foreign Policy*, Harvard University Press, 1971, pp. 44, 57, 148.
52. D. Hirst, *The Representative of the People? Voters and Voting in England under the Early Stuarts*, Cambridge University Press, 1975, p. 144; *Calendar of State Papers, Venetian, 1625-6*, p. 63; McClure, *Chamberlain Letters*, op. cit., II, p. 540. Fulke Greville had used the word in his *Life of Sir Philip Sidney*, not published until 1652 (1907 edn, p. 187). So did Bacon in 1612: J. Spedding, R.L. Ellis and D.D. Heath (eds) *Works*, 1857-72, IV, pp. 279-80.
53. T. Birch (ed.) *The Court and Times of Charles I*, 1848, I, p. 327.
54. D. Willson (ed.) *The Parliamentary Diary of Robert Bowyer*, 1606-7, Minnesota University Press, 1931, p. xiii
55. J. Dollimore, *Radical Tragedy: Religion, Ideology and Power in the Drama of Shakespeare and his Contemporaries*, Brighton, 1984; S. Shepherd, *Amazons and Warrior Women: Varieties of Feminism in Seventeenth-century Drama*, Brighton, 1981, especially Chs. 9 and 13.

cussion in plays from Marlowe and Shakespeare onwards. There are repeated contrasts between the God-given nature of the office and the all too human individuals who fill it.[56] There were other influences moulding public opinion. The powerful and witty pamphlets of Thomas Scott, smuggled in from the Netherlands, circulated widely in the 1620s and constituted a direct incitement to oppositional political action.[57] Political verses – against Buckingham, for instance – appealed to all classes and helped to increase popular participation in politics.[58] Sir Walter Ralegh's provocatively entitled *The Prerogative of Parliaments* could not be published in England before 1640, but it circulated extensively in manuscript; five illegal editions appeared in and after the critical year 1628. It was written in dialogue form – a convenient way of avoiding responsibility for dangerous views. Ralegh's Justice put forward a programme for action based on the proto-Harringtonian assumption that parliament represents forces which cannot be wished out of existence: the king must accept historical necessity.[59] 'A prince by racking his sovereign authority to the utmost extent', Ralegh observed in his *History of the World*, only brings evil consequences on his successors.[60] Ralegh's remark was topical: Chamberlain in 1610 said that James's speeches 'bred generally much discomfort to see our monarchical power and royal prerogative stretched so high and made so transcendent every way'.[61]

In a valuable article Richard Cust has demonstrated the contribution of newsletters to the polarization of opinion. Printed newspapers were illegal before 1640. John Pory's idea of an official gazette had been rejected in 1621: it would encourage popular discussion of the mysteries of state.[62] Written newsletters were expensive, but there was a demand for them; they were often shared by many subscribers, and so their effect was spread more widely. The amount of political

---

56. Dollimore, *Radical Tragedy*, op. cit., pp. 3–4. See my *Writing and Revolution in 17th-Century England*, Brighton, 1985, pp. 12–20; and Ch. 10 below.
57. My *Writing and Revolution*, op. cit., pp. 47, 78; my *People and Ideas*, op. cit., p. 306.
58. R. Cust, 'News and politics in early seventeenth-century England', *Past and Present*, 1986, 112, pp. 76–9.
59. *The Prerogative of Parliaments*, in Ralegh, *Works*, op. cit., I, pp. 242–7; cf. II, p. 318.
60. Ralegh, *History of the World*, op. cit., VI, p. 35; see R.H. Tawney, *Harrington's Interpretation of his Age*, Raleigh Lecture, 1941, for Ralegh's anticipation of Harrington's version of English history.
61. McClure, *Chamberlain Letters*, op. cit., I, p. 301.
62. Cust, 'News and politics', op. cit., p. 81; W.S. Powell, *John Pory, 1572–1636: The Life and Letters*, North Carolina University Press, 1977, pp. 52–3.

news available to the localities increased rapidly in the early seventeenth century. In the 1620s, for almost the first time, detailed and continuous coverage of national politics was disseminated. This helped electors to see local events against a background of national politics, and so to conceive of the possibility of influencing national policy.[63] The 'news' often suggested an image of government at variance with contemporary rhetoric emphasizing consensus and harmony.

For example, billeting of soldiers from 1625 onwards reached newsletters only when it became a matter of public controversy in 1628. 'Scandalous' items, then as now, were the most newsworthy. The news showed the king himself, not merely his ministers, involved in conflict – helping Catholic France against the Huguenots, defending Buckingham. 'The court' came to seem the most disruptive element within the political order, conflict as the logical consequence of the need to provide a remedy. John Glanville in 1625 was described as 'speaking for the country against the King'. The diarists Rous and Yonge came to see national problems in terms of two sides. Yonge labelled Hampden's judges as either 'pro patria' or 'pro rege'.[64]

So the heavy emphasis on consensus in parliamentary debates is not necessarily decisive evidence of absence of disagreement on major issues, or of lack of concern with matters of principle, but rather the opposite. In exactly the same way emphasis on 'the great chain of being' in literature may indicate that that traditional notion was under attack.

Yet so deceptive was the rhetoric of consensus that the government itself in 1626 called for county meetings of subsidy men, at which it hoped to win acceptance of the forced loan. In some counties at least these meetings became fora in which lesser subsidy men learnt to speak of the necessity of proceeding 'in a parliamentary way'. Divisions among the gentry contributed to the political education of lesser freeholders, who took courage from the example of their betters. Charles's naive belief that the political nation as a whole would support him, that opposition came only from a few factious spirits, led him disastrously astray, the victim of the myth of convention and harmony.[65]

Historians too easily forget the censorship on published and

63. Cust, *Forced Loan*, op. cit., pp. 150–1.
64. Cust, 'News and politics', op. cit., pp. 71–5, 83–7.
65. Cust, *Forced Loan*, op. cit., p. 328, Ch. 3 *passim*.

unpublished material. In 1626 a man was twice racked for writing a private letter which contained 'words and insinuations against His Majesty'. The Barringtons feared lest their private correspondence should be opened and read.[66] D'Ewes kept his diary in cypher; Selden employed anagrams in his correspondence.

The views which could be expressed were not the only views which were held. Men like Thomas Hobbes, Joseph Mede, D'Ewes, Fulke Greville and Sir Henry Spelman deliberately refrained from publishing (or from writing) through fear of censorship. Others (like Coke) were forcibly prevented from publishing. It is difficult even to guess how many writers said less than they thought, for prudential reasons. For 'public opinion' expressed in works published in the 1620s and 1630s is so different from what surfaced after the collapse of the censorship that it would be foolish not to suppose that many men previously held views which could be printed only after the liberation of the press. Any other assumption would have to postulate a remarkable revolution in opinion.[67]

Nevertheless, there were ways in which, whilst maintaining decorum of discourse, criticism of the monarchy could be implied. MPs might call for a fast, in order to propitiate God for the nation's sins. Among the sins to be forgiven there were always some for which it was difficult to exonerate the government – the prevalence of popery, failure to support our Protestant brethren on the continent, and so on. The ominous opening of the 1624 parliament included proposals for a fast, a committee of privileges, composed of ancient parliament men, a committee for grievances, and innumerable economic complaints.[68] The plagues of 1625 and 1635 seemed additional evidence of God's anger with England. The neatest reaction came in 1640 when the Commons called for a fast on 17 November – Queen Elizabeth's accession day. No wonder some Laudians had a principled objection to fasts.[69]

The poems of Drayton, Browne, and Wither are full of political criticism in the form of pastoral and allegory: Sidney and Spenser had indeed recommended these genres for this very purpose. The golden

---

66. Birch, *Court and Times*, op cit., I, p. 99, Searle, *Barrington Letters*, op cit., pp. 53, 100.
67. I have argued this case at some length in my *Writing and Revolution*, op. cit., Ch. 2.
68. Thompson, *Sir Nathaniel Rich's Diary*, op. cit., pp. 1–4.
69. W. Hunt, *The Puritan Moment: The Coming of Revolution in an English County*, Harvard University Press, 1983, p. 274.

age existed before monarchy was invented. 'Had all been virtuous men', wrote Chapman, 'There never had been prince upon the earth.'[70] History was useful too, especially in the House of Commons. Christopher Sherland in 1625 prudently chose an example from the reign of Henry V, when 'the Commons did desire the King he would keep his promise for execution of the laws better than heretofore. This did anger the King, but the blame rested upon them that had given him ill counsel.'[71] In the same year Sir Robert Phelips described Henry VI's Duke of Suffolk as one who 'made a marriage for the King, wholly possessed the government, caused an alteration of lands, did encroach upon the honour and dignity of the kingdom, etc.'; there was no need to name Buckingham. The conclusion followed: 'when he was laid by, the reformation followed'. Coke came even nearer home when he said 'the office of Lord Admiral is a place of greatest trust. . . . It will be well when offices are restored to men of sufficiency. If an office be granted to an unexperienced man, it is void.' The Master of Ordnance had normally been a tradesman until 20 Henry VIII; 'and since it was possessed by the nobility, was never well executed'. 'Our story mentioneth no levies against law,' mused Sherland, 'which have not bred tumults and commotions'. To cite a precedent was a polite way of saying No.[72]

History was a relatively safe source. Wentworth cited examples of tyranny from the Spanish Netherlands and France, as well as from Ezekiel and Daniel. Hoskins observed that wise princes 'put away strangers' – Canute sent away his Danes, the Palsgrave Queen Elizabeth's Englishmen; but he spoilt it by mentioning the Sicilian vespers.[73] In 1628 Sir Henry Marten used the fable of the lion and the fox for a discreet attack on the prerogative.[74] Pym in the same year was prudently unspecific when he said 'some times have produced such kings as, if they had had the whole kingdom to dispense, it had not been unlikely to have been spent.'[75] In the Short Parliament he was more precise: 'we know how unfortunate Henry II of France and other princes have been by occasion of such breaking their laws [as

70. George Chapman, *The Gentleman Usher*, in *Comedies and Tragedies*, 1873, I, p. 331.
71. Gardiner, *1625 Debates*, op. cit., pp. 124–5.
72. ibid., pp. 85, 109, 125, 130–1; cf. pp. 146, 148.
73. McClure, *Chamberlain Letters*, op. cit., I, pp. 533, 538.
74. Annabel Patterson, 'Fables of Power', in K. Sharpe and S.N. Zwicker (eds) *Politics of Discourse: The Literature and History of Seventeenth-Century England*, California University Press, 1987, pp. 279–80.
75. Johnson and Cole, *Commons Debates, 1628*, op. cit., IV, p. 104.

those which he had just listed in England]. I pray God we never see such times.'[76]

The most obvious historical example was Queen Elizabeth I, who could be praised to the skies for virtues which her successors conspicuously lacked. Ellesmere referred to the House of Commons 'seditiously looking back', and implying that 'the times past were golden days.' Phelips drew the contrast in 1625: 'It was not wont to be so when God and we held together: witness that glorious Queen.'[77] Eliot returned to 'that never-to-be-forgotten excellent Queen Elizabeth' at the crisis of the debate on the Petition of Right. Conrad Russell just missed the point when he said that 'for Eliot, saying something was a cornerstone of Elizabethan policy was normally synonymous with saying he agreed with it.'[78] Eliot was not merely agreeing with it; he was passionately advocating it in conditions of discourse which made it difficult to do so directly. Adulation of Prince Henry, before and especially after his death, had a similar function. Mention of the name of Drake was a criticism of government foreign policy.[79]

The ever-present awareness that 'we are the last monarchy in Christendom that retain our original rights and constitutions' was repeated in every parliament from 1604 onwards, and by many outside parliament.[80] Since Charles and his ministers rubbed the point home by threatening to discontinue parliaments, the eleven years of personal rule took no one by surprise: it looked like the culmination of a deliberate policy.[81] Nor should we be astonished that there appears to have been little 'constitutional' opposition to ship money in the localities. Here again we must push beyond appearances. Ann Hughes points out that 'the surface calm of the 1630s . . . seems likely to be a product of the sources generated rather than of the

---

76. E.S. Cope and W.H. Coates (eds) *Proceedings of the Short Parliament of 1640*, Camden Society, 4th series, 19, 1977, p. 259.
77. Foster, *1610 Parliament*, op. cit., I, p. 278; Gardiner, *1625 Debates*, op. cit., p. 31.
78. Johnson and Cole, *Commons Debates, 1628*, op. cit., IV, p. 144, cf. p. 62; Russell, *Parliaments and English Politics, 1621–9*, op. cit., p. 80.
79. Cf. C.V. Wedgwood, 'Oliver Cromwell and the Elizabethan inheritance', in *History and Hope*, 1987, pp. 317–35; E.K. Wilson, *Prince Henry and English Literature*, Cornell University Press, 1946; my *Intellectual Origins of the English Revolution*, Oxford University Press, 1965, pp. 213–19; my *Writing and Revolution*, op. cit. p. 57.
80. Gardiner, *1625 Debates*, op. cit., p. 110. Timothy Turner of Gray's Inn feared in 1616 that no more parliaments would be held 'et tunc valeat antiqua libertas Angliae' (quoted by W.R. Prest, *The Rise of the Barristers: A Social History of the English Bar, 1590–1640*, Oxford University Press, 1986, p. 266). Cf. M.A.E. Green (ed.) *Diary of John Rous*, Camden Society, 1st series, 66, 1856, pp. 2–3.
81. McClure, *Chamberlain Letters*, op. cit., II, p. 321.

situation itself'.[82] Men did indeed argue about the fairness of the assessment of themselves or their area rather than about the legality of ship money. They would have been very foolish to defy the king and his judges by raising the constitutional issue. Only someone as dedicated (and as rich) as Hampden could afford to do that. Silence in public about the legality of the tax is no more evidence of approval than silence about the desirability of communism in Romania before 1989 was evidence that all Romanians were enthusiastic communists.

There was 'murmuring' against ship money as early as 1633. It was the talk of London in 1637; men could not get into Hampden's trial because 'the crowd was so great'.[83] The case was widely canvassed, and stiffened opposition. Laud grumbled that 'so many hands and purses have gone to . . . the search which hath been made of records against the King'.[84] We know of principled opposition in twenty-six of the thirty-nine English counties. Many Suffolk defaulters are said to have emigrated to New England.[85] Ship money hit a large number of what Prynne called the 'middle and poor sort of people' for the first time. It took 'the burden off rich men's shoulders', Giles Randall declared from his Huntingdonshire pulpit, and laid it 'on the necks of poor men'.[86]

We do not perhaps sufficiently emphasize the sense of imminent catastrophe which many English men and women felt in the 1620s and 1630s. Thomas Brightman's belief that England was a doomed nation underlay his millenarianism.[87] To take random phrases from

---

82. A.Hughes, *Politics, Society and Civil War in Warwickshire, 1620–1660*, Cambridge University Press, 1987, pp. 100, 107–10. Cf. D. Underdown, *Revel, Riot and Rebellion: Popular Politics and Culture in England, 1603–1660*, Oxford University Press, 1985, pp. 124–6; Sommerville, *Politics and Ideology*, op. cit., p. 151; D. Hirst, *Authority and Conflict*, op. cit., p. 178.

83. Howell, *Familiar Letters*, op. cit., p. 32; *Calendar of State Papers, Venetian, 1632–6*, p. 466; B. Schofield (ed.) *The Knyvett Letters (1620–1644)*, 1949, p. 91.

84. J.S. Cockburn, *A History of English Assizes, 1558–1714*, Cambridge University Press, 1972, pp. 235–7; W. Laud, *Works*, Oxford University Press, 1860, VII, p. 382; cf. J.M. Bretnall, *William Bagshawe: The Apostle of the Peak*, 1970, p. 3: organized opposition in Derbyshire.

85. C. Bridenbaugh, *Vexed and Troubled Englishmen, 1590–1642*, Oxford University Press, 1968, pp. 458–69.

86. W. Prynne, *An Humble Remonstrance to His Majesty Against The Tax of Ship Money*, 1641, p. 23, quoted in B. Manning, *The English People and the English Revolution*, 1976, p. 154; Hughes, *Warwickshire*, op. cit., p. 149; Cust, *Forced Loan*, op. cit., pp. 259–60.

87. Avihu Zakai, 'Exile and kingdom: reformation, separation and the millenial quest in the formation of Massachusetts and its relationship with England, 1628–60', D. Phil thesis, Johns Hopkins University, 1982, p. 309. I am grateful to Dr Zakai for sending me a copy of this thesis.

the Barrington correspondence in 1628-9: 'God's heavy judgment most like to befall us'; 'God can bring upon us a worse scourge' even than Buckingham; 'we never had such need [to cry to the Lord] as now; . . . we have no other refuge to fly to'; 'these storms which in the eye of reason this sinful nation is likely to endure'. Sir William and Lady Masham besought 'the Lord to prepare us with comfort to brave what he may lay upon us'.[88] Such fears drove the Pilgrim Fathers and the Massachusetts Bay settlers to risk the horrors of the Atlantic crossing and life in the wilderness.

The Spanish marriage negotiations of the early 1620s led to intensified public interest in questions of foreign policy, stimulated by Puritan preachers, and to 'an attempt to marshal public opinion in opposition to the foreign policy of a government' for the first time in English history.[89] In 1623 Thomas Scott in exile was calling on ministers and freeholders to get godly men elected to parliament.[90]

Historians should take very seriously the evidence for Charles I's Popish Plot collected by Caroline Hibbard.[91] Many contemporaries were decisively influenced by belief in the existence of a plot against England's religion and national independence. During the civil war even royalists were alarmed.[92] On the other side Stephen Marshall was soon to refer to 'many of the nobles, magistrates, knights and gentlemen' as 'arrant traitors and rebels against God' – words even stronger than those of the Grand Remonstrance.[93] We cannot ignore the feeling behind such language, given the belief that a life-and-death struggle was going on between Christ and Antichrist. Frustrations had long been accumulating in the 'beleaguered isle'.[94] Under Grindal and Abbott there had been hope; under Whitgift, Bancroft and Laud, growing despair and desperation. The fact that Laud rejected the traditional Protestant equation of Antichrist with the Pope seemed evidence of his own antichristianity.[95]

This may help to resolve the paradox that the enemies of bishops

88. Searle, *Barrington Letters*, op. cit., pp. 29, 36-7, 56, 60, 77, 90.
89. G. Davies, 'English political sermons', *Huntington Library Quarterly*, 1939, 3, pp. 4-13; cf. my *Society and Puritanism*, Panther edn, pp. 41-2.
90. T. Scott, *The High-waies of the King*, 1623, p. 86.
91. Hibbard, *Charles I and the Popish Plot*, op. cit., *passim*.
92. Lord Henry Spencer and Captain John Fenwick, quoted in John Adair, *By the Sword Divided: Eyewitnesses of the English Civil War*, 1983, pp. 37-8, 131.
93. Stephen Marshall, *Reformation and Desolation*, 1642, p. 45; cf. Hibbard, *Charles I and the Popish Plot*, op. cit., pp. 246-7.
94. Carol Z. Wiener, 'The beleaguered isle: a study of Elizabethan and early Jacobean anti-catholicism', *Past and Present*, 1971, 51.
95. Cf. Ch. 4 of the present book.

seem to have been motivated mainly by religion, their defenders mainly by social considerations:[96] if bishops went, the attack might turn against peers and landlords. Conservatives were more aware of the revolutionary implications of Puritan ideology than the radicals: this had been true since the days of Martin Marprelate. The Marprelate Tracts offer a last example of irreverent plebeian discourse, referring to the Archbishop of Canterbury as 'nunckle Canterbury', 'that Caiaphas of Cant.,' 'that miserable and desperate caitiff'; to Bishop Aylmer as 'dumb dunsical John of good London'[97] When it became impossible to publish such tracts in England, Thomas Scott and others carried on the tradition from the Netherlands. The Marprelate Tracts were reprinted as soon as the censorship collapsed in 1640. Richard Overton echoed Marprelate; Levellers, Diggers, Ranters and early Quakers continued and developed this rival tradition of irreverent prose.

Until the government collapsed, all members of the propertied class were interested in preserving the king as the keystone of the social arch. For most of the time most of the people seem, so far as we can tell, to have accepted unquestioningly the necessity of a hierarchical society. But we must emphasize 'so far as we can tell'. I have been dealing throughout with respectable opinions. We get occasional glimpses of a different world among the lower classes. 'By God I do not care a turd neither for the King nor his laws', said an Essex man at the beginning of James I's reign; and Mr Emmison found much subversive talk attacking king, Council, officers and the church among the lower classes of this county.[98] How much significance should be attached to such letting off of steam is hard to assess. But the poverty, wars and misgovernment of the 1620s and 1630s, and the knowledge that their betters were dissatisfied, unleashed a rebelliousness which Brian Manning has documented. A country ballad singer, we are told in 1629, would have his songs 'interlarded with anything against the state, they are main helps to him and he will adventure to sing them though they cost him a whipping.'[99] Popular opinion in London was shown in the matter of bonfires. Ordered to celebrate Prince Charles's landing in Spain in 1623, they were 'thin and poor'; on his return, unmarried, they were

96. Joyce Malcolm, *Caesar's Due: Loyalty and King Charles I, 1642–6*, 1983, p. 163.
97. Martin Marprelate, *The Epistle*, 1588, p. 20; *Hay any worke for Cooper?*, 1589, p. 43; *Theses Martinianae*, 1589, Sig. C iiv; *The just censure and reproofe*, 1589, Sig. A iiv, B iiv – C ii.
98. F.G. Emmison, *Elizabethan Life: Disorder, Mainly from Essex Sessions and Assize Records*, Chelmsford, 1976, pp. viii, 39; cf. J. Sharpe, 'The people and the law', in B. Reay (ed.) *Popular Culture in Seventeenth-Century England*, 1985, p. 249.
99. Manning, *English People*, op. cit., *passim*; B. Capp, 'Popular literature', in Reay, *Popular Culture*, op. cit., pp. 227–8.

spontaneous, 'many and great'. Unofficial bonfires lit for the passing of the Petition of Right were 'such as were never seen but upon his Majesty's return from Spain'.[100]

'The whole land murmured' at the dissolution of 1622, D'Ewes told his diary; the king's reasons for it 'gave little satisfaction to any, and therefore, if the English had not altogether lost their spirits, some rebellion was expected.'[101] The 20-year-old D'Ewes no doubt exaggerated; but fear (or hope) of popular rebellion was not unique to him. Fulke Greville in 1593 had reminded MPs that 'if the feet knew their strength as we know their oppression, they would not bear as they do'.[102] In 1626 the Suffolk parson John Rous found that 'men be disposed to speak the worst of state business and to nourish discontent, as if there were a false carriage in all these things.' He thought that 'these men prepare' the way to 'an insurrection'. 'Our King's proceedings have caused men's minds to be incensed, to rove and project . . . looking towards the Lady Elizabeth' which 'is fearful to be thought of'. Rous believed this last idea could be dismissed as 'merely the conceit of the multitude', in itself a remarkable admission.[103] The French and Venetian ambassadors were aware of new tensions which might break out into rebellion once authority at the centre collapsed. So was an observer like Bacon, who said 'civil wars . . . seem to me apt to spread through many countries – because of certain ways of life not long since introduced'.[104] Fear that breakdown of ruling-class consensus might lead to social revolt was widespread. Keith Thomas collected a list of people alleged to have predicted the civil war; they included Richard Hooker, Lancelot Andrewes, Archbishops Abbott and Ussher, Nicholas Ferrar and others.[105]

Given this background, it might have been dangerous to allow even mildly critical speeches by MPs to be circulated to the general public. James I had complained that Coke 'hath made himself popular by . . . pulling down government'; he was 'held too great an oracle amongst the people', said Charles I.[106] After the dissolution of 1614

---

100. Bourcier (ed.) D'Ewes, *Diary*, op. cit., p. 162; Johnson and Cole, *Commons Debates, 1628*, op. cit., IV, p. 183.
101. Bourcier (ed.) D'Ewes, *Diary*, op. cit., p. 58; cf. pp. 64–5, 83, 130, 145.
102. D'Ewes, *A Complete Journal of the . . . House of Commons*, 1693, p. 490.
103. Green (ed.) Rous, *Diary*, op. cit., pp. 11–12, 19. 'The Lady Elizabeth' is of course the Queen of Bohemia.
104. F.H. Anderson, *The Philosophy of Francis Bacon*, Chicago University Press, 1948, p. 11.
105. Keith Thomas, *Religion and the Decline of Magic*, 1971, p. 132.
106. Spedding et al. (eds) Bacon, *Works*, op. cit., XIII, p. 95; *Calendar of State Papers, Domestic, 1629–31*, p. 490.

notes and papers of suspect members were seized and burnt; and again in 1629.[107] In 1628 Sir Dudley Digges would 'rather cover the power the subjects have than let it be openly spoke abroad, that mean men may not know it, which perhaps if they did should be inconvenient.' Sir Nathaniel Rich thought 'the meaner sort of people [were] in danger to join with [soldiers] and to fall into mutiny and rebellion'. The point was incorporated into a petition against billeting: 'the meaner sort . . . being exceeding poor . . . are not easily ruled' and were ready to cast off the reins of government. Such considerations were in the minds of MPs when they instructed Sir Henry Marten to remind the peers how undesirable it would be to refer to the limits on royal sovereignty in a document which would be printed and so made accessible to the vulgar.[108] A breach between the Commons on the one hand and the king and Lords on the other would be no less disastrous. 'Consider the consequences if we join not with the Commons', said the Earl of Clare. The popularity of Felton, Buckingham's assassin, with the lower classes must have given their betters food for thought.[109]

The fiercest quarrel in the House of Commons before the civil war arose over the proposal to appeal outside parliament by printing the Grand Remonstrance in November 1641. Sir Edward Dering was shocked by 'this descension from a Parliament to a people . . . The better sort think best of us . . . I did not dream that we should remonstrate downwards, tell stories to the people.' In the Short Parliament, Lord Keeper Finch referred to those who would be prepared to adopt 'Kett's and Cade's principles, which is to ruin the nobility, to ruin the gentry, to ruin learning and devour and eat up one another.'[110] In his Declaration in answer to the Grand Remonstrance, Charles I referred to the spate of 'seditious' pamphlets and sermons: 'We are many times amazed to consider by what eyes these things are seen, and by what ears they are heard'. Answering the Nineteen Propositions Charles predicted that 'at last the common people' will 'set up for themselves, and destroy all rights and properties'; government would 'end in a dark, equal chaos of confusion . . .

107. McClure, *Chamberlain Letters*, op. cit., I, p. 539.
108. Johnson and Cole, *Commons Debates, 1628*, op. cit., II, pp. 287, 391, 452. Cf. my *People and Ideas*, op. cit., pp. 42–4.
109. F.H. Relf (ed.) *Notes of the Debates of the House of Lords*, Camden Society, 3rd series, 42, 1929, p. 203. Cf. my *A Turbulent, Seditious and Factious People*, Oxford University Press, 1988, p. 4.
110. Rushworth, *Historical Collections*, op. cit., IV, p. 425; Cope and Coates, *Proceedings of the Short Parliament*, op. cit., pp. 131–2.

in a Jack Cade or a Wat Tyler'.[111] The king exaggerated for effect, but the repeated warnings would have been pointless if there were no basis for them. Contemporaries were not as surprised as some historians at what happened when revolution broke out.

If we think then of the ideas current in the world in which MPs lived, there were plenty which might make them sceptical of royal claims. Thomas Beard, Oliver Cromwell's schoolmaster, wrote a very popular book describing God's judgements on (among others) wicked princes. 'If you be mighty, puissant and fearful, know that the Lord is greater than you; . . . in what place soever you are, he is always above you, ready to hurl you down.' Archbishop Grindal had used similar words to Queen Elizabeth on a famous occasion. 'It is as easy with the Almighty to destroy the mightiest king as the poorest babe' said John Harington in the spirit of Beard.[112] Wallace MacCaffrey emphasizes the tension between Protestant loyalty to the sovereign and loyalty to what Puritans believed to be the the Word of God. Unfortunately the two did not always coincide.[113] This was one reason for not wanting the finer points of the dispute between Calvinists and Arminians to be 'talked of openly by the vulgar'.[114]

James I thought Ralegh's *History of the World* was 'too saucy in censuring princes'.[115] Hobbes believed that translations of the republican classics had been a significant contributory cause of the civil war.[116] There were many books on Venice, which Bacon among others admired as 'the wisest state of Europe'.[117] Above all there was the successful example of the United Provinces. Elizabethan government propaganda had stressed the 'perpetual unions of the . . . hearts together' of the peoples of England and the Netherlands.[118] Ralegh had drawn attention to the confiscation of aristocratic property in the Netherlands, and to the prosperity which resulted from merchants'

111. J. Nalson, *An Impartial Collection of the Great Affairs of State*, 1683, II, p. 747; Rushworth, *Historical Collections*, op. cit., V, p. 732.
112. T. Beard, *The Theatre of Gods Judgments*, 4th edn, 1648, title-page (first published 1597); Stieg (ed.), Harington, *Diary*, op. cit., p. 106.
113. MacCaffrey, *Queen Elizabeth*, op. cit., p. 492.
114. John Young to Samuel Ward, quoted in Peter White, 'The rise of Arminianism reconsidered', *Past and Present*, 1983, 101, p. 43 and *passim*.
115. Ralegh, *History of the World*, op. cit., I, pp. viii–xv, xxviii–xxxviii.
116. Thomas Hobbes, *Leviathan*, Penguin edn, p. 369; *Behemoth*, in Sir W. Molesworth (ed.) *English Works of Thomas Hobbes* (1839–48), VI, pp. 190–1.
117. Anon, *Cabala, Mysteries of State*, 1654, I, p. 8.
118. MacCaffrey, *Queen Elizabeth*, op. cit., pp. 340–1, 487.

control of the republic.[119] From 1604 onwards many MPs, including Coke, praised what they took to be the economic and social consequences of the Dutch revolt from Spain.[120] Hobbes indeed thought that London citizens 'were inclined to think that the like change of government would to them produce the like prosperity'. He was echoing what Nashe had said eighty-seven years earlier.[121]

The early Christian church could be held up as a model, without actually questioning the legitimacy of episcopacy. The liberty of the Anglo-Saxons before the introduction of Norman tyranny could be extolled, without specifying what if any elements of the Norman Yoke still remained. 'No subject of this realm', Coke was convinced, if he was 'truly instructed by the good and plain evidence of his ancient and undoubted patrimony and birthright . . . but will consult with learned and faithful counsellors for the recovery of the same'.[122] The appeal to the Anglo-Saxons was a call for political action. In the parliament of 1604 Sir Edwin Sandys appealed to natural rights.[123] It may or may not be coincidental that the abortive canons of 1606 anathematized those who believed civil society had originated from noble savages running about in the woods.[124] We recall James's suppression of the Society of Antiquaries, the closing of Cotton's library in 1629 and the suppression of Coke's *Institutes*. At the opposite pole of human history there was a widespread belief that the end of the world was approaching. Christ was the 'shortly-expected king' for many besides Milton. The evils which men saw around them could be attributed to 'these dead and declining times' which would immediately precede the Second Coming.[125] The fasts which the Commons called for to expiate the sins of the land were more than a formality. But speculations about the millennium could not circulate

119. Ralegh, *Works*, op. cit., II, pp. 15, 112–36; cf. pp. 89–90, 17–20.

120. S.R. Gardiner (ed.) *Parliamentary Debates in 1610*, Camden Society, 1st series 81, 1862, p. 114; Notestein et al., *1621 Debates*, op. cit., V, p. 93; J. Forster, *Sir John Eliot: a Biography*, 1865, I, p. 169.

121. Hobbes, *Behemoth*, op. cit., p. 168; Thomas Nashe, *Pierce Penilesse his Supplication to the Divell*, 1592, in R.B. McKerrow (ed.) *Works*, 5 vols, Oxford University Press, 1958, I, pp. 212–13.

122. Coke, *Fifth Reports*, 1605, Sig. A vb – A vi.

123. T.K. Rabb, 'Sir Edwin Sandys and the parliament of 1604', *American Historical Review*, 1963–4, 69, p. 668.

124. J.P. Kenyon (ed.) *The Stuart Constitution*, Cambridge University Press, 1966, pp. 11–12.

125. Searle, *Barrington Letters*, op. cit., p. 77; cf. Ralegh, *History of the World*, op. cit., I, p. 20; II, p. 650.

in print before 1640: they were thought to be dangerous and divisive. The seminal writings of Thomas Brightman were not allowed to be published in England, and Joseph Mede's scholarly work remained in Latin until a committee of the Long Parliament ordered its translation.

The logic of Protestantism called social hierarchy into question. In the 1530s some of Thomas Cromwell's protégés preached the equality of man and advocated a career open to the talents. Under Oliver Cromwell these doctrines were put into practice.[126] Ralegh thought that social rank was 'but as the change of garments in a play'. When 'every man wears but his own skin, the players are all alike'.[127] Lords Brooke and Saye and Sele were astonished when the Massachusetts Bay colonists politely but firmly refused to promise them the privileges of peers if they emigrated to New England. If they became church members they would enjoy the political rights of other church members; but no more.[128] That was an extreme position: but Beard's principles must have influenced many of the godly. 'In this Parliament', noted Yonge in 1624, 'there was not any one public bill sent to the lower house by them [the peers]. See what care they have for the commonwealth.'[129] 'I fear few lords have the main,' Lady Elizabeth Masham wrote to her mother in January 1630, 'the true fear of God which I prefer before all the honour in the world.' She was discussing a marriage proposal, but there are wider implications. Henry Oxinden wrote in 1642: 'If I see a man of what low degree or quality soever that is virtuous, rich, wise or powerful, him will I prefer before the greatest lord in the kingdom that comes short of him in these.'[130] (The words 'rich' and 'powerful' show that this is social rather than moral comment.)

Full hostility to the peerage was developed only by the radicals in the 1640s, attacking all distinction of ranks. But members of the lower house which could buy the lords up three times over must often have reflected on this disparity. Some historians tend to exaggerate the importance of the peerage in this period, because peers, like the king,

---

126. F. Caspari, *Humanism and the Social Order in Tudor England*, 1954, pp. 14–15; my *Intellectual Origins*, op. cit., pp. 266–7.
127. Ralegh, *History of the World*, op. cit., I, pp. vi, xl.
128. Zakai, 'Exile and kingdom', op. cit., p. 309.
129. Roberts, *Diary of Walter Yonge*, op. cit., p. 76. Cf. Coates (ed.) D'Ewes, *Journal*, op. cit., p. 224: 'I hope the citizens will be careful never to trust lord again, but to make them pay ready money.'
130. Searle, *Barrington Letters*, op. cit., p. 123; D. Gardiner, *The Oxinden Letters, 1607–42*, 1933, p. 279.

were still addressed with conventional respect. In that deferential society, a gentleman would ask a peer for a favour with proper humility. It does not prove that a Hampden, a Harington, or an Eliot was not equal in effective standing with many peers, nor even that a lesser gentleman like Pym would take orders from the Earl of Bedford.[131]

It was Oliver Cromwell who was said to have wished to see the Earl of Manchester but Mr Montagu again: the Montagus were parvenus even more recent than the Cromwells. It was Cromwell who pushed through the self-denying ordinance which deprived peers of their traditional right of military command; it was Cromwell who 'had rather have a plain russet-coated captain than that which you call "a gentleman" and is nothing else.'[132] Beard's and Cromwell's principles had perhaps a more decisive influence on the outcome of the civil war than is always recognized. The royalist armies suffered from what Monck called 'a rabble of gentility', who were expensive and bad for discipline. Parliament's shortage of officers helped to get Cromwell's principle of the career open to the talents enforced despite the reluctance of some commanding officers.[133]

In retrospect perhaps the most important fact about Cromwell was his irreverence, his subversion of degree. ' "The man is an Anabaptist?" What of it?' Provided he has the root of the matter in him his private opinions are as irrelevant as the colour of his blood. At Naseby, Oliver reported, 'God would by things that are not bring to nought things that are.'[134] That looks forward to the world of revolutionary democracy; but it also looks back to Foxe's conception of the godly English common people. It was Cromwell who in November 1641 proposed what was to become the militia ordinance of March 1642, the first direct challenge to the king's sovereignty.[135] He was reported as saying that if he met the king on the battlefield he would shoot him as he would any other enemy. 'We will cut off his head with the crown on it.' His irreverence was directed not only against social rank and the divinity hedging kings but also against all the formality of authority. 'Take away that bauble.' Whether or not Oliver did refer

131. J.H. Hexter, 'Power struggle, parliament and liberty in early Stuart England', *Journal of Modern History*, 1978, 50, p. 70; my *People and Ideas*, op. cit., pp. 27–8.
132. Abbott (ed.), *Cromwell's Writings*, op. cit., I, pp. 256, 262.
133. Malcolm, *Caesar's Due*, op. cit., Ch. 4, contains much useful information on this question.
134. Abbott (ed.) *Cromwell's Writings*, op. cit., I, pp. 278, 365.
135. Coates (ed.) D'Ewes, *Journal*, op. cit., pp. 97–8.

to 'Magna farta' the attribution is *ben trovato*. Such remarks would go down well with the troops.

The seventeenth century saw a turning-point in English and world history, from a deference society dominated by an aristocracy of the armigerous, whose weapons made them traditionally immune, to something beginning to look more like the modern world, a society of relative equality, of social mobility, of promotion by merit. Bacon had envisaged such a society and ineffectually recommended it to the young Sir George Villiers as 'that which I think was never done since I was born'.[136]

But the break came with revolution: Cromwell had the appropriate sentiments for leading it. Oliver was no intellectual: it is difficult to think of him as the ideologist of the English Revolution. But he gave colourful expression to ideas which motivated its most enthusiastic supporters. His irreverence dates back to his co-operation with the freemen of Huntingdon and with the Fenmen. It relates to the social changes so carefully demonstrated by Stone, Manning, Hirst, Wrightson and Hunt – decline of the aristocracy, growing class tensions, new importance of parish élites who found Puritanism sociologically as well as theologically attractive, growing importance of rank-and-file electors to parliament. As early as 1610 an MP said, apropos of taxation and control of ale-houses, 'If we bring not ease in these things home with us to our neighbours, we shall hardly be welcome.'[137]

Historians who have failed to find long-term causes of the English Revolution, as well as those who have failed to notice that there was a revolution at all, have perhaps been looking for the wrong things in the wrong places. There were no revolutionaries who willed what happened, no Lenin: there were virtually no republicans in the Long Parliament. But there were tensions in the society, slowly building up in the decades before 1640: and there was an ideology, popularized by Foxe and Beard, which in appropriate circumstances could become revolutionary, as it did in Cromwell. Men remembered Marprelate in 1641. Scholars have spoken of a 'polarization of taste'.[138] There

---

136. Anon, *Cabala*, op. cit., II, p. 71.
137. Foster, *1610 Parliament*, op. cit., II, p. 95.
138. Capp, 'Popular literature', op. cit., pp. 231–2; P.W. Thomas, 'Two cultures? court and country under Charles I', in C. Russell (ed.) *The Origins of the English Civil War*, 1975.

were also those unspeakable lower classes, some of whom expressed opinions far removed from those approved in respectable discourse.

The problem for those who wanted change was not to foment rebellion, but to prevent social revolt from below from breaking out. Sir Robert Cotton in 1628 argued that although parliament must do all it could to get rid of the Duke of Buckingham, still in the last resort opposition must not be pushed too far lest it open the gates to popular insurrection.[139] In Harrington's famous words, 'the dissolution of this government caused the [civil] war, not the war the dissolution of the government'. Charles I had lost his crown already, Cardinal Barberini informed Henrietta Maria in February 1642.[140] It is surely more plausible to see continuities than to assume that the startling shifts in opinion between 1640 and 1649 had no antecedent causes.

Consider a couple of analogous cases where contemporary modes of discourse can mislead. We often take at face value statements of the necessary subordination of women in seventeenth-century literature. Milton is firm on the point; but in *Paradise Lost* it is Eve who restores Adam to himself after the Fall and who is given the last spoken words in the epic – normally reserved, as Milton and his educated readers knew, for the hero or a deity.[141] Lucy Hutchinson told her children that the 'felicity' of Queen Elizabeth's reign 'was the effect of her submission to her masculine and wise counsellors'. But when her husband lost his nerve at the restoration, it was she who saved him from a death sentence by writing a penitent letter on his behalf, to which she forged his signature. (Or it may be that in claiming this she is covering up for her husband, who endorsed the letter as 'a copy of my letter to the House of Commons'. But whichever way we interpret it, her submissive words are belied by her actual behaviour as a wife).[142] John Bunyan, like Milton and Mrs Hutchinson, believed that the inferiority of women necessitated their subordination: 'modesty and shamefacedness becomes women at all times'. But Mrs Bunyan in 1661

---

139. R. Cotton, *The Dangers Wherein the Kingdome now Standeth*, 1628. I owe this reference to Simon Adams.

140. Harrington, *Political Works*, ed. J.G.A. Pocock, Cambridge University Press, 1977, p. 198; Notestein (ed.) D'Ewes, *Journal*, op. cit., 1923, p. 321.

141. J. Wittreich, *Feminist Milton*, Cornell University Press, 1987, pp. 107–8.

142. Hutchinson, *Memoirs*, op. cit., pp. xviii–xix, 48, 229–34, 290–2; Margaret George, *Women in the First Capitalist Society: Experiences in Seventeenth-Century England*, Illinois University Press, 1988, Ch. 1.

showed a very unwomanly initiative in fighting to save her husband from imprisonment.[143]

Some historians have argued that the passion of love was non-existent before the eighteenth century, because few talked about it and the preachers preached against it. The fact that it was not talked about was a convention of discourse: passion was not regarded as morally desirable. But the preachers would not have warned so regularly and so strongly against something that did not exist. The same is true of love for children. It too was not an invention of the eighteenth century, as a reaction of demand to an increase in supply. The preachers here too warned against excessive displays of emotion which became fashionable only with the rise of romanticism.

The restoration of 1660 was followed by a reinforcement of censorship and tacit agreement on conventions of responsible political discourse, including condemnation of anything that savoured of 'enthusiasm'. But the emphasis had subtly shifted. The king was once more immune from criticism; but now England had a 'mixed monarchy'. Royal power was indissolubly linked with that of parliament, with liberty, property and the Protestant religion, all of which the king was now deemed to support.[144] Professor Zwicker argues that in any period there are conventions of political discourse, things that can and cannot be said, and that to try to read the literature without being aware of these conventions may lead to disastrous misunderstandings. He is concerned with the special case of the post-revolutionary period, when men were anxious to preserve a consensus which they knew to be fragile. But *mutatis mutandis* there was a similar awareness, and there were similar conventions, in the period before 1640.[145] 'Platitudes and pious hopes about balance were useful in disguising the reality of disagreement on matters of substance', writes Dr Sommerville of the years before 1640. Rhetoric was used to conceal ideological conflict.[146]

143. G. Offor (ed.) *Works of John Bunyan*, 1860, II, pp. 438–9, 673–4; J. Bunyan, 'A relation of my imprisonment', in Bunyan, *Grace Abounding*, ed. R. Sharrock, Oxford University Press, 1977, pp. 125–9.
144. J. Miller, 'Charles II and his parliaments', *RHS Transactions*, 1982, 5th series, 32, p. 17; H. Nenner, *By Colour of Law: Legal Culture and Constitutional Politics in England, 1660–1689*, Chicago University Press, 1977, p. 10.
145. S.N. Zwicker, *Politics and Language in Dryden's Poetry*, Princeton University Press, 1984, esp. Ch. 1 and Epilogue; Nicholas Jose, *Ideas of the Restoration in English Literature, 1660–71*, 1984, p. 23.
146. Sommerville, *Politics and Ideology*, op. cit., pp. 137, 140–1; cf. M. Butler, 'Politics and the masque: the triumph of peace', *The Seventeenth Century*, 1987, II, 2, p. 138.

Conventions of discourse work much more subtly than censorship because they are self-imposed. To take what Dryden wrote always at its surface value, Zwicker writes, is to read his words 'with a naïveté about the character of political language in his age and an ignorance of the complexity of circumstances in which he wrote'. 'Politicians understood that after civil war and political revolution, deception would enable men to approximate civic stability.' 'All those who entered public debate . . . covered themselves with the garb of moderation, because the language of the ancient constitution, of rights and liberties, of balance and moderation, was the accepted language of political discourse'.[147] It was as treasonable, Marvell argued in 1677, to make monarchy absolute as to 'alter our monarchy into a commonwealth'.[148] Political revolution necessitated a change in the accepted terms of discourse.

There is, it seems to me, far more to explain if we abandon some such concept as the Great Rebellion, the Puritan Revolution or the English Revolution. To say it was an accident leaves army democracy, Levellers and the execution of Charles I totally inexplicable. The leaders' compulsion to act came from religion: when the breakdown of government could no longer be prevented, revolutionary Puritanism took over, first leading to revolt, then suppressing the radicals. But the breakdown was no accident: it was foreseen by the articulate few who crossed the Atlantic because 'God is leaving England.' The religious perspective, the sense of God's continuing watchfulness over England, explained in retrospect what Cromwell called 'the revolutions of Christ'. God called the Long Parliament, God created the New Model Army. Oliver Cromwell was 'the force of angry heaven's flame' [which] 'cast the kingdom old/Into another mould'.[149]

147. Zwicker, *Politics and Language*, op. cit., pp. 26, 29, 31-3, 54, 59-60, 88, 206-7; cf. 103, 218-20.
148. Andrew Marvell, *An Account of the Growth of Popery and Arbitrary Government in England*, Amsterdam, 1677, in A.B. Grosart (ed.) *Complete Works in Verse and Prose*, 1872-5, IV, p. 261.
149. I read Susan Staves's 'Where is history but in texts? Reading the history of marriage', in J.M. Wallace (ed.) *The Golden and the Brazen World: Papers in Literature and History 1650-1800*, California University Press, 1985, after this was written. What she has to say is very relevant to my argument. See now Alison Wall, 'Elizabethan precept and feminine practice: the Thynne family of Longleat', *History*, 1990, 243, pp. 23-38.

4

Archbishop Laud's place in English history

Methinks I see a cloud arising and threatening the Church of England. God of his mercy dissipate it.

> Laud, *Diary*, 29 January 1626; *Works*, op. cit., III, p. 180

William Juxon, Lord Bishop of London, made Lord High Treasurer. No churchman had it since Henry VII's time. . . . And now if the church will not hold up themselves under God, I can do no more.

> Laud, *Diary*, 6 March 1636; *Works*, op. cit., III, p. 226

It is a hard thing in this age to bring men to understand the good that is done them.

> Laud to the Vice-Chancellor of Oxford University, 10 April 1637; *Works*, V, p. 166

It has become fashionable to deny that the English Revolution had any long-term causes: what happened between 1640 and 1660 was rather the result of accident, of converging coincidences. If you start with such assumptions, naturally the role of personality looms large in historical explanation. Many have seen Archbishop Laud as the *diabolus ex machina*. Nicholas Tyacke saw 'Laudian revolutionaries'.[1] Even that great historian Patrick Collinson swam with the tide in his Ford Lectures, *The Religion of Protestants*, where he suggested that all (or nearly all) was well with the English church until the advent of Laud.

There have been attempts to clear Laud of responsibility for disrupting a previously harmonious Church of England. Rosemary O'Day and Ann Hughes, two of the most powerful historians of the

---

1. N. Tyacke, 'Puritanism, Arminianism and the counter-revolution', in C. Russell, *Origins of the English Civil War*, op. cit., pp. 121, 132–3.

younger generation, suggested that 'our perceptions of the religious history of the sixteen-thirties are still perhaps too much dominated by the confrontation between Laud and the force of Puritanism'.[2] Peter White thinks it an overstatement to describe the Church of England as solidly Calvinist before Laud. Bancroft was no Calvinist, and James I (no doubt at Bancroft's instance) promoted Andrewes and Harsnett in 1609, as well as Buckeridge in 1611 and Overall in 1614,[3] Julian Davis has suggested that it was subordinate Laudians rather than the archbishop himself who were forcing the pace on ceremonies.[4]

I shall suggest that most of Laud's actions and beliefs were quite traditional, at any rate if we look back to Archbishops Whitgift and Bancroft. Things were different under Grindal, and again under Abbott. But Grindal lasted as effective primate only for his hundred days, and Abbott for little more than ten years. It is the exceptions that call for explanation, Grindal and Abbott, rather than the norm – Whitgift – Bancroft – Laud. But the dualism is interesting, suggesting that two alternative possibilities were deadlocked.

There had been a potential split within the Church of England from its very inception. The Reformation claimed to be based on the Word of God; it was carried through by the godly princes Henry VIII, Edward VI and Elizabeth. At this stage few envisaged a conflict between the Bible and the commands of the head of the church. But such a conflict is all but inevitable in a Protestant state church. The principle of the priesthood of all believers is logically opposed to the very idea of a church controlled from on top. It sets the individual against any form of hierarchy.[5] Protestant reformers, encouraging the study of the Bible in the vernacular and criticizing papal abuses, stimulated wide-ranging discussions, which alarmed governments and the rulers of the church. Individual lay consciences will not always accept the interpretations of a priesthood; the apostolic succession as a source of authority contradicts the idea of a predestined elect. Laud was not the first to observe that the anarchical principle of

---

2. 'Augmentation and amalgamation: was there a systematic approach to the reformation of parochial finance, 1640–1660?', in R. O'Day and F. Heal (eds) *Princes and Paupers in the English Church, 1500–1700*, Leicester University Press, 1981, p. 131.
3. P. White, 'The rise of Arminianism reconsidered', *Past and Present*, 1983, 101, *passim*.
4. J. Davis, unpublished paper, 'The genesis and enforcement of the Laudian Altar Policy', which he kindly allowed me to read.
5. Cf. D. Zaret, *The Heavenly Contract: Ideology and Organization in Pre-Revolutionary Puritanism*, Chicago University Press, 1985, pp. 62–4: J.R. Knott, *Sword of the Spirit: Puritan Responses to the Bible*, Chicago University Press, 1971, p. 40.

private judgement threatened to destroy Protestant churches from within; nor was he the first to try to avert this by stifling public discussion of perplexing questions.[6] Nearly a century earlier Henry VIII had tried to abolish 'diversity of opinions' by parliamentary statute. The point was demonstrated during the English Revolution, when Presbyterians, Independents and separatists all proved incapable of agreeing on how the church should be reformed, or what should replace it: contrary to Milton's expectations in *Areopagitica*, the more free discussion, the less agreement there was.

The problems which Laud faced were *inherited* problems, only in part of his making. Over the course of a century they had accumulated and become more difficult to solve, but their roots go back at least to the Reformation. We are not dealing with a matter of personal preferences. The 'rise of Arminianism', as we feebly call it, took place in a society experiencing a crisis of confidence in the government of church and state. Some intellectually respectable answer had to be produced to the logic of Calvinism, which French and Dutch experience had shown could be put to revolutionary uses. Many theologians genuinely shrank from the full logic of Calvinist predestinarianism. As Tyacke has shown, there were 'proto-Arminians' among the parish clergy before Laud; under James and Charles there were aspiring clergymen ready – some for proper theological reasons, others because they smelt the loaves and fishes – to put their pens at the disposal of a government threatened or apparently threatened by ideas which called a hierarchical state church in question.

Early Elizabethan bishops, many of them Marian exiles, had trouble with Puritans who had been their companions in exile – not only with clerics but with laymen, who often pushed ministers into opposition to the demands of the hierarchy.[7] For Puritanism itself was never monolithic. Separatists clashed with conforming 'Presbyterians', Puritan ministers found themselves caught between their episcopal superiors and their lay supporters, much as MPs in the 1620s found themselves squeezed between the crown and the electorate.

Martin Marprelate in 1589 offended both Puritan ministers and lay sympathizers from the gentry and aristocracy by his vigorous,

---

6. Laud to Vossius, 14 July 1629, in *Works*, op. cit., VI, pp. 265–6; cf. Lancelot Andrewes, *96 Sermons*, 1629, p. 163; Bacon, Essays III, XVII, and LVIII.
7. Zaret, *Heavenly Contract*, op. cit., Chs 1, 4 and 5, *passim*.

irreverent, subversive appeal to ordinary people against bishops.[8]
Nashe (or some other government pamphleteer) summed up:

> Yes, he that now saith, Why should bishops be?
> Will next cry out, Why kings? The saints are free.[9]

The Earl of Hertford took the point: 'as they shoot at bishops now, so
will they do at the nobility also if they be suffered'.[10] 'No bishop, no
King, no nobility' was James I's more succinct version.[11] How right
they all were! The alarm of the respectable permitted Whitgift and
Bancroft to persecute clerical Presbyterianism almost out of existence. Henceforth a favourite tactic with defenders of the hierarchy
was to stress the dangers of democratic anarchy inherent in Puritanism. Parker, Whitgift and James I all opposed the seditious rabble
no less than did Laud.[12] 'Parity in the church will lead to parity in the
state' was the cry from the 1580s to the 1640s.[13] In 1640-1, when
bishops were attacked for religious and constitutional reasons, they
were defended on social grounds. It was to re-emphasize the hierarchical principle that Bancroft first proclaimed the divine right of
bishops, a claim later emphasized by the Laudians. Like James I's
doctrine of the divine right of kings, it was a response to challenges
from below.[14] Milton did not fail in 1641 to taunt the bishops with
'that old pharisaical fear that still dogs them, the fear of the people'.[15]
'Equality of persons' said Whitgift in a sermon preached on the
twenty-fifth anniversary of Elizabeth's accession, 'engendreth strife,
which is the cause of all evil'.[16]

As paths divided under Elizabeth, bishops became more and more
dependent on the royal supremacy; and the crown had increasing

---

8. The Marprelate Tracts, like the Geneva Bible and the Admonition of 1572, were
published in handy pocket editions (W. Pierce, *An Historical Introduction to the Marprelate
Tracts*, 1908, p. 40).
9. Anon, *A Whip for an Ape*, 1589.
10. Pierce, *Historical Introduction*, op. cit., p. 182.
11. Godfrey Goodman, *The Court of King James I*, 1839, I, p. 421.
12. J. Strype, *The Life and Acts of Matthew Parker*, Oxford University Press, II, p. 323;
The Life and Acts of John Whitgift, Oxford University Press, 1822, III, pp. 70–81, 126.
13. See my *Religion and Politics in 17th Century England*, Brighton, 1986, pp. 88–9 for
examples; N. Tyacke, *Anti-Calvinists: The Rise of Arminianism, 1590–1640*, Oxford,
1987, pp. 134–6. The argument had been used from the earliest days of the Reformation: see Tyndale, *Doctrinal Treatises*, Parker Society, 1848, p. 247.
14. My *Religion and Politics*, op. cit., pp. 98–101; cf. pp. 44–5 above.
15. Milton, *Complete Prose Works*, op. cit., I, p. 683.
16. Strype, *Whitgift*, op. cit., III, p. 72.

need of the church as an instrument of government.[17] Between 1567 and 1586 there had been no ecclesiastics on the Queen's Council.[18] On the whole councillors were unfriendly to bishops, often overruling their actions. In June 1584 Sir Francis Knollys complained to Burghley of 'the prelatic government of matters of state' as well as of the church. In July Burghley wrote his famous letter to Whitgift comparing the High Commission to the Spanish Inquisition.[19] But Elizabeth gave consistent support to her archbishop, and ultimately Burghley came to terms with Whitgift, accepting him on the Privy Council as an ally against Leicester's faction. Yet as late as 1593 John Penry still thought it worth while to appeal to Burghley as well as to Essex against his condemnation by the bishops.[20]

But apart from the interludes of Grindal (Burghley's nominee)[21] and Abbott, the interests of church and crown were tightly linked; there was normally close co-operation between them. Grindal's overthrow resulted from his support for prophesyings, for preaching, a dispute which recurred under every archbishop from Parker to Laud.[22] But Grindal's disgrace was also connected with foreign policy. Grindal was allied with the Leicester – Walsingham group which advocated an adventurous pro-Protestant policy.[23] The archbishop's sequestration was followed by an opening to the right – the rise of Hatton (and Whitgift, Hatton's chaplain) and by the disintegration of the Leicester faction.[24] Burghley, who had previously attempted to mediate, came down on the side of conservatism and caution.

A similar pattern can be observed in the case of Abbott after 1610. He too discreetly encouraged prophesyings,[25] and he favoured a

17. Cf. my Religion and Politics, op. cit., pp. 104-8, 111.
18. D.L. Keir, Constitutional History of Modern Britain since 1485, 8th edn, 1966, p. 114.
19. M.M. Knappen, Tudor Puritanism: A Chapter in the History of Idealism, Chicago University Press, 1939, pp. 261-2, 275.
20. A. Peel (ed.) The Notebook of John Penry, 1593, Camden Society, 3rd series, 67, 1944, pp. 53-77, 85-93.
21. J. Strype, History of the Life and Acts of . . . Edmund Grindal, Oxford University Press, 1821, p. 282.
22. Strype, Matthew Parker, op. cit., II, Ch. 37. Cf. John Morgan, Godly Learning: Puritan Attitudes towards Reason, Learning and Education, 1560-1640, Cambridge University Press, 1986, pp. 84-5.
23. P. Collinson, The Elizabethan Puritan Movement, 1967, pp. 202-5, 314, 444; Archbishop Grindal, 1519-1583: The Struggle for a Reformed Church, 1979, pp. 256-7.
24. For the anguish which Grindal's fall and the shift in foreign policy caused Spenser and the circle around Leicester, see MacCaffrey, Queen Elizabeth, op. cit., pp. 264-5, 446-7, quoting P.E. McLane, Spenser's Shephearde's Calender, Notre Dame, Indiana, 1961, Chs. 4 and 5. Cf. my Religion and Politics, op. cit., Ch. 6.
25. Collinson, Grindal, op. cit., pp. 291-2.

Protestant foreign policy – support for the Netherlands, Bohemia and the Palatinate.[26] Abbott believed that the true church had no necessary connection with institutions, and had not always been visible; during the popish Middle Ages the meanest of the people had carried it on. But since the Reformation it had become visible in international Protestantism, of which the Church of England was a part. Abbott could therefore have no truck with Laud's belief that Rome was a true church.[27] Abbott was associated with the Pembroke group in the Council and with its foreign policy. His sequestration was the consequence of his refusal to license Robert Sibthorp's sermon defending a forced loan.[28] His disgrace removed an obstacle to James's policy of appeasement of Spain, desertion of the Palatinate and the Netherlands, and non-involvement with the Calvinist international. It led to the silencing of theological discussion in England. In 1626–8 there was a rapid series of new appointments to bishoprics of a very different outlook from that of the archbishop, recalling the similar conservative appointments after Grindal's disgrace.[29]

But foreign policy entailed internal social consequences – under Whitgift the rise of Hatton, persecution of Puritans and separatists, relative lenience to Catholics, culminating in Bancroft's direct negotiations with them.[30] In 1616 Abbott was described as being in conflict with 'the court bishops and other courtiers that commonly prevail'. The issue was appointment to bishoprics.[31] In the 1620s first the Spanish marriage negotiations and then Charles I's French marriage led to non-enforcement of the penal laws and release of Catholics from gaol – *de facto* toleration for papists.

26. Cf. Abbott's forceful letter to Secretary Naunton in September 1619 (Anon, *Cabala*, op. cit., I, pp. 169–70).

27. Norbrook, *Poetry and Politics in the English Renaissance*, 1984, pp. 230–1. Abbott's criticisms of Laud were apparently made in 1603, though not published until 1624 as *A Treatise of the Perpetual Visibility and Succession of the True Church in All Ages*.

28. Rushworth, *Historical Collections*, op. cit., I, p. 431.

29. Collinson, *Elizabethan Puritan Movement*, op. cit., p. 201, gives examples. Cf. M. Schwarz, 'Arminianism and the English parliament, 1624–1629', *Journal of British Studies*, 1973, 12, pp. 57, 62–3: of 13 newly-appointed bishops in 1626–8, only one was unsympathetic to the Laudians, and that one was Joseph Hall, who defended Richard Montagu and was later the author of *Episcopacy by Divine Right*, 1640.

30. Pierce, *Historical Introduction*, op. cit., pp. 204–5. In 1602 Bancroft was accused to the House of Commons of shielding a secret Catholic printing press (H.H. Plomer, 'Bishop Bancroft and a Catholic press', *The Library*, April 1907).

31. McClure, *Chamberlain Letters*, op. cit., II, p. 44; cf. ibid., I, pp. 528–31: the bishops said to be angry with Secretary Winwood for speaking against recusants and idle churchmen (May 1614).

Thus Grindal and Abbott both stood for a Protestant foreign policy of the sort favoured by Puritans (and many others) in parliament. The 'popularity' of Grindal and Abbott was of course relative: both got on well with the gentry of Kent, as Whitgift, Bancroft and Laud did not. Whitgift was more renowned for his entertainments of the queen than of his neighbours. He was, he admitted, charged with being the first archbishop that 'set myself against the gentlemen of Kent'.[32]

So religion, foreign policy and social considerations continually worked to strengthen the alliance between the leaders of the church and the crown. The government, lacking the army and bureaucracy with which continental monarchies enforced their policies, needed the machinery of the church, including its executive organ, the Court of High Commission; and it needed the church's legitimating function, its control of heresy, of the press, and of education. 'No man can libel against' the clergy, Laud declared, 'but he libels against the King and the state'.[33] The church needed the support of the crown against continuing threats of further plunder of its landed property. Leicester, Essex and Buckingham in their time were all cast in the role of leader of the 'Puritan' aristocracy and gentry in such an attack.[34]

So there were two rival policies for the English church, one represented by Whitgift and Bancroft, the other by Grindal and Abbott. Conflict between the two involved far more than ecclesiastical or theological questions: foreign policy, the authority of the crown, prerogative versus parliament. It came to include questions of taxation to pay for policy as the crown's financial problems led to disagreements with the House of Commons.

Naturally bishops like Whitgift, Bancroft and Laud, and others with ambitions, came to support the crown in these disputes. The Canons of 1604 were attacked in the House as infringing the rights of property; bishops were viewed with suspicion by many in the Commons. In 1610 Bancroft thought that the proposition that 'the King's necessity must be supported' was a sound point in speculative divinity. In parliament the same year Marten attacked clergymen who preached up a prerogative

32. P. Heylyn, *Cyprianus Anglicus, or the History of the Life and Death of William Laud, Archbishop of Canterbury*, 1671, pp. 161, 228–30; Peter Clark, *English Provincial Society from the Reformation to the Revolution: Religion, Politics and Society in Kent, 1500–1640*, 1977, p. 172; cf. pp. 306, 366. See F. Heal, 'Archbishop Laud revisited: leases and estate management at Canterbury and Winchester before the civil war', in O'Day and Heal, *Princes and Paupers*, op. cit., pp. 134–40, 150. Dr Heal is less sure of the contrast between Grindal and Whitgift in respect of hospitality, but confirms that between Abbott and Laud.
33. Laud, *Works*, op. cit., V, pp. 43–4.
34. Collinson, *Elizabethan Puritan Movement*, op. cit., *passim*.

right to taxation; four years later he and Sir Roger Owen repeated the charge. Bishop Neile was in trouble for attacking the House of Commons, and there was 'murmuring against the bishops' for urging payment of a benevolence after the dissolution of 1610 – though they were alleged to have been less than generous in their own contributions.[35] In his conflict with the common-law courts Bancroft asserted that all jurisdiction, spiritual and temporal, belonged to the king, who must decide when there was a conflict of jurisdictions.[36] Whitgift disliked parliaments as much as Laud did, though the latter was rather more outspoken in public.

Laud and Neile tried to get the author of an anonymous pamphlet attacking the forced loan of 1626 indicted for treason. Sermons were preached in favour of the loan by Sibthorp, Manwaring, Matthew Wren and Isaac Bargrave. It has been argued that the quarrel over Richard Montagu was mainly about jurisdiction. Montagu's *Appello Caesarem* rejected the authority of parliament in religious matters. The Commons' Declaration against Manwaring in 1628, and Pym's speech to the House of Lords demanding his impeachment, were careful to stress Manwaring's subversion of parliament and the laws of England, steering clear of his theological opinions. His wicked intention was 'to avert His Majesty's mind from calling of Parliaments'. Selden in 1628 said he had never heard property attacked save in the pulpit.[37] The statement on the 'regal power' of taxation in the canons of 1640 was the culmination of a long tradition.

So far as there were theories of or leanings towards absolutism in seventeenth-century England, they were patronized by Bancroft and the Laudians. I am delighted to have the support here of J.P. Sommerville's seminal book, *Politics and Ideology in England, 1603-1640*.[38] Dr John Cowell, author of *The Interpreter* (1607), a book

35. Foster, *1610 Parliament*, op. cit., II, pp. 79, 328. Marten was probably attacking, among others, Samuel Harsnett, Bishop of Chichester. Cf. T.L. Moir, *The Addled Parliament of 1614*, Oxford University Press, 1958, pp. 116–17; McClure, *Chamberlain Letters*, op. cit., I, pp. 542, 546; Sommerville, *Politics and Ideology*, op. cit., p. 214–15.
36. Nenner, *By Colour of Law*, op. cit., p. 71; cf. H.R. Trevor-Roper, *Catholics, Anglicans and Puritans*, 1987, pp. 114–16.
37 T. Fuller, *Church History of Britain*, 1655, IV, p. 129; S.R. Gardiner, *History of England*, 1883–4, Ch. 61; Rushworth, *Historical Collections*, op. cit., I, p. 597; Schwartz, 'Arminianism', op. cit., esp. pp. 52–67; Cust, *Forced Loan*, op. cit., pp. 61–3, 304 and *passim*. Manwaring insisted that his sermon should be printed 'by his Majesty's special command'. Cf. Trevor-Roper, *Catholics, Anglicans and Puritans*, op. cit., p. 98.
38. Sommerville, *Politics and Ideology*, op. cit., esp. pp. 119, 127–31, 178, 193–4; cf. Tyacke, *Anti-Calvinists*, op. cit., pp. 158–9.

denounced in the Commons and reluctantly banned by James, was a protégé of Bancroft's. Laud allowed this book to be reprinted, unexpurgated, in 1637: this formed one of the articles against him at his trial.[39] Sibthorp and Manwaring drew on the ideas of French absolutists in the 1620s.[40] At the height of the crisis over the Petition of Right, Pym argued with much support that Arminianism, alteration in religion, was linked with a plan to alter the government.[41] An amendment from the House of Lords proposing to insert the words 'upon necessity' about taxation was rejected on 19 May precisely because 'these reasons have already been preached by Manwaring to the King'.[42] In the Lords Harsnett, now Archbishop of York, so defined royal power that the subjects were 'left little or no assurance of their property'.[43] The theorizing of the Laudians led to ideological polarization. As one side attacked 'popery', so the other denounced 'popularity'.[44]

Use of the High Commission as a regular court dates from Whitgift's primacy, and initially roused protests from Privy Councillors as well as from parliament. Whitgift claimed that use of the oath *ex officio* was necessary because of the unreliability of JPs. Brownists and Familists would never be presented in the normal procedure 'if the chief gentleman in the parish or most of the parish be so affected'.[45] Whitgift and especially Bancroft used the High Commission consistently to enforce uniformity. In 1610 the Commons petitioned against the High Commission as an innovation.[46] More and more the court came to be used interchangeably with Star Chamber, especially in enforcing the censorship, and in prosecuting those whose rank made them likely to escape normal judicial processes.[47] But Star

39. S.B. Chrimes, 'Constitutional ideas of Dr J. Cowell', *English Historical Review*, 1949, 64, p. 474.
40. White, 'Rise of Arminianism', op. cit, *passim*.
41. Johnson and Cole, *Commons Debates, 1628*, op. cit., III, pp. 411–16; IV, pp. 103–10; White, 'Rise of Arminianism', op. cit., p. 51. Cf. W. Notestein and F. Relf (eds) *Commons Debates, 1629*, Minnesota University Press, 1921, pp. 15–16.
42. Johnson and Cole, *Commons Debates, 1628*, op. cit., II, pp. 478, 536; cf. pp. 411–12, 416, 624; IV, pp. 102–8.
43. M.A. Judson, *The Crisis of the Constitution: an essay in constitutional and political thought in England, 1603–1645*, Rutgers University Press, 1949, pp. 164–5.
44. Cust, *Forced Loan*, op. cit., Chs 3–5 and Conclusion, *passim*; Trevor-Roper, *Catholics, Anglicans and Puritans*, op. cit., pp. 164–5.
45. J.R. Tanner (ed.) *Tudor Constitutional Documents*, Cambridge University Press, 1930, pp. 360, 368.
46. J.R. Tanner (ed.) *Constitutional Documents of the Reign of James I*, Cambridge University Press, 1930, pp. 149–54; Sommerville, *Politics and Ideology*, op. cit., p. 213.
47. Tanner, *James I*, op. cit., pp. 144, 146. The judges had recognized the High Commission as a legal ecclesiastical court in Cawdrey's Case, 1591.

Chamber was used when corporal penalties were demanded; Laud in 1637 reminded Strafford of the fate of Udall and Penry in Elizabeth's reign.[48] Coke made many famous attacks on the High Commission, its authority and procedure, especially its use of the oath *ex officio*. But under Abbott Richard Montagu thought the Commission's power insufficient. 'Before God', he wrote to Cosin in 1624, 'it will never be well till we have our Inquisition'.[49]

Associated with foreign policy was the question of relations with foreign Protestant churches. The Marian exiles had established close relations with Geneva, Strasbourg, Zurich and other Protestant cities; bishops among others consulted Calvin, Bullinger and others on the progress and problems of the Reformation in England. The foreign churches in England were especially warmly treated by Grindal.[50] Essex ministers in 1580 argued against the English prayer book that it was out of step with continental Protestantism; Martin Marprelate in 1588 took pleasure in pointing out that the Swiss, Scottish, French, Bohemian and Dutch churches, among others, regarded episcopal authority as Antichristian.[51]

Whitgift and Bancroft were much less enthusiastic about connections with foreign Protestant churches than Grindal had been. Whitgift challenged the ordinations of non-episcopal churches, and repudiated excessive reverence for the authority of Calvin.[52] He did not think it lawful to assist Dutch rebels against the King of Spain, and he feared that support for them might be paid for by the demolition of cathedral churches in England.[53] The Catholic martyr, Francis Throgmorton, described Whitgift in 1583 as 'the meetest bishop in the realm'.[54] Bancroft's *Dangerous Positions* (1593) was a general attack on Calvinism as an international revolutionary movement with a subversive ideology. French Huguenots, he thought,

48. Laud, *Works*, op. cit., VII, p. 329.
49. H.R. Trevor-Roper, *Archbishop Laud, 1573–1645*, 1940, p. 103.
50. P. Collinson, *Godly People: Essays on English Protestantism and Puritanism*, 1983, Ch. 9, *passim*.
51. Hunt, *Puritan Moment*, op. cit., p. 97; M.Marprelate, *Oh Read Over D. John Bridges (An Epitome)*, 1588, p. 6.
52. Peter Lake, *Moderate Puritans and the Elizabethan Church*, Cambridge University Press, 1982, pp. 208–11.
53. Strype, *Whitgift*, op. cit., I, pp. 436, 439.
54. Quoted in D.Campbell, *The Puritans in Holland, England and America*, New York, 1892, I, p. 471.

were as seditious as English Puritans.[55] Andrew Melville in Scotland called Bancroft 'the capital enemy of all the reformed churches of Europe'; many years later Francis Cheynell, preaching to the Long Parliament, spoke of 'Bishop Bancroft and the Babylonian faction'.[56] Elizabeth too regarded Dutch and Scots Calvinists as rebels; James shared this view, and found his pacifist foreign policy disrupted by Bohemian, Palatine and Dutch rebels. The Synod of Dort in 1618–19 was the first and last international Protestant Council. After 1620 the Calvinist international was in ruins, and James and Charles kept well away from it. It did Abbott no good that he continued to support the Bohemian cause. Laud opposed help to the Palatinate.

After Abbott, as after Grindal, there was a conscious reaction. Conservatives enjoyed greater influence – Hatton after Grindal, the Howards and Buckingham after Abbott, crypto-papists in the 1630s. These reactions affected policies towards Puritans, foreign policy and relations with foreign Protestants. In the 1630s Charles was seeking an alliance with Spain against Sweden and/or the Netherlands. So there was nothing unexpected in Laud's hostility to the foreign churches, which equalled Bancroft's. In 1634 Laud required the foreign churches in England to conform to Anglican ceremonies, despite protests from Kent and elsewhere.[57] His action had disastrous consequences for the Wealden and Norwich clothing industries. The Long Parliament promptly reversed this policy in 1640, religious and economic arguments neatly coinciding against Laud. It was an early example of the economic advantages of religious toleration. Laud had no use for the efforts of Comenius, Dury and Hartlib to reunite Protestants, though he once had a fleeting hope that Dury might be able to persuade the Swedish church to accept bishops.[58] He instructed the English ambassador in Paris to cease attending Huguenot worship at Charenton.[59]

As Laud's power grew, he extended his attempts to impose uniformity – on English merchant companies overseas, in Hamburg and the Netherlands,[60] on chaplains in English regiments in the Dutch

55. R. Bancroft, *Dangerous Positions and Proceedings*, 1640 edn, pp. 9–38, 44–8, 52–5, 126; Knappen, *Tudor Puritanism*, op. cit., p. 497; cf. Strype, *Whitgift*, op. cit., I, p. 504.
56. N. Sykes, *Old Priest and New Presbyter*, 1956, p. 57; F. Cheynell, *Sions Memento and Gods Alarum*, 1643, p. 30.
57. Rushworth, *Historical Collections*, op. cit., II, pp. 249–50.
58. G.H. Turnbull, *Hartlib, Dury and Comenius: Gleanings from Hartlib's Papers*, Liverpool University Press, 1947, pp. 85, 351.
59. Gardiner, *History of England*, op. cit., VIII, pp. 138–9.
60. We recall Gardiner's remark that the first action English merchants took on leaving the shores of England was to reject the Church of England and its prayer book. Cf. R. Ashton, *The City and the Court, 1603–1643*, Cambridge University Press, 1979, p. 136.

service,[61] on the Channel Islands,[62] on plantations in New England,[63] and - most disastrous of all - on Scotland. He went further than Bancroft, but in the same direction.

We can see similar continuities in areas of friction which are sometimes discussed as if they arose from Laudian innovations: Laud picked up Bancroft's attempt to reconstruct the church and to ward off the encroachments of the gentry. Bancroft may have been less successful than R.G. Usher suggested; but his had been a rational and coherent policy of economic reform and legal codification.[64] Laud's attempt to reduce lay patronage and lay ownership of impropriations followed Whitgift's and Bancroft's examples. So did his attempt to check the continuing plunder of the church by curbing the greed of bishops - for example by forbidding long leases - and by augmenting bishoprics.[65] Mary Prior has pointed out that there were long-standing tensions between the country gentry and married bishops as the latter tried to recapture the great-magnate status of their celibate predecessors - to 'live in the port of a bishop', as Archbishop Parker put it - and aspired to insert their families by marriage into the local gentry. Many gentlemen resented this; it shocked radical Protestants who stressed the democratic implications of the Reformation.[66]

Whitgift and Bancroft pursued a campaign to elevate the status of *priests* - to use the contentious word which Whitgift favoured, which the House of Commons rejected in 1606, and on which Laudians insisted.[67]

61. Heylyn, *Cyprianus*, op. cit., p. 219. Abbott had intervened to make difficulties when William Ames tried to obtain academic jobs in the Netherlands - though ultimately Abbott was unsuccessful (J. Browne, *History of Congregationalism . . . in Norfolk*, 1877, pp. 68-9).

62. Heylyn, *Cyprianus*, op. cit., p. 336.

63. A.P. Newton, *Colonizing Activities of the English Puritans*, Yale University Press, 1914, pp. 182-5.

64. R.G. Usher, *Reconstruction of the English Church*, 1910, *passim*. For Bancroft's programme, see my *Economic Problems of the Church*, Oxford University Press, 1956, esp. pp. 127-8, 246-8, 340-5.

65. My *Economic Problems*, op. cit., pp. 21, 143-4, 311-31; F. Heal, 'Archbishop Laud revisited', op. cit., pp. 129-51, esp. pp. 134-8. Whitgift offered 'a model of efficient financial administration to which Laud could refer'.

66. M. Prior, 'The position of Tudor bishops' wives', in M. Prior (ed.) *Women in English Society, 1500-1800*, 1985, pp. 140-1; Strype, *Parker*, op. cit., II, pp. 523-4.

67. J. Whitgift, *Works*, Parker Society, 1853, II, pp. 310-11; III, 350-2; cf. Strype, *Whitgift*, op. cit., I, p. 584; III, p. 219; Willson *Diary of Robert Bowyer*, p. 193; Sir Thomas Crewe, *Proceedings and Debates of the House of Commons in . . . 1628*, 1707, p. 73; cf. E. Cardwell, *A History of Conferences*, Oxford University Press, 1840, pp. 237, 307; R.A. Marchant, *Puritans and the Church Courts in the Diocese of York, 1560-1642*, 1960, p. 193; John Owen, *Works*, ed. W.H. Goold, 1850-3, XIII, pp. 20-8.

On this issue minor Laudians could be very provocative, advocating confession and absolution, speaking of clergymen as 'God's vicegerents here on earth', 'indued with a heavenly power'. Railing the altar was part of the policy of elevating the clergy's status. The laity must keep 'an humble distance from God', to whom parsons had immediate access.[68] We can understand Milton's fury. The soldiers who pulled down altar-rails in 1640 were, whether they knew it or not, proclaiming the dignity of laymen as well as denying the real presence. Even Little Gidding did not support Laud on this issue.[69]

Bancroft too had insisted that the clergy were to be sharply distinguished from the laity, and asserted the divine right of bishops – doctrine which Sir Francis Knollys held to be treasonable.[70] Divine right episcopacy continued to be preached throughout the next two reigns, by William Barlow, George Carleton, George Downame, Lancelot Andrewes, Joseph Hall and many others:[71] the doctrine had no necessary association with 'Arminian' theology. Bancroft tried to get an act of parliament passed to ensure that all beneficed clergy got their tithes in kind, and that in towns house rents should be tithed. If this had succeeded, it would have revolutionized the situation of the poorer clergy.[72] It was a policy which Laud resumed in the 1630s. Under the Scottish prayer book of 1638 the poor were to get only half of the alms allotted to them in the English prayer book: the other half went to the priest.[73] Laud made clergymen JPs, and supported cathedral chapters in their perennial quarrels with municipal authorities. Following Bancroft's example, Laud tried to restrict to those of the highest rank the right to have a chaplain, a campaign which Abbott much disliked: evicted Puritans were often chaplains.[74] Laud infuriated Abbott by trying, through Buckingham, to get taxation of the clergy reduced.[75] Like

68. Tyacke, *Anti-Calvinists*, op. cit., pp. 198–9, 204–7, 221–2; cf. Laud, *Works*, op. cit., VI, Part II, p. 573.

69. Rober Van der Weyer, 'Nicholas Ferrar and Little Gidding: a reappraisal', in Ollard and Tudor-Craig, *For Veronica Wedgwood, These*, op. cit., p. 159.

70. Strype, *Whitgift*, op. cit., I, pp. 559–60.

71. W.M. Lamont, *Godly Rule: Politics and Religion, 1603–1660*, 1969, pp. 36–59; Laud, *Works*, op. cit., III, pp. 199–200.

72. Usher, *Reconstruction*, op. cit., I, pp. 337–8; my *Economic Problems*, op. cit., Chs 12 and 13. For Bancroft see ibid., p. 273.

73. James Gordon, *History of Scots Affairs, From 1637 to 1641*, Spalding Club, 1841, II, p. 79.

74. My *Economic Problems*, op. cit., pp. 179, 221–2, 231–2; my *Society and Puritanism*, op. cit., pp. 89–90, 110.

75. Laud, *Works*, op. cit., III, pp. 150–1, VII, p. 622.

Whitgift at Cambridge, Laud took firm control of Oxford. The statutes of the two universities were revised to bring them under oligarchical control.

Bancroft's canons of 1604, it was said in parliament, 'trenched upon all courts'. The clergy had 'taken on them in pulpits to dispute of property'. The canons were never ratified by parliament: the same fate awaited the canons of 1640, and that time it mattered.[76] Bancroft's attempt to clarify the legal position of the church was as unsuccessful as James's attempt to establish his divine right claims. Abbott accepted this deadlock.

In matters ceremonial too, Laud was traditional. Hooker, Bancroft's protégé, defended the sacraments against Puritans.[77] 'There is no religion where there are no ceremonies', Bancroft was reported as saying.[78] (The Puritan William Bradshaw may have been mocking this when he said 'no ceremony, no bishop'). James I was said to be 'more vehement for these ceremonies than the bishops themselves.[79] Laud's campaign in favour of ceremonial observances, of 'the beauty of holiness', was only the last battle in a long war. Puritans had been denouncing vestments as 'conjuring garments of popery' since 1567.[80] The controversy between them and the hierarchy, both sides agreed, was not 'for a cap, a tippet, or a surplice, but for great matters concerning a true ministry and regiment of the church according to the Word'.[81] The canons of 1604 insisted on observance of saints' days (canon 13), on bowing at the name of Jesus (18), and on the wearing of ecclesiastical vestments (20-5, 58, 74). The first Book of Sports was issued by James I in 1618; as so often, Laud was only enforcing more effectively a traditional policy. In 1624 Samuel Harsnett was denounced in the Commons for setting up images and discouraging preaching, as well as for extortion.[82] Episcopal ceremonies had been popish ever since the Reformation, Lord Brooke claimed.[83] Bishop Aylmer spoke of the surplice as 'the

---

76. Usher, *Reconstruction*, op. cit., I, Book II, Chs 4-5.
77. For Usher's view of Hooker's dependence on Bancroft, see Usher, *Reconstruction*, op. cit., I, pp. 73-90. Hooker dedicated Book V of the *Laws of Ecclesiastical Polity* to Whitgift.
78. Usher, *Reconstruction*, op. cit., II, p. 124.
79. Bradshaw, *A Consideration of Certaine Positions Archiepiscopal*, 1604, Sig. A 2v: William Bedell to Samuel Ward, 16 October 1604, in E.S. Shuckburgh (ed.)*Two Biographies of William Bedell*, Cambridge University Press, 1902, p. 218.
80. Strype, *Grindal*, op. cit., p. 175.
81. *The Admonition to Parliament*, 1572, in W.H. Frere and C.E. Douglas (eds), *Puritan Manifestoes*, 1907, p. 36; cf. p. 11.
82. Thompson, *Holles Account*, op. cit., p. 90.
83. Brooke, *A Discourse opening the Nature of. . . Episcopacie*, 2nd edn, 1642, pp. 58-9, in W. Haller (ed.) *Tracts on Liberty in the Puritan Revolution*, Columbia University Press, 1933, II.

Queen's livery', and Bishop Hall defended ministers wearing 'the bishops' liveries';[84] so Laud compared the ecclesiastical ceremonies which he enforced to those of the Garter.[85]

As early as 1593 Bancroft was refuting the allegation that bishops falsely called their enemies 'Puritans'.[86] Pym made the same charge against Montagu.[87] It was a habit which ambassadors of Catholic powers shared.[88] Bacon in the early twenties had deplored the tendency to label 'honest and religious men' 'Puritans': such men were 'the greatest part of the body of the subjects'.[89] Statistically this is unverifiable; but it testifies to a long-standing awareness of ideological divisions within the political nation. At various times between July 1637 and July 1639 Venetian diplomats estimated that three out of five of the English were 'Puritans', that their number had recently greatly increased, and that they had become the strongest party in the kingdom.[90]

Bancroft, Usher tells us, believed that the Church of England would never be institutionally strong until Puritans were legally excluded from it. Police methods could succeed against Marprelate and Presbyterians, assisted by the hierarchy's claim that Puritans aimed at parity in church and state. But from the 1590s the lead in Puritanism passed from Presbyterian clerics to lay middle-of-the-road Erastians to whom the preaching which Haller depicted appealed. The Puritan discipline seemed to offer solutions to problems of law and order in the increasingly crisis-ridden and class-divided society. Bancroft's promotion to the primacy saw a significant stepping-up of pressure on the Puritan laity.[91]

Bancroft and Laud disliked Calvinism, among other things, because

84. Pierce, *Historical Introduction*, op. cit., p. 78; J. Hall, *Works*, Oxford, 1837–9, X, pp. 89–90.
85. My *Society and Puritanism*, op. cit., pp. 44–5.
86. Bancroft, *Dangerous Positions*, op. cit., p. 137.
87. Gardiner, *1625 Debates*, p. 181.
88. R.E. Schreiber, *The Political Career of Sir Robert Naunton, 1589–1635*, 1981, p. 62; my *Society and Puritanism*, op. cit., p. 18; B. Cotteret, 'Diplomatie et éthique de l'état', in *Regards sur la pensée politique de la France du premier XVIIe Siècle*, Paris, 1985, pp. 235–6. A list of unlikely persons labelled 'Puritan' would include the names of Archbishops Whitgift and Abbott, King James and Prince Charles, Secretary Naunton, the Earl of Strafford and Inigo Jones.
89. Quoted in my *Society and Puritanism*, op. cit., p. 18.
90. *Calendar of State Papers, Venetian, 1636–9*, pp. 242, 300–1, 387, 479, 559.
91. Usher, *Reconstruction*, op. cit., I, pp. 393–8.

it denied the special status and role of the clergy. Most Puritans had no objection to bishops as such, only to the divine-right claims of 'prelatical bishops' and their support of absolutist claims – and to attempts to elevate the clergy above the laity, of which Laudianism was the culmination.

What is sometimes called Laud's 'social justice policy', his opposition to enclosure because it ground the faces of the poor, is also traditional, and is not entirely altruistic. As Garrarde put it to Wentworth, 'My Lord of Canterbury hath great care of the church in this business, for by turning arable into pasture churchmen have had great loss of tithes'.[92] Laud himself was very careful to protect his own rectories from the losses which enclosure would bring.[93] Whatever its motives, Laud's social policy alienated many landowners, including, as Clarendon pointed out, courtiers.[94] But not only the gentry were affected. Many aspects of government policy in the thirties for which Laud was held responsible were detrimental to the interests of parish élites. The second Book of Sports positively encouraged junketings harmful to labour discipline and social subordination.

A new and determined governmental effort was made to seize from the localities the initiative in running the poor law, aided by pressure from assize judges on JPs. Orders in Council showered down on local authorities, already walking a tightrope between government demands and the threat of popular revolt, or at least unpopularity with their neighbours. JPs' powers of licensing maltsters and brewers (as earlier ale-houses) were taken from them.[95] Revived activities of church courts, topped by the High Commission, checked the previous trend for JPs to take over moral supervision of their parishes – in order to keep rates down, among other reasons. Laud struck against parish vestries, where in some villages a godly minister and a group of conscientious leading laymen co-operated. As Dr Hunt put it, how Laud 'imagined the English countryside could be governed without something like a parish vestry is unclear'.[96]

92. W. Knowler (ed.) *The Earl of Strafforde's Letters and Dispatches*, 1739, I, p. 491.
93. Laud, *Works*, op. cit., VI, p. 520; cf. VII, p. 645; cf. Strype, *Whitgift*, III, p. 174.
94. Clarendon, *History of the Rebellion*, Oxford University Press, 1888, I, p. 131. The crown was a leading encloser.
95. T.G. Barnes, *Somerset, 1625–1640: A County's Government During the 'Personal Rule'*, 1961, pp. 194–5.
96. Hunt, *Puritan Moment*, op. cit., p. 253; cf. my *Society and Puritanism*, op. cit., p. 422, for a similar attack on vestries in London. Cf. my *People and Ideas*, pp. 50–3.

At the beginning of James's reign William Bradshaw had pointed out how 'our parishional church-wardens and sidesmen, though instituted with other name and wanting that ordination and authority that . . . elders ought to have', nevertheless fulfilled some of their functions.[97] Introduction of the Presbyterian discipline, Bancroft warned Elizabeth, would mean that she 'must submit herself and her sceptre to the fantastic humours of her own parish governors'.[98] Canon 91 of 1604 insisted that parish clerks should be chosen by ministers, not by the parish. Dr Hunt and Messrs Wrightson and Levine have pointed out the attractions which the Puritan discipline might have for parish élites, not necessarily on theological grounds.[99]

Patrick Collinson, with whom I am always loath to disagree, has emphasized the consensus policies of Grindal and Abbott, and builds up a powerful case for seeing Laud's activities as a main cause of the breakdown in 1640. I am arguing that all Laudian policies had been anticipated by Whitgift and Bancroft. We must be a little dialectical about this. Some contemporaries did see Laud as introducing 'innovations', a word loaded with pejorative implications. But the change, I suggest, was not in Laud or the Church of England, but in the European situation (and consequently the English situation) in which Laud had to operate. The Thirty Years War polarized religious groups all over Europe. In France it led to suppression of the Huguenots and the appearance of sophisticated theories of royal absolutism from which Sibthorp and Manwaring learnt. The dangers of the foreign situation, and the pressures of war, revealed the financial inadequacies of the English political system and called for drastic reorganization. Absolutism, based on a standing army and a bureaucracy, had been the solution found on the continent. In England vested interests were too strong. As the external situation deteriorated, and governments proved increasingly incapable of coping with it, tensions within the political nation mounted. The ideology of Protestantism pulled in one direction and led to demands for greater parliamentary influence over policy.

This drift towards 'Puritanism' tightened the links between church and crown. The church hierarchy, traditionally the spokesman for the

---

97. Bradshaw, *Myld and Just Defence of Certeyne Arguments*, 1606, pp. 116–17, in R.C. Simmes (ed.) *Puritanism and Separatism*, 1972.
98. A. Peel (ed.) *Tracts Ascribed to Richard Bancroft*, Cambridge University Press, 1953, p. 47; cf. p. 93.
99. Hunt, *Puritan Moment*, op. cit., Ch. 1, pp. 21–2, 67, 134, 166, 197–8 and *passim*; K. Wrightson and D. Levine, *Poverty and Piety in an English Village: Terling, 1525–1700*, 1979, pp. 159–67, 177–84; Wrightson, *English Society, 1580–1660*, 1982, pp. 166–70; cf. Lake, *Moderate Puritans*, op. cit., p. 271.

government, backed James and Charles in their attempts to solve their financial problems, from Neile in 1614 onwards. The alliance forged between patriots, Puritans and parliamentarian constitutionalists could be resisted only by a rival ideology. Laud saw himself as an efficiency man, the exponent of 'Thorough' against Lady Mora. But efficiency now meant overcoming traditional, ill-defined legal rights and the privileges of parliament; above all tightening control over the church and censorship. As under Whitgift and Bancroft, suppression of Puritans accompanied a foreign policy of non-alignment with the Calvinist international. Only now there were more 'Puritans'. That was the only novelty: they were no great innovations in policy.

Except perhaps the 'very dangerous heresy' of Arminianism.[100] This is a difficult subject to deal with as an afterthought; but perhaps it was an afterthought historically. Was Laud an Arminian? He himself denied it. He rejected Calvinist predestination, but he distinguished his position sharply from that of Dutch Arminians, because of their lack of emphasis on the sacraments.[101] He also was horrified by 'that point of Arminianism, *libertas prophetandi*', which he thought capable of doing infinite mischief.[102] Arminianism was barely mentioned in the Short Parliament, or in the many pamphlets attacking Laud in the early forties, or in the charges against him at his trial. The label seems to have served its purpose by then.

Montagu said he had never read a word of Arminius before he was attacked in the House of Commons, and in 1628 he formally disclaimed any wish to uphold Arminius's views.[103] Neile in 1629 denied any acquaintance with Arminian writings.[104] 'There is no evidence that Manwaring was an Arminian', says Conrad Russell flatly, though Pym may have believed him to be one.[105] Arminianism was an

100. Bourcier (ed.) D'Ewes, *Diary*, op. cit., pp. 181–2.
101. Tyacke, 'Puritanism', op. cit., pp. 119, 131–2; *Anti-Calvinists*, op. cit., pp. 55, 266–70.
102. Laud, *Works*, op. cit., IV, p. 263.
103. White, 'Rise of Arminianism', op. cit., pp. 46, 51; cf. Tyacke, *Anti-Calvinists*, op. cit., pp. 126–7.
104. P.L. Thirlby, *The Rise to Power of William Laud, 1624–9*, Cambridge University Ph.D. thesis, 1958, p. 275.
105. C. Russell, 'The parliamentary career of John Pym, 1621–9', in P. Clark, A.G.R. Smith and N. Tyacke (eds) *The English Commonwealth, 1547–1640: Essays in Politics and Society Presented to Joel Hurstfield*, Leicester University Press 1979, p. 253. Cf. K. Sharpe, 'Archbishop Laud and the University of Oxford', in H. Lloyd-Jones, V.L. Pearl and B. Worden (eds) *History and Imagination: Essays in Honour of H.R. Trevor-Roper*, 1981, pp. 160–1. See also J. Sears McGee, 'William Laud and the outward face of religion', in R.L. DeMolen (ed.) *Leaders of the Reformation*, Susquehanna University Press, 1984, pp. 331–3.

enemy word, like 'Puritan', which historians have perhaps a little too uncritically taken over. It was useful in the 1620s because Dutch Arminians were believed to be insufficiently enthusiastically anti-Spanish, as well as anti-Calvinist. This view was not limited to Puritans like Sir Benjamin Rudyerd; the play *Sir John van Olden Barnavelt* (1619), attributed to Fletcher and Massinger, assumed that Arminianism was little more than popery in disguise.[106] But the social aura of Dutch Arminianism – great patrician traders, toleration and intellectual sophistication – is very unlike the smell of Laudianism. Dutch Arminianism has at least as much in common with what has been called 'radical Arminianism', 'Arminianism of the left', the Arminianism of John Goodwin and John Milton. 'Heretical Anabaptists', wrote Sir Simonds D'Ewes in 1632, 'have called themselves by a new invented and false name of Arminians'.[107]

To call the Laudians 'Arminians' smeared a 'conservative' group with a 'radical' label – a technique familiar enough the other way round, as when Anabaptists were equated with papists, Ranters were said to adore a picture of Laud and Quakers were 'Jesuits in disguise'.[108] Geyl suggested that Dutch Arminians compared the Contra-Remonstrants with English Puritans in order to enlist James I's support against them.[109] It does not make for clarity when historians adopt a contemporary label whose object was to confuse extreme right with extreme left.

There had been 'proto-Arminians' in England in the 1590s (Baro, Barret and others), though they might perhaps more properly be regarded as surviving Catholics: Barrett became a papist. Montagu's doctrines seem to be more Catholic than anything else. He did not think the Pope was Antichrist.[110] The Laudian Robert Shelford

106. Thompson, *Sir Nathaniel Rich's Diary*, p. 25; Norbrook, *Poetry and Politics*, op. cit., pp. 230-1; cf. Francis Quarles, *Complete Works*, ed. A.B. Grosart, 1881, III, pp. 205-8, 217-20, 227-30, 234.
107. Halliwell (ed.) D'Ewes, *Autobiography*, p. 65; cf. J.T. Cliffe, *The Puritan Gentry: The Great Puritan Families of Early Stuart England*, 1984, pp. 154-5; G.H. Williams, *The Radical Reformation*, Philadelphia, 1962, p. 384.
108. Cf. White, 'Rise of Arminianism', op. cit., pp. 51-2; Norbrook, *Poetry and Politics*, op. cit., pp. 231-2; M. Stubs, *The Ranters Declaration*, 1650, in J.C. Davis, *Fear, Myth and History: the Ranters and the Historians*, Cambridge University Press. 1986, p. 177.
109. P. Geyl, *The Netherlands in the Seventeenth Century*, Part I, *1609-1648*, 1961, p. 62.
110. Lake, *Moderate Puritans*, op. cit., p. 206; Collinson, *Grindal*, op. cit., p. 151; my *Society and Puritanism*, op. cit., p. 489; R. Montagu, *A Gagg for the new Gospell? No: A New Gagg for An Old Goose*, 1624, pp. 33, 74-5; cf. *Appello Caesarem* 1625, pp. 146-9. For residual popery see D.D. Wallace, *Puritans and Predestination: English Protestant Theology, 1525-1695*, North Carolina University Press, 1985, pp. 75-6, 98-105.

published to that effect in 1635.[111] To deny that the Pope was Antichrist undermined the whole ideological basis of English Protestant nationalism and of the Protestant international – as Laud cannot but have been aware. Prynne alleged that Laud's licensers struck out any passages which described the Pope as Antichrist.[112]

Laudianism then was a policy rather than a theology. 'Religion was not the thing at first contested for', said Oliver Cromwell, who should have known, and who did not underestimate the importance of religion. Defoe agreed: 'The King and Parliament fell out about matters of civil right. . . . The first difference between [them] did not respect religion but civil property.'[113] Until S.R. Gardiner invented 'the Puritan Revolution' in the late nineteenth century, few suggested that the original causes of the civil war had been religious.

We might cite on the other side John Selden,[114] political theorists like Henry Ferne, Dudley Digges, Henry Robinson and Marchamont Nedham as well as innumerable lesser pamphleteers.[115] Add the Duke of Newcastle,[116] participants in the debate in parliament in 1659 on the causes of the war,[117] early historians like Nalson, Baxter and Clarendon.[118] The diarist John Greene noted early in 1644 that '*now* 'tis made a war almost merely for religion' – in order, he thought, to be able to make a propagandist appeal to the people.[119] By this time Laud was all but forgotten. Archbishop Williams made this transformation in the nature of the war his reason for ceasing to mediate between the two sides.[120] The point is elaborated by Brian Manning's 'Religion and politics: the godly people'.[121]

111. R. Shelford, *Five Pious Learned Treatises*, 1635, p. 314; Laud, *Works*, op. cit., IV, pp. 312-13, 334, p. 577; my *Antichrist in 17th Century England*, Oxford University Press, 1971, pp. 38, 180.

112. Prynne, *Canterburies Doome*, 1646, pp. 260-79.

113. Defoe, quoted in T.H. Buckle, *History of Civilization in England*, World's Classics, I, p. 292.

114. Selden, *Table Talk*, op. cit., p. 22.

115. Jordan, *History of Religious Toleration in England (1640–1660)*, 1940, p. 167; W. Haller (ed.) *Tracts on Liberty in the Puritan Revolution*, Columbia University Press, 1933, III, pp. 118, 163; Nedham, *Case of the Commonwealth*, op. cit., pp. 5-6. Cf. D.W. Petegorsky, *Left-Wing Democracy in the English Civil War*, 1940, p. 45.

116. Clarendon, *History of the Rebellion*, op. cit., II, p. 505.

117. J.T. Rutt (ed.) *Diary of Thomas Burton*, 1828, esp. II, pp. 284-90, 451; III, pp. 34, 99, 105, 133-5, 145-8, 186-91, 271-2, 344; IV, pp. 61-2, 476-81.

118. Nalson, *Impartial Collection*, op. cit., I, p. lxxvii; M. Sylvester (ed.) *Reliquiae Baxterianae*, 1696, I, p. 26; Clarendon, *History of the Rebellion*, op. cit., III, p. 477. Johann Sommerville has some sensible remarks on this subject (*Politics and Ideology*, op. cit., pp. 140-1, 193-4, 207, 224).

119. Quoted in D. Bush, *English Literature in the Earlier Seventeenth Century, 1600–1660*, Oxford University Press, 1962, p. 7. My italics.

120. J. Hacker, *Scrinia Reserata: A Memorial . . . of John Williams*, 1693, pp. 185-97.

121. In B. Manning (ed.) *Politics, Religion and the Civil War*, 1973, pp. 83-123.

When George Morley said that the Laudians held 'all the best bishoprics and deaneries in the kingdom', he no doubt alluded also to their lack of a clear-cut theological position.[122] Nicholas Tyacke has discovered 'grass-roots' Laudians in the 1620s and 1630s as well as the proto-Laudians of the 1590s. This suggests that the basis of Laudianism was a surviving Catholicism rather than a new creed. But English history since the Reformation had equated patriotism with Protestantism: Catholicism now had to be Anglo- (as in Henry VIII's reign) rather than Roman (as under Mary). Samuel Harsnett, later a Laudian, was denounced as a papist as early as 1584, for preaching against predestination. With Overall and Andrewes he refused to condemn Baro. Fellows of the Cambridge College of which Harsnett was head accused him to James I of favouring popery.[123] He was attacked for introducing images.[124]

No one who aspired to a career in the Church of England could admit to popery, any more than today those right-wing advisers who aspire to influence Mrs Thatcher can call themselves fascists. But when Francis Rous said 'an Arminian is the spawn of a papist', 'papist' meant pro-Spanish, pro-absolutist.[125] 'There is not a policy more advantageable to the Spaniard', Rous wrote, 'than to bring divisions into a land by bringing in Arminianism', which 'almost forfeited the Low Countries to the Spaniard'.[126] Eliot is often regarded as less sensitive to religious issues than Pym. But he too was conscious of the political implications of religious views. 'Fears or dangers in religion, and the increase of popery', he wrote in *Negotium Posterorum*, naturally stirred emotions in the Commons: 'whatever is obnoxious in the state' is reckoned a consequence of unsoundness in religion.[127] The apparent contradiction between the fierce anti-popery expressed by gentlemen in the House of Commons and the relative lenience shown by JPs to their popish neighbours becomes less paradoxical if

122. Under the canons of 1640, Fuller sneered, bowing to the altar was necessary to preferment if not to salvation (*Church History*, op. cit., IV, p. 170). For Arminianism as the route to preferment see also Wallace, *Puritans and Predestination*, op. cit., pp. 95–7.
123. *Dictionary of National Biography*.
124. Hunt, *Puritan Moment*, op. cit., p. 180.
125. Russell, *Parliaments and English Politics*, op. cit., p. 407; Thompson, *Holles Account*, op. cit., pp. 14–15; White, 'Rise of Arminianism', op. cit., p. 52.
126. F. Rous, *Testis Veritatis: The Doctrine of King James . . . Of the Church of England, Of the Catholike Church*, 1626, p. 106.
127. Quoted by Ruigh, *Parliament of 1624*, op. cit., p. 6.

we reflect that attacks on popery in the Commons were mainly aimed at *court* popery, especially at the Buckingham connection. Theological polarization was a consequence of foreign policy.[128] There was an upsurge of anti-Catholicism in the elections of 1624: account had to be taken of it.[129] Part of the object of anti-papal demonstrations in the Commons was to impress outside opinion below the level of the gentry.[130]

The foreign policy and financial strains of the 1620s ended consensus in religion as in politics. Laud in 1639 claimed Charles I's authority for saying that James had changed his mind about his earlier insistence that the Pope was Antichrist. If James *did* change his mind, it was because he had changed his assessment of the international situation: this occurred 'when the King that now is went to Spain'.[131] Those who continued to believe that the Pope was Antichrist could hardly sit passively by as Catholic forces seemed to be sweeping the continent. Charles I's foreign policy in the 1630s was perhaps even more alarming to those who took Antichrist seriously. Consensus ended as traditional Elizabethan Protestant positions came to be labelled 'Puritan'. Bishop George Carleton claimed never to have heard of 'a Puritan doctrine' before 1626.[132] It is possible that Patrick Collinson underestimates the significance of this polarization over foreign policy.

Richard Montagu, who was most liberal in calling his opponents 'Puritans', himself professed doctrines which came very close to Catholicism. He told the papal agent that Laud and several other bishops 'held the opinion of Rome on dogma.' Laud, he said, believed in the real presence, turned communion tables into altars, and repaired broken images. Panzani thought that eleven bishops would favour a return to Rome if suitable terms could be agreed.[133] There was no doubt a great deal of wishful thinking here, but it tells us something about Montagu and his cronies. Cosin was said to equate the Reformation with deformation, John Pocklington to have called

128. White, 'Rise of Arminianism', op. cit., p. 45.
129. D.Hirst, *The Representative of the People?*, op. cit., p. 152.
130. Ruigh, *Parliament of 1624*, op. cit., pp. 244–5; cf. R. Clifton, 'Fear of popery', in Russell, *Origins of the English Civil War*, op. cit., pp. 144–67.
131. Laud, *Works*, op. cit., VI, pp. 577–8; cf. ibid., IV, pp. 308–9, 312–13, 334.
132. White, 'Rise of Arminianism', op. cit., pp. 57, 54.
133. Gardiner, *History of England*, op. cit., VIII, pp. 138–9; Jordan, *Religious Toleration in England (1603–1640)*, op. cit., p. 197.

Foxe's martyrs 'rebels and traitors'.[134] D'Ewes was sure that Laud, Wren 'and their wicked associates' were no Protestants; it was all that £1000 a year could do to prevent them admitting it, Falkland added.[135]

In the political crisis of the early seventeenth century all the logic of Protestantism made for a Calvinist international; so all the logic of conservative episcopalianism might seem to argue at least for an understanding with Rome. Evidence from Oxford college libraries suggests a new interest in medieval schoolmen and Catholic theology between 1585 and 1640.[136] Laud was only one of many whose interest in the early Fathers – itself no doubt a product of controversy between Protestants and Catholics – had led him to participate in a European movement of thought of which the Counter-Reformation was one manifestation, just at a time when radical Protestantism was moving in the direction of rationalism. Laud was 'troubled' when he dreamed he was reconciled to the Church of Rome in 1627. Six years later, when he had just become Archbishop of Canterbury, Laud was offered a cardinal's hat.[137]

By the 1620s 'Puritanism' had established deep grass roots: a generation of preaching the covenant theology had built up a body of beliefs which penetrated the laity to a greater social depth than the Presbyterianism of the 1580s and 1590s had been able to do.[138] Considerations of foreign policy, and the lay ascendancy in Puritanism, forced to the fore the anti-clericalism which was always latent in Protestantism. The crucial issues, from Bancroft to Laud, were tithes, impropriations, church courts, the status of the clergy and especially of bishops; and this involved their financing. Also relevant was the attempt to impose 'social justice' policies on parish élites. All these, I suspect, were more important than questions of predestination.

What we call 'Arminianism' was not a sudden import from the continent; it was the culmination of a long rivalry, going back before the Reformation, between high clerical claims and the resistance of an increasingly self-confident, because richer, laity. Sacramentalism was not just an accidental addition to 'Dutch' Arminianism; it was of the

134. Cornelius Burges, *Two Sermons Preached to the Honourable House of Commons*, 1645, p. 43. This sermon was preached on 20 March 1642.
135. Halliwell (ed.) D'Ewes, *Autobiography*, op. cit., II, pp. 112–14; Rushworth, *Historical Collections*, op. cit., IV, pp. 183–4.
136. N.P. Ker, 'Oxford college libraries in the sixteenth century', *Bodleian Library Record*, 1959, 6, p. 498.
137. Laud, *Works*, op. cit., III, pp. 201, 219.
138. Zaret, *Heavenly Contract*, op. cit., pp. 148–50.

essence of the traditional clerical position. The Calvinism of the laity – household religion, sabbatarianism, preaching and still more preaching – was becoming too dangerous to clerical supremacy. Grindal's offence had been to elevate the importance of preaching. Martin Marprelate, said Whitgift with some exaggeration, accused the bishops of persecuting 'the heresy of preaching'.[139] Bancroft thought that a praying ministry was at least equally important.[140] He recognized a connection between lectureships and Puritans.[141] Abbott disliked the campaign against lecturers – which Laud revived.[142] Laud thought a bishop might preach the gospel 'to far greater edification in a court of judicature or at a council table than many preachers in their several cures can do'.[143] The two policies – comprehension or exclusion of nonconformists, internationalism or Little Englandism – represented two rival interests, so equally balanced that no definitive solution was possible so long as the exclusive church of the old régime survived.

One argument indeed for believing that the English Revolution had long-term causes is the fact that Abbott failed no less than Grindal, Laud no less than Bancroft. Under Laud long-standing rivalries intensified. 'Yield and they will be pleased at last' was said to have been Abbott's maxim; 'resolve, for there is no end of yielding' was Laud's retort.[144] In 1604 most Puritans acknowledged the spiritual leadership of the bishops, and wanted to remain within the church. But by the late 1630s the breach was becoming absolute, not only between Laudians and men like Prynne and Bastwick but also (though never publicly expressed until 1641) between Laudians and men like Lord Brooke and Milton. Milton came to think that all bishops *ex officio*, whatever their private virtues, would be consigned to hell for all eternity – and on the whole Milton was less generous with such condemnations than many of his contemporaries – Cowley, for instance.[145] Not all Puritans felt as strongly as Milton; but his passion was only a heightened form of what many felt.

---

139. Strype, *Whitgift*, op. cit., III, p. 219.
140. Cardwell, *History of Conferences*, op. cit., pp. 191–2.
141. D. Wilkins, *Concilia*, 1737, IV, pp. 409–10. Cf. Peel, *Tracts Ascribed to Richard Bancroft*, op. cit., pp. 56–9; P.S. Seaver, *The Puritan Lectureships: the Politics of Religious Dissent, 1560–1662*, Stanford University Press, 1970, pp. 221–4.
142. P.A. Welsby, *George Abbott*, 1962, p. 137.
143. Laud, *Works*, op. cit., VI, p. 191.
144. D. Lloyd, *State-Worthies*, 1756, II, p. 312. Cf. Ch. 2 above.
145. Milton, *Complete Prose Works*, op. cit., I, pp. 616–17.

Laud was to some extent the victim of government policies not entirely in his control – Charles I's Scottish policy, for instance. The Irish rebellion of 1641 counted heavily against him at his trial, but the responsibility was not mainly his. Laud was certainly not a whole-hearted adherent of the 'popish plot' which Caroline Hibbard has so skilfully traced.[146] But by the late 1620s Catholic successes in the Thirty Years War had made the image of popery politically terrifying to inhabitants of 'the beleaguered isle'[147] – to owners of monastic lands as well as to the godly. Evidence for this comes not merely from the extremist pamphleteering of Prynne, Burton and Bastwick, or from the covert propaganda of *Lycidas*. We find it in the private correspondence of the Barrington family, for instance, or in the anxieties which drove John Winthrop, Anne Hutchinson and many others to cross the Atlantic in search of a refuge.[148] We find it too in the behaviour of rank-and-file conscripts in 1638–41 – drawn from a social class not expected to have political opinions – who attacked their popish officers and pulled down communion rails as well as hedges round enclosures, but who showed no enthusiasm for fighting our brethren the Scots.

Laud, it has been argued, was no supporter of royal absolutism, because it would conflict with the independence of the church.[149] But once secure in the favour of Charles and Buckingham, he and his allies were committed to foreign and financial policies which led inexorably away from co-operation with parliament. John Preston, who died in 1628, saw Laud as 'his greatest adversary', in foreign policy as well as in religion.[150] Laud had made his dislike and distrust of parliament clear in the 1620s, at a time when Thomas Scott was insisting that rule without parliament was Spanish.[151] The claim that Montagu's case was outside the jurisdiction of parliament elevated the prerogative just as much as did Sibthorp and Manwaring's

---

146. Hibbard, *Charles I and the Popish Plot*, op. cit., *passim*. Royalists themselves during the civil war were worried by the possible consequences of the king's connivance at popery. See p. 44 above.

147. Wiener, 'The beleaguered isle', op. cit., 51, esp. pp. 54–62.

148. Searle, *Barrington Letters*, op. cit., *passim*; Thomas Hooker, *The Danger of Desertion*, 1641, in A. Heimat and A. Delbanco (eds) *The Puritans in America: a Narrative Anthology*, Harvard University Press, 1985, pp. 66–9. See also P. Christianson, *Reformers and Babylon: English Apocalyptic Visions from the Reformation to the Eve of the Civil War*, Toronto University Press, 1978, Ch. 4. esp. pp. 152–61; Tyacke, *Anti-Calvinists*, op. cit., pp. 157–63, 227–8, 236–8, 242–4.

149. J.W. Allen, *English Political Thought, 1603–1644*, 1938, pp. 181–96.

150. Ball, *Life of Dr Preston*, op. cit., p. 53. Probably written in the late 1630s.

151. Trevor-Roper, *Archbishop Laud*, op. cit., pp. 66, 297; Scott, *Vox Populi*, 1620, Sig. B2–B3v.

defence of forced loans: the Commons' Protestation of 2 March 1629 linked 'innovations in religion' with illegal taxation.[152] Marvell, looking back from 1672, blamed Laud for persuading Charles to 'that imaginary absolute government, upon which rock we all ruined'.[153] Laud's efficiency and toughness on the government's behalf made him increasingly identified with it: he was blamed for policies which could not be attacked as the king's. Laud had, and was seen to have, more influence on policy-making than any of his Protestant predecessors; and his behaviour was as provocative as his theology. His use of his powerful position to monopolize ecclesiastical patronage, and to pack the government with his creatures, together with the savagery with which he silenced his enemies – these rather than his theology were innovations.[154]

Middle-of-the-road Protestants were caught between Laudianism on the one hand and separatism on the other, just as MPs were caught between crown and electorate. Only the prospect of rescue by the Presbyterian Scots drove the bulk of those whom the House of Commons represented to choose opposition as the lesser evil. Taken by themselves neither the Laudian ceremonies nor Laudian support of the prerogative at the expense of the property rights of the subject were novel. It was their cumulative effect, plus the deliberately provocative rhetoric of men like Montagu and Manwaring, which made them seem a break with the past. They did represent a break with the genial rule of King Log, Archbishop Abbott; but they were just a reversion to the stork-like policies of Whitgift and Bancroft.

---

152. Hillel Schwartz, 'Arminianism', op. cit., pp. 42–3, 55, 61–2, 67.
153. A. Marvell, *The Rehearsal Transpros'd*, ed. D.I.B. Smith, Oxford University Press, 1971, p. 128; cf. pp. 127–35 *passim*.
154. A. Zakai, 'Exile and kingdom', op. cit., pp. 67–8 and *passim*.

5

The word 'Revolution'

There is nothing so hard to discover in the past as that which has subsequently become familiar.

Joyce Appleby, *Capitalism and a New Social Order: The Republican Vision of the 1790s*, New York, 1984, p. 5

The revolution in trade brought about a revolution in the nature of things.

Daniel Defoe, *Robinson Crusoe*

Words and their changes in meaning are a problem for the historian. One's first reaction is naively to read the modern meaning into earlier usage. I made this mistake in relation to Dr John Cowell's use of the phrase 'absolute monarchy' in 1607. The next, more sophisticated, reaction is to look at contemporary dictionaries, and fall over backwards not to force modern meanings on old words. In the third phase, we consider specific words more closely than compilers of dictionaries have time to do, read them in context, and then see. In fact Cowell's *meaning* was not so different from what we understand by 'absolute monarchy' today.

Conventional wisdom has it that the word 'revolution' acquired its modern political meaning only after 1688. Previously it had been an astronomical and astrological term limited to the revolution of the heavens, or to any completed circular motion. This has received the stamp of approval from Braudel, though on the rather shaky authority of Hannah Arendt. Peter Laslett in 1956 dated the new meaning to the political literature of 1688-9, though he himself shows Locke using it in 1679-81.[1] V.F. Snow in 1962 appeared to accept a date

---

1. P. Laslett, 'The English Revolution and Locke's two treatises of government', *Cambridge Historical Journal*, 1956, 12, p. 55. By 'the "English Revolution"' he means the revolution of 1688. Cf. F. Braudel, *Civilisation Matérielle, Economie et Capitalisme*, Paris, 1979, III, p. 465.

after 1688, despite himself giving earlier examples.[2] Melvin Lasky, whilst rightly attributing to 'English lexicographers' a date after 1688, recognized that the changed application from astronomy to politics was a consequence of the mid-century English Revolution.[3] I wish to suggest that the transition to the modern sense occurred considerably before 1688.

The word 'revolution' at the beginning of the seventeenth century seems to have been temporarily neutral. It doesn't imply going either forwards or backwards but rotating. So usage follows the thought of those who originally looked to the distant past (the Garden of Eden, the primitive church, the free Anglo-Saxons) and then discovered that they were really looking to the future. As Winstanley put it, the Diggers' object was not just to remove the Norman Yoke but to get back behind the Fall of Man, to a period outside history – the future millennium as well as Adam's Paradise.[4]

Since the stars were believed to influence events on earth there is clearly much room for ambiguity in a shift from 'the revolution of the heavens' to a political revolution on earth. But one characteristic of the earlier sense is that a revolution is circular, returning to its starting-point: the historical process is cyclical. The modern idea of a revolution suggests a break in continuity. One important factor in bringing about the change of meaning, I believe, was the decline of cyclical history after the decisive break of the Reformation. Protestants proposed to return to the primitive church, it is true; but many radicals hoped for continuous reformation until God's kingdom had been established on earth. Millenarianism was widely preached in England after the liberation of press and pulpit in 1640. The millennium is a once-for-all occurrence: it means the end of cyclical history. And it is reached by a series of revolutions – the wars of Armageddon, the defeat of Turkish power, the raging and ultimate overthrow of Antichrist. None of these is likely to recur, because they signify the approaching end of history.

Another radical concept, that of a third age, the age of the spirit, whether or not derived from Joachim of Fiore, also pointed in the direction of linear history. The last age would be an improvement on what had gone before, not a reversion to the past. As Winstanley put it, 'the ministration of Christ in one single person is to be silent and draw back'

2. V.F. Snow, 'The concept of revolution in seventeenth century England', *Historical Journal*, 1962, 5, pp. 168–70.
3. M. Lasky, *Utopia and Revolution*, 1976, p. 246.
4. Winstanley, *A Letter to Lord Fairfax and his Council of War*, 1649, in G.H. Sabine (ed.) *The Works of Gerrard Winstanley*, Cornell University Press, 1941, p. 292.

once Christ has risen in sons and daughters.[5] John Reeve believed that his commission replaced that of Christ and the Apostles, as their commission had ended Moses's.[6] 'We look for a new earth as well as a new heaven,' the Quaker Edward Burrough told parliament in 1659, echoing what William Erbery had written earlier.[7] Millenarianism and the concept of the third age thus cut across the circularity of the historical process. God's revolutions might move in a straight or a wavy line, but they did advance along a line. Both astrologers and Puritans thought of external forces, the stars or God, impinging on the actions of men: the idea of revolutionary change being due solely to a human conspiracy was more characteristic of Charles I and the royalists generally.[8]

Seventeenth-century lexicographers adhered firmly to the old meaning of the word throughout the seventeenth century. Three things need to be said here. First, post-dating is a normal tendency in lexicographers: anyone who has tried to use the *Oxford English Dictionary* as a guide to the chronological origins of words is aware of this.[9] Second, lexicographers copy from one another, and therefore are slow to spot changes in usage. Third, seventeenth-century lexicographers were mostly scholarly men, to whom Latin was as familiar as English: this helped to fix the idea of 'return to a starting position' in defining the word 'revolution'.

To illustrate these points, consider the word 'absolute', another word which was acquiring a political sense in the seventeenth century. Mr Daly suggests that there was a shift in meaning from about 1640, after which the original sense of 'complete', 'perfect' receded and the modern sense of 'legally unlimited', 'arbitrary' began to emerge.[10] We could date the shift considerably earlier. In the 1590s Hooker spoke of 'an absolute monarch' who 'commandeth . . . that which seemeth good in his own discretion';[11] and the Earl of Essex suggested that Elizabeth was seeking 'an infinite absoluteness'.[12] Fulke Greville

5. Sabine, *Works of Winstanley*, op. cit., p. 162.
6. J. Reeve, *Remains . . . being a Collection of Several Treatises*, 1706, pp. 64–8.
7. Edward Burrough, *To the Parliament of the Commonwealth of England*, 1659, p. 3; W. Erbery, *The Testimony of William Erbery*, 1658, pp. 207–8.
8. A. Marwick, *The Nature of History*, 1972, p. 165. It was in defeat that Milton came back to a cyclical view of history in *Paradise Lost*, Book XII.
9. See my *Milton and the English Revolution*, op. cit., p. 226 n.; and my *Change and Continuity in Seventeenth-Century England*, 1974, pp. 103–5.
10. J. Daly, 'The idea of absolute monarchy in seventeenth-century England', *Historical Journal*, 1978, 21, pp. 227–50.
11. Richard Hooker, *The Laws of Ecclesiastical Polity*, Everyman edn, I, p. 194.
12. W.B. Devereux, *Lives and Letters of the Devereux, Earls of Essex*, 1853, I, pp. 501–2. Cf. Chrimes, 'Constitutional ideas of Dr John Cowell', op. cit., p. 481.

referred to 'absolute princes', with 'an absoluteness dangerous to their subjects' freedom', and feared lest 'our moderate form of monarchy' might be transformed into 'a precipitate absoluteness'.[13] Christopher Brooke in 1614 contrasted 'lawful power' with 'absolute power';[14] and Simonds D'Ewes in 1622 believed that all James I's 'actions did tend to an absolute monarchy'.[15] The *Oxford English Dictionary* cites Bacon in 1625: 'a king more absolute but less safe'. By 1649 the Ranter Joseph Salmon could refer simply to 'the darkness of absolute and arbitrary monarchy', and to parliament 'making themselves as absolute and tyrannical as ever the King in his reign'.[16]

All these examples approach the modern sense, yet seventeenth-century lexicographers do not notice the change. Robert Cawdrey's *A Table Alphabeticall* (1604, 1613) defines 'absolute' as 'perfect or upright'. Randle Cotgrave's *French – English Dictionary* from 1611 to 1673 translates 'absolute' as 'absolu, parfait'. J. Bullokar's *An English Expositor* retained the definition 'perfect, accomplished' from 1616 to 1680. Henry Cockeram's *The English Dictionarie* (1623) has simply 'perfect', expanded to 'perfect, accomplished' in his 1642 edition. Edward Philips, Milton's nephew, in *The New World of Words* (1658), defined absolute as 'perfect'; by 1671 this had been expanded only to 'perfect; as it were finished'. Elisha Coles had 'perfect' as his only definition in *An English Dictionary* (1676, unchanged to 1708). Even John Kersey, who by 1702 had caught up with the new meaning of 'revolution', still defined absolute as 'perfect; or not depending' in his *New English Dictionary*.

So it is not surprising to find that lexicographers were equally slow to note changes in the meaning of 'revolution'. Cawdrey and Bullokar define it as 'a wandering or turning about, especially in the course of time'. Cotgrave's *A Table Alphabeticall* has 'turning back to the same place'. In his *French – English Dictionary* the French 'révolution' was translated as 'a revolution, a full compassing, rounding, turning back to the first place or point: the accomplishment of a circular course'. This sense survived down to 1677, despite James Howell's helping hand in later editions. Cockeram in 1623 only slightly modified Cawdrey and Bullokar: 'a winding or turning

---

13. Fulke Greville, *Life of Sir Philip Sidney*, Oxford, 1907, pp. 48, 52, 54. First published 1652, written *c*. 1610–12.
14. J.P. Cooper (ed.) *Wentworth Papers, 1597–1628*, Camden Society, 4th series, 1973, p. 67.
15. Bourcier (ed.) D'Ewes, *Diary*, op. cit., p. 59.
16. J. Salmon, *A Rout, A Rout*, 1649, in N. Smith (ed.) *A Collection of Ranter Writings from the 17th Century*, 1983, p. 193.

about, especially in the course of time'. This was repeated down to 1642. Thomas Blount in *Glossographia* had 'a returning back to the first place or point, the accomplishment of a circular course' (1656, unchanged down to 1681). Edward Philips was even more restrictive in *The New World of Words*: 'a rolling back of celestial bodies to their first point, and finishing their circular course' (unchanged 1658–78). Elisha Coles's *An English Dictionary* has 'a turning round to the first point' in editions from 1676 to 1708. His English – Latin dictionary of 1677 distinguished between 'the revolution of heaven' = 'coeli cursus' and 'revolution' = 'revolutio', 'a revolution, a turning quite round'. The first definitely political definition which I have found comes in John Kersey's *New English Dictionary* of 1702: 'whirling about, a certain course of the planets, time, &c.; or a change of government'.

The *Oxford English Dictionary (OED)* clearly established that there were other meanings than 'a turning back to the first point' before the middle of the century. Under the definition 'alteration, change, mutation' it cites *Hamlet* as he looks at a skull: 'Here's fine revolution, an we had the trick to see't' (Act V, sc. i, 98), and Tourneur, 'The self-same course/Of revolution, both in man and beast', referring to 'birth, growth, decay and death' (*The Atheist's Tragedy*, 1611, Act I, sc. i). Under the heading 'great change or alteration, in affairs or in some particular thing' the OED cites Fynes Morison, 'every important revolution of our business . . .' and a translation by H. Cogan in 1663, 'How great the revolutions of time and fortune are'.

These senses were well established in seventeenth-century England, though contemporary lexicographers ignored them. Antony's remark in *Antony and Cleopatra*:

> the present pleasure,
> By revolution lowering, does become
> The opposite of itself
>
> (Act I, sc. ii)

like the passage from *Hamlet* quoted, above, does not seem to imply circularity, though 'the revolution of the times' in *2 Henry IV*, Act III, sc. i, may.[17] Ben Jonson in *The Fortunate Isles* (1625) has

> That point of revolution being come
> When all the Fortunate Islands should be joined.[18]

---

17. In *The Birth of Merlin* (possibly *c.* 1622), one of the plays occasionally attributed to Shakespeare, Merlin refers, more traditionally, to 'revolutions, rise and fall of nations', which are 'figured yonder in that star' (Act IV, sc. v).
18. Ben Jonson, *Works*, ed. C.H. Herford, P. and E. Simpson, Oxford University Press, 1941, VII, p. 722.

Edward Bolton in *Hypercritica* (*c.* 1618) speaks of the 'five hundred and fifty years between the Norman Conquest till the Union under King James' as 'the English Revolution'.[19] This period could hardly be thought of as a return to an earlier state: though equally it is not 'a change of government'.

A third definition given by the *OED* approximates to the modern sense: 'A complete overthrow of the established government in any country or state by those who were previously subject to it; a forcible substitution of a new ruler or form of government.' Surprisingly, the *OED* cites Edward Blount in 1600: 'assuring those quarters from all revolutions that might be feared'; and, less surprisingly, George Monck in 1660 (not 1655, as the *OED*), explaining that Sir Arthur Haslerig, just before the restoration, had been 'very jealous of the intended revolution of government to his Majesty's advantage'. The *OED* also cites examples from 1674 onwards of 'the revolution' signifying 'the overthrow of the Rump' of the Long Parliament in 1660.

J. Hatto and V.F. Snow rightly draw our attention to influences from romance languages, which seem to have preceded England in adopting the modern meaning. Upheavals in Florence of 1494, 1512, and 1527 were called 'revoluzioni' by those who witnessed them. Guicciardini (1508–12) described constitutional changes as 'revolutions'. Montaigne wrote 'many worse revolutions have been seen'. Fear of a 'revolution of the people' was expressed in Spain in 1525; in 1648 Assarino published an account of *Le Rivolutioni di Catalogna*. A. Giraffi's *Le Rivolutioni di Napoli* (1647) was translated by James Howell as *An Exact historie of the late revolutions in Naples*. By then this sense was common. Howell himself had already in January 1646–7 neatly combined the two senses of the word. 'Within these twelve years there have the strangest revolutions and horridest things happened, not only in Europe, but all the world over, that have befallen mankind . . . in so short a revolution of time'.[20] Robert Mentet de Salmonet, in his *Histoire des troubles de la Grande Bretagne* (Paris, 1649), spoke of the

---

19. Edward Bolton, *Hypercritica, or a Rule of Judgment for Writing or Reading our Historys*, in J.E. Spingarn (ed.) *Critical Essays of the Seventeenth Century*, Oxford University Press, 1908, I (1605–1650), p. 102.
20. J.H. Elliott, 'Revolution and continuity in early modern Europe', *Past and Present*, 1969, 42, pp. 40–1; Howell, *Familiar Letters*, op. cit., p. 2; J. Hatto, '"Revolution": an enquiry into the usefulness of an historical term', *Mind*, 1949, 58, pp. 502–3; Snow, 'Concept of revolution', op. cit., pp. 169–70; cf. P. Zagorin, *The Court and the Country: the Beginnings of the English Revolution of the Seventeenth Century*, 1970, pp. 13–16.

age in which he lived as 'famous for the great and strange revolutions that have happened in it'.[21]

Already the sense of change, of a significant transformation in personal or political circumstances, is present in the word: revolutions do not always have to be circular. The political crisis of the 1640s influenced this shift. The Five Dissenting Brethren in their *Apologeticall Narration* of 1644 spoke of 'these revolutions of the times', in which 'it pleased God to bring us his poor exiles back again'. The words contain the idea of restoration, but the Brethren were hardly thinking of a recurrent process.[22] We can see usage changing if we look at Fast Sermons preached before parliament. In February 1644 Thomas Young was wholly traditional: 'after the revolution of so many solemn fasts'.[23] So was Humphrey Hardwick four months later: 'after the revolution of many thoughts'. But in March the Scot George Gillespie had spoken of 'the great revolution and turning of things upside down in these our days'.[24] John Owen, two years later, used the word to describe a transformation that is not circular: 'all revolutions here below . . . are carried along according to the eternally fixed purposes of God', and so are historically inevitable. Nicholas Lockyer in the same year opposed the idea of cyclical history, whilst using 'revolution' in its traditional sense: 'an impatient man thinks that the revolution of all times should be of the same aspect: that the present times should be as full of trade, as full of friends, as full of peace and plenty, as former times'. But in Matthew Barker's Fast Sermon of 25 October 1648 a more ominous and more modern note is struck: 'The Lord knows what revolutions and changes we may see before the next monthly fast.'[25]

One way of describing what was happening in the 1640s was to speak of 'the world turned upside down'. This is half a revolution, and perhaps use of the phrase by conservatives implied a hope that the revolution would be completed by a return to normality. But some way of describing one-directional political change was needed, since it

---

21. Parker, *Europe in Crisis*, op. cit., pp. 17, 339. Parker points out that Mentet was writing at the height of the Fronde and published in the crisis of the English Revolution.
22. op. cit., p. 22, in Haller, *Tracts on Liberty*, op. cit., II.
23. T. Young, *Hopes Encouragement*, 1644, p. 1.
24. H. Hardwick, *The Difficulties of Sions Deliverance and Reformation*, 1644, p. 4; G. Gillespie, *A Sermon Preached before the . . . House of Commons* (27 March 1644), p. 9.
25. John Owen, *A Vision of Unchangeable free Mercy*, 1646, p. 3; Nicholas Lockyer, *A Sermon Preached before the House of Commons*, 18 October 1646, p. 16; Matthew Barker, *A Christian Standing & Moving Upon the true Foundation*, 1648, p. 49.

was happening. Just as today we might speak of 'revolutions of the heavenly bodies' to distinguish the astronomical use of the word, so in the seventeenth century men came to speak of 'revolutions and changes' to distinguish political revolutions, a break in continuity, from traditional circular revolutions. Astrologers of course continued to use the word in its old sense. But Lilly was speaking of 'our astrological revolution' by 1644, and of 'the great revolutions of the world' by 1647.[26]

The events of the winter of 1648–9 seem to have expedited adoption of the new meaning. Thus in March 1649 an unknown 'D.P.' wrote: 'We need not wonder at the revolutions and changes of government.'[27] Antony Ascham published in 1648 *A discourse wherein is examined What is particularly lawfull during the Confusions and Revolutions of Government*. It was expanded next year as *Of the Confusions and Revolutions of Governments*. Ascham saw 'confusions and revolutions of government' in the Wars of the Roses, when power shifted backwards and forwards from one group to another until Henry VII's *de facto* law 'concluded these contradictions and revolutions'.[28] Robert Heath in *Clarastella* (1650) has a phrase which perhaps sounds more modern than he intended:

> Nothing but fair Utopian worlds i'th moon
> Must be new formed by revolution.[29]

Milton is old-fashioned in his usage. We know that when he wrote Latin he insisted on classical forms and resisted post-classical neologisms.[30] He may for the same reason have objected to giving the word 'revolution' a new meaning; others classically educated may have shared his feeling.

Robert Boyle in 1651 seemed to think of revolution (in the singular) as a sudden change: 'I do with some confidence expect a revolution, whereby Divinity will be a loser and real Philosophy flourish, perhaps

---

26. See for instance [John Booker], *Mercurius Coelicus*, 1644, p. 2; W. Lilly, *Merlinus Anglicus Junior*, 1644, p. 14; Lilly, *Supernatural Sights and Apparitions*, 1649, p. 97; *The Worlds Catastrophe: Or, Europes many Mutations until 1666*, 1647, p. 29; *An Astrological Prediction of the Occurrences in England*, 1648, p. 43. For 'revolutions and changes' cf. John Dury, *The Reformed School*, 1650, quoted in Charles Webster, *Samuel Hartlib and the Advancement of Learning*, Cambridge University Press, 1970, p. 140. See also pp. 90–1, 93 below.
27. D.P., *The True Primitive State of Civill and Ecclesiasticall Government*, 1648 [-9], p. 3.
28. A. Ascham, *A discourse*, 1648, Sig.ˣ3, p. 93; *Of the Confusions and Revolutions*, 1649, Sig. A²v, p. 103.
29. Quoted by Marjorie Nicolson, 'English Almanacs and the "new astronomy"', *Annals of Science*, 1939, 4, p. 21.
30. Leo Miller, *John Milton and the Oldenburg Safeguard*, New York, 1985, pp. 259–61, 285–6, 322–3. For examples of Milton's traditional use of 'revolution', see Milton, *Complete Prose Works*, op. cit., II, p. 539; V, p. 403; his second Hobson poem, and *Paradise Lost*, II. 596–8, VIII. 31 and 813–15.

beyond men's hopes.' There is no suggestion here of turning back to the first point. In 1665 Boyle referred to 'the revolutions of governments'.[31] The Ranter Joseph Salmon, also in 1651, uses 'revolution' more in the modern sense, though he is referring to events in his private life. There 'happened a sudden, dreadful revolution, a most strange vicissitude'.[32] An anonymous pamphlet, also of 1651, likewise had the modern sense: 'all revolutions and changes . . . are for the perfecting of this glorious work'.[33] Arise Evans in 1653 used similar words: 'these revolutions and changes came to pass even to fulfil the words and promises of God'.[34] John Hull in New England slipped from the sublime to the ridiculous when the grand phrase 'it is best willing to submit to the governing hand of the greatest Governor of all the greater and lesser revolutions that we poor sons of men are involved in' led on without any punctuation to 'by the invoice you see the whole amounteth to £405.16.3'.[35] *Mercurius Politicus* in March 1652-3 used the word 'revolution' to signify recurrent change: 'as in the governments of the people the successive revolution of authority by their consent hath been the only bank against inundations of arbitrary power and tyranny'.[36]

From 1653, the year which saw the dissolution of the Rump, the rule and abdication of Barebone's Parliament and the proclamation of the Protectorate, we find a cluster of examples. Henry Newcome wrote, apropos the expulsion of the Rump: 'I had upon thoughts of this revolution, amongst others, this Scripture brought to hand, Isaiah 29. 14-17'.[37] Henry Marten, in a letter to Oliver Cromwell declining an invitation to sit in Barebone's Parliament, spoke of 'this and all other revolutions'.[38] George Wither resolved:

31. Quoted in J.R. Jacob, *Robert Boyle and the English Revolution*, New York, 1977, p. 97; Boyle, *Occasional Reflections upon Several Subjects*, 1665, pp. 13-14.
32. Salmon, *Heights in Depths and Depths in Heights*, 1651, in Smith (ed.) *Ranter Writings*, op. cit., p. 212.
33. Anon, *A Cry for a Right Improvement*, 1651, p. 7. I owe this reference to J.P. Laydon's 'The Kingdom of Christ and the Powers of the Earth: the political uses of apocalyptic and millenarian ideas in England, 1640-1653', Cambridge University Ph.D. thesis, 1976, p. 150.
34. Arise Evans, *Admonitions to all the People of this Kingdom*, in *The Bloudy Vision of John Farley*, 1653, p. 23.
35. L. Ziff, *Puritanism in America: New Culture in a New World*, New York, 1973, p. 150.
36. *Mercurius Politicus*, 26 February - 4 March 1652(-3), 91, p. 1442. Cf. nos 66, 102, 440, 568.
37. Henry Newcome, *Autobiography*, ed. R. Parkinson, Chetham Society, 1852, p. 44.
38. I owe this reference, from the Henry Marten papers, to the late Professor C.M. Williams.

Let not the revolutions or the changes
Or the prevarication which now ranges
Throughout the world, me from my station carry,
Or cause me from good principles to vary.[39]

The millenarian John Canne predicted for 1655 'great changes and revolutions, in respect both of persons and things', for at that time the Lord will 'most eminently appear, shaking the earth and overthrowing the thrones of kingdoms everywhere in Europe'.[40] A translation of Lieuwe van Aitzema published in 1653 was entitled *Notable Revolutions: Being a True Relation of What Happened in the United Provinces.*

Ralph Josselin in January 1654, looking backwards, noted in his diary that 'this year hath brought forth notable revolutions at home in dissolving Parliament and declaring Cromwell Protector'.[41] Here 'revolution' clearly involved innovation. Twenty-five years later Josselin had adopted the singular: 'some threat as the greatest revolution we ever saw were at the door'.[42] At the beginning of 1654, Whitehall messengers' salaries were twelve months and more in arrears, 'which hath been mainly occasioned by the uncertainty of the times through the many revolutions of government'.[43] Here again the reference is to specific change, not to turning back to the first point. A very clear instance of the modern sense comes in Christopher Feake's *The New Non-conformist* (1654), where (like the Five Dissenting Brethren) he speaks of émigrés who had returned to England 'from New England and from Holland at the beginning of the late great revolution'.[44] Roger Williams saw the sailing of the expedition which Oliver Cromwell sent to the West Indies in 1655 as the beginning of 'greater and greater revolutions approaching'.[45]

Matthew Wren wrote (probably in the 1650s) but did not publish

---

39. George Wither, *Westrow Revived*, 1653, p. 63, in *Miscellaneous Works*, Spenser Society, 3, 1874.
40. J. Canne, *A Voice from the Temple to the Higher Powers*, 1653, pp. 29–30.
41. Ralph Josselin, *Diary, 1616–1683*, ed. A Macfarlane, Oxford University Press 1976, p. 316.
42. ibid., p. 616: 8 December 1678.
43. G.E. Aylmer, *The State's Servants: The Civil Service of the English Republic, 1649–1660*, 1973, pp. 121–2.
44. C. Feake, *The New Non-conformist*, 1654, Sig. A 3v. For the stock phrase 'revolutions and changes' see also the anonymous *A Cry for a Right Improvement*, 1651, p. 7 and J. Warren, *Mere Fury*, 1656, p. 31.
45. Quoted in Kuppermann, 'Errand to the Indies', op. cit., p. 94.

Of the Origin and Progress of the Revolutions in England. The title may have been added by Gutch, who published it in 1781: but in the text Wren refers to 'those strange revolutions we have seen' and – even more to our purpose – said that 'a pack of discontented noblemen and gentlemen . . . were engaged to labour a revolution of affairs'.[46] The use of the singular is significant.

The most striking example of the new usage, appropriately enough, comes from Oliver Cromwell himself, in his speech at the dissolution of his first parliament on 22 January 1655. 'Let men take heed,' he warned, 'how they call his revolutions, the things of God and his working of things from one period to another, how . . . they call them necessities of men's creations.' To deny that 'those mighty things God hath wrought in the midst of us' have been 'the revolutions of Christ himself' was to deny God's sovereignty. 'Take heed, again I say, how you judge of his revolutions as the products of men's inventions.' 'The Lord hath done such things amongst us as have not been known in the world these thousand years.'[47] Though still using the word in the plural, Cromwell seems to employ it in its modern sense. His 'working of things from one period to another' recalls Marvell's view of Cromwell himself as 'the force of angry Heaven's flame', who 'cast the kingdom old/Into another mould'. By 1657, Cromwell could use the word casually in a letter to Blake – 'all these late revolutions'.[48]

In 1656, William Howard, on behalf of a group of former Levellers and Anabaptists, wrote to Charles Stuart in exile, referring to 'the many changings, turnings and overturnings of governors and governments which in the revolutions of a few years have been produced'.[49] Here 'revolutions' could simply mean 'successions of years'; but the singular would seem more appropriate if that was the sense intended. Zachary Crofton referred to the installation of Cromwell as Lord Protector under the Humble Petition and Advice as 'the late revolution'.[50] 'How many revolutions have we been through!' exclaimed Sergeant Sir John Maynard in Richard Cromwell's parliament.[51]

46. J.A. Gutch (ed.) *Collectanea Curiosa*, 1781, I, pp. 242 and 238.
47. Abbott, *Cromwell's Writings*, op. cit., III, pp. 590–3.
48. ibid., IV, p. 549. Cf. *Calendar of State Papers Domestic, 1656–7*, p. 272, *1657–8*, p. 48. See p. 55 above and Marchamont Nedham, quoted on p. 23 above.
49. Clarendon, *History of the Rebellion*, op. cit., VI, p. 68.
50. Quoted in R.L. Greaves, *Saints and Rebels: Seven Nonconformists in Stuart England*, Mercer University Press, 1985, p. 124.
51. J.T. Rutt, *Diary of Thomas Burton*, op. cit., III, p. 573.

After Ascham, James Harrington is the political theorist who comes nearest to using the word in its modern sense in print before 1660. In *The Prerogative of Popular Government* (1658) he wrote:

> Property comes to have a being before empire or government two ways, either by natural or violent revolution. Natural revolution happeneth from within, or by commerce, as when a government erected upon one balance, that for example of a nobility or a clergy, . . . comes to alter to another balance . . . Violent revolution happeneth from without, or by arms.

The English Revolution, as Harrington explained elsewhere, was a 'natural revolution': 'the dissolution of this government caused the [civil] war, not the war the dissolution of this government'.[52]

Various publications of 1659 refer to 'our late revolutions' – George Bishop's *Mene Tekel*,[53] R. Fitz-Brian's *The Good Old Cause Dressed in its Primitive Lustre*.[54] Rushworth, in the preface to the first volume of his *Historical Collections* (1659), gave as his object 'to learn the true causes, the rises and growths of our late miseries, the strange alterations and revolutions'. The former radical William Sedgwick used the plural in his *Inquisition for the Blood of our late Soveraign* (1660): 'in these times when there are so great and notorious revolutions'; 'these strange revolutions', 'the great revolutions of this kingdom'.[55] In January 1660 Warwickshire petitioners supporting the Good Old Cause conceived that 'the cause of our present calamities . . . proceeds from the many revolutions, through maladministration of government and want of the right constitution of Parliaments'. A penitent parliamentarian from the same county asked the new king to put 'a fair construction on intermediate accidents and revolutions of affairs'.[56]

The restoration should have offered an opportunity for applying the word 'revolution' to politics in the sense of a return to a first position. Professor McKeon says that for Dryden's contemporaries the word meant restoration or renovation, return to a former state. One example which he gives is clear enough: 'Revolution! Revolution!

---

52. Pocock (ed.) Harrington, *Political Works*, op. cit., pp. 405–6, 198.
53. George Bishop, *Mene Tekel: Or, The Council of the Officers of the Army Against The Declarations &c. of the Army*, 1659, p. 5.
54. Fitz-Brian, op. cit., 1659, p. 1 (rightly p. 2).
55. W. Sedgwick, *Inquisition for the Blood of our late Soveraign*, 1660, pp. 63, 155, 259.
56. Hughes, *Warwickshire*, op. cit., pp. 332, 221.

Our King proclaimed! restored!'[57] But it is, I think, at least possible that Henry Bold (in the passage just cited) was being deliberately provocative in appropriating the word to this conservative purpose: recall Cromwell's 'the revolutions of Christ'. Dryden in *Absalom and Achitophel* and elsewhere does not always use the word to mean restoration.[58] The Matchless Orinda puns on the two senses of the word:

> Why should changes here below surprise.
> When the whole world its revolution tries?[59]

One wonders how often apparent ambiguity in use of the word is, as here, a deliberate pun.

By 1665 Edward Waterhouse is consciously looking back to the experience of the 1640s and 1650s when he writes that money buys men 'in all revolutions': wisdom 'little avails in worldly revolutions without it'.[60] Sprat in 1667 spoke of 'those dreadful revolutions'.[61] Old Cromwellians used the word when they discussed politics together in private. The Earl of Sandwich in February 1666 confided to Pepys his fear of 'some very great revolutions' in the immediate future. Two years later Thomas Povey more optimistically anticipated 'great revolutions' in consequence of which 'a man of the old strain . . . will be up again'.[62] Lucy Hutchinson called the Reformation 'this great revolution'.[63] Sir William Temple in 1672 referred to the 'fatal revolutions' of the crown and nation between 1646 and 1660, 'the revolution of England in the year 1660'. In the Netherlands there had been 'some unavoidable revolutions', 'revolutions unparalleled in any story'.[64]

---

57. Henry Bold, *St. Georges Day*, 1661, pp. 1-2, quoted in M. McKeon, *Politics and Poetry in Restoration England*, Harvard University Press, 1975, pp. 237, 262-4.
58. J. Dryden, *Absalom and Achitophel*, lines. 252-3. 'Heaven has to all allotted, soon or late,/ Some lucky revolution of their fate'; cf. Dryden's translation of Juvenal's sixth satire, lines 56-7: 'What revolutions can appear so strange/ As such a lecher, such a life to change?' See also his translation of Virgil's ninth eclogue, lines 4-6, and *On the Marriage of the Fair and Virtuous Lady, Mrs. Anastasia Stafford*, lines 53-4.
59. Katherine Philips, 'Submission', in G. Saintsbury (ed.) *The Caroline Poets*, Oxford University Press, 1905, I, p. 568. Mrs Philips died in 1664, the year in which her poems were posthumously published.
60. Edward Waterhouse, *The Gentleman's Monitor*, 1665, in Joan Thirsk, *The Restoration*, 1976, p. 92.
61. Thomas Sprat, *History of the Royal Society of London*, 1667, p. 58.
62. Pepys, *Diary*, 25 February, 1666; 20 June, 1668.
63. Hutchinson, *Memoirs of Colonel Hutchinson*, op. cit., p. 38. Probably written in the late 1660s.
64. Sir William Temple, *Essay on Popular Discontents* and *Observations upon the United Provinces*, in *Works*, 1757, III, pp. 32-66, I, pp. 56, 59.

Henry Stubbe, former radical parliamentarian, used the word 'revolution' in the singular: 'From the apostolic and primitive times to the revolution under Constantine'.[65] As J.R. Jacob points out, Stubbe regularly employs the word in its modern sense, especially in that very modern work, *The History of the Rise and Progress of Mahometanism.* Mahomet's 'prosperous revolution' was directed against 'the ostentation and abuse' of 'arbitrary power'.[66] Stubbe's friend Charles Blount spoke of 'those revolutions which (otherwise) no human sagacity or courage could have accomplished'; 'all revolutions whatever, both in church and state . . . must still be seconded by some private temporal interest'. In the 1670s Blount had discussed with the Earl of Rochester 'the great changes and revolutions that from time to time have happened in the universe'.[67]

Andrew Marvell, another former parliamentarian, was using the word in an entirely modern sense when he wrote in 1677 of 'the tendency of all affairs and counsels in this nation towards a revolution'.[68] So was Samuel Butler, when he saw an analogy between 'revelations and revolutions'. Henry Neville spoke in 1681 of 'a natural revolution of political circumstances'. We may compare Aubrey: 'the revolution of so many years and governments'.[69] Locke, as Laslett showed, was using the word in the modern sense in 1679–81. Hobbe's *Behemoth* was not published until 1679, having been previously prohibited by Charles II. But it was probably completed not later than 1668. In it Hobbes wrote: 'I have seen in this revolution a circular motion of the sovereign power'. Monarchy – sedition – republic – sedition – monarchy: here Hobbes, like the Matchless Orinda, seems to be punning on the old and new meanings of the word. Perhaps he did so in *Leviathan* too, when he referred to 'the

65. Henry Stubbe, *Legends no Histories*, 1670, 1911 ed., p. 121.

66. Stubbe, op. cit. (1911), p. 128; cf. p. 49: 'such great revolutions': J.R. Jacob, *Henry Stubbe: Radical Protestantism and the Early Enlightenment*, Cambridge University Press, 1983, p. 66.

67. J. Treglown (ed.) *Letters of John Wilmot, Earl of Rochester*, Oxford University Press, 1980, pp. 208, 213–14; V. de Sola Pinto, *Enthusiast in Wit: a Portrait of John Wilmot, Earl of Rochester, 1641–1680*, 1962, p. 187.

68. Marvell, *An Account of the Growth of Popery*, in *Works* (ed. Thompson, 1770), I, p. 645. Marvell appears to refer to a revolution in religion.

69. Butler, *Prose Observations*, ed. H. de Quehen, Oxford University Press, 1979, p. 246; Neville, *Plato Redivivus*, op. cit., p. 182; Aubrey, *Wiltshire Topographical Collections*, ed. J.E. Jackson, Devizes, Wiltshire Topographical Society, 1862, p. 4.

revolution of states' as 'no very good constellation for truths . . . to be born under'.[70]

In 1685 Evelyn had referred to Titus Oates's reversal of fortune as 'a strange revolution' – the traditional usage. But in 1688 he spoke of 'a sad revolution' threatening 'this sinful nation'; and in December he said 'it looks like a revolution',[71] just as Louis XVI was told in 1789 that what was happening was a revolution, not a revolt. The Marquis of Halifax referred presciently in 1687 to 'the next probable revolution'; in April 1688 he assured William of Orange that 'the very Papists have . . . an eye to what may happen in a revolution'.[72] Professor Kenyon's bland note here on the word 'revolution' – 'any change of government; not "revolution" in our sense' – seems to me to beg most of the questions I have been trying to raise. How could governments be changed in seventeenth-century England (really changed, as governments were changed in 1640–2, 1649, 1653, 1659–60 and 1688: not the sort of cosmetic shuffle tried – unsuccessfully – by Charles I in 1641 and – successfully – by Charles II in 1679)? There was no His Majesty's Opposition standing patiently in the wings waiting for its cue. The 'complete overthrow of the established government . . . by those who were previously subject to it',[73] to which Ascham, Feake, Cromwell, Harrington, Pepys, Marvell and Evelyn referred, was as different from a twentieth-century 'change of government' as that is from the lexicographers' 'change of position'. The shift from circular motion to a one-way 'change of government' is decisive for our theme. For such a change could happen only if politics passed out of the control of those holding government office.

The word 'revolution' may have become more acceptable after 1688. In that year a play entitled *The Late Revolution* was put on the stage – published anonymously in 1690. Wildman, naturally enough, referred in 1689 to 'the wonderful revolution' which had rescued both 'religion and civil liberties' in 'this undeserving land'.[74] Edward Howard's *Caroloriades* was in its first edition of 1689 subtitled *or the Rebellion of 1641*. The second edition, in 1695, was called *Caroloriades*

---

70. Hobbes, *Behemoth*, op. cit., 1889, p. 204; Hobbes, *Leviathan*, op. cit., p. 728.
71. John Evelyn, *Diary*, ed E.S. de Beer, Oxford University Press, 1955, IV, pp. 445, 603, 609.
72. Marquis of Halifax, *Complete Works*, ed. J.P. Kenyon, Penguin edn, pp. 116, 338.
73. See *OED* quoted on p. 87 above.
74. M. Ashley, 'John Wildman and the Post Office', in Ollard and Tudor-Craig, *For Veronica Wedgwood, These*, op. cit., p. 214.

Redivivus, or the Wars and Revolutions in the Time of King Charles I. Burnet
said that Lady Ranelagh, sister of Roger and Robert Boyle, had cut
'the greatest figure in all these revolutions of three kingdoms for above
fifty years of any woman of her age'. Lord Wharton was said in 1696 to
have 'behaved himself with honour in all the revolutions that happened
in his time'.[75] Locke in his *Second Treatise* (published in 1690) spoke
quite casually of 'the many revolutions which have been seen in this
kingdom in this and former ages'. 'Such revolutions,' he added,
'happen not upon every mismanagement in public affairs'.[76] Walter
Moyle at the end of the century summed up: 'revolutions of empires
are the natural transmigration of dominion, from one form of government to another'. But he added, with a backward glance at the
original meaning of the word: they 'make the common circle in the
generation and corruption of all states'.[77] By 1710 a pamphlet could
be published entitled *The True English Revolutionist*.

The idea of revolution as a significant political transformation thus
appears to have emerged during the interregnum. The concept of a
revolution which God had brought about precluded the idea of such
an event being 'a necessity of men's creations', a conspiratorial *putsch*
or a revolt in blind reaction to localized grievances. Men might co-
operate with God in His 'working of things from one period to
another'; they could not initiate a revolution. Such an event had
deep roots in God's purposes for his people. It had nothing to do with
the intentions of men.

Professor Pocock once said 'men cannot do what they have no
means of saying they have done'.[78] I find this surprising. The word
'Purgatory', as Le Goff has shown, came into existence only after the
concept was well established.[79] Men and women committed suicide
before Sir Thomas Browne used the word in the 1630s.[80] There were
pantheists before Toland invented that word in 1705, and there were
minorities before the word came into use in the eighteenth century.[81]

75. J. Kent Clark, *Goodwin Wharton*, Oxford University Press, 1984, p. 369.
76. Locke, *Two Treatises of Government*, ed. P. Laslett, Cambridge University Press,
1960, pp. 432–3. Laslett here appears to date these passages to 1679–82 (ibid., p. 424).
77. W. Moyle, *An Essay on the Constitution and Government of the Roman State*, in Robbins,
Republican Tracts, op. cit., pp. 229–31.
78. J.G.A. Pocock, 'Virtue and commerce in the eighteenth century', *Journal of Inter-
disciplinary History*, 1972, 3; cf. J.S. Morrill, *Seventeenth-Century Britain, 1603–1714*,
Folkestone, 1980, pp. 108–9.
79. J. Le Goff, *La Naissance du Purgatoire*, Paris, 1981, Appendix 2.
80. *Oxford English Dictionary*.
81. P.U. Bononi, '''A Just Opposition'': the Great Awakening as a radical model', in
M. and J. Jacob (eds) *The Origins of Anglo-American Radicalism*, 1984, p. 255.

Men and women presumably were 'civilized' before they began to say they were; and it is unlikely that the word 'urbanity' preceded the thing. Nor would men think of the word 'suburb' before building one.[82] The word 'feminism', Barbara Taylor reminds us, did not appear until the late nineteenth century, but there had been people whom we can call feminists for at least a century before that.[83] Jonathan Dollimore points out that ideology existed long before the word which describes it.[84] The disease rickets came to notice a generation before it was given a name. Things precede words. Men and women find words to say what they have done or experienced in the process of doing it, or after they have experienced it. It is difficult to see how it could have been otherwise. Especially when we are dealing with terms of analysis like 'ideology' and 'revolution'.

During the Revolution, Sprat thought, the English language 'was enlarged by many sound and necessary forms and idioms which before it wanted'.[85] New words were needed because new things happened, or old concepts forced themselves anew upon popular attention. Fuller thought 'malignant', 'plunder' and 'fanatic' were new in his time.[86] Keith Thomas identified many new words dealing with change – 'epoch', 'synchronize', 'out-of-date', 'anachronism'.[87] Other new words which clearly relate to the events of the Revolution are 'anarchism' (*OED* 1642, though 'anarchy' had appeared earlier),[88] 'antinomianism' (1643), 'superstructure' (1641).[89]

The words 'nature' and 'natural' underwent a transformation in the seventeenth century. We make romantic assumptions about 'nature', but for early Protestants 'natural man' was sinful man. The word 'class', too, begins to assume its modern sense. In 1624 the deputy lieutenants of Essex referred to 'some of the better classes

---

82. J.M. Roberts, *The Pelican History of the World*, 1976, p. 525.

83. Barbara Taylor, *Eve and the New Jerusalem*, 1976, p. 10.

84. Jonathan Dollimore, *Radical Tragedy: Religion, Ideology and Power in the Drama of Shakespeare and his Contemporaries*, Brighton, 1984, p. 18.

85. Sprat, *History of the Royal Society*, op. cit., p. 42.

86. T. Fuller, *Church History*, op. cit., III, p. 443; *Mixed Contemplations in Better Times*, 1660, in *Good Thoughts in Bad Times*, 1830, pp. 294–5; cf. P.Styles, *Studies in Seventeenth Century West Midland History*, Kineton, 1978, p. 20.

87. Thomas, *Religion and the Decline of Magic*, op. cit., p. 429.

88. Milton used 'anarchy' as well as 'anarch' in *Paradise Lost* (Book X. 283, Book II. 988).

89. 'Superstructure' was used by Harrington (*Political Works*, op. cit., pp. 202, 609–10); cf. John Philips, in H. Darbishire (ed.) *Early Lives of Milton*, 1932, p. 24, and Lucy Hutchinson, *Memoirs*, op. cit., p. 6.

setting a very ill example'.[90] This will displease historians who argue that there could have been no classes in seventeenth-century England because the word was not used in its modern sense: a false conclusion from a false premise. In fact the word 'class' was well enough established for Blount to define it in his *Glossographia* as 'an order or distinction of people according to their several degrees'.[91]

Many words changed their meaning in the seventeenth century. C.L. Barber wrote a fascinating book on changing concepts of 'honour'.[92] I looked briefly at new senses of 'liberty' and 'reason'.[93] Quentin Skinner has pointed out that 'obsequious' becomes pejorative, and words like 'gentle' and 'generous' widen their original restrictive social connotations. 'Frugality', 'squandering', and 'spendthrift' are new: 'commodity' and 'honesty' narrow their meanings, and 'purchase' changes its reference.[94] So do 'value', 'worth', and 'credit'.[95] 'Society' and 'community' acquire new senses.[96] Joyce Appleby noted that 'individual' is first cited in the *Oxford English Dictionary* from 1626. In the seventeenth century 'the word market was transformed, another of those sleights of tongue obscuring a change of meaning'.[97] 'The quality' comes to mean those of good social position, independent of birth: the meaning is connected with access to high-quality goods.[98] The word 'election' ceases to include the meaning 'nominated from above' (as in 'the elect') and comes to mean exclusively 'chosen from below'.

Adam in Paradise knew the names of things intuitively. But the

90. Hunt, *Puritan Moment*, op. cit., p. 184.
91. I owe this reference to the kindness of Dr Penelope Corfield.
92. C.L. Barber, *The Idea of Honour in the English Drama, 1591–1700*, Göteborg, 1957.
93. My *Change and Continuity*, op. cit., Ch. 4; for 'liberty' see J. Appleby, *Capitalism*, op. cit., pp. 16–22. For 'reason' see her *Economic Thought and Ideology in Seventeenth-Century England*, Princeton University Press, 1978, p. 62 and *passim*.
94. Q. Skinner, 'Some problems in the analysis of political thought and action', *Political Theory*, 1974, pp. 296–8; 'Language and social change', in L. Michaels and C. Ricks (eds) *The State of the Language*, California University Press, 1980, pp. 570–2. I have drawn on correspondence from Professor Skinner on this subject. For 'honesty' see also Zwicker, *Politics and Language*, op. cit., pp. 206–7. 'Imagination' had a pejorative sense in the seventeenth century.
95. For 'credit' I am indebted to Susan Amussen, *An Ordered Society: Gender and Class in Early Modern England*, Oxford, 1988, and to discussions with her. For 'value' and 'worth' see Louise Lecocq, 'Le débat sur la valeur dans *Troilus et Cressida*', *Confluents*, 1976, 2, p. 3 and *passim*.
96. I owe this point to discussions with Peter Burke.
97. Appleby, *Capitalism*, op. cit., pp. 15, 30.
98. Nicholas Jose, *Ideas of the Restoration in English Literature, 1660–71*, 1984, p. 19.

language of fallen man, as Locke was to insist, depends on social agreement. The words used by the men of the 1640s to describe their political actions fall very far short of what they were actually doing: as Henry Marten discovered in 1643, when he was sent to the Tower for saying in the House of Commons that it was better that one family should suffer than a whole nation. It took Oliver Cromwell to break through to reality by saying he would shoot the king if he met him on the battlefield.

Hobbes had seen the vital importance of definitions for political theory, in the muddled state in which he found it. Men were quarrelling about the precise meaning of mixed monarchy, prerogative, fundamental law. Hence Winstanley's insistence on the proper definition of 'kingly power' as the power of an unrepresentative state, and of a commonwealth as an equal society, not a continuation of kingly power without a king after 'you seemingly have cut off his head'.[99]

Men groped for new words to describe what they were experiencing. 'The general revolt of a nation cannot be called a rebellion', wrote Algernon Sidney.[100] 'Innovation was the contemporary term for revolution', noted Michael Wilding.[101] Men searched the Bible for the right phrases: 'the world turned upside down', 'overturn, overturn, overturn!' Men had said that God called the Long Parliament, God created the New Model Army, long before Cromwell defined 'God's revolutions' as 'his working of things from one period to another'.[102] Authority derived from 'the people', most supporters of parliament agreed. But this word was invariably used loosely, imprecisely. 'The people' themselves had no coherent shape or form or general will. Do they include the poor? Or only heads of households? Property owners? Freeholders? Copyholders? Vagabonds? Locke managed never to define 'the people' at all, though they are basic to his political philosophy. His smudged compromises contrast sharply with Hobbes's insistence on starting from precise definitions.[103]

But then 1688 was a smudged compromise, and helped to prevent England ever having a revolutionary tradition in the sense that the USA, France and the USSR have revolutionary traditions.[104] 1688

99. See Ch. 7 below.
100. A. Sidney, *Discourses Concerning Government*, 1698, Section 36. Written long before Sidney's execution in 1683.
101. M. Wilding, *Dragon's Teeth: Literature in the English Revolution*, Oxford University Press, 1987, p. 91.
102. See p. 92 above.
103. My *People and Ideas*, op. cit., Ch. 12.
104. See pp. 3-4 above.

was 'glorious', bloodless, because fixed by an agreement between party leaders without involving 'the people' at all. If 1688 was a revolution, had there been a revolution in the 1640s? Voltaire in 1733 took for granted that the 1640s had seen 'une révolution en Angleterre',[105] and this usage continued through the French Revolution to Guizot, to Karl Marx, and to European historical writing generally. But in England, although the shift in the meaning of 'revolution' had taken place well before 1688, the events of that year created new ambiguities. So we cannot think about the evolution of the word without thinking about the evolution of the society.

There is room for serious linguistic study of the new words which appeared in the seventeenth century, and of old words whose meaning shifted. Such a study would tell us a great deal about the social changes which took place then, and might even help us in dating them. We could do with a chronologically arranged dictionary, preferably compiled by a historian. Meanwhile, I think we can put the shift in the meaning of 'revolution' well before 1688.

---

105. Voltaire, *Lettres Philosophiques sur les Anglais*, ed. G. Lanson, Paris, 1909, I, p. 91.

6

Governments and public relations: Reformation to 'Glorious' Revolution

Art became a piece of state.
Sir Henry Wootton, a propos Inigo Jones's Banqueting House at Whitehall, quoted by Jonathan Goldberg, *James I and the Politics of Literature: Jonson, Shakespeare, Donne and their Contemporaries*, Johns Hopkins University Press, 1983, pp. 39–40

I

Today we take for granted the interest of the state and politicians in PR. American presidents have fireside chats, English prime ministers change their hairstyles and are taught to modulate their voices in order to impress the electorate. But even before politicians depended upon a mass electorate, before there were mass media, rulers wished to project an image to their peoples. Down to the seventeenth-century sovereigns regularly went on progress, touring round the countryside of southern England with their court, giving the richer among their loyal subjects the dubious favour of entertaining them,[1] and being on display to humbler citizens who were encouraged to put on shows of welcome. There was personal contact, of a highly stylized kind, between monarchs and their subjects, primarily in southern England.

The age of print brought changes in monarchy's public relations, just as TV has brought changes in PR today. The impact of printing was heightened by its coincidence in time with the Protestant Reformation. The rise of an educated laity created a reading public whose

---

1. Sixteenth-century royal progresses were 'designed to shatter the finances of the regional aristocracy as much as to display the Royal Person to crowds' (T. Nairn, *The Enchanted Glass: Britain and its Monarchy*, 1988, p. 85). If this was not the design, it could on occasion be the consequence.

hunger could now be satisfied. Religious changes led to extended use of the printing press, as well as to the introduction of state censorship. *Foreign* public relations acquired a new importance. Henry VIII personally entered the lists against Luther, in order to establish his orthodoxy. Later his 'divorce' from Catherine of Aragon gave rise to an international propaganda campaign. The Reformation statutes represented an appeal to public opinion, an appeal which extended beyond the political nation. Lollard heretics, with their secretly circulated manuscript translations of the Bible, had prepared for the popular Protestantism of the Book. Thomas Cromwell rightly saw the uses of the Bible in the vernacular as government propaganda. The Mexican revolutionary government in the 1920s found it equally valuable.

The marginal notes in the Geneva Bible made political points about God's judgements on tyrants and persecutors. God often revealed his truths to men of inferior social status. 'When they linger which ought to be the chiefest preachers [God] will raise up other extraordinarily, in despite of them (Luke xix. 39)'. That could be applied to bishops. The Geneva notes were not reprinted in the Authorized Version, because they were thought doctrinally and politically unsound. But they were missed, and the Long Parliament set up a committee to revise them. This did not turn out to be a useful PR exercise: the *Annotations* of the learned divines spilt over from the margins into two large folio volumes.

In Henry VIII's reign Cromwell's bureaucratization, if it was his, helped to depersonalize government. From being solely the administration of the king's household it becomes the government of the state. This was a long, slow process, extending from the king's two bodies in the Middle Ages to the charge in 1649 that Charles I was a traitor to the people of England. The royal supremacy was an important milestone on the road, a new national symbol. It led to 'a propaganda campaign without precedent'.[2] Patriotism in sixteenth- and early seventeenth-century England was linked with Protestantism and the Church of England as well as with the monarchy. Elizabethan governments made especial use of the press for propaganda purposes, helping to make Foxe's *Book of Martyrs* a bestseller, censoring Holinshed's *History*.

In the rapid transitions of 1547–58 printed propaganda for foreign consumption – Goodman, Ponet, Knox – centred round the monarch,

2. Scarisbrick, *Henry VIII*, op. cit., pp. 385–6, 392.

the state and the church. Internal propaganda drew on the Lollard tradition in Edward VI's reign, though under Elizabeth Martin Marprelate utilized this tradition for popular opposition, as did Thomas Scott and others in the early seventeenth century.

The myth of Elizabeth the Virgin Queen attempted to supplant that of the Virgin Mary. England the beleaguered isle under threat from international catholicism, England the defender throughout history of God's cause against Antichrist – these were central propaganda themes. (The identification of the Pope with Antichrist was taken over by many Anglicans, not always very enthusiastically, from the Lollards.) Foxe stressed the role of the common people in this struggle, supported by the evidence of the Marian martyrs. This supplied a useful source for parliamentarian propaganda in the 1640s. Elizabeth prudently left defence of her religious settlement to John Jewell and other bishops. James I, perhaps less wisely, followed Henry VIII's example by himself taking part in the theological battles of the day. His *Apologie for the oath of allegiance* (1607) was distributed, in specially bound copies, to all the crowned heads of Europe. Catholics among them refused to receive it, and it did James no good. 'The writing of books was no fit business for a King', said the wiser Henri IV, who had decided that Paris was worth a mass.[3] Henry VIII's condemnation of Luther proved inconvenient after England's breach with Rome: James's positive identification of the papacy with Antichrist in his bid for leadership of the European Protestant interest became embarrassing when his foreign policy changed. Laud had to assert that James had altered his views on this all-important subject.[4] No subsequent English sovereign has been so imprudent as to publish a work of theological controversy.

Increasingly in the sixteenth century royal courts were becoming centres of artistic and literary patronage, an important source of prestige. The resources of continental absolute monarchies were far greater than those of the English court. But portraits of Elizabeth played a significant role as patriotic icons. Court pageantry, tournaments, royal entries etc. helped to familiarize at least citizens of London with the royal person, with her or his glamour and power.[5]

---

3. Leona Rostenberg, *The Minority Press and the English Crown*, Nieuwkoop, 1971, pp. 9, 152–3.
4. Laud, *Works*, op. cit., VI, pp. 577–8; cf. p. 77 above.
5. Sir Roy Strong, *Splendour at Court: Renaissance Spectacle and Illusion*, 1973; *The Cult of Elizabeth: Elizabethan Portraiture and Pageantry*, 1977; *Gloriana: the Portraits of Elizabeth I*, 1987.

Elizabeth's well-timed speech at Tilbury, after the Armada had been safely defeated, earned her a glory which she hardly deserved; and her Golden Speech to parliament in 1601 was equally felicitous.

Elizabeth was much more adept at this aspect of public relations than either James I, who could not bear crowds, or Charles, who withdrew into the secure privacy of Whitehall. Touching for the king's evil was one public ceremony which James reluctantly undertook, and he was followed in this by both his son and the more easily cynical Charles II. The Stuarts simply could not emulate continental monarchies in conspicuous expenditure: attempts to do so only increased tensions between king and parliament – for example Charles I's extravagant plans for rebuilding Whitehall and his lavish purchases of paintings. In the 1630s masques celebrating royal omnipotence were in such manifest conflict with reality that it hardly needed the civil war to make the point. Charles I may have regarded the masque as 'a duty, a ritual no less than his participation in the services of the Anglican church'; but not even courtiers can have taken too seriously the idea that 'the royal government is love', that 'the government of Charles and Henrietta Maria engenders virtue because it is founded in love', and that 'kingship, the rule of the soul over the body politic, might lead man back to his earthly paradise'. After the civil war, Dr Sharpe observes sadly but accurately, 'the language of love was no longer a recurrent voice of the discourse of politics'.[6] Charles II had been divorced from his kingdom for so long that he could hardly be identified with it as his father's sycophants had identified Charles I. Marvell indeed differentiated between Charles II and England, whom the king wishes to seduce or rape.[7]

The legend of Elizabeth, the staunch defender of Protestantism and of England's interests, became a useful means of criticizing the weaker policies, especially the foreign policies, of her two successors. Fulke Greville's *Life of Sidney*, unpublishable before 1640, is the *locus classicus*; but the technique was familiar in the parliaments of James and Charles. The memory of Prince Henry, who had devoted much thought and energy to constructing his own PR image,[8] the misfortunes of Elizabeth, the Winter Queen of Bohemia, were put to analogous uses. After 1660 nonconformists similarly appealed to the

6. Kevin Sharpe, *Criticism and Compliment: The Politics of Literature in the England of Charles I*, Cambridge University Press, 1987, pp. 204, 211, 272–4.
7. A. Marvell, *Last Instructions to a Painter*, 1667, in H.M. Margoliouth (ed.) *Poems and Letters*, Oxford University Press, 1927, I, pp. 162–3.
8. R. Strong, *Henry, Prince of Wales, and England's Lost Renaissance*, 1986.

myth of the united and firmly Protestant church under Archbishops Grindal and Abbott.

'We princes,' Elizabeth told MPs in 1586, 'are set upon stages in sight and view of all the world'.[9] Theatres were new in her reign, and rapidly became very important for public relations. They needed royal approval, and under James I they came under direct royal patronage – the King's Men. They were, consequently, subject to censorship, which became stricter as tension increased under Charles I. Margot Heinemann, Dollimore, Norbrook, Martin Butler and Simon Shepherd, among others, are beginning to elucidate the political role which the theatres played. They were at once controlled by the government and subject to popular control through the box office. They offered the one forum, apart from the equally censored pulpits, where ordinary citizens could hear political matters discussed, however indirectly. In theory political questions were far above the heads of common people, and they were to be kept from them. In theory too the theatres were censored. But it was possible to discuss current political questions in a play set in – say – Sicily, or in a play about the distant past. Plays celebrating the institution of monarchy might have the effect of contrasting the actual occupant of the throne – in some far away country and epoch, of course – with the ideal. Shakespeare's *Richard II* was regarded as a seditious play despite – or because of – its high-flown divine right of kings rhetoric.

Margot Heinemann has shown from Middleton's *A Game at Chess* of 1624, and Martin Butler has shown even from the strictly censored theatre of the 1630s, that plays might raise political problems when the court itself was divided. In the 1630s the popular theatres became increasingly difficult to control.[10] After 1660 they were not reopened; the others – the King's theatre and the Duke's – were under supervision.

The parliamentary disputes of the 1620s led to appeals to different abstractions – on the one side to the impersonal authority of the law, or the supremacy of parliament, on the other to the personal prerogative of the sovereign, his divine right. Hence the House of Commons refused to accept an amendment to the Petition of Right from the House of Lords which would have 'saved the royal prerogative'; hence

9. James I repeated the remark: Steven Mullaney, *The Place of the Stage: License, Play and Power in Renaissance England*, Chicago University Press, 1988, pp. 96–7.

10. Margot Heinemann, *Puritanism and Theatre: Thomas Middleton and Opposition Drama under the Early Stuarts*, Cambridge University Press, 1980, *passim*; Martin Butler, *Theatre and Crisis, 1632–1642*, Cambridge University Press, 1984, *passim*.

Charles I's insistence that *he* was responsible, personally, not his ministers, when the Commons attacked the latter. They on the contrary argued that 'the King can do no wrong' meant that if wrong was done a minister must be held responsible. It was a struggle for impersonality in government, opposing the corporate to the personal capacity of the crown. Taxation must be granted 'in a Parliamentary way', not by forced loans or ship money based on the personal prerogative.

Protecting the property of the subject (including property in his own person) against the royal prerogative, against unparliamentary taxation or arbitrary arrest, meant protecting the rights of the propertied class, who believed that the state existed to protect them, against the personal needs of the king. Again this is to depersonalize the state. Under Charles II the issues came to be Habeas Corpus and the independence of judges from the king's *personal* influence. Two concepts of the state are in conflict.

Theories of the divine right of kings were evolved in England in the early seventeenth century: the theory was needed here more than in France, where the personal authority of the king was unquestioned. [11] 'Princes are not bound to give account of their actions but to God alone', declared Charles I in 1629; 'yet for the satisfaction of the minds of our loving subjects, we have thought good' to give an account of the reasons for dissolving parliament in that year. [12] Already the public relations battle was on: the king did not wish to explain himself. That he did so was a victory for public opinion. There was a great outburst of propagandist pamphlets in 1641 and after, when both king and parliament were seeking for support and legitimation. Such competition was novel in English history, though it had occurred in the French wars of religion and the Revolt of the Netherlands. Parliamentarians drew on ideas from both these upheavals: the Wars of the Roses had had no comparable social or political implications, and anyway occurred before the spread of printing.

II

Charles I ceased effectively to be king over the whole English people in 1642 if not earlier. Civil war only made this obvious. The king tried to communicate with his subjects by declarations and proclamations

11. J.N. Figgis, *The Divine Right of Kings*, Cambridge University Press, 1914, Ch. 6.
12. *The King's Declaration showing the Causes of the late Dissolution*, in S.R. Gardiner (ed.) *Constitutional Documents of the Puritan Revolution, 1625–1660*, Oxford University Press, 3rd edn, 1906, p. 83.

in the early forties: these were mainly directed to the political élite, and the king continued to deplore the necessity for taking part in such altercations. ('We are many times amazed to consider by what eyes these things [seditious parliamentarian publications] are seen and by what ears they are heard'.)[13] He appealed to the population as a whole only at the very end of his life. In his trial he addressed public opinion directly : if they can do this to me, which of you is safe? Immediately after his execution *Eikon Basilike* was published by John Gauden, for whom Charles may have supplied material. This work hit a note which not even Milton could silence with his sneers in *Eikonoklastes* at Charles's 'masquing scene'.

English monarchy seemed doubly dead when *Eikon Basilike* appeared in February 1649. Charles I's head had been severed, the 'Young Pretender' Prince Charles was in exile, and the English republic had been proclaimed. Yet the image of the king prevailed over the impersonal state and its spokesman. Milton might expose *Eikon Basilike* as spurious, but it was, he admitted, 'the best advocate and interpreter' of Charles's actions, of which his party made full use.[14] In contributed mightily to the restoration in 1660 of 'a King with plenty of holy oil about him', to the manipulated monarchy which has survived down to our time. Milton's eloquence impressed the European intelligentsia more than the English people. Charles II 'touched' for the king's evil with less reluctance than his father or grandfather. This particular survival of the *personal* magic of monarchy died out soon after the end of the century, when the hereditary succession was finally broken.

As early as 1608 Lord Herbert of Cherbury in 'The Progress of the State' was philosophizing about why we obey the state, of which monarchy is only one form.[15] In James I's reign men were distinguishing between the king and the commonwealth.[16] The civil war furthered the depersonalization of government. Dr Ann Hughes, in a perceptive article, points out that on the royalist side the progress of the war led to greater personal authoritarianism and arbitrariness, whilst on the parliamentarian side it led to an insistence on greater accountability, of individuals and institutions: authority had to come

13. Nalson, *Impartial Collection*, op. cit., II, pp. 747–8.
14. Milton, *Complete Prose Works*, op. cit., III, pp. 338–42; cf. pp. 596, 601.
15. R.G. Howarth (ed.) *Minor Poets of the 17th Century*, Everyman edn, 1931, pp. 8–10.
16. See p. 29 above.

from the bottom upwards, from parish élites, not from the top down-wards as in absolute monarchy.[17]

A further contributory factor was the irreverence of parlia-mentarian propaganda.[18] This propaganda catered for social groups new to politics, who lacked traditional reticence about the mysteries of government. The breakdown of controls allowed common people to discuss and criticize government; at Putney rank-and-file soldiers argued with generals about the future constitution of England. Mil-lenarianism, widespread among the parliamentarian rank and file, was by definition critical of all existing governments. From the 1640s the royal supremacy, and indeed the Church of England, ceased to be the focus for patriotic loyalty. The church and the royal supremacy as restored in 1660 never acquired the old glamour. Bishops ceased to occupy high state office; the last time bishops played a significant political role was in opposition to James II.[19]

Hobbes's theory of sovereignty in *Leviathan* is intended to be applicable to either a monarchy or a republic; whether the sovereign is a man or a body of men, there are certain powers which he must have in order to do his job of protecting his subjects. The purged parliament which ruled the English republic after 1649 asserted a sovereignty as absolute as that which Charles I had claimed. At the same time as it succeeded to the theoretical claims of the monarchy the Commonwealth was taking over functions hitherto left to private enterprise.[20] The Commonwealth and Oliver Cromwell gave full state backing to the East India Company, as the Stuart kings had never done. This policy survived the restoration, symbolized by the founda-tion of the *Royal* African Company, with the king, the queen and the Duke of York among its shareholders.

The power of the press was recognized at the restoration, itself a great public relations event.[21] The king became not only head of the Church of England but (hardly less important now) patron of the Royal Society, picking up his uncle Prince Henry's interest in science.[22] The Declarations of Indulgence issued by Charles and James were last attempts to recover *personal* royal authority, to appeal over

---

17. Ann Hughes, 'The king, the parliament and the localities during the English civil war', *Journal of British Studies*, 1985, 24, p. 263.
18. See pp. 51–2 above.
19. See p. 21 above.
20. See pp. 11–12 above.
21. Jose, *Ideas of the Restoration*, op. cit., *passim*.
22. Strong, *Henry, Prince of Wales*, op. cit., pp. 211–19.

the heads of parliament and bishops to middle- and lower-class dissenters. The attempts failed.

Censorship, that important instrument of state control, had been indisputably the king's prerogative before 1640. In 1662 the Licensing Act was passed by parliament – a recognition of the importance of who controls the media. This was further illustrated in the party struggle to draw propaganda benefits from the Popish Plot, when censorship temporarily broke down. An opposition press functioned freely for a short time as the crown struggled to resume control. A solution was found only when restored consensus after 1688 meant that publishers themselves censored authors in the interests of sales.[23]

A feature of the whole period was the public relations significance of show trials and public executions. Henry VIII made an important political statement when he burnt Anabaptists and papists at the same time. Mary's burnings overreached their objective of inspiring terror: the courage and eloquence of the martyrs destroyed the effect. Similarly public executions lost their terrorizing effect as the ideology of the Good Old Cause gave courage to the victims which they expressed in speeches from the scaffold. Legate and Wightman in 1612, Charles I in 1649, the regicides in 1660–2, all probably achieved more by their deaths than the governments which condemned them. Public executions ceased not for humanitarian reasons but because they were failing to achieve the desired public relations effect. This became true eventually of the victims of the Popish Plot in 1678–82.

Charles I in 1649 was condemned as a traitor to the people of England, to the Commonwealth. Although this particular example fell from favour, the concept of treason against the commonwealth as well as against the person of the king remained. Marvell in 1677 said that to attempt to establish absolute monarchy was no less treasonable than to try to convert monarchy into a republic. He and Rochester opposed the government in the name of the state; Marvell differentiated between Charles and England.[24] The rhetoric of monarchy is changing: Charles II was deemed to support liberty, property and the Protestant religion.[25] We move slowly from the personal public relations of the monarch and his court to the public relations of the state, to the *idea* of English monarchy.

---

23. See pp. 240–2 below.
24. Marvell, *An Account of the Growth of Popery*, in *Works* (ed. Grosart), op. cit., IV, p. 261; *Last Instructions to a Painter*, p. 105 above.
25. See pp. 54–5 above.

III

The greatest PR man was John Milton. His first public relations job for the government of the Commonwealth was to combat *Eikon Basilike*, much the most effective work of propaganda on behalf of Charles I. Gauden compared the royal martyr with Christ, to Milton's disgust; and he drew skilfully on traditional images of the radical-heretical opposition. Foxe's martyrs were justified *because of* their sufferings; their separatist successors knew they were godly *because* they had to endure persecution. Jesus Christ was a king; even before 1640 increasing emphasis had been laid on his suffering by poets like George Herbert:

> A King my title is, prefixt on high;
> Yet by my subjects am condemned to die . . .

> Herod in judgment sits, while I do stand;
> Examines me with a censorious hand:
> I him obey, who all things else command:
> Was ever grief like mine? . . .

> Weep not, dear friends, since I for both have wept
> When all my tears were blood, the while you slept:
> Your tears for your own fortunes should be kept:
> Was ever grief like mine?[26]

In a curious way Herbert seems to have anticipated circumstances which arose only after 1649, when the pathos which clung to the suffering Christ was transferred to Charles. The point was more obvious when Vaughan wrote, about 1646, of 'The King Disguis'd':

> A king and no king! Is he gone from us
> And stolen alive into his coffin thus?[27]

Gauden's appropriation of arguments hitherto the property of radical sectaries was not a propaganda line applicable to monarchy in general, but it was superbly relevant to the interregnum. In *Eikonoklastes* Milton tried, unsuccessfully, to counter the effects of the king's demeanour at his trial, and the pathos of *Eikon Basilike*. Milton thought that Gauden's mawkish stress on Charles's personal piety

---

26. G. Herbert, 'The Church: Superliminare'; cf. 'The Thanksgiving': – 'Oh King of grief! (A title strange, yet true), / To thee of all kings only due'.
27. L.C. Martin (ed.) *Works of Henry Vaughan*, Oxford University Press, 1914, II, pp. 605–6.

was a shameless way of evading the grandeur of the Revolution's achievements, which he celebrated in his two *Defences of the People of England* (1651 and 1654) as 'the most heroic and exemplary . . . since the creation of the world'.[28] We do not know whether Milton's job was originally intended to embrace the task of propagandist in chief for the Commonwealth, its spokesman to the whole of Europe; or whether 'John Milton, Englishman' created it for himself. But he was sensationally successful in getting his message across. The Revolution, Milton thought, had created a new state of *European* significance. Idolatry like that in *Eikon Basilike* distracted attention from serious matters, from glorifying God by *activities* on behalf of humanity.

Milton looks to the future because he exclusively defends the Commonwealth and what it stands for, not an individual ruler, as Marvell was to defend Cromwell in *The First Anniversary*. Milton was dazzled by the novelty and importance of his task. His approach was defensive, but it was also a trumpet-call to his own nation and beyond to an international community.[29] Nothing quite like his *Defences* had appeared, for kings since Henry VIII thought that they did not need to be defended, or disdained the mere idea of an appeal to European public opinion. International communication in Latin was still possible, at least at the level of the learned élite: though this would not long remain true; and Milton wished to appeal beyond the élite. Different propaganda techniques had to be evolved for the American and French Revolutions.

Milton used his uniquely privileged position to play party politics, recommending to Cromwell for instance that he should re-employ old republicans like Bradshaw and Robert Overton. This shows how far from united the English revolutionary nation was; we may contrast Milton's failure to obey orders to attack Levellers whilst gladly writing against royalists. But with the protectorate Milton ceased to be the herald of a new state, a new European order. His tasks faded into the common day-to-day diplomacy of obtaining a safeguard for Mylius.[30]

But the glimpse of the modern world which Milton offered was not unique to him. Marchamont Nedham in *The State of the Case of the Commonwealth* (1654) and in his journalism pressed similar themes:

---

28. J. Milton, *Second Defence*, in *Complete Prose*, op. cit., IV, p. 549.
29. See David Loewenstein, 'Milton and the politics of defense', in D. Loewenstein and J.G. Turner (eds) *Two-Handed Engine: Politics, Poetics and Hermeneutics in Milton's Prose*, Ch. 9 (forthcoming).
30. Miller, *Milton and the Oldenburg Safeguard*, op. cit.

his reputation as a republican thinker was as great in the eighteenth century as that of Milton or Marvell. Harrington too had envisaged a republican internationalism which would liberate oppressed peoples.[31]

Marvell tried to recapture some of the millenarian fervour in *The First Anniversary of the Government under O.C.* (1655): but by then his was defensive propaganda primarily for home consumption: it was not addressed to the people of Europe. Still less so was Dryden's *Annus Mirabilis* (1666), with its glorification of London and its trade. In both we can see the commercial interest fusing with the state. Both Marvell and Dryden – and many after them – were self-appointed to the role of spokesman for their country – unlike Milton. The official appointed by Charles II who comes nearest to such a spokesman was Roger L'Estrange. L'Estrange was more concerned to censor 'the great masters of the popular style', and to slander and hunt down hostile elements *within* the English state than to proclaim its grandeurs abroad. With Dryden's *Absalom and Achitophel* defence of the monarchy sinks to the level of party politics. The monarchy could again be depersonalized only after 1688. William III could never have said 'L'Etat, c'est moi', still less George I. In the eighteenth and early nineteenth centuries the symbol of the bellicose English state came to be not the insignificant occupant of the throne but John Bull, the yeoman with his cudgel. (The more genial but equally plebeian Uncle Sam was perhaps a deliberate foil). Only with Queen Victoria and Prince Albert did the monarchy begin to treat PR as a serious matter to be seriously cultivated. It never looked back.[32]

From George II's reign Englishmen could sing either 'God save the King!' or 'Rule Britannia!' to celebrate their monarch's or their country's power. The successors of Winstanley might have thought this a distinction without a difference, since 'oppression is a great tree still, and keeps off the sun of freedom from the poor commons still; he hath many branches and great roots which must be grubbed up before everyone can sing Sion's songs in peace'.[33]

31. Harrington, *Political Works*, op. cit., pp. 329–33.
32. See Nairn, *Enchanted Glass*, op. cit., Chs 2 and 3.
33. Winstanley, *The Law of Freedom*, op. cit., p. 166.

7

Gerrard Winstanley and freedom

If thou pray, it must be for freedom to all; and if thou give thanks, it must be because freedom covers all people. . . . If, when thou hast power to settle freedom in thy country, thou takest the possession of the earth into thy own particular hands, and makest thy brother work for thee as the kings did, thou hast fought and acted for thyself, not for thy country.
Gerrard Winstanley, *The Law of Freedom in a Platform*, 1652, 'To the Friendly and Unbiased Reader', in *'The Law of Freedom' and other Writings*, Penguin edn, pp. 292–3

It is not the changings of government, and its new titles and names, but it is truth and perfect freedom that the best of men delights in, and it is that, that will satisfy the hungry people.
Grace Barwick, *To All Present Rulers, Whether Parliament or Whosoever, of England*, 1659, pp. 3–5*

The clothing county of Lancashire supplied more than its quota of radicals to the seventeenth-century English Revolution. Samuel Gorton, born near Manchester in 1592, became a clothier in London. He was one of New England's most active heretics. Lawrence Clarkson, born in Preston in 1616, was described as a tailor. He became a leading Ranter. Gerrard Winstanley, born in Wigan in 1609 into a middle-class Puritan family of clothiers, also came to London. He was apprenticed to a clothier, married, and set up in business just before the outbreak of civil war. The war, severing communications between London and Lancashire, ruined him; he

---

* I owe this reference to a paper delivered by Phyllis Mack to the Conference of the American Historical Association at Chicago in December 1986, which she was kind enough to let me read.

withdrew to the Surrey countryside, where his father-in-law lived. There he herded other men's cows, as a hired labourer.[1]

The 1640s were years of religious and political turmoil – the civil war, leading to the defeat of the king; Levellers in London and the army, arguing for a republic and a wide extension of the parliamentary franchise. In 1647 the army seized the king, hitherto a prisoner of parliament, and in January 1649 he was tried and executed as a traitor to the people of England. An MP for Wigan was one of the regicides. The House of Lords was abolished, and England was proclaimed a Commonwealth. Millenarian expectations ran high: almost anything seemed possible, including the return of King Jesus as successor to King Charles. There was a ferment of political and religious discussion.

But the forties were also years of great economic hardship for the lower classes. Over the century before 1640 real wages had halved. The years between 1620 and 1650, Professor Bowden has said, were among the most terrible the English lower classes have ever endured. The economic disruption of the war, leading to unemployment, was accompanied by exceptionally high taxation, billeting and free quartering of soliders, and plunder. On top of all this there was a series of exceptionally bad harvests, famine and disease. The problem of poverty was acute. Rioting crowds seized corn. Men were said to lie starving in the London streets.

In the years 1648-9 a spate of pamphlets was published advocating use of confiscated church, crown and royalist lands to provide for the poor, and even fresh land confiscations; there were those who suggested expropriating the rich and establishing a communist society. Many predicted the second coming of Jesus Christ, and foresaw a thousand-year rule of the saints in which a materialist utopia would be established on earth – egalitarian, just to the poor at the expense of the rich. So Winstanley, who brooded deeply over these matters in his poverty, was not alone. But he was the only thinker we know of to break through to a systematically worked-out theory of communism which could be put into immediate effect. More's *Utopia*, published in 1516, had been in Latin, and More rejected with horror any idea of making it accessible to ordinary people by translating it into English.

---

1. Philip F. Gura, *A Glimpse of Sion's Glory: Puritan Radicalism in New England 1620-1660*, Wesleyan University Press, 1984, especially Ch. 10. For Clarkson see Chapter 9 of the present book; for Winstanley, see J. Alsop, 'Gerrard Winstanley's later life', *Past and Present*, 1979, 82.

But Winstanley wrote, at a time of acute social and political crisis, in the vernacular, and appealed to the common people of England to take action to establish a communist society. 'Action is the life of all', he wrote; 'and if thou dost not act thou dost nothing'.[2]

It started, as so much seventeenth-century thinking did, with a vision, in which Winstanley received the messages 'Work together, Eat bread together', 'Let Israel go free: . . . Israel shall neither give nor take hire'. Winstanley decided he must 'go forth and declare it in my action' by organizing 'us that are called the common people to manure and work upon the common lands'.[3] This was two months after the execution of Charles I. Winstanley, with a handful of poor men, established a colony on St George's Hill, near Cobham, to take symbolic ownership of the uncultivated common and waste lands. It lasted a year.

Winstanley wrote a series of pamphlets defending the Digger colony and calling on others to imitate their example. At least ten more colonies were established. In the process Winstanley elaborated a quite original theory of communism. It is not possible to do full justice to the theory as a whole since we are concerned with Winstanley and freedom; but freedom was crucial to his thinking. It had indeed been crucial for the revolutionaries from the start. 'Liberty and property' was the slogan of the moderates; 'back to Anglo-Saxon freedom' the cry of the radicals. But the word 'liberty' was hopelessly ambiguous. The close association of liberty and property in orthodox parliamentary discourse is not fortuitous, for the Latin word *libertas*, like the French word *franchise*, came very close to meaning a property right; a 'liberty' is something you can exclude others from. To these Norman words Winstanley preferred the more plebeian Anglo-Saxon 'freedom'. Throwing off the Norman Yoke, as John Hare argued in a pamphlet published in 1647, involved a linguistic as well as a political revolution. There was no agreement on what liberty was, or should be.

'All men have stood for freedom', wrote Winstanley;

2. Winstanley, *Law of Freedom*, op. cit., pp. 127–8; G.E. Aylmer, 'The religion of Gerrard Winstanley', in J.F. McGregor and B. Reay (eds) *Radical Religion in the English Revolution*, Oxford University Press, 1984; my *Religion and Politics*, Ch. 11; K.V. Thomas (ed.) 'A Declaration . . . [from] Iver', *Past and Present*, 1969, 42; Petegorsky, *Left-Wing Democracy*, op. cit., *passim*.
3. Sabine, *Works of Winstanley*, op. cit., pp. 190, 194, 199; cf. Winstanley, 'Englands Spirit Unfoulded', 1650, ed. G.E. Aylmer, *Past and Present*, 1968, 40, p. 9.

and now the common enemy is gone, you are all like men in a mist, seeking for freedom and know not where nor what it is. . . . And those of the richer sort of you that see it are ashamed and afraid to own it, because it comes clothed in a clownish garment. . . . Freedom is the man that will turn the world upside down, therefore no wonder he hath enemies.[4]

He summed up in *The Law of Freedom* (1652): 'The great searching of heart in these days is to find out where true freedom lies, that the Commonwealth of England might be established in peace'. (A few years earlier Edward Hyde, in exile, had observed from a more conservative viewpoint that 'though the name of liberty be pleasant to all kinds of people, yet all men do not understand the same thing by it'.)[5]

Winstanley listed four current versions of freedom; and the order in which he discusses them is perhaps significant:

1 'Free use of trading, and to have all patents, licences [i.e. monopolies] and restrictions removed' – freedom for businessmen;
2 Freedom of conscience, no constraints 'from or to any form of worship' – the sort of freedom the sects called for;
3 'It is true freedom to have community with all women, and to have liberty to satisfy their lusts' – Ranter libertinism;
4 Absolute freedom of property, for landlords and their eldest sons – the freedom the gentry most wanted.

Curiously, there is no mention of constitutional liberty. None of these, Winstanley thought, is 'the true foundation freedom which settles a commonwealth in peace'.[6]

So Winstanley was aware that his concept of freedom differed from that of most parliamentarians. He insisted on economic freedom for the poor as well as the rich, on social as well as religious freedom. 'If thou consent to freedom to the rich in the City, and givest freedom to the freeholders in the country and to priests and lawyers and lords of manors . . . and yet allowest the poor no freedom, thou art there a declared hypocrite.' All men had a 'creation birth-right' of access to cultivate the land.[7] In his final pamphlet, published in 1652 after the defeat of the Diggers, Winstanley was quite specific: 'True freedom

4. Winstanley, *Law of Freedom*, op. cit., p. 128.
5. ibid., p. 294; Edward Hyde's Commonplace Book, 1646–7, quoted by F. Raab, *The English Face of Machiavelli. A Changing Interpretation, 1500–1700*, 1964, p. 148.
6. Winstanley, *Law of Freedom*, op. cit., p. 294.
7. ibid., pp. 129, 306; cf. p. 124, below.

lies where a man receives his nourishment and preservation, and that is in the use of the earth. . . . A man had better to have no body than to have no food for it. . . . True commonwealth's freedom lies in the free enjoyment of the earth'.[8] Living in a preponderantly agrarian society, Winstanley uses 'the land', 'the earth', to signify property in general; but he knew from his own experience in Wigan and London that England was already becoming an industrial country. He had interesting things to say about the desirability of abolishing commercial secrets, and the need in a communist society for a state monopoly of foreign trade.

In 1646 the Leveller John Lilburne had asserted that 'the poorest that lives hath as true a right to give a vote as well as the richest and greatest'.[9] Levellers were agitating for a wide extension of the parliamentary franchise. Next year there were debates at Putney in the Army Council between generals, elected representatives of junior officers and of the rank and file – a remarkable occasion. Discussing the parliamentary franchise, Colonel Rainborough echoed Lilburne in memorable words: 'the poorest he that is in England hath a life to live as the greatest he, and therefore . . . every man that is to live under a government ought first by his own consent to put himself under that government'. This led to a long debate with Commissary-General Ireton, who argued that 'liberty cannot be provided for in a general sense if property be preserved'. If the right to a vote derived from 'the right of nature', then 'by the same right of nature' a man 'hath the same right in any goods he sees, . . . to take and use them for his sustenance'. Natural right leads to communism: 'constitution founds property'.[10]

This argument nonplussed the Levellers at Putney, because most of them wanted to retain the institution of private property. William Walwyn was believed to be a theoretical communist, and the boundary line between Levellers and True Levellers (Diggers) was never clearly drawn. But Lilburne and other Levellers leaders repudiated the communism of the Diggers.[11] Many of them were prepared to exclude servants and paupers from the franchise. Winstanley, on the other hand, insisted uncompromisingly that 'the common people' are

8. ibid., p. 295.
9. John Lilburne, *The Charters of London*, 1646, quoted by Wolfe, *Leveller Manifestoes of the Puritan Revolution*, Columbia University Press, 1944, p. 14.
10. A.S.P. Woodhouse (ed.) *Puritanism and Liberty*, 1938, pp. 53, 58, 69, 73.
11. My *World Turned Upside Down*, Penguin edn, p. 119.

'part of the nation'; 'without exception, all sorts of people in the land are to have freedom', not just 'the gentry and clergy'.[12]

Winstanley alone grasped Ireton's theoretical nettle. He agreed that a natural right to accumulate property was incompatible with liberty. 'There cannot be a universal liberty till this universal community be established.'[13] 'I would have an eye to property', Ireton had insisted.[14] Winstanley preferred liberty. For him the introduction of private property – and he speaks especially of property in land – had been the Fall of Man. 'In the beginning of time the great Creator Reason made the earth to be a common treasury'; and all men were equal, none ruling over another. But covetousness overcame Reason and equality together. 'When self-love began to arise in the earth, then man began to fall.'[15] 'When mankind began to quarrel about the earth and some would have all and shut out others, forcing them to be servants: this was man's fall.'[16] 'Murdering property' was founded on theft; and the state was set up to protect the property of the plunderers: 'You hold that cursed thing by the power of the sword.' Property is the devil, and to support it is 'rebellion and high treason against the King of Righteousness'.[17] Buying and selling, hiring wage labour, the laws regulating the market, are all part of the Fall.

So long as private property survives, 'so long the creation lies under bondage'. The government that maintains private property is 'the government of . . . self-seeking Antichrist', 'the government of highwaymen'.[18] Exploitation, not labour, is the curse of fallen man. Property and wage labour, Winstanley thought, must be abolished before all can enjoy freedom.

The Levellers and many in the army argued that parliament's victory in the civil war over the Norman Yoke of king and landlords ought to lead to the establishment of political democracy. Winstanley held that it must lead to a restoration of economic equality. 'Everyone upon the recovery of the [Norman] conquest ought to return into freedom again without respecting persons. . . . Surely all sorts, both gentry in their enclosures, commonalty in their commons, ought to

---

12. Winstanley, *Law of Freedom*, op. cit., pp. 182, 116.
13. Sabine, *Works of Winstanley*, op. cit., p. 199.
14. Woodhouse, *Puritanism and Liberty*, op. cit., p. 57.
15. Winstanley, *Law of Freedom*, op. cit., pp. 77–8, 193.
16. Sabine, *Works of Winstanley*, op. cit., p. 424.
17. Winstanley, *Law of Freedom*, op. cit., pp. 85, 99, 120–1, 141, 222, 266–8; Sabine, *Works of Winstanley*, op. cit., p. 201.
18. Winstanley, *Law of Freedom*, op. cit., pp. 244, 306–7.

have their freedom, not compelling one to work for another?' 'The laws that were made in the days of the kings . . . give freedom' only 'to the gentry and clergy; all the rest are left servants and bondmen to those task-masters'. 'If the common people have no more freedom in England but only to live among their elder brothers [landlords] and work for them for hire, what freedom then can they have in England more than we can have in Turkey or France?'[19]

This would necessitate wholesale change. 'All laws that are not grounded upon equity and reason, not giving a universal freedom to all but respecting persons, ought . . . to be cut off with the King's head'.[20] What Winstanley called 'kingly power' had survived the king: 'that top bough is lopped off the tree of tyranny, and kingly power in that one particular is cast out. But alas, oppression is a great tree still, and keeps off the sun of freedom from the poor commons still'.[21] 'Everyone talks of freedom, but there are but few that act for freedom, and the actors for freedom are oppressed by the talkers and verbal professors of freedom.'[22]

Winstanley thus insisted that formal political liberty was inadequate unless accompanied by economic freedom, by equality. When J.C. Davis says that 'to Winstanley the only freedom that mattered was freedom from economic insecurity', he is, I think, quite wrong.[23] Winstanley said, indeed, that 'free enjoyment' of the earth 'is true freedom';[24] and that heaven is a 'comfortable livelihood in the earth'. 'There cannot be a universal liberty till this community be established.'[25] But freedom for Winstanley meant intellectual as well as economic freedom, meant the rule of Reason, the beginning of civilized life for all. 'When men are sure of food and raiment, their reason will be ripe, and ready to dive into the secrets of the creation.'[26] He foresaw a commonwealth in which science would flourish. Hitherto 'fear of want and care to pay rent to task-masters hath hindered many rare inventions'. In a free commonwealth, men would be encouraged to 'employ their reason and industry'; inventions would benefit all, not just the inventor. Kingly power had 'crushed

19. Sabine, *Works of Winstanley*, op. cit., pp. 287–8.
20. ibid., p. 288.
21. Winstanley, *Law of Freedom*, op. cit, p. 166.
22. ibid., p. 129.
23. J.C. Davis, 'Gerrard Winstanley and the restoration of true magistracy', *Past and Present*, 1976, 70, pp. 78, 92.
24. Winstanley, *Law of Freedom*, op. cit., p. 296.
25. Sabine, *Works of Winstanley*, op. cit., p. 199.
26. Winstanley, *Law of Freedom*, op. cit., pp. 365–6.

the spirit of knowledge'; now it could 'rise up in its beauty and fullness'.[27] His belief in the possibilities of democratically controlled science is one of the most attractive features of Winstanley's thought.

In his final pamphlet, Winstanley declared that 'all the inward bondages of the mind, as covetousness, pride, hypocrisy, envy, sorrows, fears, desperation and madness, are all occasioned by the outward bondage that one sort of people lay upon another'.[28] 'No true freedom can be established for England's peace . . . but such a one as hath respect to the poor as well as the rich.' But economic freedom is the beginning, not the end. 'Freedom', he declared, 'is Christ in you and among you.'[29]

For Winstanley, Christ was not a person. The biblical stories are allegories, not history. 'Whether there was any such outward things or no', he remarked nonchalantly, 'it matters not much.'[30] In a pamphlet written in his pre-communist phase, Winstanley explained that he preferred to use the word Reason rather than God, because he had been 'held in darkness' by the word God.[31] Reason is 'the great Creator', not a personal God beyond the skies but the law of the universe which will ultimately prevail among all men and women. For Winstanley, the Second Coming is 'the rising up of Christ in sons and daughters' – Christ, the spirit of Reason entering the hearts of all men and women, 'comes to set all free'. Freedom 'is Christ in you'.[32]

And what will Reason tell us? 'Is thy neighbour hungry and naked today, do thou feed him and clothe him; it may be thy case tomorrow, and then he will be ready to help thee.'[33] Reason teaches co-operation, and the rising of Reason in all men and women will lead to recognition of the necessity of a communist society. The ethos of existing society was the negation of co-operation, of sharing. Here Winstanley drew on his own rudimentary version of what was later to be called the labour theory of value:

> No man can be rich, but he must be rich either by his own labours, or by the labours of other men helping him. If a man have no help from his neighbours, he shall never gather an

27. ibid., pp. 355–6.
28. ibid., p. 296.
29. ibid., pp. 128–9.
30. ibid., p. 232.
31. Sabine, *Works of Winstanley*, op. cit., p. 105.
32. Winstanley, *Law of Freedom*, op. cit., pp. 216, 128; Sabine, *Works of Winstanley*, op. cit., pp. 114–15, 162, 204–5, 225.
33. Winstanley, *The Saints Paradise*, 1648?, p. 123.

estate of hundreds and thousands a year. If other men help him
to work, then are those riches his neighbours' as well as his; for
they be the fruit of other men's labours as well as his own. . . .
Rich men receive all they have from the labourer's hand, and
what they give, they give away other men's labours, not their
own.[34]

Men and women will be truly free when Reason 'knits every
creature together into a oneness, making every creature to be an
upholder of his fellow, and so everyone is an assistant to preserve the
whole'.[35] 'To live in the enjoyment of Christ . . . will bring in true
community and destroy murdering property.'[36] 'True freedom . . .
lies in the community in spirit and community in the earthly treasury;
and this is Christ . . . spread abroad in the creation'.[37]

This commonwealth's freedom will unite the hearts of Englishmen together in love, so that if a foreign enemy endeavour to
come in we shall all with joint consent rise up to defend our
inheritance, and shall be true to one another. Whereas now the
poor . . . say . . . 'We can as well live under a foreign enemy
working for day wages as under our own brethren, with whom
we ought to have equal freedom'.[38]

Many of the ringing and oft-quoted Leveller declarations of human
rights – Lilburne's 'the poorest that lives . . .', Rainborough's 'the
poorest he . . .', 'every man . . .' – appear to be restricted to one sex
only. So does Winstanley's 'the poorest man hath as true a title and
just right to the land as the richest man'. But Winstanley continually
surprises us. In his first pamphlet defending the Diggers he declared
'Not one word was spoken in the beginning, that one branch of mankind should rule over another. And the reason is this, every single
man, male and female, is a perfect creature of himself.' In *Fire in the
Bush* (1650) he spoke throughout of 'mankind' rather than of 'men'. I
quoted him above insisting on freedom for 'all sorts of people'.[39] So it
is possible that when Winstanley says 'every man' he may mean 'every
man and woman'. Whether Levellers speaking of 'every man' were

---

34. Winstanley, *Law of Freedom*, op. cit., p. 287.
35. Sabine, *Works of Winstanley*, op. cit., p. 105.
36. Winstanley, *Law of Freedom*, op. cit., p. 222.
37. ibid., p. 129.
38. Sabine, *Works of Winstanley*, op. cit., p. 414.
39. Winstanley, *Law of Freedom*, op. cit., pp. 131, 77, 213, and *passim*; see also Ch. 1
above.

similarly inclusive we do not know. Winstanley is unique in his continual emphasis on Christ rising in sons *and daughters*.

For Winstanley every man subject to Reason's law becomes a Son of God. His ruler is within, whether it is called conscience, or love, or Reason, or Christ. After the Second Coming, when Reason has risen in sons and daughters, 'the ministration of Christ in one single person is to be silent and draw back' before the righteousness and wisdom in every person.[40] Religion will wither away.

But kingly power proved stronger than the Christ within. After the destruction of his communist colony in 1650, a less optimistic Winstanley asked why 'most people are so ignorant of their freedom, and so few fit to be chosen Commonwealth's officers?' His answer was that 'the old kingly clergy . . . are continually distilling their blind principles into the people and do thereby nurse up ignorance in them'. He had a virulent anti-clericalism worthy of Milton. It made Winstanley almost anticipate Marx's 'opium of the people':

> While men are gazing up to heaven, imagining after a happiness or fearing a hell after they are dead, their eyes are put out, that they see not what is their birthrights, and what is to be done by them on earth while they are living. . . . And indeed the subtle clergy do know that if they can but charm the people . . . to look after riches, heaven and glory when they are dead, that then they shall easily be the inheritors of the earth and have the deceived people to be their servants. This . . . was not the doctrine of Christ.[41]

'The upshot of all your universities and public preachers . . . is only to hinder Christ from rising', 'a cloak of policy' to cheat the poor of 'the freedom of the earth'. Only when the clergy have been deprived of their privileged position will each of us be free to 'read in your own book, your heart'.[42]

The 'murdering God of this world', 'the author of the creatures' misery', who defends property and ensures that the clergy get their tithes, is covetousness. Any external God must be rejected: the Diggers would 'neither come to church, nor serve their [the clergy's] God'. The true God is within, and each man has 'his God'.[43]

---

40. Winstanley, *Law of Freedom*, op. cit., pp. 222, 227; Sabine, *Works of Winstanley*, op. cit., p. 162.
41. Winstanley, *Law of Freedom*, op. cit., pp. 324, 353–4.
42. Sabine, *Works of Winstanley*, op. cit., pp. 238–42, 213–14.
43. Winstanley, *Law of Freedom*, op. cit., pp. 138, 144, 196–8, 225–6, 271–2, 307–8, 310, 379; Sabine, *Works of Winstanley*, op. cit., pp. 197, 434.

Winstanley originally envisaged the transition to a communist society in ingeniously simple and peaceful terms. The example of the Digger community inspired ten or more similar communities in central and southern England. Winstanley believed that 'the work of digging' is 'freedom or the appearance of Christ in the earth'.[44] 'For the voice is gone out, freedom, freedom, freedom.'[45] The rising of Christ in men and women would be irresistible, starting from the lowest classes. 'The people shall all fall off from you, and you shall fall on a sudden like a great tree that is undermined at the root.' The poor would take over and begin to cultivate the commons and wastes everywhere.[46] Then a universal withdrawal of wage labour would be organized. The gentry would find themselves possessed of large estates which they were unable to cultivate. In time, they too would be influenced by the rising of Christ in them, would see that the only rational course was for them to throw the lands they could not farm themselves into the common stock and share in the advantages of a communist society. Winstanley even envisaged facilitating the transition by giving them specially favourable compensatory terms.

It was deliciously simple; but it failed to allow for the continued existence of 'kingly power' even after the abolition of kingship. Landlords, lawyers, clergy, all stood together to preserve the status quo and their privileged position. So, by the time he published *The Law of Freedom* in 1652, the experience of harassment, persecution, and finally violent suppression, had convinced Winstanley that Christ would be prevented from rising by lords of manors, priests, lawyers and their state. *The Law of Freedom* was dedicated to Oliver Cromwell: 'you have power . . . to act for common freedom if you will: I have no power'.[47] Whether or not Winstanley really hoped that Cromwell would help to set up a communist society in England, he was right in thinking that it could not be done without the support of the revolutionary army. And Oliver had not yet adopted the conservative posture he found appropriate after 1653.

Previously Winstanley had attacked all forms of state authority and punishment. 'What need have we of imprisoning, whipping or hanging laws to bring one another into bondage?' To execute a murderer is

44. Thomas, 'A Declaration', op. cit., pp. 57–60; Sabine, *Works of Winstanley*, op. cit., p. 437.
45. Winstanley, *Law of Freedom*, op. cit., p. 217.
46. ibid., p. 203.
47. ibid., p. 285.

to commit another murder.[48] But now the title of his pamphlet, *The Law of Freedom: Or, True Magistracy Restored*, shows a new recognition that the state will have to be used if kingly power is to be overcome. Winstanley looks forward to a transitional period in which 'it is the work of a Parliament to break the tyrants' bonds, to abolish all their oppressing laws, and to give orders, encouragements and directions unto the poor oppressed people of the land'. Then 'the spirit of universal righteousness dwelling in mankind' and 'now rising up' would be able to take over.[49] 'In time . . . this Commonwealth's government . . . will be the restorer of long lost freedom to the creation.' But till then, landlords, priests and lawyers must be curbed; so must be the 'rudeness of the people' from which the Diggers had suffered. Christ, 'the true and faithful Leveller', 'the spirit and power of universal love' 'or the law written in the heart',[50] would not rise in all men and women as quickly as Winstanley had hoped. Meanwhile the law of the Commonwealth must 'preserve peace and freedom'.[51] The battle had still to be fought, education and political education carried on (a subject on which Winstanley is very interesting). Choices had to be made. 'There is but bondage and freedom', he wrote, 'particular interest or common interest'.[52]

For some especially grave offences, the death penalty would have to be retained as a deterrent during the transitional period: and it is interesting to see what these offences were. They were murder, 'buying and selling' (which 'killed Christ' and hindered his resurrection), taking money as a lawyer ('the power of lawyers is the only power that hinders Christ from rising') or as a priest, and rape.[53]

But Winstanley was well aware that 'freedom gotten by the sword is an established bondage to some part or other of the creation'.[54] 'Tyranny is tyranny . . . in a poor man lifted up by his valour as in a rich man lifted up by his lands.'[55] Experience had taught Winstanley that a standing army separate from the people could swiftly lose its political ideals. Instead he wanted government by a really representative parliament and magistrates, elected annually and responsible to

48. Sabine, *Works of Winstanley*, op. cit., pp. 193, 283; cf. p. 197, and Winstanley, *Law of Freedom*, op. cit., p. 192.
49. Winstanley, *Law of Freedom*, op. cit., pp. 340, 312.
50. ibid., pp. 199, 203–4, 312.
51. ibid., p. 222.
52. ibid., p. 342.
53. ibid., pp. 171, 366, 383, 388; Sabine, *Works of Winstanley*, op. cit., p. 238.
54. Winstanley, *Law of Freedom*, op. cit., p. 190.
55. Sabine, *Works of Winstanley*, op. cit., p. 198.

'their masters, the people, who chose them'. The ultimate check was that the people retained arms in their hands and had a right of insurrection.[56] Winstanley rejected in advance the theory of forcing them to be free, of dictatorship in the interests of democracy, which has defaced some later communist practice.

Winstanley's ideas were unprecedented. What is astonishing is the sophistication of his analysis, the distance he covered in the years from 1649 to 1652. At Putney, Rainborough and the Levellers could find no answer to Ireton's 'Liberty cannot be provided for in a general sense if property be preserved.' Basing political democracy on natural rights would leave no logical argument against a natural right to equality of property: the right to property derived from substantive laws, not natural rights. This was conventional wisdom by Ireton's day. Thomas Hedley had said in the Parliament of 1610 that property existed not by the law of nature but by municipal law.[57] But then, how did the state which passed these substantive laws get its authority?

Forty years later, Locke thought he had solved the problem. A right to property arises in the state of nature, anterior to the state. 'As much land as a man tills, plants, improves and can use the product of, so much is his property. He by his labour does, as it were, enclose it from the common.'[58] All men by mutual agreement then set up a state to guarantee their property: all men were property-owners. Locke's theory is all very well as an explanation of the *origins* of property, avoiding the danger of giving all men a natural right to it; and it had its advantages in justifying expropriation of colonial peoples – in Ireland or America – who did not 'till, plant and improve' their land. But how had gross inequalities of property developed? Could they be justified? Enclosed land whose produce was not utilized, Locke thought, 'was still to be looked upon as waste, and might be the possession of any other'. Locke attributed inequalities of property to the invention of money, which allowed some men to amass more property than they needed to sustain life; and the state protected them in their unequal ownership in the interests of law and order, of social peace. But what about those with no property at all? Locke seems always to have been uneasy about this part of his argument, insisting

56. Winstanley, *Law of Freedom*, op. cit., pp. 318–20.
57. Foster, *1610 Parliament*, op. cit., II, pp. 189, 194–6.
58. Locke, *Two Treatises*, op. cit., Second Treatise, p. 325.

that the poor had a *right* to subsistence in time of dearth, and to maintenance in old age. What kind of right?[59]

Unlike the Levellers, Winstanley was able to answer this poser, adumbrated by Ireton before being worked out by Locke. Money, buying and selling land, led to inequality. That was for Winstanley part of the Fall. 'Thereby . . . man was brought into bondage and became a greater slave to such of his own kind than the beasts of the field were to him. . . . The earth . . . was hedged into enclosures by the teachers and rulers, and the others were made servants and slaves.' Property ever since has been held 'by the power of the sword'; even if the present owners 'did not kill or thieve', yet their ancestors had done so.[60] This state of affairs can be reversed only by abolishing buying and selling which, Winstanley agreed with Locke, was the source of inequality. 'This will destroy all government and all our ministry', Winstanley imagined someone objecting; and he replied 'it is very true'.[61] It meant a total overthrow of kingly power and a reconstruction of society and the state on the basis of communal property. There was no other solution. It was a difficult programme, which could be put into effect only when Christ – the power of Reason – had risen in all men and women. Then there would be a decent society.

Winstanley seems to have had an equally effective answer to Hobbes. *Leviathan* was not published until 1651, but in 1650 Winstanley seems to be answering Hobbist arguments. He was hardly likely to have read Hobbes in Latin, but Hobbism was in the air; the economic and political situation gave rise to Hobbist theories, in others as well as in Hobbes.[62] Hobbes based the state on an original contract into which all men had entered in order to escape from the state of nature. In the state of nature the competitive drives of individualistic men, all roughly equal in physical strength and enjoying equal individual rights, inevitably produced anarchy until they agreed to elevate a sovereign with, in the last resort, absolute authority.

59. ibid., p. 313; cf. p. 135 below. Locke's views are usefully summarized in J. Dunn, *Locke*, Oxford University Press, 1984, especially pp. 29–41. They were perhaps not altogether original. Aquinas described appropriation as a dictate of natural reason and denied that uncorrupted reason dictated communal ownership (Beryl Smalley, '*Quaestiones* of Simon of Henton', in R.W. Hunt, W.A. Pantin and R.W. Southern (eds) *Studies in Medieval History Presented to F.M. Powicke*, Oxford University Press, 1948, p. 219).
60. Winstanley, *Law of Freedom*, op. cit., pp. 77–8, 99.
61. ibid., p. 243.
62. Cf. *World Turned Upside Down*, op. cit., appendix I; Q. Skinner, 'Conquest and consent: Thomas Hobbes and the engagement controversy', in G.E. Aylmer (ed.) *The Interregnum: The Quest for Settlement, 1646–1660*, 1972.

Winstanley agreed with much of Hobbes's analysis, but drew different conclusions. If you abolish competitive individualist property relations, you abolish the problem. Property was not created by sinful human nature but vice versa; so only the abolition of property could get rid of the coercive state and the preachers of sin, both of which had come into existence to protect property. Winstanley saw that Hobbes's system was based on challengeable psychological assumptions: 'This same power in man that causes divisions and war is called by some the state of nature, which every man brings into the world with him'.[63] Winstanley rejected the competitive spirit which Hobbes pushed back from his own society into the state of nature as something universal. Winstanley had a rival psychology. 'Look upon the child that is new-born, or till he grows up to some few years; he is innocent, harmless, humble, patient, gentle, easy to be entreated, not envious.' He is corrupted by the competitive world in which he grows up.[64] But Reason governs the universe; when Reason rules in man he lives 'in community with . . . the spirit of the globe'. Man stands in need of others, and others stand in need of him. He 'dares not trespass against his fellow-creature, but will do as he would be done unto'.[65]

This strikes us as a fairly obvious criticism of the competitive psychology on which Hobbes's philosophy was based. But in the seventeenth century Hobbes seemed more difficult to refute on that plane. For his psychology was that of the almost universally accepted Calvinism, and was reinforced by the pressures of early capitalist society. Only someone who had emancipated himself from the ethos of that society (and from Calvinism) could attack Hobbes at what then seemed his strongest point.

One further point on Winstanley's refutation of Hobbes: 'Winstanley', says Dr Eccleshall, 'rejected, more fully and explicitly than any previous writer, the assumption that human nature was a fixed datum of which the established political system was the natural and invariable counterpart. Human nature . . . was an historical artefact', and was 'historically modifiable' as social relationships changed.[66] In his recognition that you *can* change human nature, Winstanley, unlike Hobbes and Locke, was in the modern world.

---

63. Winstanley, *Law of Freedom*, op. cit., p. 268; cf. p. 309.
64. ibid., p. 269.
65. Sabine, *Works of Winstanley*, op. cit., pp. 109–12; Winstanley, *The Saints Paradise*, op. cit., p. 123.
66. E. Eccleshall, *Order and Reason in Politics: Theories of Absolute and Limited Monarchy in Early Modern England*, Oxford University Press, 1978, pp. 174–6.

In the context of what mattered in the seventeenth century, a word on Filmer and patriarchialism is required. His argument, that the authority of kings derives by direct descent from Adam and is therefore absolute over all subjects, seems puerile to modern readers; yet Locke felt it necessary to answer him seriously, and historians have pointed out what strong roots patriarchialism had in that society where (not to mention the Bible) the household was also the work-place (family farms, family businesses) and the father was responsible for the conduct and discipline of his apprentices and servants, no less than of his children. The father of a family indeed wielded over his dependants all the powers of the state except that of life and death. He could flog, fine and imprison his dependants. (Pepys locked up one of his maids in a cellar for the night.) He was also responsible for their education, technical training, religious and moral behaviour. In the countryside, where the vast mass of the population lived, with no police force, no state educational system or social services, the author-ity of the head of the household could be beneficial as well as on occasion tyrannical. Recall too the deference still shown to fathers. In this society, where symbols mattered, Quaker sons who kept their hats on and thou'd their fathers had a painful time of it. The commandment, Honour thy father and thy mother, was regularly used in sermons and treatises discussing political obligation. As late as 1700, Mary Astell argued from the example of 1688 that if monarchical tyranny in the state was wrong, male tyranny in the family must be wrong too.[67]

The household plays an important part in the community which Winstanley sketched in *The Law of Freedom*. But he totally rejected the political conclusions which Filmer drew from the authority of heads of households. Authority for Winstanley is based on the social functions which the father performs and acceptance of them by his dependants. The only justification of authority is 'common preservation, . . . a principle in everyone to seek the good of others as himself without respecting persons'. For a magistrate to put self-interest above the common interest 'is the root of the tree of tyranny', which 'is the cause of all wars and troubles'. 'A true commonwealth's officer is to be . . . chosen . . . by them who are in necessity and judge him fit for that work', just as 'a father in a family is a commonwealth's officer

---

67. Mary Astell, *Some Reflections upon Marriage*, 1706, Preface. This work was first published in 1700. For Filmer, see Laslett's Introduction to *Patriarcha and other Political Works of Sir Robert Filmer*, Oxford, 1949.

because the necessity of young children chose him by joint consent'. The chain of authority goes *upwards* from the family to the parish or town, each of which is governed by elected officers, to MPs – all to be chosen annually. The implied contract is 'Do you see our laws observed for our preservation and peace, and we will assist and protect you'. And these words 'assist' and 'protect' imply in the last resort the rising up of the people by force of arms to defend their laws and officers against 'any invasion, rebellion or resistance', or any who 'are fallen from true magistracy'[68] – for example, by trying to restore private property. So the paternalism of the society, which Filmer used to justify absolute monarchy, becomes for Winstanley an argument for communities in his ideal state to defend their rights.

Only one of his contemporaries seems to have entered directly into controversy with Winstanley. This was Anthony Ascham. In 1648 he published *A Discourse Wherein is examined What is particularly lawfull during the Confusions and Revolutions of Government*. In the following year, after the execution of Charles I, an expanded version appeared under the title *Of the Confusions and Revolutions of Governments*. This included a new chapter called 'The Originall of Property'. 'Some authors of this age', Ascham said, 'by a new art of levelling, think nothing can be rightly mended or reformed unless the whole piece ravel out to the very end, and that all intermediate greatness betwixt kings and them should be crumbled even to dust.' Such men say 'the law enslaves one sort of people to another. The clergy and gentry have got their freedom, but the common people are still servants to work for the other.' 'I wonder not so much at this sort of arguing', Ascham continued patronizingly, 'as to find that they who have such sort of arguments in their mouths should have spades in their hands.'[69] The reference to the Diggers could hardly be more explicit.

Ascham's arguments against Winstanley are intellectually rather disappointing. He was critical of what he took to be the Diggers' primitivism. In Hobbist vein he argued that the state of nature would have been a state of perpetual war. It was inequality that 'perfectly bred dominion, and that [bred] property'. Men are bound by the contract which got them out of this state of nature and legitimized private property. Significantly perhaps, in view of Locke's later argument, Ascham followed his chapter on property with another inserted chapter, 'Of the Nature of Money'. Property, Ascham

68. Winstanley, *Law of Freedom*, op. cit., pp. 314–20.
69. Ascham, *Of the Confusions*, op. cit., pp. 18–19.

thought, had good as well as evil consequences: 'that some faultlessly lead indigent lives in a state is no argument of tyranny in property, but of the ill use of it'. The rich 'are unhappier than the poor', who do not suffer from diseases like gout and the stone.[70] It is possible that he wrote this chapter in rather a hurry!

My claims for Winstanley are being pitched high, setting him up against the greatest political thinkers to emerge from the fertile soil of the English Revolution – the Levellers, Hobbes, Filmer, Ascham, Locke. One remains – James Harrington. Both Winstanley and Harrington recognized the economic basis of society and of political change. Russell Smith speculated over seventy years ago that Harrington might even have been influenced by Winstanley. It is an interesting coincidence that Richard Goodgroom, who signed one of the Digger manifestos in 1649, wrote a tract (probably in 1654) which incorporates many of the ideas elaborated in Harrington's *Oceana* two years later.[71]

Harrington argued that the land transfers of the century before 1640 necessitated a commonwealth – by which he meant a state ruled by property-owners, who alone constitute 'the people'. 'Robbers or Levellers', servants and paupers, cannot be free and so are excluded from the franchise; representation in Harrington's ideal state would be tilted to favour the well-to-do. Harrington himself disliked anything like the oligarchy which complete freedom for capitalist development was to produce in eighteenth-century England. He thought to safeguard against oligarchy by two devices: an agrarian law – no one to inherit more than £2,000 per annum – and secret ballot to prevent the domination of elections by money.

Harrington dedicated *Oceana* to Oliver Cromwell in 1656, when it seemed as little likely that the Lord Protector would establish an 'equal commonwealth' as it was likely in 1652, when Winstanley dedicated *The Law of Freedom* to him, that he would establish a communist society. In this sense, both writers were utopians. Harringtonianism was very influential in the later seventeenth and eighteenth centuries, when England was (in Harringtonian terms) not a monarchy but a commonwealth headed by a prince. Harrington was interpreted as arguing that the men of property *ought* to rule, thus

---

70. ibid., pp. 20–5. Ascham was assassinated in 1650 by royalist exiles when he was acting as agent for the parliamentary Commonwealth in Madrid.
71. H.F.R. Smith, *Harrington and his Oceana*, Cambridge University Press, 1914. For Goodgroom, see Harrington, *Political Works*, op. cit., pp. 11–12, 58.

justifying the Whig oligarchy; and his prediction that a common-wealth would be far more effective than absolute monarchy 'for increase', for aggressive colonial expansion, proved well founded.[72]

Complete freedom for private property was incompatible with Harrington's 'equal commonwealth' – as Winstanley could have told him. Winstanley rejected Harrington's starting point no less than he did that of Hobbes, from whom Harrington no doubt derived it. For Harrington, reason taught self-interest, not co-operation. (Primary allegiance is due to ourselves, Ascham thought.[73]) Whether Winstanley's system would have proved any more workable than Harrington's is debatable; unlike Cromwell, Winstanley was never tested by having to exercise power;[74] but at least he had faced head on the intellectual problems which made Harrington's 'equal common-wealth' utopian.

Winstanley is arguably the most intellectually respectable and consistent of the great political theorists who emerged from the English Revolution. (Milton cannot be included in this context, since he was not an original political thinker.) Central to Winstanley's vision was his argument that 'there cannot be a universal liberty till this universal community be established'.[75] True freedom and true equality can be guaranteed only when 'community . . . called Christ or universal love' rises unimpeded in sons and daughters and casts out 'property, called the devil or covetousness'.[76]

Winstanley failed; but his writings justify the words he prefixed to one of his Digger pamphlets:

When these clay bodies are in grave, and children stand in place,
This shows we stood for truth and peace and freedom in our days.[77]

72. See my *The Experience of Defeat: Milton and Some Contemporaries*, 1984, Ch. 10, section 5.
73. Ascham, *Of the Confusions*, op. cit., pp. 106–7.
74. Roger Howell, 'Cromwell and English liberty', in R.C. Richardson and G.M. Ridden (eds) *Freedom and the English Revolution*, pp. 25, 44.
75. Sabine, *Works of Winstanley*, op. cit., p. 199.
76. Winstanley, *Law of Freedom*, op. cit., p. 268.
77. ibid., p. 125.

8

Seventeenth-century English radicals
and Ireland

Whoso England will subdue, with Ireland must begin.
William Warner, *Albions England*, 1586, Book 10, p. 242.
I cite from the edition of 1596

Great force must be the instrument, but famine must be the
means, for until Ireland be famished it cannot be subdued.
A Briefe Note of Ireland, attributed to Edmund Spenser, quoted by
Ciaran Brady, 'Spenser's Irish crisis: humanism and experience
in the 1590s', *Past and Present*, 1986, III, p. 48

England's Irish problem in its modern form dates from the seventeenth-
century English Revolution. It is an old and wry observation that
whenever Englishmen are most successfully establishing liberty at
home they are most ruthlessly denying it to the Irish. This was never
more true than of the seventeenth century. My subject is the attitude
of radical groups to Ireland during the English Revolution. Why did
they not do more to oppose the brutal subjugation of Ireland under
Oliver Cromwell?

We must start from the Reformation, which an American historian
called Henry VIII's Declaration of Independence from the papacy.
Throughout the rest of the sixteenth century England felt itself to be a
beleaguered isle,[1] isolated in a world dominated by the great Catholic
powers of Spain, Austria and France. These powers were, it was
feared, liable at any time to combine to conquer England and restore
the old religion – and monastic lands. In these circumstances protestantism and patriotism came to be closely interwoven, not only in
government propaganda but also in educated public opinion. John
Foxe's best-selling *Book of Martyrs* popularized a view of history as a

---

1. Cf. Wiener, 'The beleaguered isle', op. cit., pp. 27–62.

continuing struggle between the forces of good and evil, with God's Englishmen foremost in the battle against Antichrist, the Pope. Popery was associated with treachery and cruelty. Starting with the burnings under Mary, plenty of evidence was produced to support the allegation – Alva's Council of Blood in the Netherlands in the 1560s, the massacre of St Bartholomew's Day in 1572, Gunpowder Plot in 1605, Spanish cruelty to the Indians in South America (though, as Professor Canny has suggested, English colonizers in Ireland and North America, may have learnt a thing or two from Spanish practice).[2] The Spanish Armada, defeated in 1588 when God blew with his winds and scattered them, was believed to have been filled with racks, whips and other instruments of torture to be used in the reconversion of England.

Ireland's place in this cosmic drama was that of back door for a foreign invasion of England. In the reign of Henry VII the pretenders Lambert Simnel and Perkin Warbeck had both invaded by way of Ireland. Powerful forces, mainly composed of Italian and Spanish troops, landed there in 1579 and 1580.[3] Spaniards were in Ireland in 1601, James II with French troops in the 1690s. English rulers rightly assumed that almost any army that was not English would be welcomed in Ireland.

The English had been in Ireland since the twelfth century. Over the centuries the original settlers had adapted themselves to Irish customs. No serious attempt had been made to extend English law to the whole island, and English rule had been indirect. But things began to change in the later sixteenth century. Pressure of relative over-population in England led to emigration to Ireland – initially sponsored by private enterprise. This meant seizures of Irish land, removals of population, local fighting and periodic massacres. Ireland was easily accessible from south-western England, Wales or Scotland, and it has been suggested that in the seventeenth century there was more English and Scottish emigration to Ireland than to any trans-Atlantic colony.[4]

From the 1580s onwards English governments began to be alarmed by the infiltration of Counter-Reformation priests aiming at the

2. Canny, *Elizabethan Conquest* op. cit., p. 103; 'The ideology of English colonisation: from England to America', *William and Mary Quarterly*, 1973, 3rd series, XXX, pp. 593–4.
3. MacCaffrey, *Queen Elizabeth*, pp. 129–30, 266.
4. Canny, *Elizabethan Conquest*, op. cit., especially Ch. IV; Donald Jackson, 'Violence and assimilation in Tudor Ireland', in Eoin O'Brien (ed.) *Essays in Honour of J.D.H. Widdess*, Dublin, 1978, pp. 113–26; N.P. Canny, 'The Anglo-American colonial experience', *Historical Journal*, 1981, XXIV, p. 489.

reconversion of England, just when the long-postponed war with Spain was seen to have become inevitable. This and the possibility of disputes over the succession when the ageing Elizabeth should die raised sharply the strategic issue. It combined with increased pressure from the New English settlers in Ireland for outright military conquest and the enforcement of English law on Ireland.

For some Englishmen in Ireland the motives behind this were not wholly discreditable. Once the Irish aristocracy was removed, it was argued, the two populations could merge; the Irish would enjoy the advantages of regular and disciplined labour, and improved agriculture would in the long run be to the advantage of the Irish common people themselves. Men like the first Earl of Cork, Professor Canny has told us, believed that profits for him could be combined with benefits to the Irish.[5] But all such ideas presumed military conquest first. They totally disregarded Irish habits and traditions in the interests of economic progress, whose main advantages would go to Englishmen. It is the classic colonial situation, looking forward to all those well-intentioned colonial civil servants in nineteenth-century India and Africa.

Even relatively liberal thinkers *assumed* the total inferiority of the Irish and their culture. The gentle Edmund Spenser spoke of 'their savage brutishness and loathsome filthiness which is not to be named'. He was referring especially to the clothes they wore, their sexual habits, and their lack of any fixed abode.[6] Spenser's account was based on a historical analysis and explanation already familiar to Englishmen. He made a similar point about the ancient Britons in *The Faerie Queene*:

> They held this land, and with their filthiness
> Polluted this same gentle soil long time,

until Brutus came, representative of a higher civilization, 'and them of their unjust possession deprived'. People who fail to make full economic use of the land have no right to it: the same argument was to be used against the American Indians.[7] Spenser therefore wanted to

5. N.P. Canny, *The Upstart Earl: a Study of the Social and Mental World of Richard Boyle, First Earl of Cork*, Cambridge University Press, 1982, *passim*. Francis Bacon had less horrific views on Ireland than most English politicians: see H.R. Trevor-Roper, 'The lost moments of history', *New York Review of Books*, 27 October 1988.
6. E. Spenser, *A View of the Present State of Ireland*, in *Works*, Globe edn, p. 632. First published 1633.
7. E. Spenser, *The Faerie Queene*, Book II, canto x, stanza 9; cf. Canny, *Elizabethan Conquest*, op. cit., pp. 160–3; Canny, 'Ideology', pp. 588–9, 595. Cf. Locke, quoted on p. 126 above.

'reduce things into order of English law'. Everybody must be drawn into labour, so that the old attitudes could be transformed. This must be preceded by thorough military conquest, and removal of most of the Irish from areas to be occupied by the English. Until the military power of the lords had been broken, as it had in England, those Irish who remain must be cut off from their old connections. For 'all the rebellions that you see from time to time in Ireland are not begun by the common people, but by the lords and captains of countries'.[8]

Another poet, Sir John Davies, in 1612 shared this attitude. The nature of Irish customs is such that 'the people which doth use them must of necessity be rebels to all good government, destroy the commonwealth wherein they live, and bring barbarism and desolation upon the richest and most fertile land of the world'. 'To make a commonweal in Ireland', he said, necessitated 'settling of all the estates and possessions' by English law, establishing 'lawful matrimony to the end they might have lawful heirs', and insisting that 'every man shall have a certain home', so that he could manure his lands and provide for posterity. Only the English could 'make a commonweal in Ireland'.[9]

There were various reasons for looking down on the Irish. Their religious practices seemed to English settlers to be as much pagan as Christian. It had always been possible to compare the semi-nomadic Irish with masterless vagabonds in England, or with rightless American Indians. The wild Irish and the Indians do not much differ, declared Hugh Peter, just back from New England, in 1646.[10] Inculcation of religious hatred and contempt had long been used to discourage the fraternization with the Irish to which some masterless English colonists were regrettably prone. Professor Canny has shown that the same problems and the same answers arose in New England.[11] However unattractive we may find it, there is a consistent philosophy behind the denial of rights in the land to those who had for so long occupied it undisturbed.

8. Spenser, *A View*, op. cit., pp. 672–4, 677; *A Briefe Note of Ireland* (attributed to Spenser: but see Viola Hulbert, 'Spenser's relation to certain documents on Ireland', *Modern Philology*, 1936–7, XXXIV, pp. 345–53) See also a paper presented to James I in 1615, which advocated strict segregation until the Irish had been freed from the tyranny of their lords and then re-educated (Canny, 'Edmund Spenser and the development of an Anglo-Irish identity', *Year-Book of English Studies*, 1983, XIII, pp. 16–17). For Spenser and Ireland see also Norbrook, *Poetry and Politics*, op. cit., Ch. 2; A. Low, *The Georgic Revolution*, Princeton University Press, 1985, Ch. 2. Cf. the second epigraph to this chapter.
9. Sir John Davies, *A Discovery of the True Causes why Ireland was never entirely subdued*, 1612, in H. Morley (ed.) *Ireland under Elizabeth and James I*, 1890, pp. 290, 336, 379, 385–6.
10. *Mr. Peters Last Report of the English Warres*, 1646, p. 5.
11. Canny, *Elizabethan Conquest*, Chs VI and VIII; 'Ideology', *passim*.

After the peaceful succession of James I in 1603, the ending of the Anglo-Spanish war and the termination of O'Neill's rebellion, English panic about Ireland diminished. The main concern of English rulers of Ireland was to keep costs down after this ruinous war. But Thomas Wentworth as lord deputy in the 1630s pursued a more active policy, an experiment in direct rather than indirect colonial rule. He tried to persuade the Old English to pay for his taking the New English off their backs, but he was still balancing the two interests, papists against Protestants, and was trusted by neither.

Meanwhile in England Protestant anxieties had been roused by James I's policy of appeasing Spain whilst the Thirty Years War seemed to be threatening protestantism all over Europe. Charles caused even greater alarm by his devotion to his Catholic wife, by receiving a papal nuncio in London for the first time since the reign of Bloody Mary, by supporting Archbishop Laud's ceremonial innovations which struck Protestants as a reversion to popery, and supporting the enforcement of Laudianism on Scotland by military means. As Catholic power advanced on the continent, the English government seemed to be at best half-hearted in opposing it, if not indeed positively co-operating with it. Alarm was intensified by the fact that Wentworth was building up an army in Ireland whose soldiers were not subject to the customary religious tests. When the lord deputy – now Earl of Strafford – promised that this army was ready for use against 'this kingdom', it seemed to alarmed Protestants to matter little whether 'this kingdom' was England, or in the first instance Scotland. In 1640–1 Strafford was negotiating for a military alliance with Spain, under which the latter would be allowed to raise troops in the British Isles in return for financial support.[12]

The collapse of Charles I's government with the assembly of parliament in November 1640, followed by the trial and execution of Strafford in May 1641, led to the breakdown of English authority in Ireland and to the revolt of 1641 – the catalyst which forced civil war in England because neither king nor parliament would trust the other with command of the army which all agreed must be sent to restore English power in Ireland. The rebels issued a proclamation in the king's name, calling on Catholics to take up arms in his defence. It was a forgery, but it was widely believed. The last parliamentary bill to which Charles agreed was an act for the subjugation of Ireland.

12. J.H. Elliott, 'The year of the three ambassadors', in Lloyd Jones et al., *History and Imagination*, op. cit., especially pp. 170–81.

The Irish revolt and alleged massacres of Protestants became one of the great myths of history. Nobody knows exactly how many English and Scottish Protestants were killed – probably quite a lot, some of them unpleasantly. But English propaganda exaggerated this beyond all bounds. John Cook, the lawyer who was to prosecute the king at his trial in 1649, said that 154,000 people had been 'barbarously murdered in one province of Ireland' – more than the total of English and Scots settlers. The grotesque exaggerations of propagandists were accepted by perfectly rational and balanced Englishmen, including John Milton. Richard Baxter, a middle-of-the-road man, believed that religion had been the main cause of the civil war in England. There had been an international Catholic conspiracy against England with which Charles I had connived.[13] 'Arise, O Lord and scatter the Irish rebels', cried Edmund Calamy in a sermon preached to the House of Commons in December 1641: 'arise, O Lord and confound Antichrist'.[14] The second prayer merely repeated the first. Towards the end of the civil war the king did empower the Earl of Glamorgan to negotiate with the Irish. The discussions came to nothing, but Charles, with typical ineptitude, allowed his correspondence to be captured after his final defeat at Naseby in 1645, and his participation in the international Catholic conspiracy seemed to be established.

Further confirmation of the antichristian conspiracy was not lacking. The Pope sent money to the Irish rebels. Non-participant Catholics were excommunicated.[15] From 1645 to 1649 effective command of the revolt was taken over by Archbishop Rinuccini, the papal nuncio. The Earl of Glamorgan, who was regarded as Charles I's lord lieutenant, swore submission to the nuncio. Such facts were used to assert *national* responsibility for the Irish rebellion and for all the unpleasantness which resulted from it.

Meanwhile money for the reconquest of Ireland had been subscribed by a group of London adventurers, who no doubt promised themselves ultimate handsome returns on their investment. Again private enterprise rather than the government was looking after

---

13. John Cook, *Monarchy No Creature of Gods Making* 1652, p. 96; W.M. Lamont, *Richard Baxter and the Millennium: Protestant Imperialism and the English Revolution*, 1979, pp. 29, 80-1, 292.

14. Edmund Calamy, *Englands Looking-glasse*, 1642, p. 10.

15. Patrick J. Corish, 'The rising of 1641 and the Catholic confederacy, 1641-5', in T.W. Moody, F.X. Martin and F.J. Byrne (eds) *A New History of Ireland*, III, *Early Modern Ireland, 1534-1691*, Oxford University Press, 1976, Chs XI and XII, especially pp. 298, 321-4.

English interests in Ireland. But the adventurers' money was diverted to pay for the civil war against Charles I. Hence after the king's defeat increased pressure from the City was added to the strategic reasons for reconquest.

Parliament debated the matter at length in 1646-7, urged on by Puritan preachers of Fast Sermons calling for help to be sent to poor Ireland.[16] The final decision neatly linked the Irish problem with the problem of getting rid of the increasingly radical New Model Army. Parliament voted that part of the army should be sent to Ireland and the remainder disbanded. Unfortunately they failed to provide for payment of wages – and the army's pay was many months in arrears. Mutiny resulted, which soon acquired political overtones. The rank and file took the lead, chasing non-cooperative officers out of the army, electing 'agitators' to represent their views, linking up with the London democratic party, the Levellers, and forcibly taking the imprisoned Charles I away from the custody of parliament's commissioners. Cromwell and the generals put themselves at the head of the mutiny. Officers wanted to be paid their arrears too, and the generals were well aware of the suspicion with which parliament viewed them. Conniving at mutiny was risky; attempting to smash it would have been even riskier, and would have left the generals – and the cause of religious toleration – at the mercy of a hostile parliament. The reunited army advanced on London, and parliament submitted.

Then came the second civil war. Charles escaped from captivity, a Scottish army invaded England in his support, and former parliamentarians in Wales, Kent, East Anglia and elsewhere joined in. When the royalists were finally defeated, feeling in the army was so intense that the generals again had to act. Parliament was purged, Charles tried and executed, monarchy and House of Lords abolished, and a republic proclaimed. Having co-operated with the Levellers and their allies in London and the army for these purposes, the now all-powerful generals turned on them, provoked and suppressed mutinies in the army, and by May 1649 were in supreme control.

One stimulus to these drastic actions was concern about Ireland. Unlike the French and Russian Revolutions, the English Revolution had known none of the foreign intervention which so embittered the later conflicts. The main reason for this was that throughout the 1640s

---

16. At least six such appeals were made in Fast Sermons preached between July 1646 and November 1647, by Samuel Bolton, William Bridge, Thomas Horton, Matthew Newcomen, Simeon Ash and Richard Kentish.

the major European powers had all been involved in the Thirty Years War. But in October 1648 this was ended by the Treaty of Westphalia. France and Spain remained at war, but in Germany many professional troops were suddenly forced to look for employment. What more natural than to use some of them to restore the English monarchy via Ireland? Negotiations did in fact take place between royalists and the Duke of Lorraine, one of the *condottieri* leaders who hoped to use his unemployed troops to carve out for himself a principality in Ireland. The royalist commander in Ireland confirmed the suspicions of Protestants by coming to terms with the Irish rebels in January 1649. Newsbooks of the time reveal that alarm in England was great. It therefore seemed essential to finish with Ireland quickly and finally, to shut the wide-open back door. This is the background to the Cromwellian campaign that began in 1649. 'Send all the pack of Babylonish trash' back from Ireland, 'to Rome, after the nuncio,' William Cooper urged parliament in a sermon of August 1649.[17]

So the year 1649 saw attitudes towards Ireland hardening in England. The military government was very conscious of its unpopularity. But it commanded vast resources from confiscated church, crown and royalists' lands, and had a powerful army at its disposal, which might again become dangerously radical if it was not used. The solution was obvious. As early as 1575 Lord Deputy Sir Henry Sidney had pointed out that the military subjugation of Ireland was 'no subject's enterprise: a prince's purse and power must do it'.[18] But neither Elizabeth, James nor Charles had the resources for such a conquest, though English settlers repeatedly called for it. But now conquest had become not only possible but necessary, and the demand was reinforced by pressure from the City to milk Ireland to pay the debts outstanding to the adventurers. Confiscations of Irish land could also be used to make the army self-supporting. Public opinion had for years been nurtured in anti-popery: the time seemed ripe for going over to the offensive against the international forces of Antichrist before they should strike through Ireland. The legend of Irish national responsibility for the exaggerated horrors of 1641 had intensified the feelings of religious and cultural hatred for the Irish, which had long been fostered. After the conquest and total overthrow of traditional stability in Ireland, the routed Irish looked more like vagabonds than ever.

---

17. W. Cooper, *Jerusalem fatall to her assailants*, 1649, p. 30.
18. Canny, *Elizabethan Conquest*, op. cit., p. 90; 'Edmund Spenser', op. cit., p. 17.

All this may help to explain the acquiescence in, indeed enthusiasm for, the conquest of Ireland among radical supporters of the Revolution. They were trapped in the assumptions of their age. If Levellers and Diggers were alive today we could hold a rational discussion with them about politics and economics; we could argue about sex with Ranters. Pym, Cromwell and Ireton would be old-fashioned by any modern standards; we must always set them in a historical context if we are to be fair to their ideas. But on Ireland we no longer have the illusory sense that the radicals are our contemporaries; they too have to be understood historically. The object of the preceding background sketch was to suggest how the Irish came to be cast for the role of supporters of Antichrist, the enemy of all that the revolutionaries stood for.

The radicals were the most fiercely anti-Catholic, the most anxious to defend the Revolution against what they saw as the forces of reaction. Their strength depended on the army, which many of them believed was God's instrument for the final overthrow of Antichrist. So, for a whole variety of reasons, most of the radicals accepted the necessity of conquest. Vavasor Powell, in a Fast Sermon of February 1649, hailed 'the concurrence of God's Providence in effecting those great things which you have undertaken, both in this land and in Ireland' as evidence that the Lord had smiled on parliament 'since you have appeared and acted for Him of late so impartially and courageously'.[19] Powell was a Fifth Monarchist, relatively very radical. So was Christopher Feake, who in 1659 spoke of 'the work of justice in Ireland . . . prospering under the standard of the interest of Christ'.[20] Quakers too (not pacifists before 1661): Francis Howgil and Edward Burrough after their visit to Ireland in 1656 declared 'to the natives of that nation': 'You are shut up in blindness and covered with darkness which may be felt, and you . . . are become wild and brutish as the beasts of the field . . . The indignation of God is against you . . . Cease from your filthy, nasty, polluted ways of idolatry.'[21] The Quaker George Bishop praised the army's conquest of Ireland 'with wonderful success and hard service'; he thought "insufficient thanks had been rendered to God for that deliverance'.[22] There were many Quakers in the army in Ireland.

19. V. Powell, *Christ exalted above all creatures*, 1651, pp. 87–8.
20. C. Feake, *A beame of light shining in the midst of much darkness*, 1659, p. 30.
21. F. Howgil and E. Burrough *The visitation of the rebellious nation of Ireland*, 1656, pp. 37–8.
22. Bishop, *Mene Tekel*, op. cit., p. 37.

So radical supporters of parliament applauded the conquest. Colonel Axtell, just before his execution as a regicide in 1660, gloried in his share. 'When I consider their bloody cruelty in murdering so many thousands of Protestants and innocent souls that word was much upon my heart, "Give her blood to drink for she is worthy"; and sometimes we neither gave nor took quarter'.[23] National responsibility again.

It is remarkable that any voices were raised on the other side, but some were. By 1646 men were asking whether it was lawful to fight in Ireland. A colonel said the Irish did but fight for religion and liberty of conscience and for their lands and estates. Some sectaries even justified the rebellion of 1641, Thomas Edwards tells us; others argued against and hindered the sending of help to Ireland.[24]

The Leveller William Walwyn, according to Edwards, said 'the Irish did no more but what we would have done ourselves if it had been our case'. 'What had the English to do in their kingdom?', he asked: 'why should not they enjoy the liberty of their consciences?'[25] The charge is repeated in the anonymous *Walwins Wiles* (April 1649), where he was alleged to have said that English troops had been sent to Ireland in 'an unlawful war, a cruel and bloody work to go to destroy the Irish natives for their consciences . . . and to drive them from their proper natural and native rights'. The author spoke of Walwyn's 'constant endeavour to hinder the relief of Ireland, . . . arguing that the cause of the Irish natives in seeking their just freedoms, immunities and liberties, was the very same with our cause here, in endeavouring our own rescue and freedom from the power of oppressors'.[26] Walwyn never committed himself to such views in print. But he never repudiated them. His son-in-law Humphrey Brooke and he himself replied at great length to *Walwins Wiles*, but both ignored the charges about Ireland.[27]

The Levellers as a group did not take up Walwyn's generous position. This and Walwyn's public silence may indicate how unpopular

---

23. Anon, *A complete collection of the lives and speeches of those persons lately Executed*, 1660, p. 83.
24. T. Edwards, *Gangraena*, 1646, III, pp. 23, 239–40.
25. ibid., ii, p. 27.
26. Op. cit., in W. Haller and G. Davies (eds) *The Leveller Tracts, 1647–1653*, Columbia University Press, 1944, pp. 288–9, 310; and cf. p. 315.
27. Humphrey Brooke, *The Charity of Church-Men*, May 1649, and *Walwyn's Just Defence*, June 1649, in Haller and Davies, *Leveller Tracts*, op. cit., pp. 329–49, 350–98. Walwyn likewise ignored the accusation that he had spoken in favour of communism, which Brooke tried to brush aside.

and dangerous it might be to speak up on behalf of the Irish in the 1640s. *Walwins Wiles* suggested that Lilburne and Prince, two of the Leveller leaders, would not 'be persuaded to hinder the relief of Ireland': by implication the charge of being pro-Irish was limited to Walwyn and Richard Overton.[28] The latter had argued in 1645 that persecution had caused the rebellion of 1641, as Roger Williams had done the year before;[29] but I am not aware that Overton otherwise committed himself on Irish questions. Prince did express views on Ireland, but they are less radical than those attributed to Walwyn. In June 1649 he urged a moderate settlement and conscientious government by 'faithful men' who would not try to enforce 'their own domination, a taste whereof you know is exercised in England'. If the Agreement of the People were introduced into England, the Irish would be so impressed by 'the goodness of the government' that 'there would be some hopes . . . that the Irish would soon be reduced, as being willing to change their condition of bondage for freedom'. But apart from that utopian aspiration, Prince gave no precise indication of what exactly the Irish would get in return. He is really more concerned to make propaganda against the English government: 'For keeping out of rebels I am not only against any that shall invade the land from abroad, but I am against all that any ways invade our liberties within the nation'.[30]

In December 1648 a very interesting near-Leveller, Lt.-Col. John Jubbes, urged army officers that 'the Irish may not still be proceeded against as to execute cruelty for cruelty'. Irishmen who had not been 'beginners and fomentors of the war' should be allowed to compound for their delinquency on the same terms as English royalists.[31] The rights and wrongs of sending English troops to Ireland caused running

---

28. ibid., pp. 314–15.
29. W. Walwyn, *The Araignement of Mr. Persecution*, in Haller, *Tracts on Liberty*, op. cit., III, p. 222; cf. p. 238; Roger Williams, *The Bloudy Tenent of Persecution*, 1644, in Woodhouse, *Puritanism and Liberty*, op. cit., p. 278.
30. Prince, *The Silken Independents Snare Broken*, June 1649, pp. 6–7; H.N. Brailsford, *The Levellers and the English Revolution*, 1961, p. 500; C. Durston, '"Let Ireland be quiet": opposition in England to the Cromwellian conquest of Ireland', *History Workshop Journal*, 1986, 21, p. 106. See now Norah Carlin, 'The Levellers and the conquest of Ireland in 1649', *Historical Journal*, 1987, 30.
31. J. Jubbes, *Several Proposals for Peace and Freedom*, printed (without attribution) in Wolfe, *Leveller Manifestoes*, op. cit., p. 318. For Jubbes see R.L. Greaves and R. Zaller (eds) *Biographical Dictionary of British Radicals in the Seventeenth Century*, Brighton, 1982–4, II. George Wither's *Prosopopeia Britannica* a month or two earlier had called for mercy to all of the Irish who had not been 'murderous rebels' (*Miscellaneous Works*, Spenser Society, 3, 1885, p. 92).

controversy throughout 1649. There was much voting with the feet. Only some 7 per cent of the officers volunteered for the service. There were desertions and mutinies among the other ranks. *The English Soul-diers Standard to repair to* tried to persuade against fighting in Ireland: 'it will be no satisfaction to God's justice, to plead that you murdered men in obedience to your general'; but its concern was again merely that soldiers should look after their own liberties in England; it entered into little discussion of Irish rights and liberties.[32] *The Levellers Vin-dicated* (August 1649), signed by six troopers who had been involved in the mutiny which was crushed at Burford, said they had been 'designed by lot to be . . . sent over into Ireland, . . . in order to the peace and safety of this Commonwealth, which we think necessary to be per-formed'.[33] They actually accepted the necessity of reconquest.

So far then we have made no attempt to look seriously at the Irish point of view apart from words attributed to Walwyn by Edwards: for it is highly likely that *Walwins Wiles* derived from *Gangraena*. Now Edwards, though a virulently hostile witness, took pains to be accurate in his facts. Walwyn's failure to declare himself in public must be due to strong pressures of public opinion on the other side. But in August 1649 an anonymous pamphlet, *Tyranipocrit Discovered*, sometimes attributed to Walwyn, was more radical and more generalizing. It denounced the robbery, killing and enslaving of 'the poor Indians' by English merchants, as well as national wars in which 'we will send our slaves to kill some of their slaves', and all sorts of persecution – of the Waldensians by the French, of the Moors and the Dutch by Spaniards, of Dutch Arminians by Dutch Calvinists, and 'how the English hunted the poor Irish'.[34] Three months earlier *The Soldiers Demand* had been published in Bristol, written presumably by a soldier on his way to Ireland. 'What have we to do in Ireland', he asked, 'to fight and murder a people and nation . . . which have done us no harm? . . . We have waded too far in that crimson stream already of innocent and Christian blood'.[35]

Most significant of all was a Leveller leaflet of April 1649, which has not survived but which can be reconstructed from a reply in the government newspaper, *The Moderate Intelligencer*, extending over six

32. In A.L. Morton, *Freedom in Arms: A Selection of Leveller Writings*, 1975. Brailsford attributed this pamphlet to Walwyn, but Morton thought that all four leaders had a hand in it (Brailsford, *Levellers*, op. cit., pp. 169–70); cf. Durston, op. cit., pp. 107–10.
33. In Morton, *Freedom in Arms*, op. cit., p. 305.
34. In G. Orwell and R. Reynolds (eds) *British Pamphleteers*, 1948, I, pp. 90–1, 105.
35. Quoted in Brailsford, *Levellers*, op. cit., pp. 508–9.

numbers in May and June. Much more intellectually satisfying than any other Leveller statement, it called in question the right of Englishmen 'to deprive a people of the land God and nature has given them and impose laws without their consent'. The author asked 'whether it be not a character of a true patriot to endeavour the just freedom of all as well as his own? . . . Whether . . . the Irish are not to be justified in all that they have done . . . to preserve and deliver themselves from the usurpations of the English?' It is 'as unjust to take laws and liberties from our neighbours as to take goods one from another of the same nation'. A conquered people cannot 'be accounted rebels, if at any time they seek to free themselves and recover their own'. It was therefore 'the duty of every honest man' to oppose Cromwell's expedition to Ireland. This stands in very remarkable contrast to the assumption which had prevailed since Spenser and Davies, that a people has no right to land which it has not fully developed in private ownership.

But the leaflet went even further, insisting that the English government should 'proclaim Ireland a free state, repenting of all the evil themselves have acted and intended and that our kings have formerly acted against that nation'. The two nations should join in a 'mutual league as friends', though England should retain 'some considerable seaports or towns for security and bond to tie the Irish to performance of covenants' and as a strategic guarantee. Brailsford, who first drew attention to the significance of this leaflet, commented that its approach to international relations was in advance even of Grotius. Brailsford stressed no less the hard-headed practicality of the policy outlined. Many Irishmen had no love for the Stuarts as such, and might have been prepared to accept a neutral status in return for English withdrawal under guarantees. The leaflet was perhaps less realistic in ignoring the economic reasons for the presence of Englishmen in Ireland.[36]

If the Levellers were half-hearted in their public utterances about Ireland, their enemies did not fail to attribute pro-Irish sentiments to them. John Owen, preaching to parliament on 28 February 1649, referred to 'some mountains of opposition that lie in the way against any success' in Ireland. He denounced 'the strivings and strugglings of . . . people . . . totally obstructing . . . any deliverance for Ireland', and especially 'that mighty mountain (which some misnamed a level) that thought at once to have locked an everlasting door upon that expedition'. He 'could heartily rejoice that the Irish might enjoy

36. ibid., pp. 501-5.

Ireland so long as the moon endureth, so that Jesus Christ might possess the Irish'. It is not 'the sovereignty and interest of England that is alone to be transacted there'. Ireland must not be left to Antichrist.[37] Just over three months later, preaching to parliament to celebrate the defeat of the mutineers at Burford, Owen rejoiced not only 'that our necks are yet kept from the yoke of lawless lust, fury and tyranny' of the Levellers, but also in the 'hope that a poor distressed handful in Ireland may yet be relieved'.[38] This sermon was preached just before Owen left for Ireland with Cromwell.

Cromwell had taken a keen interest in Irish affairs since at least 1642. He accepted the Irish command on 29 March 1649, the day after the arrest of Lilburne, Walwyn, Overton and Prince signified the end of the Leveller movement. Cromwell's preparations were careful and thorough, and he did not leave for Ireland until 13 August, nearly five months later. On arrival he announced to the Irish 'We come (by the assistance of God) to hold forth and maintain the lustre and glory of English liberty in a nation where we have an undoubted right to it'.[39] There is a significant dualism in his attitude towards the conquest of Ireland. On the one hand, holding all Irish Catholics responsible for the rebellion, Cromwell saw the slaughter and repression both as strategically necessary and as part of a religious war against Antichrist. In his thinking Rinuccini and the Duke of Lorraine contributed to the massacre of Drogheda. On the other hand, the conquest was also a commercial operation. 'If we should proceed by the rules of other states', he told the Speaker, getting towns to surrender 'would cost you more money than this army hath had since we came over. I hope, through the blessing of God, they will come cheaper to you.' He had told the Irish that the English government would hardly spend five or six million pounds 'merely to procure purchasers [of confiscated Irish lands] to be invested in that for which they did disburse little above a quarter of a million' – though he hoped and believed the adventurers would receive reasonable satisfaction.[40] The commercial attitude recalls – symbolically – words which Lilburne said he had heard Cromwell use to the Council of State in April 1649,

37. Owen, *Works* op. cit., VIII, pp. 230–6.
38. ibid., IX, p. 216.
39. Snow and Young, *Private Journals*, op. cit., pp. 268, 275; Abbott, *Cromwell's Writings*, op. cit., II, p. 205.
40. ibid., pp. 234, 204. In fact perhaps £ ¾ million rather than £5 or £6 millions had been spent when he wrote, though of course more bills were to come in.

that if the Levellers were not broken in pieces 'they will break you; and bring all the guilt of the blood and treasure shed and spent in this kingdom upon your heads and shoulders, and frustrate and make void all that work that with so many years' industry, toil and pains you have done'.[41] The defeat of the Levellers was necessary to realize returns on this investment – in Ireland as in England.

Not until 1655, after massacres, transportation and emigration, did an English settler in Ireland, Vincent Gookin, reject the concept of national guilt and show some compassion for the Irish common people. He argued that only landlords and priests should be transplanted; then the Irish, an industrious people, would soon adapt to English rule and English customs. This revival of Spenserian policies was wildly optimistic; and by then it was too late. There had been much voluntary emigration from Ireland to the West Indies before 1640, and large numbers were forcibly transported there in the 1650s. By the late sixties there were some 20,000 Irish in the West Indies, some of whom were liable to join in slave revolts.[42]

Many were the schemes for carrying out the Spenserian programme of improving Irish agriculture, now that the Spenserian policy of forcible conquest had been put into effect. Samuel Hartlib published in 1652 Gerard Boate's *Irelands Natural History . . . with the several ways of Manuring and improving the same.* Ireland was important for England in the first instance as a source of plundered wealth: the first English colony. The vast land fund at the disposal of the state after expropriating Irish landlords was used to pay not only the English adventurers but also the army. Leveller-led mutinies in England in 1647 and 1649 had been fomented in large part by arrears of pay: there was no danger of that happening again.

The Elizabethan and Jacobean settlements in Ireland had been financed by private enterprise, just as colonial trade and the colonization of North America and the West Indies were, just as the navy which defeated the Spanish Armada was. What was new from the 1650s was the central role of the state. As Sir Henry Sidney, Spenser, Davies and others saw, only the state could finance a thorough conquest, just as only the state could finance the war against the Netherlands which

---

41. Lilburne *The Picture of the Council of State*, 1649, in Haller and Davies, *Leveller Tracts*, op. cit., p. 204.
42. Gookin, *The Great Case of Transplantation in Ireland Discussed*, 1655; Moody et al., *A New History of Ireland*, III, pp. 363–5, 601–2. Cf. Petty, quoted by P. Linebaugh, 'All the Atlantic mountains shook', in G. Eley and W. Hunt (eds) *Reviving the English Revolution*, 1988, pp. 203–4.

guaranteed English merchants' monopoly of trade with the colonies promised by the Navigation Act, and only the state could produce the naval force which seized Jamaica and guaranteed English naval pre-eminence in the Caribbean as well as in the Mediterranean. But when we say 'the state' it must be borne in mind that it was a new state, the product of the Revolution, with vastly greater financial resources at its disposal; the governments of the old regime could never have undertaken any of these activities.[43]

Marx in 1869 said that the English republic met shipwreck in Ireland. When he said 'the English reaction in England had its roots . . . in the subjugation of Ireland',[44] he meant, I take it, that Ireland split the radicals on the religious issue, and so ended any possibility of united opposition to the dominance of Cromwell and the generals. Seeing the Irish as part of the international forces of Antichrist united a section of the radicals with the commercial interests and isolated those who thought, like Walwyn and the authors of the lost leaflet of April 1649, that the Irish people might become allies of the English people against their mutual oppressors.

What is difficult for us to grasp is the crucial role of the army in so dividing the radicals. Without the army religious toleration could never have been established, and so the radical minority would have been unable to organize and propagandize freely. Without the army Charles I would never have been brought to trial, nor the republic proclaimed, nor the House of Lords abolished. The Levellers, more prescient than most, foresaw that military dictatorship would lead back to the supremacy of the propertied class and ultimately to a restoration of monarchy. But once the Leveller challenge to the generals had been defeated, and the social basis of the republic correspondingly narrowed, other radicals saw that the army, with all its faults, stood between them and a return of intolerance and unfreedom. In particular the occupation of Ireland was a guarantee against a restoration of monarchy by foreign papist arms. That is why millenarians, Quakers and Baptists, and Milton, William Erbery and William Sedgwick, saw the army as the lesser evil even while it was being converted from a collection of liberty-loving citizens with arms in their hands into a police force for the men of property. There was no way out of their impasse. In consequence Cromwell and the conservative wing, in

43. Cf. Ch. 2 of this book.
44. K. Marx and F. Engels, *Correspondence*, Selected and edited by Dona Torr, 1934, pp. 279, 281; cf. p. 264.

alliance with the City of London, got the upper hand in England, where the plunder of Ireland helped to finance the stabilization of the regime.

Among the more reputable of Cromwell's supporters we may take Andrew Marvell. His *Horatian Ode* was written 'upon Cromwell's return from Ireland'. The date is significant: the all-important mission has been completed, and Marvell is looking to the future. The conquest of Ireland had sealed the triumph of the new military–commercial state, had guaranteed England from foreign intervention and had ensured the colonial status of Ireland. Like the conquest of Scotland which followed, it was a triumph for the new ruthless state power, which ' 'tis madness to resist or blame'. By comparison Charles I, 'the royal actor', was a mere butterfly crushed on the wheel, worthy of a moment's compassion. Like Milton, Marvell in 1650 foresaw a new order arising for the whole of Europe. In this perspective the subjugation of the Celtic fringe, in Ireland and the Highlands of Scotland, was a mere preliminary. Cromwell had

> Cast the kingdom old
> Into another mould.

The Commonwealth's task now was to extend the new order to France and Italy: Cromwell

> To all states not free
> Shall climacteric be.

There were jobs here for forward youths to take up, accepting the republic and its army:

> The same arts that did gain
> A power must it maintain.

When monarchy was finally restored in 1660, to preside over the victory of the propertied revolutionaries, the Cromwellian policy for the military subjugation and colonial exploitation of Ireland was taken over: England's liberating role in Europe was forgotten. Worse than that: under the protectorate Ireland had been incorporated within the English economic system, and so might have expected to get the benefits of the Navigation Act and increasing British prosperity. But after 1660 Ireland was excluded from these advantages, with all the consequences that we know so well. Irish industries which competed with English were deliberately destroyed; export of sheep, cattle, butter and cheese to England was prohibited. Absentee landlords took most of what agrarian profit there was. Repeated famines anticipated that of the 1840s.

Looking back with Marx's dictum in mind we can see that even the relatively good intentions of some English rulers of Ireland were bedevilled by the strategic problem. In the early 1650s Colonel John Jones, one of four parliamentary commissioners for governing Ireland, hoped (like Gookin) that in Ireland 'all men of estates' would 'be banished, and the Irish ploughman and the labourer admitted to the same immunities with the English'. Then the two peoples would 'cohabit peaceably'. But he accepted that this was a policy of 'doing the people good though against their wills'.[45]

From Spenser and Bacon through Jones and Gookin to Maria Edgeworth in *Castle Rackrent*, there were English men and women who hoped by a combination of coercion and education to force the Irish people to be free in the sense of accepting the work ethic and all that goes with it. Jones had had a similar policy for Scotland – 'to break the interest of the great men . . . and to settle the interests of the common people upon a different foot from the interest of their lords and masters; . . . to propound freedom to the people and relief' against the 'tyranny' of 'the great men'.[46] In Scotland this policy worked. The Cromwellian conquest of the 1650s, followed by the corrupt union of 1707, did in fact work to Scotland's ultimate economic advantage, if not to the advantage of all Scots. Maria Edgeworth and others like her hoped that the defeat of the rebellion of 1798 corresponded to Culloden in 1746, and that the union of 1800 would be accepted as final and advantageous to the Irish. But all Irish history, and particularly the events of the seventeenth century, were against these hopes.

So I have attempted, I hope not altogether unconvincingly, to suggest that the Irish problem of the seventeenth century must be seen in an international context: the Irish people, through no fault of their own, found themselves on the wrong side in a world war between England and Antichrist. What is disturbing for an Englishman is that this situation helped to confirm an attitude of mind among most ordinary Englishmen, and even poets like Spenser, Milton and Marvell, which disposed them to put lesser breeds – including all

---

45. A.H. Dodd, *Studies in Stuart Wales*, Wales University Press, 1952, pp. 104–6.
46. Spedding et al. (eds) Bacon, *Works*, op. cit., XIII, pp. 156–7; J. Mayer (ed.) 'Inedited letters of Cromwell, Colonel Jones, Bradshaw and other regicides', *Transactions of the Historical Society of Lancashire and Cheshire*, new series, I, p. 192.

non-Protestant Christians – without the law. Given also the survival of Calvinist predestinarianism, against which the radicals had protested, this contributed to John Bull's national arrogance and to a racialism which is no less a problem for England today than is Ulster. The gods are just, and of our once-off vices make instruments to plague us.

In principle the only solution – in the seventeenth century as today – would have involved taking full account of the Irish people in trying to solve England's Irish problem, difficult and complex though that would have been even then. Some Levellers grasped the point, but not even the Leveller movement as a whole ever made alliance with the people of Ireland a main point of its platform. Presumably the Levellers knew the society of which they were part, and believed that it would have been hopeless to try to overcome the passionately held association of English patriotism with protestantism. But some of them at least had more realistic as well as more humane ideas than most politicians who have failed to solve the problem over the past three centuries. Walwyn and the author of the lost leaflet of April 1649 deserve to be remembered, both by Irishmen and by English radicals.

9

Abolishing the Ranters

It is too easy to be original by doing the opposite of what everyone else is doing. . . . People try to be original and have a personality on the cheap.

Antonio Gramsci, *Selections from Cultural Writings*, 1985, p. 124

A name is not the thing, but the thing is the name and thing.

Thomas Tany, *The Nations Right in Magna Charta discussed with the thing Called Parliament*, 1650, in Tany, *The Nations Right . . . with other writings*, ed. Andrew Hopton, 1988, p. 19; cf. pp. 14, 17, 22

Most historians believe that the Ranters flourished at the height of the English Revolution, around 1649–52. Professor Colin Davis has written a book, *Fear, Myth and History: the Ranters and the Historians* (Cambridge University Press, 1986), whose object is to abolish the Ranters. He suggests that they were invented by contemporary propagandists for their own ideological purposes, and re-invented by twentieth-century historians, some of whom had different but analogous ideological motives. I am one of the historians listed in the latter category, so I am an interested party. But if we can establish that Ranters did exist in the seventeenth century, the question of who invented them in the present century becomes less urgent and can be deferred. I believe that Davis's arguments about the seventeenth century can be shown to be fallacious, and that people whom we can usefully call Ranters did exist.

My criticisms of Davis's arguments are threefold: methodological, chronological and historiographical.

152

METHODOLOGICAL

'Ranter' is a term of opprobrium, like 'Leveller', 'Quaker', 'Puritan' and indeed 'Arminian'. In the 1640s and 1650s Levellers and Quakers accepted only that they were 'Levellers so-called', 'Quakers so-called'. There were men and women whom contemporaries called Ranters, from 1649 or so onwards; and from their usage it is possible to arrive at some sort of a definition of what they meant by the word. Historians so far have followed this rough and ready procedure. Professor Davis is not prepared to accept contemporary practice. He starts from what he calls a 'paradigm' of Ranter beliefs, allegedly drawn from other historians (*Fear, Myth and History* pp. 24-5, 28; all textual page references in this chapter are to this work). But it is a very selective paradigm. It excludes some beliefs which contemporaries thought characteristic of Ranters – mortalism, for instance, the belief that the soul dies with the body, a belief which Bunyan, who knew them well, thought 'the chief doctrine of the Ranters'.[1] It ignores the political element in most Ranter thinking – opposition to a state church, to tithes, to political authority, whether that of king or parliament or army (pp. 24-5). It also excludes Ranter subversion of the subordinate position of women, which outraged Bunyan and many others.

This dubious 'historical paradigm', for which there is no contemporary authority, soon becomes 'the received model', 'the received stereotype', though no one is cited as receiving it. Ranters, Davis claims, did not agree on this or any other definition (pp. 30, 42, 48, 57). This is true, but it may suggest that there is something wrong with Davis's paradigm. He wants to find 'a closely bonded group', 'a coherent cohesive group' of 'like-minded Ranters' (pp. 33, 36, 63, 74-5). Of course he doesn't find them. He would not have found anything like that among *any* religious grouping in the mid-seventeenth century. Indeed, arguments similar to his could easily be used to demonstrate that Levellers, Baptists, Fifth Monarchists and early Quakers did not exist. Fox and Nayler, Fox and Burrough, disagreed. Lilburne became a Quaker pacifist, Fox urged Cromwell's army to sack Rome. There were open- and closed-communion Baptists. Some favoured total immersion, others sprinkling; some insisted on baptism in running water. Some accepted tithes in the Cromwellian

---

1. Bunyan, *Of the Resurrection of the Dead* (1665?), in *Miscellaneous Works*, Oxford University Press, 1976-, III, p. 247.

state church, others did not. There were Fifth Monarchist congregations and groups: no Fifth Monarchist party. Levellers disagreed about the franchise. Lilburne denounced Winstanley, the 'true Leveller'; the Leveller newspaper *The Moderate* wrote sympathetically of him and his ideas. Walwyn was accused of favouring communism, and never denied it. In mid-seventeenth century England there were no buildings labelled 'Baptist church', 'Leveller party', 'Society of Friends'. There were individual groups gathered around a charismatic preacher or leader. From this milieu of free discussion Baptists, Muggletonians and Quakers ultimately emerged, after many disputes. We can see them as sects, retrospectively, because they survived. Ranters, like Levellers, Diggers and Fifth Monarchists, were suppressed because they were thought dangerous. They never achieved the degree of organization which was forced on Baptists, Muggletonians and Quakers later in the century.

The fact that a parliamentary committee spoke in 1650 of 'a sect called Ranters' is troublesome for Davis's thesis. It warns us not only that Ranters existed, but also that words change their meanings. 'Sect' means something precise to us after three centuries of organized nonconformity: a group which cut itself off or was cut off from the national church. Like most such labels, it originated as a term of abuse. But in the 1640s and early 1650s there were no clear-cut lines of division, no organized sects.

Davis is right to insist that the Ranters had no 'clear leaders, authoritative tests on entry, and control over numbers' (p. 43). They were not a sect in the modern sense, though the word was used to describe them by John Reeve, founder of what later became the sect of the Muggletonians, as well as by the parliamentary committee. No group in the 1640s or 1650s met Davis's anachronistic demands. But he is quite wrong in thinking this is a new discovery of his. In 1986 a very well-informed and judicious Soviet historian, Professor Tatiana Pavlova, declared that 'We know that the Ranters were not a sect in the exact meaning of that word; they had no organization of any kind, no membership, no visible church, dogmas or ceremonies.'[2] That is an

---

2. T.A. Pavlova, 'The Ranters and Winstanley', in *Istoriya Sozialisticheskikh Ucheniy*, Moscow, 1986, p. 114; in Russian. Professor Pavlova refers to A.L. Morton, *The World of the Ranters* 1970; N. Smith, *A Collection of Ranter Writings from the 17th century*, 1983; T.W. Hayes, *Winstanley the Digger: A Literary Analysis of Radical Ideas in the English Revolution*, Harvard University Press, 1979, and to my *World Turned Upside Down*, op. cit. She makes some shrewd criticisms of Morton and myself, though not such as will bring comfort to Davis.

accurate statement of received scholarly opinion – at least in the northern hemisphere – and it was published in the year in which Davis's book appeared. A.L. Morton, who knew more about the Ranters than anyone else, said they were not a sect but a movement: I said there was never 'an organized movement' of Ranters, the emphasis being on 'organized'.[3] But we can get into silly semantic arguments here. I have always preferred the word 'milieu'. Jacob Bauthumley in 1650 used the first person plural and claimed to speak for 'a certain generation of men and women' in order to influence public opinion in their favour. To that extent he was aware of some sort of collectivity. So was Thomas Tany, who in 1652 felt that he could speak for 'me and my brethren'.[4]

There undoubtedly was what contemporaries accepted as a Ranter milieu, with a series of shared beliefs and attitudes – hostility to organized churches and to any centralized state power and inequalities in property, materialism, mortalism, rejection of hell and the devil, scepticism about the special sanctity of the Bible, which did not preclude the use of arguments drawn from it: that was the way discussion was conducted in the seventeenth century. Some believed in the eternity of matter, and so denied divine creation of the world. (Milton's rebel angels believed they were 'self-begot', one of his many allusions to Ranter beliefs.)[5] Or God was equated with Reason or Nature, or was located within human beings: some saw him in all things, pantheistically. Ranters rejected the gloomy doctrines of original sin and eternal punishment for the mass of mankind; they preached and some apparently practised sexual permissiveness; and they used deliberately violent and shocking language. Women played a part in this milieu, and seem to have enjoyed more equality than in most of the dissenting congregations, in theory and in practice. In the new conditions of free discussion which existed in the 1640s and early

---

3. Morton, *World of the Ranters* op. cit., pp. 92, 102; C. Hill, B. Reay and W. Lamont (eds) *The World of the Muggletonians*, 1983, p. 95; my *The Experience of Defeat*, op. cit., p. 50. If anyone is tempted to take Davis's criticisms of Morton seriously, I urge him or her to read what that pioneer historian actually wrote. He is alas no longer able to defend himself; but he was always meticulously careful to avoid overstating the case when discussing the numbers or influence of the Ranters. I followed him in this as carefully as I could. So did McGregor, quoted by Davis, *Fear, Myth and History*, op. cit., p. 20.
4. J. Bauthumley, 'The Light and Dark Sides of God', in Smith, *Ranter Writings*, op. cit., p. 229; T. Tany, *Theauraujohn, High Priest to the Jewes*, in *The Nations Right*, op. cit., p. 29.
5. My *Milton and the English Revolution*, op. cit., pp. 397–8.

1650s, men and women pursued all sorts of heretical ideas, provocatively. The word Ranter was used to describe those who participated in, and justified, these discussions: it is difficult to be more precise.[6]

On the basis of his 'paradigm' Davis refuses the name Ranter to any but a tiny group of individuals – at most Lawrence Clarkson, Abiezer Coppe, Jacob Bauthumley. Now we can, like Humpty Dumpty, make words mean anything we wish; but we cannot compel others to accept our rulings. Davis excludes Joseph Salmon, who was imprisoned with Coppe and was associated with Richard Coppin, Thomas Webbe and probably Jacob Bauthumley.[7] None of these was a member of 'a coherent group', but they seem to have remained in contact until at least 1655 (p. 39). Davis also excludes Joshua Garment and John Robins, whom Thomas Collier described in 1657 as 'the old Ranters'. They were arrested together in May 1651. Muggleton described Robins and Thomas Tany as 'the heads' of the Ranters and Quakers. Davis says Robins cannot be a Ranter because he claimed to be a reincarnation of Jesus Christ (pp. 25–6). The same accusation was made against James Nayler, but this does not stop him being recognized as a Quaker. Davis also excludes Tany, whom John Reeve in 1653 called King of the Ranters.[8] Davis's reason was that Tany wrote 'as the mouthpiece of God' (p. 27). So did Coppe, whom Davis accepts as a Ranter; it is often difficult to decide whether Coppe or the Almighty is speaking. George Foster is also ruled out on grounds that would exclude Coppe (pp. 30–1).

More arguable is Richard Coppin, whom Davis does not accept as a 'paradigmatic Ranter'. I once described him as a 'near-Ranter'. But Jerome Friedman, who devotes more space to Coppin than to any other Ranter, calls him 'the theologian-philosopher of the Ranter movement', author of 'the best systematic presentation of Ranter beliefs'. Coppe wrote a laudatory preface to Coppin's *Divine Teachings* (1649), and Friedman thinks that while Coppin was not himself 'a typical Ranter', he nevertheless 'laid the intellectual foundations from which all other Ranter tendencies might draw'.[9] Coppin was

6. My *Religion and Politics*, op. cit., pp. 194–200.

7. Morton, *World of the Ranters*, op. cit., pp. 97–8; Smith, *Ranter Writings*, op. cit., pp. 12–13, 117, 201–2; C.E. Whiting, *Studies in English Puritanism from the Restoration to the Revolution*, 1931, p. 281.

8. Thomas Collier, *A Looking-Glasse for the Quakers*, 1657, p. 16; J. Reeve, *A Remonstrance from the Eternal God*, 1719, p. 4. First published 1653. Cf. Muggleton, *The Acts of the Witnesses of the Spirit*, 1764, pp. 48, 99. First published 1699, though written earlier.

9. J. Friedman, *Blasphemy, Immorality, and Anarchy: The Ranters and the English Revolution* Ohio University Press, 1987, Ch. 2 *passim*.

denounced in 1657 by Edward Garland, a minister in Kent, where Coppin was said to have 'followers', and to have 'done much mischief to the church of Christ'. 'A more dangerous wolf and heretic was not in the church from the days of the Apostles until this time.' His heresies included treating all the Scriptures as an allegory, preaching universal salvation and – perhaps worse – exposing 'the practice of magistrates and ministers, . . . how they uphold one another, to serve not the Lord but themselves'.[10]

Coppin himself denied being a Ranter, but Friedman discusses at some length the subterfuges and double-talk to which he resorted to save himself from jail during his many prosecutions under the Blasphemy Act of 9 August 1650.[11] To exclude him from the Ranter milieu demands stricter definitions than I think possible. It seems to me safer and less arbitrary to look at what contemporaries said – unless our object is to abolish the Ranters altogether.

CHRONOLOGICAL

Davis tries to discredit two principal sources for our knowledge of Ranters – anti-Ranter propaganda tracts of 1650–1, and the writings of early Quakers. These two types of evidence must be sharply distinguished. The decisive event was parliament's act of 9 August 1650 against blasphemy. The Blasphemy Ordinance of May 1648 had denounced many ideas which would later be called Ranter; the act of 1650 was aimed more specifically against them. They are not named in it, but it resulted from the report of 21 June presented by a committee set up to consider the 'abominable practices of a sect called Ranters', and its provisions were clearly directed against them. Coppe said that this act, and that of 10 May 1650 against adultery, 'were put out because of me'.[12] In the parliament of 1656 Francis Rous was referring to the act of 9 August 1650 when he said 'the laws against blasphemy and Ranters are still in force'. These laws had been reinforced by a proclamation of 15 February 1655 against

---

10. Edward Garland, *An Answer To a Printed Book, falsely Intituled, a Blow at the Serpent*, 1657, Sig. A 2v, pp. 3–4, 28, 52–8, 63.
11. Coppin, *Truths Testimony* (1655), Chs VI–XV, *passim*; Friedman, *Blasphemy*, op. cit., pp. 45–7, 53–8.
12. N. Cohn, op. cit., pp. 325–7; Morton *World of the Ranters*, op. cit., p. 102; Smith, *Ranter Writings*, op. cit., pp. 14, 119. Cohn reprints the relevant sections of the act of 9 August. Both acts, Coppe added, followed his imprisonment.

'Quakers, Ranters and others'.[13] The main body of anti-Ranter propaganda comes from the months immediately before and after the act of August 1650.

As Cohn and Morton stressed long ago, this propaganda is not to be taken too seriously. It often uses words and concepts taken directly from the act: hence they are stereotyped, and many of the authors give full rein to their fantasy.[14] Davis rightly wishes to discount charges based on these scandalous news-sheets and pamphlets. The nature of the allegations, with their lurid sexual overtones, is highly conventional: similar stories had been told about sixteenth-century Familists, about mechanic preachers and their congregations when they were first able to appear in public in the early 1640s, about women preachers. They represent the sort of smear that tended to be made against any unorthodox group which met privately. We should not believe them; but it would be silly to carry scepticism to the point of denying the existence of Familists or mechanic or women preachers – or for that matter of the early Quakers. Nor should we assume that all the press was 'yellow' when it came to describing the Ranters. There were many relatively unslanted factual accounts, cited by Morton, Smith and Andrew Hopton.[15] These early critics of Ranters included Levellers, Baptists and Presbyterians as well as royalists.[16] What distinguishes Ranters from earlier victims of such smears is that some of them – Coppe and Clarkson in particular – rather enjoyed and played up to their scandalous reputation.

Davis's second source of evidence, Quaker attacks on Ranters, is to be sharply distinguished from the attacks of the yellow press in 1650-1. 'The Northern Quakers', as they were regularly called, did not move into the south of England until the summer of 1654. Howgil and Burrough reached London early in July, and by September regular Quaker meetings were being held.[17]

Initially Quakers spoke in friendly terms of former Ranters. Fox in 1654 witnessed to the Ranters' 'pure convincement',[18] and in 1655 he

---

13. Rutt, *Diary of Thomas Burton* op. cit., I, p. 29; cf. pp. 49–50 (Major-General Skippon); Abbott, *Cromwell's Writings*, op. cit., III, pp. 626–7.
14. Cohn, *Pursuit of the Millennium*, op. cit., p. 328; Morton *World of the Ranters*, op. cit., pp. 104–7.
15. Morton, *World of the Ranters*, op. cit., *passim*; Smith, *Ranter Writings* op. cit., pp. 18–19; A. Coppe, *Selected Writings*, ed. A. Hopton, 1987, notes on p. 13.
16. Morton, *World of the Ranters*, op. cit., pp. 101–2.
17. W.C. Braithwaite, *The Beginnings of Quakerism*, 1912, pp. 155–61.
18. The phrase 'pure convincement', 'as the Quakers call it', was quoted in 1657 by Edward Garland (*An Answer*, op. cit., p. 25): see pp. 163–4 below.

found himself in amicable agreement with Jacob Bauthumley.[19] Anthony Pearson, also in 1654, agreed that 'some that are joined to the Ranters are pretty people', though he added that they attracted too many 'rude savage apprentices and young people'.[20] James Parnell in 1655 criticized Ranters, but admitted that 'some of them have tasted of the love of God.[21] Richard Farnsworth agreed: 'You did run well, but you have lost the right way'. 'Many [Ranters] were once tender and simple-hearted . . . and were zealous for the truth'.[22] Edward Burrough at one stage 'followed only to hear the highest notionists', from whom he learnt 'fleshly liberty to the carnal mind'. But in 1656 he admitted that the Ranters 'have scorned self-righteousness'. Theirs had been the house of prayer, though it is so no longer.[23]

1656 was the year in which James Nayler was accused of blasphemy for re-enacting in Bristol Christ's entry into Jerusalem. After their suppression in 1650–1 many Ranters attached themselves to the Quakers, who in their early days were given to making extravagant symbolic gestures. Only gradually, and especially after the Nayler scandal, did Quaker leaders come to differentiate themselves from Ranters. They denounced Nayler's supporters as Ranters. By 1657 Burrough was warning Quakers to beware of the Ranter spirit.[24] Quaker leaders was especially anxious to free themselves from the 'libertine' reputation of Ranters, and spent many weary years trying to draw lines of distinction. Nevertheless, even in 1660 Samuel Fisher, whilst denouncing 'that old spirit of the Ranters', continued to list them as one of the seven Protestant churches, the others being pre-latists, Presbyterians, Independents, Baptists, Seekers and Quakers.[25]

19. G. Fox and J. Nailor (sic), *A Word from the Lord*, 1654, p. 13; Swarthmore MSS., quoted by R.M. Jones, *Studies in Mystical Religion*, 1909, p. 473. The account of this incident in Fox's *Journal* is much less sympathetic to Bauthumley. It has no doubt been rewritten. Fox has an entry in his *Journal* for 1649 recording a meeting with Joseph Salmon and other Ranters in Coventry jail. Coventry was a Ranter stronghold, but Fox's use of the name 'Ranter' for those whom he initially described as 'people that were in prison for religion' may be an afterthought (*Journal*, 1902, I, pp. 47–8).
20. A.E. Wallis, 'Anthony Pearson (1626–1666)', *Journal of the Friends' Historical Society*, 1967, LI, p. 85.
21. James Parnell, *A Shield of Truth*, 1655, p. 39.
22. Farnsworth, *The Ranters Principle and Deceits Discovered*, 1655, pp. 1–2.
23. Burrough, *A Trumpet of the Lord*, 1656, pp. 26–8; *The Memorable Works of a Son of Thunder and Consolation*, 1672, pp. 15, 26. 'Notionists' normally means Ranters.
24. ibid., pp. 108–9, 138, 143, 208, 279–80, 319–20, 746; cf. J.F. McGregor, 'Seekers and Ranters', in *Radical Religion*, op. cit., p. 131.
25. S. Fisher, *The Rusticks Alarm to the Rabbies*, 1660, in *The Testimony of Truth Exalted*, 1679, pp. 543, 621; cf. pp. 91–2, and Burrough, *Memorable Works*, op. cit., pp. 96–114 (1655).

So when Davis says 'the Quakers provide the most substantial evidence for the existence of Ranters after 1651 . . . but it is not evidence to be taken at face value', he must be interpreted as meaning 'after 1654–5,' though his statement is not true for that period. For the years both before and after 1656 there is a great deal of very substantial evidence for the existence of Ranters. I give a few examples, the product of casual reading. These, I am sure, could be greatly extended by a little more research.

As early as March 1649, before the word Ranter had gained currency, the Leveller William Walwyn refers to ideas which would soon be called Ranter – rejection of 'a Christ crucified at Jerusalem', 'the Scriptures were but a dead letter', there is no sin or day of judgement, heaven is attainable on earth, God is in all things, including men and women.[26] Gerrard Winstanley in February–March of the following year (before the clampdown on either Diggers or Ranters had started) wrote a pamphlet criticizing 'the ranting practice'. He was particularly concerned with Ranter libertinism. At about the time when the Digger colony started (April 1649) there had been a demonstration nearby when half a dozen soldiers invaded the parish church of Walton-on-Thames, burnt a Bible and abolished the Sabbath, tithes, ministers and magistrates. They sound more like Ranters than Diggers.[27] But the Digger colony was apparently later infiltrated by a group of Ranters, whose practice of 'excessive community of women' was used to slander the Diggers. Ranter behaviour, said Winstanley, proved 'a peace-breaker', 'a breeder of much distemper, wars and quarrels'. 'By seeking their own freedom' in sexual relations, Ranters 'imbondage others'. 'The mother and child begotten in this manner is like to have the worst of it, for the man will be gone and leave them.' Ranter rejection of the work ethic was 'the support of idleness'. But Winstanley was careful to add, well before persecution of the Ranters had started, 'let none go about to suppress that ranting power by their punishing hand'. Reason, not force, must be the corrective. 'But if thou wilt needs be punishing, then see thou be without sin thyself, and then cast the first stone at the Ranter.'[28] It

---

26. Walwyn, *The Vanitie of the Present Churches*, in J.R. McMichael and B. Taft (eds) *The Writings of William Walwyn*, Georgia University Press, 1989, pp. 317–19.
27. Clement Walker, *The Compleat History of Independencie*, 1649, Part II, pp. 152–3. Tany became notorious for symbolically burning the Bible in public.
28. Winstanley, *A Vindication of those . . . . called Diggers*, in Sabine, *Works of Winstanley*, op. cit., pp. 399–403; cf. Winstanley, 'Englands Spirit Unfoulded', ed. G. Aylmer, 1968, 40, p. 14.

was a note that Coppe was to echo in his 'recantation' a year later. In a postscript to a pamphlet published in the same year Winstanley's disavowal was more specific: 'if any of the Diggers fall into the practice of ranting, they fall off from their principles, as some in all churches does'.[29] The last six words, and the note of urgency in the text, suggest that some Diggers, like John Bunyan for a time, may have been attracted by Ranter libertinism. Davis, who claims to be something of an expert on Winstanley (see p. 189 below), is significantly silent on his anti-Ranter pamphlets. They would have been difficult to explain away.

Where we have church books for congregations during this period, they record the presence of Ranters. The Warboys church (Huntingdonshire) refers to Ranters from 1648 onwards. The Fenstanton church in the same county in 1653 excommunicated many holders of views that 'savoured of Rantism'.[30] Robert Gell preached a sermon against 'rantists' in 1650; he returned to the theme five years later.[31] The astrologer William Lilly quoted Gell's first sermon. Lilly was very hostile to Ranters, perhaps because his rival John Gadbury was said to be one.[32] Nicholas Culpeper referred to Ranters and their views in astrological writings of 1652, 1653 and 1654.[33] In 1651 Richard Baxter had spoken of 'Mr. Coppe and his followers, called by some the Ranters'.[34] In the same year John Osborne, vicar of Bampton, Oxfordshire, mentions Coppe as well as describing a public debate he himself had with Richard Coppin.[35] Evidence that Ranters existed and had views which could be cited with approval rather than ritual disgust comes from a ballad of 1652. It was written by Lionel Lockier, who describes himself as physician of Southwark. Lockier defends the poor against the hypocritical godly who oppress them, and who call 'all that hold community' Ranters. The really sinful Ranter, Lockier thought, was the rich man who

29. ibid., pp. 14–15.
30. E.B. Underhill (ed.) *Records of the Churches . . . at Fenstanton, Warboys and Hexham*, Hanserd Knollys Society, 1854, pp. 269–71, 73–9, 89–90; cf. pp. 330–1 (Hexham).
31. Robert Gell, *A Sermon Touching Gods Government of the World*, 1650, p. 39; *Noahs Flood Returning*, 1655, p. 11.
32. William Lilly, *Astrological Predictions for the Year 1651*, Sig. A8; *History of his Life and Times*, ed. K.M. Briggs, 1974, p. 64; D. Parker, *Familiar to All: William Lilly and Astrology in the 17th Century*, 1975, p. 54; K. Thomas, *Religion and the Decline of Magic*, op. cit., pp. 375, 377.
33. N. Culpeper, *Catastrophe Magnatum: Or, The Fall of Monarchie*, 1652, p. 17; *The English Physitian Enlarged*, 1653, Sig. B 4; *Pharmacopoeia Londinensis*, 1654, Sig. A 3v.
34. R. Baxter, *Plain Scripture Proof of Infant Church-membership and Baptism*, 1651, p. 148.
35. J. Osborne, *The World to Come, or the Mysteries of the Resurrection Opened*, 1651, Sig. A 2.

riotously hath spent
That which his fellow-creatures want[36]

'Fellow-creature' was the favoured Ranter form of address.

In 1653 Rapha Harford in his Epistle Dedicatory to John Everard's posthumous *Some Gospel Treasures Opened* was careful to explain that Everard was no 'licentious Ranter'.[37] In the same year Samuel Fisher called Part IV of his *Baby Baptism meer Babism* 'Anti-Rantism', and the whole bulky treatise would be pointless if Fisher at least did not believe, and expect his readers to believe, in the existence of Ranters.[38] Two years later he was still denouncing, alliteratively, 'the rabble of the ruder sort of Ranters'.[39]

Samuel Sheppard was not on oath when in 1651 he said 'all the world now is in the Ranting humour'.[40] But John Pordage in 1655 assumed general agreement that in 1650-1 'notions of Rantism . . . were everywhere frequently discussed of'. He even accused his arch-enemy Christopher Fowler of entertaining 'some notions of Rantism'.[41] Bunyan was speaking of the same period when he tells us of a man who had been his 'religious intimate companion' but then 'turned a most devilish Ranter' and assured Bunyan that all the godly would soon follow his example.[42] Robert Abbott attacked the Ranter belief in human perfectibility in 1652.[43] In 1653 the radical William Dell used the phrase 'savouring of the Ranters' religion' to mock a conservative adversary.[44] The royalist poet Nicholas Hookes, also in 1653, referred to Ranters in the conventional pejorative way, as did Marvell in 'The First Anniversary of the Government under O.C.' in 1655.[45] In 1654 the prophetess Anna Trapnel, who had been in Bridewell with 'a

---

36. H.E. Rollins (ed.) *Cavalier and Puritan Ballads*, New York, 1923, pp. 320-4; cf. Tany, *The Nations Right*, op. cit., pp. 21-2: cf. ibid., p. 28: *Theauraujohn, High Priest to the Jewes*.

37. R. Harford, 'To the Reader', in J. Everard, *Some Gospel Treasures Opened*, 1653, quoted by R.M. Jones *Spiritual Reformers in the 16th and 17th centuries*, 1914, p. 214.

38. *Rusticks Alarm*, op. cit., pp. 466-522.

39. Fisher, *Christianismus Redivivus*, 1655, pp. 466-7, 482, 492, 513. By 1660 Fisher, now a Quaker, distinguished sharply between Ranters and Quakers (*Rusticks Alarm*, op. cit., pp. 91-2, 537, 543, 621).

40. S.S., *The Joviall Crew or the Devil turned Ranter*, 1651, Prologue.

41. Pordage, *Innocencie appearing Through the Dark Mists of Pretended Guilt*, 1655, pp. 11, 23, 25. Contemporaries counted Pordage as a Ranter, and so does Friedman, though this is not generally agreed. See my *Experience of Defeat*, op. cit., Ch. 8, section i, and p. 172 below.

42. Bunyan, *Grace Abounding*, op. cit., pp. 16-17.

43. Abbott, *The Young Mans Warning-piece*, 1652, Sig. A 3v - A 4.

44. Dell, *Several Sermons*, 1709, p. 607. First published 1652-3.

45. Hookes, *Amanda*, 1923, p. 83. First published 1653. Margoliouth (ed.) Marvell, *Poems and Letters*, op. cit., I, pp. 110-11.

company of ranting sluts . . . who have spoke a great many good words', rejoiced that she had nevertheless been preserved from 'those Familistical ranting tenents'.[46] Sir Henry Vane was not much more favourable in *The Retired Mans Meditations*.[47] John Trapp, headmaster of what had been Shakespeare's school in Stratford-upon-Avon, spoke in his *Commentary on the New Testament* (2nd edn, 1656) of 'our Ranters (as they call themselves)'.[48] The legal reformer William Sheppard thought that Ranters should be declared incapable of holding office in the commonwealth, along with 'Quakers, murderers, thieves, whoremongers' and seven other categories of malefactors.[49] No one has ever doubted the existence of the other eleven categories. Most interesting of all, perhaps, is the enlarged second edition (1655) of Alexander Ross's *View of all Religions in the World*, first published in 1653. In this edition Reeve, Muggleton, Quakers and Ranters all appear for the first time. The account of Ranters is hostile, naturally, but it is seriously documented. Theauraujohn and Coppin are described as Ranters. Ross particularly stresses the Ranters' disrespect for magistracy as well as ministry.[50]

Thomas Fuller, in his *Church History of Britain* (1655), suggested – like Anna Trapnel – that the 'modern Ranters' derived from Familists, though they are now grown much more numerous.[51] It will be noted that the communist Winstanley, the law reformer William Sheppard, the royalists Samuel Sheppard and Nicholas Hookes, the moderate Anglican Fuller, the conservative Baxter,[52] the heresy-hunting Ross, the Calvinist Bunyan, the Behmenist Pordage, Samuel Fisher in both his Baptist and Quaker phases, the astrologer Lilly and the ballad-writer Lockier, all independently testify to the prevalence of Ranters and Ranterism in the early 1650s. None of them was a propagandist journalist, and most of them refer to a period before the Quaker attack on Ranters had begun. As late as 1657 Edward Garland thought it worth while answering Coppin's *A Blow at*

---

46. *Anna Trapnels Report and Plea*, 1654, p. 38: the words quoted are those of the 'matron' of Bridewell; [Anna Trapnel], *The Cry of a Stone*, 1654, pp. 8–10. I owe the first reference to Dr Valerie Drake.

47. 1655 edn, p. 201.

48. 1958 edn, p. 721.

49. W. Sheppard, *Englands Balme*, 1656, pp. 41–2.

50. *View of All Religions*, op. cit., pp. 377–89.

51. *Church History* op. cit., III, p. 211. I cite from the reprint of 1842.

52. My quotations from pamphlets published by Baxter in 1651 and 1655 (see p. 161 above, n. 34 and p. 166 below, n. 65, for titles) may cast some doubt on Davis's attempt to discredit his testimony in *Reliquiae Baxterianae* (1696) as 'recalled in some confusion', 'in part dependent on stories culled from Thomas Edwards' (Davis, *Fear, Myth and History*, op. cit., pp. 92, 129).

the Serpent of 1656; and Coppin replied in *Michael Opposing the Dragon.* [53]

Some of the strongest evidence for Ranters in the early fifties comes from the followers of John Reeve, later known as Muggletonians. Mr Davis tries to laugh off the 'crude retrospective characterization' of Ranters in Lodowick Muggleton's *Acts of the Witnesses* (1699). It is indeed a late source. But it is based on first-hand evidence, dating from before 1652. Reeve and Muggleton themselves came from the Ranter milieu. John Reeve's elder brother, Thomas, was a disciple of John Robins and remained a Ranter until, we are told, he died – appropriately – a drunkard. [54] Both brothers came from Wiltshire, a Ranter area. John Reeve also became a disciple of Robins. We know about Robins mostly from his enemies, so we may be sceptical about stories that he 'called himself the God and Father of the Lord Jesus Christ'. Robins clearly had charisma and managed to collect many disciples, including Mrs Attaway, who claimed to have been influenced by Milton's divorce pamphlets when she separated from her first husband. John Robins 'changed his first wife . . . for an example', which 'many of his disciples followed'; and he insisted on vegetarianism 'until many a poor soul was almost starved under his diet'. Reeve alleged that Robins, like twentieth-century American prophets, took over 'their whole estates' from many of his disciples. [55] Closely associated with Robins was Thomas Tany ('prince and head of the atheistical lie held forth by all the filthy sodomitical Ranters', 'King of the Ranters'). [56]

So involved was Reeve with Robins and the Ranters that he needed a divine command to escape from them. In February 1652 the Lord commissioned Reeve as his 'last messenger for a great work unto this bloody and unbelieving world'. The first part of this great work was to denounce 'the heads' of the Ranters, Tany and Robins. [57] (The fact that God clearly thought that Ranters existed in 1652 appears to

---

53. *Mercurius Politicus*, No. 572 (16–23 June 1659), p. 525; No. 278 (7–14 July 1659), p. 588. (Something seems to have gone wrong with the numbering hereabouts.) Coppin was much less openly political here than other Ranters had been; but Friedman nevertheless describes *Michael Opposing the Dragon* as 'vintage Rantism' (*Blasphemy*, op. cit., p. 34).

54. Hill et al., *World of the Muggletonians*, op. cit., pp. 67, 103. A Ranter named Thomas Reeve was arrested in London in November 1650 (Cohn, op. cit., p. 329; Morton, *World of the Ranters*, op. cit., p. 105). Cf. Reeve and Muggleton, *Spiritual Discourses*, 1820, p. 114. First published 1755.

55. J. Reeve, *A Transcendent Spiritual Treatise*, 1711, pp. 8–14. First published 1652.

56. Reeve, *Remonstrance*, op. cit., pp. 4–5.

57. Reeve, *Transcendent Spiritual Treatise*, op. cit., pp. 4–6. The hymn-book, *Divine Songs of the Muggletonians*, in 1829 still celebrated the victory over Robins and Tany (pp. 85, 119–20).

cast troublesome doubts on his omniscience; but since all time is present with God, he would know that the Ranters were to be invented in the mid-twentieth century).

In the early days of Reeve's commission 'Ranters were the most company we had'. A victualling house in the Minories was run by a Ranter; and there large numbers attended discussions between believers in the commission and a group of Ranters.[58] In 1668 Muggleton wrote that 'the Ranters, when we came out first, sixteen years ago, were very high in their elevations'.[59] Reeve specifically rejected the Ranter doctrines that there was no resurrection (though he remained a mortalist); that the world had no beginning, that there is no God but nature. (The last of these ideas attracted George Fox at one stage.) Reeve also rejected the sexual ethic of Clarkson and Coppe.[60] Nevertheless in 1665 Muggleton, like Samuel Fisher, counted the Ranters as one of the seven churches.[61]

After the suppression of the Ranters, many from their milieu ultimately were absorbed by Muggletonians and Quakers. Because of this fact, each of these sects (if we may begin so to call them) wanted to differentiate its members from the Ranter milieu in which they originated. For this purpose it was convenient to identify libertinism, rejection of the work ethic or excessively enthusiastic behaviour with Ranters. J.F. McGregor, in his seminal article on the Ranters, accurately summed up by saying that for Quakers the word 'Ranter' 'was often a convenient description of the unwelcome by-products of their missionary activities rather than an autonomous movement or an endemic religious mood'. The name could also be applied to 'doubtful converts . . . who were reluctant to submit themselves to Quaker discipline', especially after 1660.[62]

But this is a description of Quaker practice long after Ranters had been suppressed and silenced: it cannot be used, as Davis tries to use it, to argue against the very existence of Ranters in 1649–51, when there were no organized Quakers. Quakers and Muggletonians each used

---

58. Muggleton, *Acts of the Witnesses*, op. cit., pp. 52–3, 56–8.

59. Muggleton, *A Looking Glass for George Fox*, 1756, p. 98. First published 1668.

60. Reeve, *Transcendent Spiritual Treatise*, op. cit., p. 73; Reeve, *A Divine Looking-Glass*, 1719, pp. 133–4, 180. First published 1656.

61. Muggleton, *A True Interpretation of the Eleventh Chapter of the Revelation of St. John*, 1751–2, pp. 60–2. First published (?) 1665.

62. McGregor, 'Ranterism and the development of early Quakerism', *Journal of Religious History*, 1977, 9, p. 345.

the Ranter stick to beat the other.[63] But there would have been no point in this sort of name-calling if there had never been any Ranters. A modern analogy would be attacks by Labour Party or Communist Party members on 'Trotskyites', 'Maoists', 'Militants'. It would have been no good inventing such labels if there had never been any Trotskyites, Maoists or Militants. When government spokesmen today attack bishops for their 'Marxist' ideas, this shows they are ignorant and foolish; it does not prove that Marxists do not exist.

The Quakers, Muggleton said, 'are but the spawn of John Robins', and they inherited Tany's 'witchcraft fits'. When Tany appeared in the lobby of parliament with his sword drawn in December 1654 he was described as a Quaker.[64] 'Seekers, Ranters, Familists, and now Quakers' was how Baxter described the progression in 1655.[65] This recognition that Quakers took their doctrines from Ranters became commonplace. Francis Higginson of Kirby Stephen near Kendal in 1653 published one of the earliest tracts against 'the northern Quakers', saying 'there are none professing Christianity more irreligious than they are, Ranters excepted'.[66]

Bunyan in 1657 distinguished: 'the very opinions that are held at this day by the Quakers are the same that long ago were held by the Ranters. Only the Ranters had made them threadbare at an ale-house, and the Quakers have set a new gloss upon them again, by an outward legal holiness and righteousness'.[67] It seems a fair discrimination. Pagitt's continuator in 1654 had been more concise: 'the Ranter is more open and less sour than the Quaker'.[68] Coincidentally, the Baptist Thomas Collier, also in 1657, said that 'the Quakers' principles were

63. Cf. e.g. George Fox, *Something in Answer to Lodowick Muggleton's Book . . . The Quakers Neck Broken*, 1667, pp. 9, 15, 18, 31; Muggleton, *Looking Glass*, op. cit., pp. 21, 55, 74, 99–100, and *passim*. The point had been clearly made by the best early Quaker historians – Jones, *Mystical Religion*, op. cit., Ch. XIX; Braithwaite, *Beginnings of Quakerism*, op. cit., pp. 22, 69, 181; H. Barbour, *The Quakers in Puritan England*, Yale University Press, 1964, Ch. 4.
64. Muggleton, *True Interpretation*, op. cit., pp. 180–3; *Looking-Glass*, op. cit., pp. 98–100; Bulstrode Whitelocke, *Memorials of the English Affairs*, 1682, p. 592.
65. R. Baxter, *The Quakers Catechism or The Quakers Question*, 1655, quoted in H. Barbour and A. Roberts, *Early Quaker Writings*, Grand Rapids, Michigan, 1973, p. 266. Tany stresses what was later the Quaker principle that 'true teaching came . . . from the light within' (*Theous Ori*, 1651, quoted in *The Nations Right*, op. cit., p. 12).
66. Higginson, *A Brief Relation of the Irreligion of the Northern Quakers*, 1653, in Barbour and Roberts, *Early Quaker Writings*, op. cit., p. 78.
67. Bunyan, *A Vindication of Some Gospel-truths*, in *Miscellaneous Works*, op. cit., I, pp. 138–9.
68. Pagitt, *Heresiography*, 5th edn, 1654, p. 143. Pagitt died two years after the first edition of this work was published in 1645 – too early for the Ranters.

those of the old Ranters. . . . Any that know the principles of the Ranters may easily discern it.' Only the Quakers 'smooth it over with an outward austere carriage before men'.[69] Also in 1657 Claudius Gilbert, a minister at Limerick in Ireland, made precisely the same point: 'the Ranters were merrily, the Quakers are melancholically mad: those had more of the fire, these more of the water'. Behind all the 'Levelling, Ranting and Quaking principles' he saw popery.[70] Muggleton in 1669 agreed that the 'Quakers have taken up the doctrinal part of the Ranters but left their practice'.[71]

When parliament was debating the case of James Nayler in December 1656, Colonel Sydenham said that his doctrines came near to 'a glorious truth, that the spirit is personally in us'.[72] The fundamental Protestant doctrine of the priesthood of all believers underlay Nayler's demonstration. The Ranters had extended the same doctrine a little further. The savagery and near-hysteria of MPs when discussing Nayler in 1656 derived from this: Nayler was dangerous because his case reopened a dispute that appeared to have been settled by the 1650 Blasphemy Act. Oliver Cromwell, whilst claiming to 'abhor James Nayler's principle', nevertheless reminded his officers that 'the case of James Nayler might happen to be your own case'. Strong passions were aroused because the distinction to be drawn between 'a glorious truth' and 'blasphemy' was narrow and yet politically and socially vital.[73]

Some of the best evidence for the existence of Ranters as something more than bogys comes from those who were at one time close to their views but later dissociated themselves. William Erbery, for instance, had many Ranterish views, and came to visit Clarkson in jail. He was examined by parliament as a suspect Ranter in 1652. He was careful after that to differentiate himself; but both he and his editor and biographer John Webster in 1658 still recognized his affinity with Ranters. Erbery insisted that what had been 'nicknamed Puritanism' was now 'called Ranting'. Like Winstanley, and like Coppe in his 'recantation', Erbery drew unflattering comparisons between the

69. Collier, *Looking-Glasse*, op. cit., p. 7.
70. C. Gilbert, *The Libertine School, Or a Vindication of the Magistrates Power in Religious Matters*, 1657, p. 25, Sig. Bv; cf. pp. 19, 24, 54.
71. Muggleton, *An Answer to Isaac Penington, Esquire*, 1719, p. 20. First published 1669.
72. Rutt, *Diary of Thomas Burton*, op. cit., I, p. 69.
73. Abbott, *Cromwell's Writings*, op. cit., IV, pp. 417, 419. For Nayler and the Ranters see also my *World Turned Upside Down*, pp. 231–58, 370–1, 377–9; *Experience of Defeat*, pp. 138–42.

'profane people called Ranters' and the prosperous and lustful self-styled saints. Erbery's sympathies were always with the poor.[74] John Bidle, who spent many years in prison for his anti-Trinitarian views, was careful in 1654 to condemn 'the licentious opinions and practices of the Ranters'.[75] Why should so many persons of principle bother to disavow connections with non-existent bogymen?

Magnus Byne was a parson of the state church, drawing tithes from two parishes. Quakers accused him of being a Ranter, and of still associating with 'drunkards, Ranters and profane persons'. Byne replied that he 'abhorred the blasphemies and filthy talk and practice of Ranters. . . . Yet let not the high-minded Quaker glory over these poor deluded Ranters', many of whom 'have tasted of the heavenly gift'. Another Quaker critic said that, 'Ranter-like', Byne 'must talk still of Eden, Paradise . . .' etc. These exchanges tell us something about surviving Ranters, about Quakers, and about nostalgia for Ranter notions even in a conformist minister, even in 1656. Between the 'over-wickedness' of the Ranters and the 'over-righteousness' of the Quakers, Byne may have preferred the former.[76]

Peter Sterry, Cromwell's chaplain, was also aware that his beliefs could be interpreted as akin to those of the Ranters. The Epistle Dedicatory to his Fast Sermon of New Year's Day, 1649, preached to celebrate the surrender of Drogheda and Wexford, has been described as 'the first intellectually structured presentation of Ranter doctrine, not based on gossip and hearsay' and aiming not at mere denunciation but at rational discussion 'for the discovery of the truth'. As late as 1675 Sterry had to admit that parts of his *Discourse of the Freedom of the Will* 'seem . . . to confirm the Ranters in their licentious principles and practice'; and he went to great lengths to make the necessary distinctions.[77]

William Sedgwick spoke favourably of Ranters, and was on friendly terms with Coppe as well as with John Reeve. Sedgwick too used the

74. William Erbery, *The Testimony of William Erbery*, 1658, pp. 259, 312–16, 331. L. Clarkson, *The Lost sheep Found*, Exeter University Press, 1974, p. 19. First published 1660.

75. John Bidle, *A Twofold Catechism*, 1654, Sig. A 5v.

76. Magnus Byne, *The Scornfull Quakers Answered*, 1656, pp. 32, 63–4, 120; cf. p. 78. Byne attributed his double tithes to Providence: 'your murmurings are not so much against me as against the Lord' (p. 51).

77. Peter Sterry, *The Commings Forth of Christ*, 1650, esp. Sig. A 2v, A 3, aa 4v; *A Discourse of the Freedom of the Will*, 1675, pp. 156–66; Sterry to Colonel John Jones, 24 October 1653, in Mayer, 'Inedited letters', op. cit., I, pp. 248–51; V. de Sola Pinto, *Peter Sterry: Platonist and Puritan*, Cambridge University Press, 1934, pp. 108–9; N.I. Matar, 'Peter Sterry and the Ranters', *Notes and Queries*, 1982, 227, new series 29, pp. 504–5.

Ranters as a stick with which to beat the godly rich.[78] Isaac Penington was 'upon the Ranting principle' long before there were any Quakers; he only slowly distinguished himself from them. His *Light or Darkness* (1650) and other pamphlets of this period contain many Ranter ideas and images; they were never reprinted by Quaker editors of his collected works.[79] What is interesting is that some observers – Erbery, Byne and Sedgwick, for instance – found things to praise in the Ranters, unlike the muck-rakers and the later Quakers, unlike the orthodox godly. They would hardly invent the Ranters for this purpose though.

Fox came in contact with Ranters in Cleveland and Staithes (Yorkshire) in 1651. They are not mentioned in his *Journal* for the next three or four years, no doubt because Ranters were lying low. But in 1654–5 he encountered them in large numbers in Nottinghamshire, Cleveland, York and its environs, the Peak District, Leicester (Bauthumley and many others) and Sussex ('a band of Ranters'), Reading and Weymouth, as well as London. He tells us of many Ranter groups which ultimately became Quaker.[80] Then there is another gap until 1659, when Ranters reappear in Norwich. All these examples cast doubt on the idea that Quakers invented Ranters as straw whipping boys in the process of their own evolution as a society. Much more probable, it seems to me, is that Ranters and Quakers emerged from the same milieu, Ranters first; and that differentiation was slow. The Quaker John Whitehead had previously been a Ranter; so, it was alleged, had Margaret Fell. Anthony Pearson may have gone through a Ranter phase: Burrough and Penington certainly did.[81] In 1654 Ranters as well as Quakers were accused of interrupting church services.[82] After the suppression of the Ranters a Ranter wing continued in the Quaker movement.[83]

The case of James Nayler forced the necessity of coping with this

---

78. My *Experience of Defeat*, op. cit., p. 101; Clarkson, *The Lost sheep Found*, op. cit., p. 119; Smith, *Ranter Writings*, op. cit., pp. 109–10.
79. Reeve, *The Prophet Reeves Epistle to his Friend*, 1654, pp. 15–20; Muggleton, *Answer to Penington*, Sig. A iv, pp. 22–3, and *passim*; my *Experience of Defeat*, op. cit., pp. 118–28. Salmon ultimately became a Quaker (Smith, *Ranter Writings*, op. cit., p. 66).
80. Fox, *Journal*, op. cit., I, pp. 84–6, 194–5, 198–200, 212, 230–1, 263; cf. pp. 451, 516, II, pp. 7, 95–7, 170.
81. Burrough, *Memorable Works*, op. cit., p. 15; see my *Experience of Defeat*, op. cit., p. 141; cf. pp. 167–8, and *World Turned Upside Down*, Ch. 20, *passim*; Braithwaite, *Beginnings of Quakerism*, op. cit., pp. 112–13.
82. *Mercurius Politicus*, op. cit., Nos 245 and 246 (1654), pp. 5142, 5164.
83. My *World Turned Upside Down*, op. cit., 253–4; cf. p. 170 below.

Ranter wing.[84] Anything not acceptable to the leadership after the Nayler débâcle tended to be dismissed as 'the rotten principles of the old Ranters'.[85] After the proclamation of the peace principle in 1661, and the new discipline which necessarily accompanied it, Quakers were right, I think, to trace continuities from Ranters to Nayler's supporters to Perrot and to the Story–Wilkinson separation.[86] As late as 1668 Fox wrote of 'a rude company of Ranters' in Southampton: 'though they were Ranters, great opposers of Friends and disturbers of our meetings, some people that did not know them would be apt to say they were Quakers'.[87] Whether they were 'really' Ranters, or whether they were Ranterish Quakers is no easier to determine today than, in all probability, it was in 1668. It was in and around Southampton that the Ranters William Franklin and Mary Gadbury had won a large following in 1649–50. (See p. 172 below).

This, the traditional picture, is confirmed by many contemporary estimates. Robert Gell, no friend to the Ranters, said 'Had not the Quakers come, the Ranters had overrun the nation.' Durant Hotham, like Bunyan and Collier, distinguished between Ranters and Quakers: the former 'would have said as we said and done as we commanded, and yet have kept their principle still'. But for the Quakers, 'the nation would have been overrun with Ranterism'. All these independent witnesses seem to confirm not only that the Ranters existed but that there was an 'abundance of those they call Ranters . . . in several parts.'[88]

A.L. Morton in his great pioneering study found Ranters in London, Berkshire (Abingdon), Cornwall, Derbyshire, Dorset (Poole, Weymouth), Essex (Ilford), Gloucester, Hampshire (Winchester, Andover, Southampton), Lancashire, Leicestershire, Middlesex (Uxbridge), Norfolk (Norwich, King's Lynn), Nottinghamshire, Sussex (Horsham), Warwickshire (Coventry), Yorkshire (all three

84. For Nayler and later Quaker splits, see ibid. pp. 248–58; cf. Rebecca Travers, *A Testimony Concerning the Light and Life of Jesus*, 1663, p. 1. I owe this reference to the kindness of Dr Valerie Drake.

85. Fox, *Journal*, op. cit., I, p. 519 (1661). Cf. Fisher, *Testimony*, op. cit., p. 621: Nayler revealed 'that old spirit of the Ranters'. Nayler himself blamed Ranters for his fall after the event (my *World Turned Upside Down*, op. cit., p. 251).

86. Fox, *A testimony in that which separates between the pretious and the vile* (? 1667), p. 3; K.L. Carroll, *John Perrot, early Quaker Schismatic*, Friends' Historical Society, 1971, pp. 57, 61, 90. The subject was discussed by Stephen Crisp in 1684 (*A Faithful Warning and Exhortation to Friends: To Beware of Seducing Spirits*).

87. Fox, *Journal*, op. cit., II, p. 96.

88. ibid., I, p. 95; Jones, *Mystical Religion*, op. cit., p. 481; *Leybourne – Popham Papers*, Historical Manuscripts Commission, 1899, p. 78.

Ridings). We may add Bedfordshire, Cambridgeshire, Cheshire, Huntingdonshire, Kent, Northamptonshire (Wellingborough), Oxfordshire (Banbury), Somerset (Wells), Staffordshire, Suffolk, and Wiltshire.[89] This is two-thirds of the English counties. We may add Edinburgh and elsewhere in Scotland, and Ireland. A lot of places to be peopled by imaginary characters.

What seems to me significant about this list is the wide geographical distribution of people whom contemporaries called Ranters. In many cases we are dealing with pre-existent groups, who either became or were called Ranters in the late forties and early fifties. Thus 'the seat of the old Ranters, Garment and Robins', was Poole and Wells.[90] In 1650 Poole was 'the main centre in Dorset' for Ranters, under the protection, it was said, of a lieutenant-colonel. Wells is in Somerset: there were Ranters and Ranter ideas there in the forties and fifties.[91] Neighbouring Wiltshire was another Ranter centre. Scepticism about the authenticity of the Bible had been reported in the county in 1607 and 1619.[92] John Reeve was born in Wiltshire: the antinomian Tobias Crisp had a living at Brinkworth from 1627 to 1642. Edwards spotted Thomas Webbe in Wiltshire in 1646, and there may have been other Ranter groups there: one still existed in 1656.[93] In October 1660 we learn that 'Anabaptists and Quakers swarm in every corner of the county'.[94]

Coppe had connections in Coventry and Warwickshire generally, as well as in Gloucestershire and Oxfordshire. Coppin and Clarkson in Kent, the former also in Oxfordshire, the latter in East Anglia, Bauthumley in Leicestershire, William Rainborough in Essex – all these gathered groups around them. Many Cambridgeshire Ranters

---

89. Morton, *World of the Ranters*, op. cit., p. 111; my *Religion and Politics*, op. cit., pp. 95-6, 108; my *People and Ideas*, op. cit., p. 162; McGregor, 'Seekers and Ranters', op. cit., p. 133; Hill et al., *World of the Muggletonians*, op. cit., p. 97; D. Underdown, *Somerset in the Civil War and Interregnum*, Newton Abbot, 1973, pp. 186-7; *Mercurius Politicus*, 29 May-5 June, 1651; my *World Turned Upside Down*, op. cit., pp. 238, 257.
90. Collier, *Looking-Glasse*, op. cit., p. 16.
91. Underdown, *Revel*, op. cit., pp. 235, 249; Underdown, *Somerset*, op. cit., pp. 146, 156, 186-8.
92. Underdown, *Somerset*, op. cit., p. 267; M. Hunter, 'The problem of "atheism" in early modern England', RHS *Transactions*, 1985, pp. 150-1, citing M.J. Ingram, 'Ecclesiastical justice in Wiltshire, 1600-1640', D.Phil., University of Oxford, 1976.
93. My *World Turned Upside Down*, op. cit., pp. 227-8; *Religion and Politics*, op. cit., pp. 141-2, 152-3; Underdown, *Revel*, op. cit., pp. 249-50, 285.
94. *Calendar of State Papers, Domestic, 1660-1661*, p. 319.

followed Clarkson when he joined the Muggletonians.[95] 'That blasphemous villain of Andover', William Franklin, with Mary Gadbury, 'his trull', won a following in Hampshire until 'the execution-lash reclaimed them out of their madness'.[96] Jerome Friedman has usefully studied them.[97] In Cornwall, we are told, in 1656 'many Baptists' 'fall off to the Ranters'.[98] Bunyan encountered groups of Ranters in the Bedford neighbourhood.[99] There were others in Ely. In the early 1650s Henry Denne's Baptist church at Fenstanton, Huntingdonshire, was busy coping with near-Ranters.[100] Ranters remained strong in Staffordshire: Robert Hickock was disputing with them there in 1658 and published a tract against them in 1659.[101] In London Tany was 'head of the sodomitical Ranters': Robins had his own circle. There was 'my one flesh', of which Coppe was perhaps the leading figure after he came to London. Clarkson became 'Captain of the Rant', which may be the same or a different group. Ranters were still strong to the south of London in the late fifties.[102]

This was a highly mobile society, in which links were maintained by itinerant preachers like Webbe (before he got his living), Coppe, Clarkson, Coppin, Salmon, Franklin. There were personal links between Coppe and Coppin, Coppin and Salmon, Salmon, Webbe and Coppe, Coppe, Clarkson and Rainborough, Tany and Robert Norwood. Whether or not John Pordage is to be counted a Ranter, he welcomed Coppe, Coppin and Tany to his house at Bradfield, Berkshire.[103] Men and women were prepared to travel long distances to seek out influential preachers. Thus Andrew Wyke, a preaching mechanic from Colchester and a friend of Salmon's, went to visit

95. Morton, *World of the Ranters*, op. cit., p. 133; Smith, *Ranter Writings*, op. cit., p. 112.
96. Gilbert, *Libertine School*, op. cit., p. 26.
97. Friedman, *Blasphemy*, op. cit., Ch. 11.
98. *Mercurius Politicus*, 17–24 April, 1656, 306, p. 6909.
99. Bunyan, *Grace Abounding*, op. cit., *passim*.
100. Underhill, *Records*, op. cit., pp. 2, 8, 33–4, 73–9, 88–93.
101. Robert Hickock, *A Testimony against the People called Ranters*, 1659; cf. Braithwaite, *Beginnings of Quakerism*, op. cit., pp. 128, 392. Hickock accused the Ranters of swearing, of walking after the manner of the world, of opposing preaching, of rejecting 'thou' and 'thee' – all well-documented Ranter habits. He seems to have lapsed as a Quaker in the early sixties.
102. Braithwaite, *Beginnings of Quakerism*, op. cit., p. 397.
103. Morton, *World of the Ranters*, op. cit., p. 98; Smith, *Ranter Writings*, op. cit., pp. 11–16, 117, 201; Friedman, *Blasphemy*, op. cit., Ch. 16; Tany, *The Nations Right*, op. cit., pp. 4–5.

Coppe in jail in Coventry in March 1650, accompanied by a lady friend.[104]

So there were Ranters all over England, in the countryside as well as in towns. Rural support for the Ranters can no doubt be explained in part by their opposition to tithes, which Davis hardly mentions: the word is not in his index. This was a part of the heretical tradition which had a continuing appeal from the time of the Lollards till the Quakers took it over and made more of it than the largely urban Ranters.[105] A long-standing anti-clericalism had been reinforced by the fundamental Protestant doctrine of the priesthood of all believers, which had spread rapidly with the rise of an educated and propertied laity. The idea that there should be a university-educated, officially accredited exponent of religious truth in every parish conflicts with the idea that some parishioners are predestined elect, still more with the radical view that something of God may be in all men and women. The existence of a superior caste of priests is, on these assumptions, an insult to humanity. We do not need to take at face value the accounts by Coppin, Coppe, Clarkson and others of the popular success of their preaching, especially among rank-and-file soldiers. But, if you think about it, it is not inherently improbable: Baxter cited letters from Abingdon which confirm it.[106] Army officers seem often to have protected Ranters, as later they protected Quakers. The re-radicalization of the army in 1659–60 reinforced the hatred of respectable Puritans for the army as for Quakers.

Tithes would also explain the existence of much contemporary hostile comment on Ranters from clergy of the state church who were neither yellow-press journalists nor Quakers – John Osborne, Richard Baxter, John Tickell, Edward Hide, Francis Higginson, Robert Gell, William Dell, Thomas Fuller, Edward Garland, Claudius Gilbert. John Trapp in his *Commentary on the New Testament* went out of his way to refer disapprovingly to the Ranters' 'most prodigious opinions and practices'.[107] In all surviving accounts of Ranter trials the clergy were invariably more savage in denunciation of the accused than laymen were; judges and constables seem frequently to have taken a more sympathetic attitude than JPs. In Chester there was so much local support

---

104. *Leybourne-Popham Papers*, op. cit., pp. 57, 59. They were alleged to think 'the Scriptures . . . were no more than a ballad', a phrase which Bunyan echoed. Cf. Smith, *Ranter Writings*, op. cit., pp. 117–18.
105. Pavlova, 'Ranters and Winstanley', op. cit., p. 122; Tany, *The Nations Right*, op. cit., p. 12 and *passim*.
106. Sylvester (ed.) *Reliquiae Baxterianae* op. cit., p. 77.
107. Trapp, *Commentary*, op. cit., 1958 edn, p. 721.

even in 1652 for a man who sounds like a Ranter that it took 'a full bench of fine gentlemen' before the local clergy could get him imprisoned.[108] The genial pluralist Magnus Byne was exceptionally tolerant.[109]

Ranter 'libertinism' also had deep historical roots. Attempts to enforce monogamous church marriage on a population which had its own traditional but different marriage customs extends from at least the fifteenth to the eighteenth centuries. Lollards opposed church marriage; from the introduction of parish registers in the 1530s to Hardwicke's Marriage Act of 1753 there is a long and imperfectly recorded conflict, of which the establishment of civil marriage by Barebone's Parliament in 1653 is one manifestation. Until the seventeenth century the church was always more tolerant of informal marriages than the state; the state and the common law were interested in the sanctity of property, which as Dr Johnson remarked depended on the chastity of women.[110] And from the fifteenth century more and more of 'the people' are property owners.

The combination of a rapid rise in population in the sixteenth century, enclosure, and periodic unemployment, made poor relief necessary for the destitute, and created vagabondage. From this arose the vast problem of preventing the production of illegitimate children which might become a charge on the parish. This was a main point of parish registers, and of trying to stop the very poor marrying – at least in their own parish. Ranter 'libertinage' inherits a long tradition here in exacerbated circumstances. It is a rejection of state and state-church control over personal relations, a rejection of official notions of 'sin' (invented by the ruling class to keep the poor down); it is also an assertion of male human freedom (and only male, in the absence of reliable contraceptive methods: Winstanley was quite right to point this out). Milton's advocacy of divorce he regarded as a challenge to 'papist' usurpations of male rights.

When I first read Davis's book I was working on Bunyan, and I was struck by the impossibility of reconciling his abolition of the Ranters with Bunyan's lengthy account of his relations with people whom he called Ranters. Bunyan was neither a pornographic scandalmonger nor a Quaker. Ranters were important for him because of their ideas, which first attracted and then repelled him, but which preoccupied him for the whole of his life.

---

108. Coppin, *Truths Testimony*, op. cit., Chs VI–XV; R. Parkinson (ed.) *Autobiography of Henry Newcome*, Chetham Society, 1852, pp. 37–40.
109. See p. 168 above.
110. See my 'The poor and the people', in *People and Ideas*, op. cit., Ch. 12; cf. Ch. 9.

Our main source is Bunyan's spiritual autobiography, *Grace Abounding*, published in 1666. It is confirmed by pamphlets which Bunyan published from 1656 onwards, so his evidence is nearly contemporary with the facts he describes. Bunyan returned from the army to his village of Elstow, just outside Bedford, in 1647. *Grace Abounding* tells the story of his battle with Ranter ideas until his conversion around 1653. Bunyan dates most of what he has to say about Ranters to the years before the Quakers came to Bedfordshire – 1655;[111] so the Ranters of whom he speaks cannot have been dissident Quakers. (Similarly Henry Denne found Ranter ideas in Cambridgeshire in 1653, before a Quaker mission had arrived there.)[112]

Bunyan read 'some Ranters' books' which were 'highly in esteem with several old professors' (i.e. religious people). One poor man in particular, who 'did talk pleasantly of the Scriptures and of the matters of religion' and was Bunyan's 'religious intimate companion', 'turned most devilish Ranter'. Bunyan dropped him, but 'several people . . . strict in religion formerly . . . were also swept away by these Ranters'. They condemned Bunyan as 'legal and dark, pretending that they only had attained to perfection that could do what they would and not sin'. He found this doctrine – Coppe's and Clarkson's – seductive, 'I being a young man and my nature in its prime'. 'Turning the grace of God into wantonness, . . . Ranter-like', he put it in 1658.[113]

But it was not only sex. Bunyan wrestled with familiar Ranter puzzles. 'How if all our faith, and Christ, and Scriptures, should be but a think-so too? . . . a fable and cunning story'. Paul, 'a subtle and cunning man', might be a deceiver. In a tract published in 1658 Bunyan made a damned soul in hell remember calling the Bible 'a dead letter, a little ink and paper'. Was it 'written by some politicians on purpose to make poor ignorant people submit to some religion and government?'[114] Other 'conclusions that atheists and Ranters use to help themselves withal' tempted Bunyan: 'that there should be no

111. John Bunyan, *The Doctrine of the Law and Grace Unfolded*, 1659, in *Miscellaneous Works*, op. cit., II, pp. 156–8; Braithwaite, *Beginnings of Quakerism*, op. cit., pp. 185–6.
112. M. Spufford, *Contrasting Communities: English Villagers in the Sixteenth and Seventeenth Centuries*, Cambridge University Press, 1974, p. 283.
113. Bunyan, *Grace Abounding*, op. cit., *passim*; *A Few Sighs from Hell*, in *Miscellaneous Works*, op. cit., I, pp. 381–2.
114. Bunyan, *Grace Abounding*, op. cit., p. 31; *Some Gospel-truths Opened*,1656, in *Miscellaneous Works*, op. cit., I, p. 33; *A Few Sighs*, op. cit., ibid., p. 343; cf. *Prison Meditations*, 1663, and *One Thing is Needful*, 1665, in John Bunyan, *Poems*, ed. G. Midgley, Oxford University Press, 1980, pp. 44, 64. Cf. the Ranter Andrew Wyke, quoted on pp. 172–3 above.

such thing as a day of judgment, that we should not rise again, and that sin was no such grievous thing'.[115]

Bunyan continued his battle against the Ranters throughout his life. Even in the allegories they are not forgotten. In *The Pilgrim's Progress* (1678) the bones of those who deny the resurrection of the body 'lie dashed in pieces' at the bottom of the Mountain of Error. Talkative and Atheist sound like Ranters. Hopeful describes his past in terms very reminiscent of the phase when Bunyan was listening to Ranters. Self-Will in Part II is identified as a Ranter by Roger Sharrock.[116] In *The Life and Death of Mr. Badman* (1680), Badman asked – Ranter-like – how do you know the Scriptures to be the Word of God? and – apropos holy matrimony – 'who would keep a cow of their own that can have a quart of milk for a penny?', as well as playing other 'vile and ranting tricks'. In *The Holy War* the character Atheism virtually quoted Clarkson: ' 'twere as good to go to a whore-house as to go to hear a sermon'. Some have seen the Doubters as Ranters.[117]

Most revealing of all is Bunyan's opposition to women's demands for greater responsibilities in his church, which arose in 1682-3. He saw this as a question of 'power'. If he agreed that women 'should minister to God in prayer before the whole church, . . . then I should be a Ranter or a Quaker'.[118] Davis cites 'yellow-press' allegations that Ranters thought husbands should give sexual liberty to their wives, that Ranter women took the sexual initiative (pp. 105-7). He seems here to give far more credit to the scandal sheets than he should. Salmon, Coppe and Coppin all stressed the equality of women; Mary Gadbury demonstrated it in practice. Friedman seems quite unnecessarily to suggest that Ranters treated women as fundamentally inferior, owing to Eve's transgression. This would be only to say that they were no less sexist than their contemporaries. But most of Friedman's evidence results from confusing 'the Whore of Babylon', who is no more a woman than Antichrist is a man, with women generally.[119]

115. Bunyan, *Grace Abounding*, op. cit., p. 49; cf. p. 11.
116. John Bunyan, *The Pilgrim's Progress*, ed. R. Sharrock, Oxford University Press, 1967, pp. 84, 120-1, 135, 137-8, 255-7, 348-9.
117. John Bunyan, *The Holy War*, ed. R. Sharrock and J.F. Forrest, Oxford University Press, 1980, pp. 121, 227.
118. John Bunyan, *A Case of Conscience Resolved*, 1683, in Offor (ed.) *Works of Bunyan*, op. cit., II, p. 664.
119. Salmon, *Antichrist in Man*, 1647; Friedman, *Blasphemy*, op. cit., pp. 142-4, Ch. 11, and *passim*.

Of all Bunyan's works, *Of the Resurrection of the Dead* (1665?) seems most directly aimed against the Ranters.[120] But attacks on them and their doctrines are to be found scattered throughout his writings published from 1665 to 1685.[121] Finally, in a commentary on Genesis on which Bunyan was working when he died, he was still at pains to refute in the most emphatic terms the Ranter heresy that matter was eternal, that God did not create the universe.[122] This continuing concern and heavy stress would suggest that Ranter ideas were not dead in the Bedford neighbourhood. They still seemed to offer a real threat.

If the Ranters did not exist, they cannot have been suppressed. This taxes Davis's ingenuity. The act of 9 August 1650, by general consent of contemporaries, was directed against Ranters. It was followed by a short, sharp – and successful – drive against leading Ranters. 'Evidence is hard to find', says Davis; 'no systematic evidence' (pp. 125, 134: there is virtue in 'systematic'). Illegal and persecuted movements have a habit, regrettable for the simple-minded historian, of not leaving around too much written evidence of their organization (if any) and contacts. This helps Davis to argue that when Coppe, Salmon and others were arrested in Coventry this was not part of a round-up of Ranters but a coincidence. However, documentation of the round-up which Davis regards as a 'fabrication' of mine, can be found in the well-researched *Treason against God: A History of the Offence of Blasphemy* by Leonard W. Levy (New York, 1981); though he would agree that more research is needed.

If there was suppression, Davis reassures us, it was mild. Only Bauthumley was so unlucky as to have his tongue bored through with a hot iron (p. 136). This, not altogether surprisingly, had a discouraging effect on others. If we reflect a little, boring through the tongue is more than just a barbarously cruel punishment. Could a mechanic preacher continue after it to exercise his God-given vocation? Bunyan chose twelve years in jail rather than give up his call to preach. Bauthumley, equally dangerous, was even more effectively

---

120. Bunyan, *Resurrection*, op. cit., in *Miscellaneous Works*, III, pp. 228, 247; cf. pp. 218, 234, 242, 269–70.
121. See Bunyan, *The Holy City*, 1665, ibid., III, p. 157; *The Heavenly Foot-man*, c. 1670–1, ibid., V., pp. 152–3; *The Barren Fig-tree*, 1673, ibid., V, p. 15; *Light for them that sit in Darkness*, 1675, ibid., VIII, p. 128; *Saved by Grace*, 1676, ibid., VIII, pp. 208–9; *A Treatise of the Fear of God*, 1679, ibid., IX, p. 109; *The Greatness of the Soul*, 1682, ibid., IX, p. 221; *A Discourse of the Pharisee and the Publicane*, 1685, ibid., X, p. 135.
122. Bunyan, *Works*, op. cit., II, p. 417.

silenced. Joseph Salmon expressed shocked horror at Bauthumley's fate in a letter to Thomas Webbe: but then neither of these was a Ranter under Davis's 'paradigm'.[123] Salmon got six months in jail, the statutory penalty, and was cashiered from the army. Coppe, Coppin, Tany and Franklin were also sentenced to imprisonment; the last three are also non-Ranters for Davis. Dozens of others were imprisoned, though exact figures are difficult to come by. Clarkson was sentenced to banishment by the House of Commons (illegally); but this sentence, as so often, was not carried out once it had achieved its object by producing a recantation.

In November 1650 'a soldier rode the wooden horse . . . with two muskets at each heel; another was whipped . . . 30 stripes for expressing some ranting opinions', a third was hanged by the thumbs.[124] Many others were flogged, including *officers* as well as army rank and file. At York 'W. Smith' was hanged; so was Alexander Agnew ('Jock of Broad Scotland') in Dumfries in 1656, for broadcasting what appear to be Ranter doctrines.[125] Cromwell cashiered Captain Covell in Scotland in October 1650: he may have been the William Covell who was to publish near-Digger pamphlets in 1659–60. In May 1651 Cromwell committed another Ranter, a lieutenant's wife, to the Marshall, telling her that she was too vile to live. We know no more of her fate.[126] Lt.-Col. Read was removed from the governorship of Poole in 1651 because he was accused of sheltering Ranters and Levellers. Major William Rainborough, brother of the Leveller Colonel Thomas, after being examined by a parliamentary committee, was discharged from the army and from the commission of the peace, and prohibited from executing the latter office in future. Captain Francis Freeman was cashiered (no Ranter for Davis).[127]

Recantations were what the authorities wanted, and in the long run

---

123. Smith, *Ranter Writings*, op. cit., p. 201.
124. *Leybourne-Popham Papers*, op. cit., p. 78; Morton, *World of the Ranters*, op. cit., p. 104.
125. *Mercurius Politicus*, 26 June–3 July 1656, 316, pp. 7064–6; cf. my *World Turned Upside Down*, op.cit., p. 209.
126. *Mercurius Politicus*, 29 May–15 June 1651, 52,p. 831; Abbott, *Cromwell's Writings*, op. cit., II, pp. 353–4, 420. For Covell see my *World Turned Upside Down*, op. cit., pp. 126, 345–6.
127. Levy, *Treason against God*, op. cit., pp. 253–64; Smith, *Ranter Writings*, op. cit., pp. 15–17; S.R. Gardiner, *History of the Commonwealth and Protectorate*, 1903, II, pp. 2–3; D.S. Katz, *Philo-Semitism and the Readmission of the Jews to England, 1603–1655*, Oxford University Press, 1982, pp. 198, 115–16; Thomas, *Religion and the Decline of Magic*, op. cit., p. 373; Morton, *World of the Ranters*, op. cit., pp. 98, 107; my *Experience of Defeat*, op. cit., pp. 40–1.

they usually got them. Since Ranters did not believe in the afterlife, they could not expect their reward there. Sixteenth-century Familists, from whom many thought Ranters derived, had practised and defended Nicodemism – recanting in the face of overwhelming power.[128] Readiness to recant was one of the big differences between Ranters and Quakers, and helps to explain their divergent reactions to persecution. It also shows how shrewd – if unrealistic – Hobbes was to insist that Leviathan would only become secure if belief in the afterlife could be abolished.[129] Most Ranters succumbed after a few months in the lethal jails that private enterprise provided. Robins held out for a year. His recantation had a devastating effect on his followers. So did Franklin's 'reclamation' by 'the execution-lash'. Salmon earned his release from prison in Coventry by recanting – with the usual Ranter ambiguity, though Davis tries to take what he said at face value (p. 35).[130]

Coppe had at least two shots at finding an acceptable form of words, aided by the drafting skills of John Dury and Marchamont Nedham – important figures, whose involvement testifies to the significance the government attached to Coppe. The final version of his recantation is a masterpiece of double-talk, which must have given that artist in words great pleasure to produce. He spoke of himself as 'the (supposed) author of the *Fiery flying Roll*', and admitted that 'some difficult, dark, hard, strange and almost unheard-of words and expressions of mine' had led to complaints, 'from a kind of zeal in some, from inveterate malice in others', 'who are by the author much pitied and dearly beloved'. Nevertheless, Coppe was satisfied with his way, 'the Lord by his spirit (in his word) revealing and opening to me many glorious things', 'unfathomable, unspeakable mysteries and glories being clearly revealed to me'. Although he admitted to having 'been strangely acted and by the devil deluded' yet 'in many things I have been injuriously dealt withal' by false reports. 'Yet if I might gain a kingdom, I could neither act nor speak [but] as I have done'.[131] Not much penitence here.

---

128. J.W. Martin, 'The Elizabethan Familists: a separatist group as perceived by their contemporaries', *Baptist Quarterly*, 1982, XXIX, p. 278. For Familist antecedents of Ranters, see Jean D. Moss, ' "Godded with God": Hendrik Niclaes and his Family of Love', *Transactions of the American Philosophical Society*, 1981, 71, pp. 58, 61–3; and *Reliquiae Baxterianae*, op. cit., p. 76.

129. Cf. p. 186 below.

130. Salmon, *Heights in Depths*, op. cit., *passim*; Smith, *Ranter Writings*, op. cit., p. 15; Friedman, *Blasphemy*, op. cit., p. 141, 149, 165. Webbe had recanted in 1646 (ibid., p. 233), but he remained of the same opinions still.

131. Smith, *Ranter Writings*, op. cit., pp. 118, 124–31.

Turning to specific accusations, Coppe asked how he could deny that sin exists when 'we, our kings, our rulers, our priests, our judges, all have sinned and gone astray?' How could he assert that man is God, when God's omnipotence permitted him freely to contradict himself in his actions? Coppe denied ever suggesting that God was 'in man or in the creature only, and nowhere else'. On the contrary: he held that God is in all things. He had been guilty of swearing; but far worse was the imposition of oaths of allegiance during the civil war, which led to 'false swearing, forswearing, and forced swearing', for which 'the land mourns. And I mourn'.[132] So always the 'Zealous and sincere Protestation Against several Errors' turns back on itself like a boomerang. Coppe repeatedly insisted that we are all sinners, and that the sins which he half-heartedly renounced (e.g. 'that community which is sinful or destructive to the well-being of a commonwealth' – not presumably the 'community' of which Coppe approved) were no worse than the sins to which his well-to-do adversaries were inclined. Not surprisingly, the only hearer who reported on the sermon of recantation which Coppe was made to preach was unconvinced by it.[133] This sermon was delivered at Burford. One wonders whether Coppe chose the place. Only two years earlier 'Judas Denne' had preached a more grimly serious recantation there to his former comrades in revolt.[134] Coppe was brave and resourceful, but he was also lucky in his timing.

Davis takes Coppe's ironical 'recantation' totally seriously, and imagines him to have undergone some sort of religious conversion (pp. 53–7). Few readers with a sense of humour and an appreciation of seventeenth-century prose will arrive at the same conclusion. Davis is clearly deaf to the subtler virtues of Ranter prose, which Morton stressed and Smith and Hopton have more recently demonstrated. Some Ranter writing shows skilled craftsmanship. The ironical, sometimes rumbustious prose of Coppe and Clarkson, the more elegiac writings of Bauthumley, Coppin and Salmon, are worth their place alongside those of Walwyn, Overton, Winstanley and Fox. All

---

132. ibid., pp. 137–45. Cf. my *Experience of Defeat*, op. cit., pp. 44–5.
133. John Tickell, *The Bottomless Pit Smoaking in Familisme*, 1651, p. 35. The full text of Coppe's recantation, together with his letter to Dury, is in Smith, *Ranter Writings*, op. cit., pp. 124–57. cf. Cohn, op. cit., pp. 327–8, 356. I tried to analyse Coppe's irony in *Experience of Defeat*, op. cit., pp. 44–5.
134. Cf. Coppe's reference in Part I of *The Fiery flying Roll*, published in 1650, to 'all the blood that hath ever been shed, from the blood of the righteous Abel to the blood of the last Levellers that were shot to death' (Smith, *Ranter Writings*, op. cit., p. 88). They were shot at Burford.

come out of the melting pot of the discussions of the forties, but the Ranters have their own special virtues. John Carey recently said that Ranter prose 'widens our understanding of human potential . . . at times . . . more fully than any other literary artefacts that have survived from the mid-17th century'.[135] High praise from the Merton Professor of English Literature at Oxford! Davis, who refuses to recognize the irony of Coppe's writing, is necessarily silent on this aspect of the Ranters. If no Ranters, how can there be Ranter prose?

Davis recognizes the existence of a long pre-history for Ranter ideas (pp. 92–100). The classic Ranter doctrines – mortalism, the eternity of matter, 'all comes by nature', heaven and hell are within us, God is in all men and women – were being denounced two generations before the name Ranter is heard – by William Perkins, Arthur Dent, Jeremy Cowderoy, Thomas Taylor, and in ballads.[136] Views which could be labelled 'Ranter' are to be found everywhere in Edwards's *Gangraena* (1646). The author of *The Ranters Bible*, one of the anti-Ranter tracts which Davis reprints, spoke in December 1650 of having associated with such 'diabolical meetings' for seven years (p. 172). But there is no reason why he should be believed.

For a long time we hear of such ideas only from their enemies, and so it is easy to underestimate their extent and their sophistication. But they erupted with the collapse of censorship and church courts, when ordinary people could discuss in public ideas which had long circulated underground. Muggleton speaks of the disintegration after 1640 of Puritanism into Presbyterians, Independents and Ranters – the latter including 'several . . . that were zealous before towards God'; an observation similar to those of Bunyan and early Quakers. This explains Muggleton's otherwise apparently odd remark that 'the Levellers were a branch that sprouted forth of the Ranters'. It makes sense if we think of an intellectual milieu from which Levellers, Ranters, Muggletonians and Quakers all emerged. Muggleton was clear at least that 'the Quakers, for the most part of them, they proceed from the Ranters.'[137]

135. John Carey, Foreword to Smith, ibid. Smith's Introduction contains a good analysis of Ranter literature. See now Postscript 2, pp. 191–2 below.
136. Cowderoy, *A Warning for Worldlings*, 1608, pp. 202–3: A. Dent, *The Opening of Heavens Gates*, 1617, p. 6; Thomas Taylor, *Works*, 1653, p. 106 (Taylor died in 1633); *The Roxburghe Ballads*, vol. III, ed. W. Chappell, 1880, pp. 109–10.
137. Muggleton, *Answer to Penington*, op. cit., p. 20; *Acts of the Witnesses*, op. cit., pp. 16–18; *True Interpretation*, op. cit., p. 106; *Looking Glass*, op. cit., pp. 55, 98. Cf. Gilbert, *Libertine School*, op. cit., Sig. Bv, pp. 19. 22.

Davis treats this body of ideas as theological (which it was) not as social and political (which it also was). He ignores the insistence of all the sources (Edwards as well as Perkins and Dent) that the ideas appealed especially to the lower classes – as Morton saw in the case of the Ranters, and as Lionel Lockier, Anthony Pearson and William Erbery confirmed.[138] The ideas also appealed, in the late forties, to the young, who had grown up to take free speculation for granted. Gerrard Winstanley, Robert Abbott, Anthony Pearson, Lionel Lockier and Bunyan testify to this.[139]

The years 1649–51, the Ranter years, were indeed traumatic, as Davis recognizes: army takeover, regicide, republic, abolition of House of Lords – all these burst on a society already expecting a better world, habituated to thinking in millenarian terms. The liberty of the forties had released hitherto suppressed plebeian irreligion and anti-clericalism. Capp comments on the anti-clericalism of popular almanacs – publications not permitted before 1640.[140] But why invent Ranters as a scapegoat for this breakthrough into print of traditional heresies? Here Davis gets into difficulties. He postulates that attempts were deliberately made to identify Ranterism with the cause of the Stuarts – *because* 'Ranterism was a powerful and dangerous slur' (p. 81). 'Powerful and dangerous'? How it became that is never explained except by circular arguments.

If we can agree that Ranters were neither fantasies of the imagination of contemporaries, nor of later historians, and that they were not straw men and women invented in order to be shot down: then the historian owes to them what he or she owes to all men and women studied in the past – sympathy and an attempt to understand. It is very difficult to enter into the minds of seventeenth-century Ranters. Some of their ideas seem bizarre and even repulsive. But we can imaginatively recapture some of the atmosphere of the crisis years 1649–51, during which Ranters most obviously flourished.

Millenarianism was widely shared among Puritans and sectaries, but Ranters lacked what Puritans and most sectaries enjoyed –

138. See pp. 159, 161, 167–8 above. Richard Sibbes in 1639 thought that antinomianism was an error 'of the meaner, ignorant sort of people' (*The Returning Backslider*, in *Works*, Edinburgh, 1862–4, II, p. 316).
139. Winstanley, 'England's Spirit Unfoulded', op.cit., p. 14; Abbott, *Young Mans Warning-Piece*, op. cit., Sig. A4; cf. Baxter, quoted by Robert Barclay, *The Inner Life of the Religious Societies of the Commonwealth*, 1876, p. 331. See also pp. 161–3 above, 183–6 below.
140. B.S. Capp, *Astrology and the Popular Press: English Almanacs, 1500–1800*, 1979, especially pp. 29, 47, 101, 155–6, 181.

religious faith and a confidence in the ways of God to men which enabled them to survive disappointments, postponements, delays. Ranters, having no such sheet anchor, drifted easily into hysterical extremism, either crying for instant divine intervention or rejecting God altogether. The Ranter years were those in which Independents and most sectaries aligned themselves with the apparently godly army generals against the less visibly godly Levellers. They accepted army and Cromwellian dictatorship at the price of postponing – it proved to be *sine die* – radical political and social reform. Ranters wanted immediate and far-reaching changes. 'It is the pleasure of the Father to turn the world upside down', wrote George Foster.[141] Most Ranters lacked sufficient confidence in God to wait and hope indefinitely.

We can catch perhaps something of the Ranter mood of impatience when we read Bunyan – who fiercely rejected the Ranters – admitting that men complained of 'seeming delays'. Christ 'accomplished all the first part of his priesthood in less than forty years'; but now 'he has been above in heaven above sixteen hundred years, and yet has not done'.[142] Some, like Milton, ceased to anticipate the millennium in the near future but continued to hope for better times on earth even if they had to come by a miracle. Milton's Samson – defeated, blinded, imprisoned, degraded – was able through faith to destroy the Philistine aristocracy and clergy, leaving a chance for the Hebrew people to regain their freedom.

> let but them
> Find courage to lay hold on this occasion.[143]

Bunyan was hoping that kings might after all cast out Antichrist, unlikely though that seemed under Charles II and James II – until James ended the antichristian persecution of God's people and began to eject the Anglican gentry from the commission of the peace.

We must think ourselves back into days when rational and sober men like Milton and Bunyan held such ideas if we are to understand how Ranters – superficially clever but ungrounded in religion and human learning – reacted to the experience of defeat.

The Ranter years saw the culmination of a decade of wide-ranging discussion; they intensified fears that religious toleration would lead to a collapse of all authority, social hierarchy and deference. The

---

141. Foster, *The Pouring Forth of the Last Vial*, 1650, p. 8.
142. Bunyan, *Solomon's Temple Spiritualized* (posthumous), in Offor, *Works of Bunyan*, op. cit., III, p. 507.
143. John Milton, *Samson Agonistes*, lines 1715–16. Cf. p. 222 below.

respectable were appalled by Ranter ridicule of the new rulers of England, the hypocritical godly rich as they saw them; and by the Ranter challenge to male supremacy. Davis tries to reassure himself that even after 1649 'there was little that was genuinely revolutionary, at least in intention, about the revolution' (p. 131). Those words between commas make the point: the activities and propaganda of Ranters went far beyond the intention of ruling groups and threatened to escape from their control, just as separatist congregations had escaped from control by parson and squire. Levellers and Diggers had been forcibly suppressed in 1649–50 because they appeared to present a challenge from the lower orders to existing social hierarchies: the Quakers were soon to be persecuted for similar reasons.[144] Coppin's followers in Rochester in 1653 were called 'church and state Levellers'.[145]

From the point of view of the orthodox, Ranters posed in its sharpest form the question of religious toleration. It was not merely that they expressed heretical views, but that they did so in such a provocative way that these views had to be countered. But the counter-attack was almost as dangerous to orthodoxy as anything the Ranters themselves wrote. The yellow-press pamphlets indulged the sexual fantasies of their authors, and so presumably won a wide popular readership. By this popularity they disseminated the Ranter ideas which they were denouncing. Treating the resurrection, heaven and hell as allegories, denying the authority of the Scriptures, replacing the oligarchy of the elect by God in all men and women, attacks on private property, a state church, and government in general, whether of king, parliament or army – these picked up socially and politically threatening ideas which had a long history but had rarely appeared in print. All publicity is good publicity in so far as it draws attention to something which many had not previously thought about. Perhaps the anti-Ranter pamphlets worried the orthodox even more than Ranter literature. Merely to think about the topics the Ranters raised seemed abominable not only to the rulers of England in the early fifties but also to their royalist opponents and to many of the sectaries. Ranter literature and anti-Ranter pamphlets ensured that Ranter ideas were made known to a far wider public than itinerant preachers could have reached. It was time to draw a line. 'Before the late act against the

---

144. B. Reay, *The Quakers and the English Revolution*, 1985, *passim*.
145. Walter Rosewell, *The Serpents Subtilty Discovered*, 1656, p. 16.

Ranters, they spake boldly', gloated Tickell; 'now they dare not'.[146] This was an important victory.

The Ranters indeed were talkers rather than doers. The violent and provocative language of some of them got no further than abstract threats of divine wrath to come, after which utopia would arrive. Because they had no organization, the implicit threats contained in their writings never became part of a social and political programme like those of Levellers, Diggers or Fifth Monarchists. Ranter ideas were spread sufficiently widely for Winstanley to think it necessary to attack them; but this was a *succès de scandale* rather than the deeply rooted popularity of a Lilburne or the more limited influence of Winstanley himself. Ranters could relatively easily be stopped from preaching and publishing, could be made to recant: the ideas were driven back underground.[147]

What can we conclude? My object has been to cite witnesses who encountered Ranter groups and individuals not in hostile pamphlets but in private conversations, in discussions in taverns and alehouses, or in mass meetings. I believe I have established that there were enough of them to prove the existence of Ranters. Royalists blamed them on Puritans, Puritans accused Ranters of royalism, of adoring Laud's portrait. All conservatives blamed religious toleration for allowing natural man to speak naturally. Ranters were caricatured and vilified – and they themselves often asked for trouble by their provocative assaults on conventional respectability. Much later, Muggletonians and Quakers, whose ideas and personnel were drawn from the Ranter milieu, joined in the attack. The social and political content of Ranter ideas, of which Davis takes little account, seems to me an adequate explanation of the deep hostility which they aroused among the respectable classes. Alexander Ross in 1655, and Edward Garland in 1657, both laid special stress on Coppin's critique of magistracy and ministry.[148] Claudius Gilbert, also in 1657, emphasized in his title *The Magistrates Power in Religious Matters*; he

146. Tickell, *Bottomless Pit*, op. cit., p. 37; Friedman, *Blasphemy*, op. cit., Ch. 17, *passim*. Cf. pp. 230–2 below. Tickell's evidence confutes Davis's suggestion – otherwise implausible – that the act was not directed against the Ranters.
147. Winstanley, 'Englands Spirit Unfoulded', op. cit., pp. 14–15; Sabine, *Works of Winstanley*, op. cit., 399–403. In this and the preceding paragraph I have drawn on ideas in Pavlova, 'Ranters and Winstanley', op cit., pp. 118, 128–9, 133 and *passim*. See also the doctoral thesis of Elizabeth Tuttle, *Discours Puritaines et Processus Révolutionnaire en Angleterre au XVII Siècle*, University of Paris, I, 12, 1987, Ch. 18. I am grateful to Dr Tuttle for giving me a copy of this thesis.
148. For Ross, see p. 163 above; Garland, *An Answer*, op. cit., pp. 52–4; see p. 158 above.

used the recantation of William Franklin and Mary Gadbury under 'the execution-lash' as an argument for violent repression. In 'this libertine age', 'external reformation is better than none at all, and the form of godliness is good though formality be naught'.[149] Many must have shared such views in the years after Nayler's flogging.

We should not stress Ranter libertinism, or their rejection of the work ethic, to the exclusion of their political and social views, including their opposition to tithes. Contemporaries saw social dangers in Ranter theology. Mortalism, for instance, 'the chief doctrine of the Ranters', was described by *Mercurius Politicus* in February 1657 as 'destructive to the conveniency of government, seeing it at once destroyeth both the hope of reward and the fear of punishment after this life is ended'.[150] Bunyan, who also attacked the rich, was no radical; but he too was damned as 'a downright Ranter', and 'an outlaw to human society'.[151] Ranters had dangerous ideas, which they were confident would spread given free discussion. 'In little time I should see all professors turn to the ways of the Ranters', one of Bunyan's Ranter friends told him.[152]

HISTORIOGRAPHICAL

Let us praise Davis where we can. He usefully reprints the anonymous *A Justification of the Mad Crew* (1650) (pp. 138–55). He asks some interesting questions, whatever we may think of his answers. His discussion of the theology of individual Ranters is the best part of his book. He has studied exhaustively the anti-Ranter propaganda literature of the late 1640s and early 1650s. He is less secure in his historiography. That all-seeing historian, S.R. Gardiner, by no means 'passed over in silence' the Ranters, as Davis states.[153] Even before Gardiner, David Masson, who was extremely well informed about mid-seventeenth-century England, had firmly distinguished between Ranters and the myth of the Ranters. 'Some low printers and booksellers made a trade on the public curiosity about the Ranters.' 'There is plenty of testimony, however,' he continues, 'that there was

149. Gilbert, *Libertine School*, op. cit., pp. 26, 42, 49. *Mercurius Politicus* in 1659 carried an advertisement for Edward Reynel's *An Advice against Libertines* (2–9 June 1659, 570, p. 492).
150. *Mercurius Politicus*, 12–19 February 1656–7, 349, p. 7064. I owe this quotation to Barry Reay.
151. My *Turbulent, Factious and Seditious People*, pp. 132–3; cf. pp. 174–7 above.
152. Bunyan, *Grace Abounding*, op. cit., pp. 16–17.
153. Gardiner, *History of the Commonwealth*, op cit., II, pp. 2–3; cf. III, pp. 260–1. See Davis, p. 4.

a real sect of the name, pretty widely spread in low neighbourhoods in towns.' That gets all the main points – the yellow press, the widespread existence of Ranters, especially among the poor and in towns. And Masson concludes 'there were probably variants of Ranters theologically'.[154] If Professor Davis had read and pondered over that remarkably accurate summing up we might have been spared his book.

Robert Barclay's great book, *The Inner Life of the Religious Societies of the Commonwealth*, published as long ago as 1876, has a chapter on the Ranters, 'large numbers' of whom 'were swept into the ranks of the Quakers'. He prints extracts from the writings of Salmon and Bauthumley. He wisely cites mainly John Holland Porter ('a temperate writer') from the Ranters' critics, as well as Reeve and Muggleton.[155] Rufus Jones in 1909 and William Braithwaite in 1912 have a great deal to say about Ranters. Jones recognized that the Ranters were not a sect, and got the chronology right when he said that Fox 'out of Ranter communities . . . built up strong meetings'.[156] Firth discusses the Ranters in his continuation of Gardiner.[157] C.B. Whiting in *Studies in English Puritanism from the Restoration to the Revolution, 1660–1688* (1931) found the Ranters sufficiently important even in that later period to discuss them in a chapter on 'the minor sects'. He too recognized that the Ranters were 'not an organized body', and did not agree among themselves.[158] So it was not really necessary for Cohn to invent the Ranters in 1957. In 1972 Norman Burns devoted much of the second chapter of his invaluable *Christian Mortalism from Tyndale to Milton* to a searching analysis of the peculiar Ranter combination of antinomianism, pantheism and annihilationist mortalism.[159]

Davis ignores the pioneer Theodor Sippell, whose *Zur Vorgeschichte des Quäkertums* (Giessen, 1920) prepared for his *Werdendes Quäkertum* (Stuttgart, 1937) which surveys the whole Ranter literature. Davis castigates the anthropologist James Mooney, who in 1896 'sadly' confused John Robins with the Ranters, thus 'perpetuating' a 'muddle'

---

154. Masson, *The Life of John Milton*, 1859–80, V, pp. 17–19.
155. Barclay, *Inner Life*, op. cit., Ch. XIX and appendix, especially pp. 409, 418, 420–1. The tone of Davis's references to Barclay suggest that he has not read his book (pp. 4–5).
156. Jones, *Mystical Religion*, op. cit., pp. 462, 481, and Ch. XIX, *passim*; Braithwaite, *Beginnings of Quakerism*, op. cit., *passim*.
157. C.H. Firth, *Last Years of the Protectorate*, 1909, I, pp. 81, 84, 88.
158. Whiting, *Studies in English Puritanism*, op. cit., especially pp. 171–3, 243–4, 272–83.
159. Burns, *Christian Mortalism*, Harvard University Press, 1972.

shared by most of Robins's contemporaries (and most historians) (pp. 5, 20). Davis rebukes serious historians like David Underdown and Philip Gura for not anticipating his abolition of the Ranters (p. 12). He is painfully condescending to Anne Laurence, who was so foolish as to discover and publish Ranter poems (p. 11). He uses Frank McGregor's seminal thesis when it suits him, but more often suppresses its well-considered arguments when he dislikes them (p. 31). He is rude about McGregor's reference to the usefulness of Edwards's *Gangraena*, and laughs at me for saying we need a critical edition because so many of its facts stand up to investigation (pp. 126-9). On p. 130 a quotation is wrongly attributed to me; and the 'fabrication' on p. 34 is Professor Davis's rather than mine. He misspells the names of two writers who have contributed much to our understanding of seventeenth-century history – Dona Torr and C.B. Macpherson.

As I was doing the research which culminated in *The World Turned Upside Down*, analogies between the cultural circumstances of the period I was describing and of the period in which I was writing forced themselves upon me. I found some Ranter ideas interesting in that connection – not least their detestation of holy conservative humbug, not extinct today. I admitted recently to having perhaps overstressed Ranter libertinism, at the expense of the political principles which Coppe, Clarkson, Foster and others expressed. I was still fighting an old battle against 'the Puritan Revolution', and enjoyed emphasizing that libertinism was preached at the height of this revolution. I was also enchanted by the vigour and resonance of most Ranter prose.

Jerome Friedman's *Blasphemy, Immorality and Anarchy: The Ranters and The English Revolution* (Ohio University Press, 1987) clearly went to press before Davis's book appeared. Friedman's is not the definitive work on the Ranters which we need; but it contains some useful points. Friedman carefully studies and analyses the ideas of fifteen individual Ranters, and concludes that 'despite significant differences, it would appear that Ranters recognized one another and the common core of views that each expressed' (p. 74). This is a valuable corrective to Davis. Friedman stresses the political component of Ranter thinking – an attack on *all* churches and all governments, parliamentary and army rule being no better than that of the king and much more expensive. Many Ranters, he insists, wrote from the point of view of the poor, and called for expropriation of the rich. Friedman emphasizes – as Davis does not – that this aspect of their thought was given prominence in the anti-Ranter literature. He draws attention to the influence, or alleged influence, of Ranters on rank-and-file soldiers in the army, and to the alarm which this naturally caused the authorities (pp. 57–8, 131–4, Part II, *passim*, especially Conclusion). (In 1650 Tany incited the army to dissolve the Rump of the Long Parliament.)[160] Wiser than Davis, Friedman stresses Ranter expertise at double-talk as a means of evading the intention of the Blasphemy Act (Chapter 17, *passim*).

But Friedman's main interest hitherto has been in medieval and Reformation theology: he is not strong on the seventeenth-century historical background. For the definitive work on the Ranters we still have to wait for Frank McGregor's revision of the thesis on which Davis relied so heavily and which he misused so flagrantly. Fortunately we shall not have to wait long. And then the ghost of the abolished Ranters can be laid to rest.

CONCLUSION

A final problem remains: why did Professor Davis think it worth while expending so much time and scholarly effort on so dubious a project? The book tells us something about his prepossessions: he thinks the loaded word 'deviance' appropriate to the Ranter image (pp. 85, 95). It reminds us of his earlier idiosyncratic interpretation of the gentle communist Gerrard Winstanley, whom Davis clearly regards as a pre-incarnation of Josef Stalin. In Winstanley's ideal community, Davis argued, 'slavery replaced imprisonment'; 'flogging, judicial violence and torture . . . were accepted as essential and continuing parts of the machinery of social discipline'.[161] In the present book he still refers to Winstanley's 'utopianized totalitarianism' (pp. 24, 135). This is unlike anything that anybody else has ever read into Winstanley: it tells us more about Davis than about the Digger. He clearly does not like the seventeenth-century radicals.

After my brief historiographical survey it is not necessary to comment at length on Davis's allegation that the rediscovery (or invention) of the Ranters in the 1970s was part of a conspiracy between members of the Historians' Group of the British Communist Party. This is insulting to the late A.L. Morton and myself, and it will hardly commend itself to Norman Cohn, the scholar who preceded

---

160. Tany, *The Nations Right* op. cit., p. 24.
161. Davis, 'Gerrard Winstanley', op. cit., pp. 78, 92. I gave my reasons for rejecting this interpretation in *Religion and Politics*, op. cit., Ch. 11.

Morton and who was never in any way connected with the Communist Party – far from it. It is also demonstrably untrue. Morton published *The World of the Ranters* thirteen years after I had ceased to be associated with him in the Historians' Group; my *World Turned Upside Down* came two years later still. We were an unconscionable time in executing our nefarious plot, which must have been hatched before 1957. Worse: Davis himself points out that in *The Century of Revolution* (1961), published four years after I had left the Communist Party, I dismissed the Ranters as 'associated with the lunatic fringe' (Davis, p. 4). Apparently I had forgotten then about our plot, though I recollected it again when I wrote *The World Turned Upside Down*. Even fiction should make chronological sense.

In any case, the idea that the Ranters offered a model acceptable to Communist Party propagandists in the second half of the twentieth century is implausible. Morton and I disagreed on our seventeenth-century favourites. He liked the Levellers, I preferred the Diggers – not the Stalinist Winstanley invented by Davis but the Winstanley of the seventeenth century. But we were neither of us in the business of inventing models for the twentieth century. On the assumption that all Cretans are liars, Davis will not be impressed by my categorical assertion that his idea of a Communist Party plot is ludicrous; but anyone who coolly considers the likelihood of a serious and dedicated scholar like A.L. Morton taking part in such a plot (not to mention Cohn) will I think agree that it is absurd.

There are those who, regardless of the evidence, will think any stick good enough to beat Marxist historians with: they will take comfort from Davis's book, though some may regret having to beat Norman Cohn too. There are others who, not being experts on seventeenth-century history themselves, will be confused by Davis's appearance of scholarship, and by his question 'If there were no Ranters, why did so many Englishmen apparently believe that there were?' (p. 76). That is why I have tried at perhaps excessive length to set the record straight. The real mystery for me is Davis's motivation. The analogy between the supposed invention of Ranters in the seventeenth and twentieth centuries may tell us something about his mode of thought. Conservative conspirators (and Quakers) invented the Ranters in the mid-seventeenth century; communist conspirators (plus the inexplicable Norman Cohn) rediscovered (or reinvented) them in our own day. The opposing arguments are both necessary if we are to avoid the just possible alternative, that the Ranters did in fact exist. Why is it so important for Davis to prove that they did not? What is he frightened of?

POSTSCRIPT 1

For the record, and to show how easy it is, here are a few more examples of persons who discussed Ranters and their views in and after 1660. The list could be vastly extended. Clarkson mentioned Ranters together with Baptists and Quakers in *The Lost sheep Found* (1660). Samuel Butler's 'Character of a Ranter' suggests some knowledge of the type.[162] Samuel Pordage, son of John, criticized Ranters in 1661.[163] Muggleton reported that a Ranter whom he had sentenced to eternal damnation in 1653 was still alive fifteen years later, and still a Ranter.[164] John Goodwin, in a work published posthumously in 1670, had a tolerant comment on the Ranters.[165] If the Ranters didn't exist, it would help us to understand restoration comedy if we invented them. Laura Brown has illustrated the influence of their ideas on the playwrights, though so far few have followed up her insight.[166] Aphra Behn wrote a comedy about *The Widow Ranter*, and throughout her *Love Letters from a Nobleman to his Sister* she is conducting a serious discussion of sexual relations outside church marriage. In *Oroonoko* and elsewhere her work shows traces of utopian primitivism and sceptical libertinism which also might have been influenced by Ranter ideas. Oroonoko 'ever made a jest' of the Trinity.[167] Elsewhere I have suggested that such influences can be found in Rochester and Charles Blount.[168] Traherne in his posthumous *Christian Ethicks* attacks 'self-conceited but shallow Ranters', who wanted to abolish religion and thought there was no distinction between vice and virtue, that sin was feigned to awe the world.[169]

162. Clarkson, *The Lost sheep Found*, op. cit., p. 39; Butler, *Characters and Passages from Notebooks*, Cambridge University Press, 1908, pp. 67–8; cf. *Poetical Works*, 1854, II, p. 286. See my *Writing and Revolution*, op. cit., p. 285.
163. Pordage, *Mundorum Explicatio*, 1661, pp. 95–6, quoted in my *Experience of Defeat*, op. cit., p. 230.
164. Muggleton, *Spiritual Epistles*, op. cit., p. 241.
165. Goodwin, *A Being filled with the Spirit*, 1867 edn, p. 473.
166. L. Brown, *English Dramatic Form, 1660–1760: An Essay in Generic History*, Yale University Press, 1981, pp. 41–8. See pp. 225–7 below.
167. Maureen Duffy, *The Passionate Shepherdess: Aphra Behn, 1640–89*, 1977, pp. 131, 177; Aphra Behn, *Love Letters*, 1684–7, *passim*; *Oroonoko*, in Aphra Behn, *Works*, ed. M. Summers, 1915, pp. 131–2, 139, 160–6, 175, 196. I return to Aphra Behn in Chapter 11.
168. My *Writing and Revolution*, op. cit., pp. 231–5, 238–41, 274–5, 304–9; *World Turned Upside Down*, op. cit., pp. 410–14. For Rochester, see M. Neill, 'Heroic heads and humble tails: sex, politics and the Restoration comic rake', *The Eighteenth Century: Theory and Interpretation*, 1983, 24, p. 131.
169. I cite from M. Bottrall's 1962 edition, to which she gives the title *The Way to Blessedness: Thomas Traherne's Christian Ethics (1675)*, p. 179. See also Julia J. Smith, 'Attitudes towards conformity and nonconformity in Thomas Traherne', *Hobbes Studies*, 1988, I, p. 31.

Milton, like Bunyan, fought a running battle with Ranters in his last great poems, as I am not alone in suggesting.[170] William Penn was busy criticizing Ranter errors in 1673 as was Sterry in 1675; the Quakers' most professional theologian, Robert Barclay, in 1676 published a whole treatise on *The Anarchy of the Ranters*. In his Preface to Fox's *Journal* in 1694 Penn was still attacking Ranters. Whiting cites references to Ranter groups in the 1670s and 1680s: they were still in existence in the early eighteenth century. There was a sect of 'Coppinists' in 1706. The French prophets in Queen Anne's reign were accused of 'ranterism' as well as of 'levelling'.[171]

At the turn of the century there were people called Ranters in Cumberland, the Midlands, Nottingham, near Inverness, and elsewhere.[172] In the 1740s and 1750s John Wesley encountered Ranter beliefs in Birmingham and Dublin.[173] George Horne, future Bishop of Norwich, was familiar with them in the 1750s when he was a Fellow of Magdalen College, Oxford.[174] Morton suggested Ranter influences on Blake: Burns may also have known about the Ranters.[175] Ranter doctrines were being taught in London in the 1780s, and there was a Swedenborgian with the interesting name of Joseph Salmon.[176]

After the restoration, as we should expect, religious radicals emigrated to the New World. I gave some examples of Ranters in the West Indies.[177] Claudius Gilbert in 1657 described 'whimsy's island (vulgo Road-Island near New England)' as 'the receptacle of notionists'.[178] D.S. Lovejoy, who has traced Ranters in America, confirms their presence on Rhode Island, as well as on Long Island and

---

170. My *World Turned Upside Down*, op. cit., pp. 395–404; *Milton and the English Revolution*, pp. 112–15, 160–1, 243–50, 298–303, Ch. 24 *passim*, pp. 329–33, 343–6, 396–8; J.G. Turner, *One Flesh: Paradisal Marriage and Sexual Relations in the Age of Milton*, Oxford University Press, 1987, especially pp. 37, 84–96, 164, 168, 177; K.W.F. Stavely, *Puritan Legacies: Paradise Lost and the New England Tradition*, Cornell University Press, 1987, especially pp. 55, 70–1, 77–8, 121–2.

171. Penn, *The Spirit of Alexander the Coppersmith*, 1673, pp. 8–9; Whiting, *Studies in English Puritanism*, op cit., pp. 277, 283; Hillel Schwartz, *The French Prophets: The History of a Millenarian Group in Eighteenth Century England*, California University Press, 1980, pp. 128, 131, 143. For Sterry see p. 168 above.

172. My *Religion and Politics*, op. cit., p. 108.

173. Wesley, *Journal*, 1864, I, pp. 10–11, 173, 270, 308.

174. Margaret Jacob, *The Radical Enlightenment: Pantheists, Freemasons and Republicans*, 1981, p. 98.

175. Morton, *The Matter of Britain*, 1966, pp. 98–121.

176. J.F.C. Harrison, *The Second Coming: Popular Millenarianism, 1780–1850*, 1979, pp. 14, 233.

177. *People and Ideas*, op. cit., pp. 167–75. For Ranter-type ideas in America before 1660 see Philip Gura, *A Glimpse of Sion's Glory*, op. cit., *passim*.

178. Gilbert, *Libertine School*, op. cit., p. 35.

elsewhere. Their history in America, he thinks, was more continuous than in England.[179] Some of our information about these Ranters comes from Quakers, and to that extent may be open to Davis's scepticism (p. 90); but by no means all. Norman Burns noticed surviving Ranter attitudes in early nineteenth-century American Quakerism.[180] Aphra Behn's *The Widow Ranter* was set in Virginia; Edward Taylor at the end of the seventeenth or early in the eighteenth century was still concerned with 'Ranting' and recognizable Ranter doctrines.[181]

POSTSCRIPT 2

Since I finalized this chapter in October 1988 Nigel Smith has published *Perfection Proclaimed: Language and Literature in English Radical Religion, 1640-1660* (Oxford University Press, 1989). Dr Smith has read Davis's book and refers courteously to his 'subtle and astute attempt to show that the Ranters were not a movement or even a collection of individuals with broadly similar ideas'. Smith does not bother to refute this view. 'If the Ranters were a fiction,' he observes, 'they were one of their own as well as others' making. It is the connections which can be made between those called Ranters and other radical Puritans which are significant' (pp. 8-9). In the remaining 340 pages Smith ignores Davis's views. He discusses Ranter ideas on a par with those of other unorganized groups for whose existence there is solid evidence – Seekers, Familists, Behmenists (pp. 109, 133, 181, 185, 188). He deals, learnedly and intelligently, with Ranter theology and 'the mystical element in Ranter writing' (p. 25), with their 'doctrine of an inner divine presence' (p. 240), 'the monism of the Ranters' (p. 216), 'Ranter pantheism' (p. 246), 'the Ranters' hypostasy' (p. 70),[182] 'the intuitive "reason" of the Ranters' (p. 250), 'Ranter prophets' and 'prophetic writing' (pp. 25, 65-72, 250), 'Ranter experience' (p. 325), the Ranters' 'register of social

179. Lovejoy, *Religious Enthusiasm in the New World: Heresy to Revolution*, Harvard University Press, 1985, especially pp. 141-3; cf. P. Linebaugh, 'All the Atlantic mountains shook', in *Reviving the English Revolution*, op. cit., p. 205.

180. Burns, *Christian Mortalism*, op. cit., p. 85.

181. E. Stanford (ed.) *The Poems of Edward Taylor*, Yale University Press, 1963, pp. 299-300, 309.

182. 'Hypostasy', the *Oxford English Dictionary* tells us, is 'obsolete', 'rare'. It can mean 'the substance of the urine'; or 'personality', personal existence, as distinguished from 'nature' and from 'substance' – e.g. the three hypostases of the Godhead. I assume the latter sense applies here.

complaint' (p. 69), 'the Ranter imagination', 'Ranter language', 'Ranter terminology' (pp. 174, 250).

Throughout Smith refers to 'Ranter writings', 'Ranter tracts' (pp. 15, 66, 68, 181, 316–17), as though such things actually existed. He discusses 'the rhythmic intention in Ranter discourse' (p. 337), 'the Ranter interest in gesture' which inspired their 'collective and ritually celebrative' dancing (p. 338). Smith contrasts Ranter use of parentheses as 'a means of exploring prophetic identity in relation to the speaking subject' with Winstanley's use (pp. 335–6). His book greatly advances our knowledge and understanding of the Ranters. It will be difficult to dissent from his conclusion that 'the image of the Ranters which was used to exclude or vilify the more extreme Quakers had actual roots in the pamphlets of Coppe, the early Clarkson and Salmon, as well as in Nayler and Perrot' (p. 346).

Smith produces two quotations which I had missed, showing how contemporaries visualized the Ranters. Francis Fullwood in 1651 accused 'the perfectionist Robert Wilkinson . . . of going beyond the heights of Socrates, Plato and the Ranters'. Smith uses this to illustrate 'what radical religious discourse was trying to do'.[183] He also cites the publisher of John Everard's sermons, Rapha Harford, who in 1653 placed Everard at 'a mid-point on the scale of "experimental" religion, between "Rationalist" and "Formalist" on the one hand, and "Familist" and "Ranter" on the other'.[184]

---

183. Fullwood, *Vindiciae mediorum et mediatoris*, 1651, p. 86, quoted by Smith, *Perfection Proclaimed*, op. cit., p. 17.
184. Everard, *Some Gospel-Treasures Opened*, op. cit., cited by Smith, *Perfection Proclaimed*, op. cit., p. 133.

10

Literature and the English Revolution

> Bureaucratic output of ink-soiled paper does not and never
> has embraced all the parameters of human life with which an
> historian might appropriately concern himself.
> W.H. McNeill, 'A defence of world history', *Transactions of the
> Royal Historical Society*, 1982, p. 76

My object is to ask how far literature can help us to understand the
mid-seventeenth-century crisis in England. Keith Thomas, best of
English historians writing today, said in his latest book that although
it is unfashionable for historians to use literary sources, 'there is
nothing to surpass [imaginative literature] as a guide to the thoughts
and feelings of at least the more articulate sections of the population'.
J.H. Hexter, with whom I don't often have the pleasure of agreeing,
wrote 'Sometimes a passage from an imaginative genius provides one
with an intensity of insight quite unattainable any other way'.[1] Lauro
Martines has recently written a book, *Society and History in English
Renaissance Verse* (Oxford, 1985), to argue for a discipline combining
history and literature, with its own philosophy and techniques. Well,
perhaps.

But there is a formidable amount of opposition to overcome. One
respected seventeenth-century historian who shall be nameless compiled a useful bibliography for students in which he quite unashamedly
declared that his acquaintance with and feeling for cultural history
(including literature) was 'vestigial'; and the bibliography reflected
this. Need I add, I think his history lacks a dimension? No doubt there

---

1. Keith Thomas, *Man and the Natural World: Changing Attitudes in England, 1500–1800*,
1983, p. 16; J.H. Hexter, 'Property, monopoly and Shakespeare's *Richard II*', in
P. Zagorin (ed.) *Culture and Politics: From Puritanism to the Enlightenment*, California
University Press, 1980, p. 18.

are similar areas of opposition from 'the-words-on-the-page' school of literary critics, if it still exists.

Pressure for the fusion of literature and history seems to come from the literature side, rather than from historians – as the editors of *Literature and History* ruefully admitted recently, and as was shown at a recent history workshop in Oxford. Historians have long been inoculated against literary sources: they are not impartial, not factual, individual imaginations cannot be objectively tested. But recently – great revelation – it is beginning to be recognized that the official documents on which administrative and political historians rely, and even the private correspondence of the gentry, may be subject to exactly the same criticisms. Such sources convey what ruling persons wanted to believe, not necessarily what actually happened. For that we have to go to other sources, including literary. Tudor legislation, we are told, was an essay in the optative mood. Not that this is true only of Tudor legislation. When I was in the army there used to be things called ACIs – army council instructions. These were thought up by great men in the War Office, and sent round to all units. There, if they happened to order something that the C.O. or the adjutant thought desirable, they would be put into operation. If not, they remained fluttering on the notice board, totally disregarded. Tudor and Stuart JPs had a similar attitude.

Take for instance peasant and popular disturbances. Accounts in state papers come normally from local JPs, who happened also to be local landowners. Of course they don't give the peasant point of view; but that could be allowed for. Worse is the myth which almost all of them share – that behind every popular disturbance there must be a hidden leader from the gentry, who has either a private or a political or religious grudge to work off. Now literary historians can cope with this more sceptically. They know the dramatic convention that any successful plebeian leader will turn out in Act V to be a prince either in disguise or unbeknown to himself. Even Robin Hood becomes Earl of Huntingdon. We are beginning to see that history from on top has its own assumptions, which history from below calls in question. We must not forget Blake's wise remark, 'Only a scoundrel believes public records to be true.' That is why some administrative/political historians hate and fear history from below. Edward Thompson – poet as well as historian – has stood archive history on its head by taking seriously a group of documents that previous historians rejected – the reports of *agents provocateurs*.[2] Historians relying on archive documents ought to subject

2. Professor R.L. Greaves has made equally effective use of similar material in *Deliver Us from Evil: The Radical Underground in Britain, 1660–1663*, Oxford University Press, 1986.

them to the same *sort* of criticisms as those who use literary sources. Literary historians have the great advantage that they know a myth when they see one; they recognize the truth of Mencken's definition of a platitude: 'It is universally accepted, and it is not true.' They can see through (or some of them can see through) not only Coriolanus but also the self- and class-interested patriotism of Volumnia and Menenius – which does not mean accepting the tribunes, who are shown leading their followers after the event, and working behind the scenes rather than in public.

Study of seventeenth-century English history is in its normal state of crisis. There has been a loss of nerve by English historians in face of controversies over the seventeenth-century Revolution. It is – or was – fashionable with one group of historians to say that there was no revolution in seventeenth-century England. The civil war had no long-term causes. It was the result of a series of accidents and coincidences. Now this is not an easy argument to refute. If you concentrate your gaze on the years 1640–2, or even a few years earlier, because you *know* there are no long-term causes, then of course it all seems accidental, the product of ruling personalities. This school of historians looks mainly at public documents, debates in parliament, the expressed views of the gentry, all of which are subject to the conventions of seventeenth-century political discourse and therefore potentially misleading. Study of the archives of church courts in the 1630s convinced Peter Laslett that 'all of our ancestors were literal Christian believers, all of the time'. It was bad luck that within a year or two Keith Thomas's majestic *Religion and the Decline of Magic* proved this totally wrong. But the merest sampling of literary evidence from the 1640s and 1650s could have saved Laslett from his bloomer. Similarly the fact that 'witnesses in ecclesiastical courts . . . left no doubt that sexual intercourse outside marriage was *universally* condemned'.[3] No doubt witnesses before courts in eastern Europe used to leave no doubt that they thought socialism superior to capitalism. Again the uncensored literature of the forties and fifties could have taught Laslett better.

Some of the best history of seventeenth-century England recently has been written by literary critics and literary historians. Faced with a crisis in English culture, they have not wished (or many of them have not wished) to explain it away as a series of accidents and coincidences. I am thinking especially of Muriel Bradbrook, Harriett

3. P. Laslett, *The World We Have Lost*, 1965, pp. 71–3, 130; my italics.

Hawkins, J.N. King, Alan Sinfield, Barbara Lewalski, Joseph Wittreich, Jonathan Dollimore, Margot Heinemann, Simon Shepherd, David Norbrook, Martin Butler, Dena Goldberg, Stephen Greenblatt, Michael Wilding, Catherine Belsey, Christine Berg and Philippa Berry. For the restoration period there are Michael McKeon, Stephen Zwicker, Annabel Patterson, Warren Chernaik, Raman Selden, Susan Staves, Laura Brown, James Turner, Keith Stavely. These are the names I happen to have come across: no offence is intended to the many I have not so far encountered.

Not much is left now of the traditional picture of pre-revolutionary English literature as dominated by an acceptance of conservative values. 'The Great Chain of Being,' stretching upwards from immaterial objects through the vegetable and animal creations to man, to angels, to God, was the world picture favoured by those who benefited by a hierarchichal society: king, landlords and gentlemen on top, merchants, artisans, yeomen and peasants below. But the theory of degree, Conrad Russell observed, does not go well with an inflationary spiral.[4] Some merchants were becoming richer than some peers, many yeomen were thriving to gentility while others and some gentlemen, even some peers, sank into poverty. The old ideology was queried as social reality changed. Statements of it in Elizabethan literature no doubt caught the eye because they were heavily emphasized. But we can see now that the emphasis was defensive, a reaction to challenge. J.N. King, Sinfield, Lewalski and Norbrook have shown the potentially radical implications of protestantism from the start, the tensions between the supremacy of the individual conscience and any form of political authority. Sinfield has plotted the way in which protestantism led to secularism and to Hobbes, and suggests that Elizabethan tragedy contributed to raising questions about the existence of a benevolent God. Dena Goldberg, in a most impressive study, stresses Webster's 'philosophical anti-authoritarianism', his 'aversion to . . . all venerable, reassuring and self-evident truths'. In his plays, 'the more didactic the speech is, the more suspicious is the message'. The speaker is 'usually either out of touch with reality or up to no good'.[5]

Joseph Wittreich has pointed out that 'the common tendency to read *Lear* and others of Shakespeare's plays as containing "conservative

---

4. See p. 203 below.
5. Alan Sinfield, *Literature in Protestant England, 1560–1660*, 1983, especially pp. 101, 128–30, 140–1; Goldberg, *Between Worlds*, op. cit., pp. 8–13. See now David Morse, *England's Time of Crisis: from Shakespeare to Milton*, 1989, pp. 16, 24, 30, 173 and *passim*.

answers to radical questions" obscures the possibility, noted by Katharine Stockholder, that "the play may be asking radical questions of the conservative answers within it".' Through the Elizabethan and Jacobean poets, 'the whole apocalyptic drama, once regarded as a struggle involving only divine figures, is reconceived to allow for, indeed to require, human participation'. Joan Rees has shown Samuel Daniel reacting away from traditional providentialist history.[6] John Davies of Hereford in 1603 put forward theories of the relationship of political power to property which anticipate Harrington fifty years later. By 1641 Francis Quarles was able to be much more specific: 'If thou endeavourest to make a republic in a nation where the gentry abounds, thou shalt hardly proceed in that design. And if thou wouldest erect a principality in a land where there is much equality of people, thou shalt not easily effect it. The way to bring the first to pass is to weaken the gentry . . .'.[7]

J.N. King's *English Reformation Literature* and David Norbrook's *Poetry and Politics in the English Renaissance* look back to the popular poets of Edward VI's reign, notably Crowley. Their subsequent eclipse, they suggest, was in part due to their use of popular ballad metres rather than the Italian measures which became fashionable at court. Puttenham urged the aspirant courtly poet to construct intricate rhyme schemes beyond the capacity of the vulgar.[8] In his edition of Bunyan's *Poems* Graham Midgley has convincingly argued that Bunyan writes in his 'homely' style, quatrains and end-stopped couplets, not because he could do no better but because he was deliberately employing a style popular with the middling sort though long out of fashion at court – the style of ballads, broadsides and chapbooks, of Thomas Tusser and metrical Psalms, including Sternhold and Hopkins. Midgley sees Bunyan as 'the inheritor and refiner of a folk-tradition of verse, and not as the unlettered hanger-on of the courtly and witty', not a failed Herbert, Vaughan, Crashaw or Herrick.[9] The examples Midgley gives

---

6. J. Wittreich, *'Image of that Horror': History, Prophecy and Apocalypse in King Lear*, San Marino, California, 1984, pp. 87, 129; K. Stockholder, 'The multiple genres of *King Lear*: breaking the archetype', *Bucknell Review*, 1968, p. 44; Joan Rees, *Samuel Daniel: A Critical and Biographical Study*, Liverpool University Press, 1964, pp. 144–6, 152–5.

7. John Davies, *Microcosmos*, in A.B. Grosart (ed.) *Complete Works*, 1878, I, pp. 58–9; Quarles, *Enchyridion*, p. 13, in *Complete Works*, op. cit., I; and my *Intellectual Origins*, op. cit., pp. 195–203.

8. J.N. King, *English Reformation Literature: The Tudor Origins of the Protestant Tradition*, Princeton University Press, 1982, *passim*; Norbrook, *Poetry and Politics*, op. cit., pp. 48–9, 78.

9. Bunyan, *Poems*, op. cit., pp. xxix–xxxvi, xlvii.

of this tradition do not go back to Crowley; nor do they include the poems of Gerrard Winstanley, which thanks to King and Norbrook we can now see falling into an alternative lower-class Protestant tradition stretching from Crowley to Bunyan, often with a radical political slant. Such verse was prominent in the revolutionary decades, not least in newspapers. How right Puttenham had been to fear that popular preachers would 'preach all truth to the rascal sort', and so 'pull people and their prince assunder'.[10]

With this lower-class verse tradition we may perhaps compare the tradition of popular and radical prose which extends from Tyndale and the Edwardians through Martin Marprelate and Thomas Scott to the Levellers and Winstanley. Miss Muriel St Clare Byrne noted that as early as Henry VIII's reign lay English men and women could write lively, colloquial workmanlike prose, 'uncontaminated by the conscious excitement of literary experiment'.[11] The age of Lyly, Shakespeare and Nashe introduced a more conscious art, but began a process in which popular and élite cultures pulled apart. The 1640s saw a vigorous reassertion of the popular culture, Overton personifying the transition from popular theatre to radical pamphleteering in the Marprelate tradition.

Also timely is Norbrook's emphasis on the Spenserian succession of poets – Daniel, Drayton, John Davies, Giles and Phineas Fletcher, William Browne, Christopher Brooke, Wither and Milton. Norbrook adds Fulke Greville, and Margot Heinemann in her turn adds the young Middleton.[12] There are also Sir Arthur Gorges, though not published in his own day, and Joshua Sylvester. Norbrook dismisses those critics who have seen Spenser as a 'conservative'.[13] 'Conservative' is a relative term: unless it is carefully defined it is a risky word to use. If we compare Spenser with, say, the Levellers, then he is conservative. Spenser had no use for the many-headed monster, whether Catholics or radical sectaries. But he was associated with the forward-looking party at Elizabeth's court, with Walsingham, Leicester, Ralegh. Spenser accepted, Norbrook argues, an apocalyptic interpretation of the Netherlands revolt. In 1591 his *Mother Hubberds Tale* was called in by the authorities for its attacks on Burghley and Robert Cecil: George Peele

10. Quoted by Norbrook, *Poetry and Politics*, op. cit., p. 70. Puttenham believed the language of poetry should be confined to the usage of court and City.

11. M. St C. Byrne (ed.) *The Lisle Letters*, Chicago University Press, 1980, I, pp. 67–84, 106; My *Writing and Revolution*, op. cit., Ch. 3.

12. Heinemann, *Puritanism and Theatre*, op. cit., pp. 57, 72.

13. Paul McLane, Vergil K. Whittaker and, more recently, Lauro Martines.

two years later said Spenser had been a victim of 'Court's disdain, the enemy to art'. Spenser was critical of Elizabeth's Irish policy as insufficiently radical. Patrick Collinson goes so far as to speak of 'Spenser's barely concealed republicanism'.[14]

'The rhetoric of *The Shepheardes Calender*,' Norbrook argues (following King), 'is at least superficially similar' to that of the radicals of Edward VI's reign.[15] It 'established a political rhetoric that was to remain popular until the civil war. The figure of the shepherd poet became associated with a militant protestant foreign policy' and toleration for Puritans at home. Norbrook sees a revival of Spenserian pastoral for political purposes after 1610, first centring on Prince Henry, believed to be in favour of an aggressive Protestant foreign policy. After his untimely death plain-speaking shepherds became alarmed at the direction of government policy and looked back to an idealized Elizabethan age. In 1614 *Englands Helicon* (1600) was reprinted, with a new motto,

> The courts of kings hear no such strains
> As daily lull the rustic swains.[16]

All the Spenserian poets were critical of dominant tendencies at court. Daniel associated his Henry VI with a sentiment which anticipates George Wither and the Levellers:

> He sees, what chair soever monarch sate
> Upon, on earth, the people was the state.[17]

The plebeians in *Coriolanus* likewise claim that the people are the city. Drayton's *Polyolbion*, with its glorification of the English countryside, was dedicated not to James I but to Prince Henry. And when Webster wanted to symbolize the perfect ruler for his City pageant of 1624 he chose neither the reigning monarch nor the heir apparent, but the dead Prince Henry.[18]

William Browne linked 'the symbolic figure of the shepherd as

---

14. Norbrook, *Poetry and Politics*, op. cit., pp. 135, 131; P. Collinson, 'The monarchical republic of Queen Elizabeth', *Bulletin of the John Rylands Library*, 1987, 69, p. 408. Cf. pp. 135–6 above.

15. Norbrook, *Poetry and Politics*, op. cit., p. 60.

16. ibid., pp. 89, 202, 207–8.

17. Daniel, *The Civil Wars*, 1609, Book VIII, stanza 31 (Rees, *Samuel Daniel*, op. cit., p. 142).

18. For Drayton and the 'opposition gentry' see R.F. Hardin, *Michael Drayton and the Passing of the Elizabethan Age*, Lawrence, Kansas, 1973; Heinemann, *Puritanism and Theatre*, op. cit., p. 258; Goldberg, *Between Worlds*, op. cit., p. 153.

protestant prophet and the celebration of the English countryside'. Browne certainly packed a great deal of politics into *Britannia's Pastorals*, dedicated to the Earl of Pembroke. Christopher Brooke attributed to Browne the sentiment

> Thought hath no prison, and the mind is free
> Under the greatest king and tyranny.[19]

In the 1620s, under Buckingham, Browne attacked peers and favourites; in the 1630s he published nothing. Brooke had attacked impositions in the Parliament of 1614; the king, he said, had no absolute power 'to make any law touching the prejudice of his subject, either for life, liberty or goods'. 'England obeys no laws but such as themselves make.'[20]

All the major Spenserians, Norbrook suggests, were associated with Sir Edwin Sandys, advocate of American colonization and patron of the Pilgrim Fathers, who believed monarchy had originally been elective. In 1621 he said he had never been more afraid for the future, since 'all things in the country are out of frame'.[21] Milton greatly admired Browne, and read *Britannia's Pastorals* carefully. His marginalia include 'poor labour to feed the luxury of the rich' – taken up by the Lady in *Comus* – and 'parasites are enlightened by the beams of kings'. Norbrook's book puts Milton's early poetry into perspective: it is radical not only in its explicit political content, but also in its stylistic affiliations and its underlying visionary utopianism. By the time Milton came to write *Lycidas* pastoral was becoming unfashionable: no really important allegorical eclogues were produced until *Adonais*, Norbrook concludes.[22]

Jonathan Dollimore's title, *Radical Tragedy: Religion, Ideology and Power in the Drama of Shakespeare and his Contemporaries* (Brighton, 1984), highlights the fact that the drama of Shakespeare's age shows us not complacent acceptance of orthodox values but a profound questioning.

---

19. Norbrook, *Poetry and Politics*, op. cit., pp. 208, 210, 213.
20. Cooper, *Wentworth Papers*, op. cit., p. 67; cf. Norbrook, *Poetry and Politics*, op. cit., pp. 211, 223, 276.
21. ibid., pp. 211–12; T.K. Rabb, 'Sir Edwin Sandys', in Greaves and Zaller, *Biographical Dictionary of British Radicals*, op. cit., III. Brooke and Wither shared Sandys's enthusiasm for Virginia. Fulke Greville and Giles Fletcher were members of Sandys's Virginia Company, Sylvester its secretary. Drayton, like Richard Sibbes, George Herbert, Henry Vaughan and many others later, saw the course of empire as westwards (Norbrook, *Poetry and Politics*, op. cit., p. 220; Sibbes, *Works*, op. cit., I, pp. 100–3; Martin, *Works of Vaughan*, op. cit., II, p. 655).
22. Norbrook *Poetry and Politics*, op. cit., pp. 213, 272, 285.

There is so much evidence for this, and some of it is so familiar, that it is tedious to rehearse it. From Tamburlaine and Faustus through Richard III, Macbeth, Iago, Volpone, Vittoria and Flamineo, and many others, we are aware of powerful aspiring individuals up against the limitations of a hierarchical society bound by custom and precedent. As Conrad Russell put it, 'the notion of every man in his place was hard to combine with the effect of inflation on the social structure'.[23] Feudal loyalties succumbed. 'My master is my master and I love him', said Manasses in *The Ile of Guls* (1606); 'but gold's my God and I honour it.'[24]

The theatre gave some expression to the ideology that accompanied social mobility. 'Measure me what I am, not what I was', cried Mosbie in *Arden of Feversham* (1592) – not, admittedly, a 'good' character.[25] 'Shepherds are men, and kings are no more', declared the hero of *The Comedie of Mucedorus* (1598).[26] *The Historie of the whole life and death of Thomas, Lord Cromwell*, acted and printed when Oliver Cromwell was three years old, gives a very favourable account of the social rise of the virtuous son of a Putney blacksmith.[27] The existence of the thriving Dutch republic was a living example of a state run by a commercial aristocracy, which Hobbes thought had an unfortunate influence.[28] References in plays to the 'birthright' even of slaves,[29] and to freeborn lower-class Englishmen, can hardly have escaped the notice of audiences.[30] Social mobility extended to marriage. The permissibility or impermissibility of great ladies marrying beneath then is at issue in *Cymbeline* and *The Duchess of Malfi*. Middleton's *Women Beware Women* deliberately contrasts court and City values (an Italian court, of course), not to the advantage of the court.

Something like two cultural traditions were forming, at least from the reign of Elizabeth. We should not forget the optimism which men could derive from Francis Bacon's and George Hakewill's conviction that the Moderns could improve on the Ancients, and Bacon's vision

---

23. Conrad Russell, *The Crisis of Parliaments, 1621-1629*, Oxford University Press, 1971, pp. 195-6, quoted to good effect by Dollimore, *Radical Tragedy*, op. cit., p. 284; cf. Goldberg, *Between Worlds*, op. cit., pp. 8-11.
24. Act III, sc. 1.
25. Act I, lines 322-5; cf. Act III, sc. v.
26. Act III, sc. i. Cf. Butler, *Theatre and Crisis*, op. cit., pp. 47, 67.
27. See my *Intellectual Origins*, op. cit., pp. 266-8, for some evidence of literary stress on the superiority of virtue to birth.
28. Hobbes, *Behemoth*, op. cit., VI, p. 618.
29. Massinger's *The Bondman*. But the leader of the slaves was an aristocrat in disguise.
30. Gabrieli and Melchiori, *Book of Sir Thomas More*, op. cit., pp. 90, 125.

of endlessly expanding co-operative use of science for the relief of man's estate: it created a divine discontent with the status quo and held out the possibility of abundance in what had always been a world of scarcity. Most of Bacon's works were printed or translated into English only after 1640. But, even though little discussed in print before then, they were already a source of influence. Serious criticism of long-standing institutions, however intolerable they may have become, finds expression only when some alternative is *seen* to be possible: which in England was not until after 1640. Earlier there are many cries of pain, but constructive alternatives cannot be put forward in print. Meanwhile it is the job of the church and the censorship to preserve appearances. So we should not necessarily take silence for consent.

Some historians, including literary historians, regard the period before 1640 and after 1660 as 'normal', because then censorship ensured that only a limited range of opinions, mostly agreeing with one another, could be expressed. During what they call 'the interregnum' this was not the case: there was an exceptionally wide spectrum of very conflicting opinions until the censorship was clamped down again in 1660, together with other repressive legislation. A censored society is 'normal'; the period in which there was no censorship can be ignored. Such historians enter into a tacit conspiracy with seventeenth-century censors. I think, on the contrary, that the period free from censorship, with its unprecedentedly large outpouring of ideas, and the unique freedom of discussion in the forties which Milton's *Areopagitica* celebrated, can tell us a great deal about the secret history of the English people: Leveller democracy and republicanism, Digger communism, sects and mechanic preachers proclaiming the rights of ordinary people, women preachers insisting on the rights of women, Ranter free love. The political ideas of Levellers, Winstanley, Hobbes and Harrington make this the greatest age in the history of English political thought: the eighteenth-century European Enlightenment drew on these ideas.

If we leave all that out of account, it is possible not to notice that there was a revolution. The pamphlets of this Revolution, I think, not only tell us what men and women were thinking in that exceptional period, but can be used, cautiously, to throw light on the years before 1640 and after 1660, when a 'normal' censorship prevailed, and only views acceptable to society's rulers could be expressed; when the hegemony of these ideas was challenged only by a few 'troublemakers'. But why do you need a censorship if everybody agrees with the accepted ideas? If historians lack the imagination to ask such questions about the seventeenth century, they might look around them in the world they live in. Robert Burton makes my point. 'We . . . hold them most part wise men that are in authority, princes, magistrates, rich men, they are wise men born, all politicians and statesmen must needs be so, for who dare speak against them?'[31] The censorship brought English satire to a halt in 1599: it did not revive until the revolutionary decades, when ample opportunity offered. Experiments made then prepared for Marvell, Dryden, Bunyan and Rochester. English history plays were also banned in 1599: the writing of recent English history became a dangerous occupation.[32]

Dollimore's *Radical Tragedy* uses drama to explain the collapse of crown, court, government and church in 1640. He postulates 'a connection in the early seventeenth century between the undermining of these institutions and a theatre in which they and their ideological legitimation were subjected to sceptical, interrogative and subversive representation'. 'The crisis of confidence in those holding power is addressed in play after play.' And he makes the valuable point that the corrupt courts in which dramatic action is so often set are not 'a transhistorical symbol of human depravity' but a very specific 'focus for a contemporary critique of power relations'.[33] Most kings succumb to flattery, Sir Arthur Gorges warned Prince Henry.[34] Dollimore analyses plays by Marlowe, Marston, Shakespeare, Jonson, Chapman, Webster and Fulke Greville to illustrate his points. The existence of the censorship, he adds, is itself evidence that 'the theatres were a potentially subversive context'. And he demonstrates how the drama was leading to 'the disintegration of providential history'.[35]

The contrast between the ideal of kingship and the inadequacy of the

31. Robert Burton, *Anatomy of Melancholy* (Everyman edn), I, p. 41.
32. My *Writing and Revolution*, op. cit., pp. 5, 34-5.
33. Dollimore, *Radical Tragedy*, op. cit., p. 4; cf. Robert Weimann, 'Autorität und Gesellschäftliche Erfahrung in Shakespeares Theater', *Shakespeare Jahrbuch*, 1983, 119, pp. 86-113.
34. H.E. Sandison (ed.) *The Poems of Sir Arthur Gorges*, Oxford University Press, 1953, pp. 172-3.
35. Dollimore, *Radical Tragedy*, op. cit., p. 38; Goldberg, *Between Worlds*, op. cit., pp. 12-13, 39, 52, 60. I received A.H. Tricomi's *Anticourt Drama in England, 1603-1642*, Virginia University Press, 1989, too late to be able to take account of his important argument. I should wish to modify and amplify some of my points in the light of his analysis. See especially his p. xiv (varieties of anti-court drama), Chs. 1-5 (the Children of the Revels and the influence of Queen Anne), Ch. 6-9 (Daniel and Greville, Jonson and Chapman), Ch. 12 (Webster), pp. 126-7 (Wilkins and wardship), Ch. 16 (Massinger), Ch. 17 (the 1630s).

actual occupants of thrones occurs again and again in Elizabethan and Jacobean drama, as Dollimore shows. I have discussed and illustrated this point elsewhere.[36] It is the contrast between Richard II and Henry IV, between Richard III and Henry VII, between Prince Hal and Henry V.

Plays about history, and especially about English history, contributed to scepticism about the divine right of kings. If the deposition of Richard II was the original sin which led to the anarchy of the Wars of the Roses, the accession of the usurper Henry VII, which led to the glorious Tudor age, was hardly a triumph for divine right. Yet gentlemen kept their criticisms of James and Charles to themselves. James reminded JPs that their authority could be challenged if his was; monarchy was the keystone of the social arch, Sir Thomas Wentworth said. There was enough social unrest in Jacobean and Caroline England to make men observe strict decorum when attributing blame to the king's ministers, but never to the king himself.

Caution had to be used even when criticizing ministers. Sir Robert Cotton in a paper of 1628 advocated opposition in parliament to the Duke of Buckingham but warned that it must not be pushed too far lest it give rise to revolt by 'the loose and needy multitude'.[37] This fear was nearer the surface in early Stuart England than we sometimes realize. In 1621 an illegal pamphlet depicted the Spanish ambassador warning James against the danger of a *democratia* of mechanics.[38] In 1622 the staid Simonds D'Ewes spoke of a 'hoped-for rebellion'.[39] Many others referred to the possibility of revolt in the 1620s.[40] Divine right had to be proclaimed because it was being challenged. In Sir Francis Hubert's poem, *The Historie of Edward the Second* (?written 1598-9), Piers Gaveston attacked peers who 'raise men that are popular',

36. My *Writing and Revolution*, op. cit., pp. 12-20.

37. Cotton, *The Dangers*, op. cit., p. 19. Cf. p. 53 above.

38. T. Gainsford, *Vox Spiritus, or Sir Walter Raleighs Ghost*, 1620, quoted by P. Steffens in a research paper presented to the West Coast Journalism Historians' Conference, March 1980. I am indebted to him for sending me a copy.

39. Bourcier (ed.) D'Ewes, *Diary*, op. cit., p. 64; cf. pp. 58, 122-3.

40. Notestein et al., *1621 Commons Debates*, op. cit., I, p. 105 (George Sandys); J. Thirsk and J. Cooper (eds) *Seventeenth-Century Economic Documents*, Oxford University Press, 1972, p. 15 (possible revolt of unemployed in 1622); Russell, *Parliaments and English Politics*, op. cit., p. 251; cf. p. 339 (Sherland, 1625; Cotton, 1628); Zagorin, *Court and Country*, op. cit., p. 111 (the Venetian ambassador, 1626; the agent of the Grand Duke of Tuscany, 1626-8); Green (ed.) Rous, *Diary*, op. cit., pp. 12, 19, 42-3, 132; K.V. Thomas, *Religion and the Decline of Magic*, op. cit., p. 132. In the 1630s the censor kept a special look-out for undesirable references to the poverty of the common people and the possibility of revolt (Heinemann, *Puritanism and Theatre*, op. cit., p. 142).

> Make pretences (for the Common weal)
> Of Reformation, of religious zeal

but are only self-interested.[41] The reader is not intended to approve of Gaveston; but his criticism is very relevant to Elizabethan and Jacobean politics, just as Exeter in *Henry VI* echoes anxieties about the succession to Elizabeth:

> No simple man that sees
> This jarring discord of nobility . . .
> This factious bandying of their favourites,
> But that it doth presage some ill event . . .
> There comes the ruin, there begins confusion. (IV.i)[42]

Elsewhere I have suggested some ways in which the drama foreshadowed tragedies that were to be played out in the 1640s. Richard II anticipates Charles I, Lear's passionate awareness of the reality of poverty became social protest with Levellers, Coppe and Winstanley.[43] In *Hamlet* the tone is set by the heir to the throne:

> The time is out of joint. O cursed spite
> That ever I was born to set it right. (I.v)

It is a world of insoluble problems facing men with 'double hearts'. A generation gap is suggested between, on the one hand, Polonius (often compared to Lord Burghley), who has all the platitudinous answers but no real solutions, and on the other Hamlet and Horatio, who are better at rejecting old nostrums than at discovering new solutions. The wisest political commentators are the grave-diggers – men who have no share in politics. In *King Lear* a Fool and a madman discuss popular grievances which were not to be aired in public discussion until the 1640s. Imogen in *Cymbeline* proclaimed that all men should be brothers. Stirringly patriotic speeches are given to the two nastiest characters in the play, Cloten and the Queen. The more acceptable Cymbeline advocates appeasement of Rome. Whatever we make of that, something has changed in the 12–15 years since *Henry V* and the Bastard in *King John*.

---

41. B. Mellor (ed.) *The Poems of Sir Francis Hubert*, Hong Kong University Press, 1961, p. 62; cf. pp. 17–19, 132–3, 147.
42. Cf. the 'Hobbist' acceptance of *de facto* claims to rule in *3 Henry VI*, Act III, sc. i.
43. My *Writing and Revolution*, op. cit., pp. 10–12, 16–17. Cf. Guiderius in *Cymbeline*, Act IV, sc. ii.

Perhaps we may now try to answer my initial question – does the literary evidence help us to decide whether the Revolution had any causes?

I hope that with the assistance of Norbrook and Dollimore I have made out a case for suggesting that monarchy – its role in the state, its strengths and weaknesses, what was to be done about the latter – was a focal point of discussion. The dramatists do not produce solutions, of course: they cannot. But by putting before a popular audience plays depicting such matters they helped to bridge the time-honoured gap between the political nation and groundlings, who hitherto had existed only to be ruled.[44] The young Welshman Arise Evans used to think the Bible dealt with far-off matters in other countries. But after moving to London he learnt in the 1630s that Biblical history was 'a mystery to be opened at this time, belonging also to us'.[45] The Bible and the theatre combined to pose questions which remind us that the most obvious achievement of the Revolution was to be the transition from would-be absolute monarchy to parliamentary sovereignty.

But sovereignty to do what? Here perhaps Fulke Greville, to whom I referred briefly in Chapter 3, can help us. Chancellor of the Exchequer to James I and Charles I, ennobled by James: Greville nevertheless had a secret life of deep hostility to everything the court stood for. In his *Life of Sidney*, probably written 1610–12, he contrasts the achievements of Elizabeth and her successors so blatantly that it could not be published before 1640: so did Sir Arthur Gorges, who also prudently left his poems unpublished. Greville had wanted to write a history of Elizabeth's reign, but Cecil would not allow him access to the relevant documents. So he wrote plays and poems, which he realized were mostly unpublishable during his lifetime. He himself destroyed one play at the time of the downfall of the Earl of Essex in 1601, because it was 'apt enough to be construed or strained to a personification of vices in the present governors and government'. His plots concern tyranny. They are set safely within the Turkish empire but are not irrelevant to the way Greville thought things were going in England. In *Mustapha* the chorus compares the people to a blinded Samson who suddenly becomes aware of his own strength, 'and so pluck down that Samson's post on which our Sultans stay'.

44. I owe this point to Margot Heinemann's forthcoming article, 'Political drama', in M. Hathaway and A. Braunmuller (eds) *The Cambridge Companion to Elizabethan and Stuart Drama*, Cambridge University Press, forthcoming.
45. Evans, *An Eccho to the Voice from Heaven*, 1653, p. 17; my *Change and Continuity*, op. cit., p. 54.

Greville is equivocal on popular revolt, of which tyranny inevitably creates the possibility. A character in *Mustapha* cries

> No, people, no. Question these thrones of tyrants;
> Revive your old equality of nature.

But – typically – he soon backs down.[46]

In *The Life of Sidney* and in his poems Greville put forward an alternative long-term programme for representative government and parliamentary control of the taxation which would pay for a forward foreign policy in the interests of God and England. He acclaimed 'the heroical design of invading and possessing America'. Ralegh had declared that 'whoever commands the sea commands the trade . . . of the world, and consequently the world itself'.[47] Bacon agreed: 'the wealth of both Indies seems in great part but an accessory to command of the sea'.[48] Ralegh had recognized that parliamentary control of taxation would be necessary if a fleet capable of enforcing an aggressive foreign policy was to be kept up. It would involve, as Ralegh and Greville appreciated, war against Spain in alliance with the Dutch republic. Greville held out the Dutch as models of – to use a later phrase – the link between protestantism and capitalism.[49] This policy was carried out by the Commonwealth and Oliver Cromwell, after the Revolution had made a huge fleet possible. Together with the Navigation Act of 1651, Cromwell's Western Design presaged a century and a half of commercial and colonial aggression, which left England top nation. If anyone had been thinking of revolution before 1628 – when Greville died – this is the programme he would have postulated. When Massinger in *The Maid of Honour* (1620) gave a *Sicilian* a stirring speech about the necessity of sea-power to resolve the island's problems of overpopulation and under-endowed younger sons of the gentry, its relevance to England must have been obvious to the audience. The point was underlined by a reference to England's *past* naval greatness under Elizabeth. The prevalence of plays set in

---

46. G. Bullough (ed.) *Poems and Dramas of Fulke Greville*, Edinburgh, n.d., II, pp. 125, 131; Norbrook, *Poetry and Politics*, op. cit., Ch. 6, *passim*, p. 282.
47. Ralegh, 'A Discourse of the Invention of Ships', in *Works* op. cit., II, p. 80. The point is spelt out at length in Ralegh's *The Prerogative of Parliaments in England*, Middelburgh, 1628: written c. 1615, ibid., I, pp. 171–248. Greville may well have read this work in manuscript. Passages in Greville, *Life of Sidney*, op. cit., are closely parallel to *The Prerogative of Parliaments*: see 1907 edn, p. 77. (See pp. 27, 37, 84–5, 105 above).
48. Bacon, Essay XXIX.
49. Greville, *Life of Sidney*, op. cit., p. 56; Norbrook, *Poetry and Politics*, op. cit., p. 127.

the ancient world or in Mediterranean countries is not entirely unconnected with the existence of censorship.

Literary historians are beginning to reveal to us the political background of many Elizabethan and Jacobean plays. History plays showing 'the King as common man' form a distinctive genre throughout the period.[50] 'The plays do not forbear to present upon their stage the whole course of this present time, not sparing either King, state or religion', wrote Secretary Calvert to Ralph Winwood in 1605.[51] Massinger's *The Bondman* draws on *Vox Coeli* and *Robert Earl of Essex his Ghost*, two seditious tracts printed overseas by the exiled Thomas Scott and smuggled into England in 1624.[52] Scott denounced gentry control over parliamentary elections, and called on the godly to organize to resist it.[53]

Margot Heinemann's splendid study of Middleton explodes the idea that all Puritans opposed the theatre, and shows with many examples that if there had been no censorship Jacobean and Caroline drama would have been much more directly critical of court and government. Middleton's *A Game at Chess* got past the censor in 1624, at a time when Prince Charles and the royal favourite Buckingham were in effect temporarily leading opposition to the king's pro-Spanish policy. Like Massinger, Middleton drew on Thomas Scott's illegal pamphlets for his play, which guys the Spanish ambassador, who was believed to have the king in his pocket. The players apparently acquired a cast-off suit of Gondomar's from a 'mole', and portrayed him to the life. At the end Gondomar was beaten and kicked into hell, followed by the King and Queen of Spain. Even more daringly, the audience was encouraged to laugh at the Fat Bishop – a Catholic renegade who had been (temporarily) a pluralist clergyman of the Church of England. That was unprecedented. The play ran for nine days before James found out and at once suppressed it. During that time it had played to packed houses: Puritans flocked to see it. It conclusively establishes Heinemann's point that 'the repertory of the early Stuart theatres as we know it is not a completely reliable index of

50. Marie Axton, *The Queen's Two Bodies: Drama and the Elizabethan Succession*, 1977, p. 26.
51. Quoted by Rees, *Samuel Daniel*, op. cit., p. 121.
52. J. Limon, *Dangerous Matter: English Drama and Politics, 1623-1624*, Cambridge University Press, 1986, pp. 65, 84-6. See pp. 200-3, 206 above for more examples, and my *Writing and Revolution*, op. cit., pp. 12-20.
53. Scott, *Vox Populi*, op. cit., Sig. B 3v; *High-waies*, op. cit., p. 86; cf. *The Second Part of Vox Populi*, 1624, *passim*. Cf. L.B. Wright's seminal article, 'Propaganda against James I's "appeasement" of Spain', *Huntington Library Quarterly*, 1942-3, 6.

the tastes of audiences, or even of the dramatists themselves'. The fact that the author and actors of *A Game at Chess* escaped relatively unscathed shows powerful support for a 'Puritan' foreign policy.[54] The Earl of Pembroke patronized Middleton, as he did Massinger and Browne. Alternative policies like Ralegh's and Greville's had high-placed backers.

Middleton's *Women Beware Women* deliberately contrasts court and City values (an Italian court, of course) to the disadvantage of the court. Moralists had often preferred virtue to birth. De Flores in Middleton's *The Changeling* drew the logical conclusion: the vicious actions of Beatrice-Joanna pulled her down to his plebeian level:

> Fly not to your birth, but settle you
> In what the act has made you.
> You're no more now. (Act III, sc. iv)

The other great economic transformation which resulted from the English Revolution was the abolition of the Court of Wards and feudal tenures, which had consequences for English agriculture as great as changes in foreign policy were for trade. One of its side-effects was to end the abuse of marriages forced upon wards during their minority by their guardians; this contributed to the slow movement towards establishing freedom of choice in aristocratic marriages. George Wilkins's interesting play, *The Miseries of Inforst Marriage*, was published in 1607, just before the first major discussion between king and parliament of the abolition of wardship and feudal tenures. It is a powerful critique of the abuses of the system. I shall discuss later the play's remarkably radical overtones.

Another area in which we might expect Elizabethan and Jacobean literature to tell us something about pre-revolutionary society is in revealing lower-class discontent. There was, we saw, much fear of revolt. How far are ideas of plebeian opposition reflected? Spenser's portrait of a communist giant in Book V of *The Faerie Queene* gets close to what I suspect some ordinary people may have been saying. The giant was of course destroyed; but his arguments were sufficiently plausible to be reprinted in 1648 as anti-Leveller propaganda: they still needed answering.[55] The censorship and the court orientation of

---

54. Heinemann, *Puritanism and Theatre*, op. cit., Chs. 10 and 12; Butler, *Theatre and Crisis*, op. cit., p. 329.
55. Anon., *The Faerie Leveller, or King Charles his Leveller described in Queene Elizabeths dayes*, in J. Frank, *Hobbled Pegasus*, New Mexico University Press, 1968, p. 209.

dramatists prevent us seeing much of the viewpoint of ordinary people
except in a distorting mirror; but something comes across. Cade and
his 'clouted shoon' anticipated the attack on the universities by radical
reformers in the forties and fifties, when they denounced education
because it led to class privilege. *Coriolanus* raises problems resulting
from popular claims to a share in government and the deceptions used
to prevent them being realized. The citizens in *Coriolanus* anticipate
anti-gentry arguments put forward by Overton and Clarkson in the
1640s ('our sufferance is a gain to them').[56] The levelling realism of
Lear's 'I am a very foolish fond old man' let a startling breath of fresh
air blow in upon kings who, James I claimed, by God himself are called
gods. I quote Victor Kiernan, always wise in literary matters: 'we can
hear the voice of bourgeois rationality . . . in *Troilus and Cressida*, with
Hersites's derision of war and lechery as the two chief occupations of
courts'.[57]

Wilkins's *The Miseries of Inforst Marriage* goes out of its way to pillory
the unfortunate consequences for younger brothers and sisters of
primogeniture, as well as of marrying wards against their wishes.
Primogeniture was to be an especial target of the Levellers. The play
is particularly notable for its social overtones. The Butler, a sort of
Figaro and Admirable Crichton combined, expresses remarkably
radical views.

> To steal is bad, but taken where is store
> The fault's the less, being done to help the poor. (lines 1652–3)

He rebukes his master to his face in extremely disrespectful terms:

> I'll rather be a beggar than your man;
> And there's your service for you. (2534–5)

His master comments that this

> Turns the world upside down, that men o'erbear their masters.
> (2572)

It is also an anti-clerical play. The only character who possesses no
good qualities is Dr Baxter, Chancellor of Oxford, who in the final
scene is admonished

---

56. My *World Turned Upside Down*, op. cit., p. 214.
57. V.G. Kiernan, *State and Society in Europe, 1550–1650*, Oxford, 1980, p. 267.

Let not promotion's hope be as a string
To tie your tongue, or let loose it to sting. (lines 2887–9)[58]

Wilkins's play is very sympathetic to women. I do not wish to make too much of this, but there was a lively literary controversy about the position of women in the 1620s, which perhaps looks forward to the outburst of women's activities and claims in the 1640s.[59] The phrase 'custom is an idiot' used by one angry defender of women suggests the line of thought that might be stimulated in reaction to defences of traditional positions. We do not always recall how very unusual Webster and Milton were in making a lady the heroine and centre of action in *The Duchess of Malfi* and in *Comus*. 'The Duchess is a perfect Puritan heroine', writes Goldberg.[60] Did contemporaries fail to notice this?

I am not arguing that Shakespeare, Middleton or Wilkins were proto-Levellers, any more than I think Shakespeare was a card-carrying Great-Chain-of-Being man, or a Christian Humanist. Both points of view existed in the society, along with many others; and they come into the plays. Why should we isolate the conservative philosophy, except to gratify twentieth-century ideological prejudices, when radical points of view are no less plausibly and sometimes sympathetically expressed in the plays? It does not surprise me that in the 1640s parliamentarian pamphleteers quoted Shakespeare and Jonson twice as often as royalists did.[61]

Martin Butler's *Theatre and Crisis, 1632–1642* gives a stimulating new view of the decade of Charles's personal rule. Many historians, myself included, had fallen into the trap of assuming that because of tighter censorship the drama of the thirties can be written off as negligible. Butler shows that playwrights used a period in the mid-thirties, analogous to 1624, when Henrietta Maria for her own political reasons supported an anti-Spanish group at court. And

---

58. See also lines 455–6, 2726–2803. It would be nice to think that the lines quoted here were aimed at William Laud, who in December 1605 had blotted his copybook by marrying the divorced Lady Penelope Rich to his patron, the Earl of Devonshire. Cf. line 2831, stressing a rather Puritan view of the supremacy of conscience.
59. The best account of this is in L.B. Wright's *Middle-Class Culture in Elizabethan England*, North Carolina University Press, 1935, Ch. 13.
60. Anon., *Haec Vir: Or, The Womanish Man*, 1620, Sig. B 2v; Norbrook, *Poetry and Politics*, op. cit., pp. 249–51; Goldberg, *Between Worlds*, op. cit., pp. 106–7; cf. p. 22 for an implied criticism of arranged marriages in Webster's *The White Devil*.
61. E. Sirluck, 'Shakespeare and Jonson among the pamphleteers of the first civil war', *Modern Philology*, 1955–6, 53, quoted by Heinemann, *Puritanism and Theatre*, op. cit., p. 256. See now Annabel Patterson, *Shakespeare and the Popular Voice*, Oxford, 1989.

Butler argues that throughout the decade plays were written for the élite theatres under the patronage of 'opposition' peers which voiced the anxieties and concerns of the independent gentry at the direction of government policy.[62] He analyses and illustrates the many ways in which politics could be discussed without saying so. He confirms Susan Staves's point that the adultery of a king could be an emblem for the defilement of the state and the abdication of responsible government.

> In justice, Sire, she is your wife, if contracts
> Can stand in force with princes.[63]

That got to the root of the matter: the marriage contract is strictly analogous to the contract between king and people. Butler gives other examples from Massinger, Shirley, Davenant, Cartwright and Brome.

'The great voicing from the professional stage of grievances and demands which Charles was failing to conciliate or to appease does illuminate . . . the way that a court forfeited the confidence of the nation.' It explains how men could begin to entertain political alternatives.[64] *A fortiori* this applies to plays written for private presentation, like Quarles's anti-Laudian *The Virgin Widow*, in which the common people were said to think that the ailing Lady Albion was 'troubled with a liturgy'. 'A lethargy, you mean', corrected the doctor nervously.[65] Quarles was nevertheless a future royalist.

Butler also demonstrates the continuing existence of a popular drama, often suppressed, censored and harassed by the government, but still giving some expression to popular grievances – satirizing Laud again, for instance, putting on, provocatively if briefly, *The Valiant Scot*, a play ostensibly about William Wallace but applicable to the Scottish rebellion of the late 1630s.[66] Butler supports a suggestion made by Margot Heinemann that the theatres were closed by parliament in 1642 less because of Puritan hostility than from fear of a too radical critique of politics from an uncensored stage. Both Heinemann

---

62. Francis Quarles had similarly opposed the interests of private gentry to the court in *Argalus and Parthenia*, 1629, in *Complete Works*, op. cit., III, p. 264.
63. J. Rutter, *The Second Part of The Cid*, quoted by Butler, *Theatre and Crisis*, op. cit., p. 62. Susan Staves, *Players' Scepters*, op. cit., p. 50.
64. Butler, *Theatre and Crisis*, op. cit., p. 285.
65. Quarles, *Complete Works*, op. cit., III, p. 309. The play also attacked sectaries.
66. Butler, *Theatre and Crisis*, op. cit., p. 231; Wedgwood, *History and Hope*, op. cit., p. 173. *The Valiant Argies* would have been an equivalent title in the 1980s.

and Butler show that many playwrights and actors became pamphleteers for the parliamentarian and indeed sometimes Puritan cause.
'The historical continuities of the drama of citizen heroism and aristocratic villainy do seem very strongly to be with the popular radicals of
the 1640s and 50s, the Levellers, Ranters and libertines.' The fact that
the popular theatres were not restored after 1660 marked a major break.
'There was much going on in the drama before 1642 which would find
no place on the stage after 1660.' 1642 was 'a moment . . . of real discontinuity'.[67] Even the court masque, sometimes taken too portentously
by scholars these days, can tell us a great deal about tensions in the
society. 'Realism in the public theatre,' Professor Kiernan observes,
'make-believe in the court masque, diverged into separate arts.'
Anticipating Butler, he sees this as evidence that 'court and nation
were drifting apart'.[68] Most masques were expected to end with all
problems solved by a *rex ex machina*, and even writers who wished to
criticize royal policy had to wrap their message up in so much flattery
that there is every likelihood that the king missed the point. Milton's
reference to Charles I's final performance at Whitehall as 'a masquing
scene' and Marvell's 'the royal actor' make the point. Nevertheless,
study of the masque has its uses for the historian, as Martin Butler
showed in a recent article on Shirley's *The Triumph of Peace*. This was
presented *at* court but *by* the lawyers of the Inns of Court. Its object
was to placate the king for the lawyer William Prynne's rude remarks
about despotic rulers and royal actresses in *Histriomastix*, which had
cost him his ears. So discretion was called for. The lawyers mounted a
vast 'parade . . . through the City streets' which may have been read
by the citizens 'as a statement of the wealth and importance of one
section of the gentry, England's Parliamentary class'. Butler shows
that Shirley 'identified problems which are central to his age, but he
lacks language which would allow him fully to confront them'.[69] The
nature of the occasion might well explain that.

For a brief moment after 1640 courtiers' pens were liberated, and
Suckling's *Brennoralt* and *The Sad One*, Denham's *The Sophy*, dealt
openly with issues hitherto taboo.

---

67. Butler, *Theatre and Crisis*, op. cit., pp. 286, 282. See pp. 225, 228–9 below.
68. Kiernan, *State and Society*, op. cit., p. 125.
69. Butler, 'Politics and the masque', op. cit., pp. 136–8. For the masque see also
Stephen Kogan, *The Hieroglyphic King: Wisdom and Idolatry in the Seventeeth-century Masque*,
1986, Cf. pp. 104–5 above.

Sire, when subjects want the privilege
To speak, then kings may have the privilege
To live in ignorance.[70]

So before 1640 there was a profound malaise at both the élite and the popular level. The idea that the Revolution was an accident seems to Butler 'patently false; there clearly were vast and deeply-rooted disagreements about fundamental issues in church and state'. It was 'a society at one in its desire for political change, but deeply torn over what that change should be. . . . The 1640s would make the difficult transition . . . to a modern world.'[71] It was a pre-revolutionary society, even if there were not yet two clear-cut sides. The fact that so many people did not want civil war to happen, and that it nevertheless did happen, suggests to me not that it was 'an accident' – how do we explain accidents? – but that long-term impersonal causes, rather than human volition, were at work.

Literary evidence thus suggests that if we look beyond the narrow circles of court and parliament we can trace long-term sources of tension in English society, going back to the Reformation itself, proceeding through the divisions at Elizabeth's court, and continuing with the Spenserian poets, patronized by Sir Edwin Sandys and the Earl of Pembroke, both associated with forward-looking policies in James's reign. The Spenserian tradition culminates in Milton, who succeeded to the role of outspoken shepherd poet-prophet. Milton adds a new cultural disgust at the Laudian régime in the church and what Peter Thomas calls 'the growing isolation, exclusiveness and repression of the court', its 'narrow snobbery and effete indulgence', which he contrasts with earlier literature of 'patriotic high seriousness and protestant nationalism'.[72] Michael Wilding has shown the contemporary relevance of *Comus* and *Lycidas* – the former attacking the court, social hierarchy and Charles I's encouragement of pagan rural sports; the latter attacking bishops and (like *Comus*) the corrupt and idle clergy. George Herbert abandoned his excellent prospects of a

70. Denham, *The Sophy*, Act II, sc. i. I owe these points to an unpublished paper by A.H. Tricomi which he kindly allowed me to read. See now note 35.
71. Butler, *Theatre and Crisis*, op. cit., pp. 287–8: Goldberg, *Between Worlds*, op. cit., p. 143 and Ch. 8 *passim*.
72. P.W. Thomas, 'Two Cultures?' op. cit., especially pp. 174–5, 184–90.

court career because the court was 'made up of fraud and titles and flattery'. They are Herbert's words.[73]

These days we are taught not to speak of 'an opposition' in parliament, and rightly. Martin Butler wisely tells us not to look for two sides even in the 1630s. 'The playwrights were dramatizing the conflicts and tensions at work in their society, embodying men's dilemmas and voicing their grievances, anxieties and frustrations. They were able to . . . shape and educate new forms of political consciousness.' 'Their drama was not merely the product of its society but was itself part of the historical process, an agent of change as much as the mirror of change, a participant engaged with society's compromises and not merely an observer of them'.[74] We cannot ignore literature if we are to understand the society.

73. Wilding, *Dragon's Teeth*, op. cit., especially pp. 10–13, 46, 52–4, 67–8, 86–7; Izaak Walton, 'Life of Mr. George Herbert', in his *Lives* (World's Classics), p. 289. Cf. Leah Marcus, *The Politics of Mirth*, Chicago University Press, 1986, Ch. VI. Contrast Annabel Patterson's interpretation of *Comus* and *Lycidas* in '"Forc'd fingers": Milton's early poems and ideological constraint', in C.J. Summers and T.L. Pebworth (eds) *'The Muses Common-Weale': Poetry and Politics in the Seventeenth Century*, Missouri University Press, 1988, pp. 15–19.
74. Butler, *Theatre and Crisis*, op. cit., pp. 279, 281.

11

The Restoration and literature

The liberty of these times hath afforded wisdom a larger passport to travel than was ever able formerly to be obtained, when
the world kept her fettered in an implicit obedience by the threefold cord of custom, education and ignorance.

Francis Osborn, *Advice to a Son*, 1656, in *Miscellaneous Works*,
11th edn, 1722, I, Sig. B 3

What prudent men a settled throne would shake?

Dryden, *Absalom and Achitophel*, 1681, line 596

Any discussion of the restoration and literature must begin with the
Revolution, to which the return of monarchy, House of Lords and
bishops in 1660 marked the end. For the years between 1640 and 1660
had been unique in the history of English culture. Censorship and
church courts had broken down in 1640, and for the best part of two
decades ordinary people had been free to meet together and discuss
not only matters of high politics but also varying (and conflicting)
forms of religious belief. A tendency towards anarchism had always
been present in protestantism's appeal to the individual conscience
against authority; freedom from ecclesiastical controls gave full rein
to discussion and dispute. The popular heretical tradition, which had
survived from Lollards through Familists and sectaries, surfaced. A
tinker John Bunyan and the son of a north-country yeoman Edward
Burrough had a fierce dispute about the relative importance of the
spirit and the letter of the Bible, and about the historical existence of
Christ: and it got into print.[1] Before 1640 it would have been

---

1. Bunyan, *Some Gospel Truths Opened*, op. cit., and *A Vindication of Gospel Truths Opened*,
op. cit.; Burrough, *The True Faith of the Gospel of Peace*, 1656, and *Truth the Strongest of all*,
1657.

impossible for such subjects or such plebeian authors to be published. In the 1640s and 1650s scores of similar local arguments were reported: hundreds were carried on verbally.

The printing explosion was the most remarkable feature of these decades. Milton's friend, the bookseller George Thomason, sensing the historical significance of the times, started in 1640 to collect a copy of every book, pamphlet and newspaper published. The figures are familiar but remain startling. In 1640 he collected 22; in 1642, 2104, and a total of over 20,000 for the twenty years 1640–60. In 1640 there were no newspapers; there were four in 1641, 722 by 1645, with an average of 350 a year for the twenty years. And Thomason's collection is not complete.[2] Books hitherto prohibited were now printed, some by order of parliament – Coke's *Institutes*, Mede's work on the end of the world. Many of Francis Bacon's writings were published in English for the first time. There were translations of previously unpublishable books – radical heresy from the continent, the Koran. Many who had previously been afraid to publish could now do so. Whole new areas of discussion were opened up. It needed little capital to set up a printing press, and the long-starved market was apparently insatiable. The informal congregations which sprang up everywhere after the fall of Archbishop Laud provided discussion centres, uncontrolled from above: so did the New Model Army. For most of two decades ordinary men and women became accustomed to liberty of debate and liberty of printing.

Censorship and control were partially restored after 1649; but they broke down again in 1659–60. Containing this ferment of debate was one of the major headaches of post-restoration governments. A strict censorship was restored; the only newspapers permitted were a couple of official sheets. Nonconformist congregations were persecuted. Coffee-houses were supervised, and one attempt was made to suppress them. But enforcing such laws was difficult. Charles II's government had only a limited bureaucracy, and could not afford a large standing army. The precedent of the very radical parliamentarian army of the forties was alarming: when James II did acquire an army its rank and file also showed radical tendencies.

During the 1640s and 1650s the fundamentals of Christianity had been discussed, and every known heresy – mortalism, antinomianism

2. F.S. Siebert, *Freedom of the Press in England, 1476–1776*, Illinois University Press, 1952, p. 203; S. Lambert, 'The beginnings of printing for the House of Commons', *The Library*, 1980, 6th series, III, p. 45n. Dr Lambert slightly modifies Siebert's figures.

and anti-Trinitarianism. The Koran worried Bunyan, the Socinian catechism licensed by Milton worried parliament. Both Clement Writer and the Quaker Samuel Fisher discussed in print the contradictions and inconsistencies of the Bible, and decided that it could not be the Word of God. Ideas of comparative religion were mooted by the Leveller John Wildman, by Francis Osborne: after 1660 Henry Stubbe wrote (but could not publish) a history of Islam which compared that religion favourably with Christianity. Ranters advocated free love and promiscuity as religious duties. All this diversity, all these quarrels and contradictions, led to scepticism. Slowly but surely in educated circles the Bible ceased to be used as an irrefutable authority on all subjects. In the Parliament of 1657 an MP who quoted the Bible too often was laughed at.[3]

For nearly twenty years the country had been ruled without king, lords or bishops. During this period the fundamentals of politics had been discussed too. Hobbes had undermined both the divine right of kings and parliamentary constitutionalism appealing to precedent. For Hobbes the sovereign was legitimate if he could protect his subjects; he needed no other legitimation than their acceptance. So far from justifying absolutism, Hobbes's theory contains an implicit warning for all rulers. Subjects have no *right* to rebel, in any circumstances, on any pretext; but if the sovereign ceases to protect them they will desert him *de facto*, as Charles I had been deserted in the 1640s (rightly, Hobbes thought), and as the republican government was to be deserted in 1659–60. Few admitted to agreeing with Hobbes, who was branded an atheist. But nobody could ignore what he had written: his amoral utilitarianism fitted the facts too well.

Politics then were secularized and pragmatized. But other, more radical, ideas had been thrown up during the Revolution. Levellers had argued for a democratic republic ruled by a more representative single chamber, and with wide social and legal reforms. The Diggers advocated a communist society, in which private property, wage labour and an established clergy would all be abolished, together with lawyers. Milton had defended divorce for incompatibility of temperament, and wide freedom of the press; he argued that subjects had the right to call their rulers to account. Barebone's Parliament in 1653 established civil marriage: Milton covertly defended it in *Paradise Lost*. James Harrington, in a plausible historical analysis, asserted

3. J.D. Ogilvie (ed.) *Diary of Sir Archibald Johnston of Wariston*, III, *1655–60*, Scottish History Society, 1940, p. 71.

that power followed property, and that the civil war had been adjusting a balance by extending power to those who now owned property. He predicted that even if monarchy was restored, it would not be able to rule in the old way except by means of a standing army. 1688 proved him right. Henceforth the English monarch was, in Harrington's phraseology, 'a prince in a commonwealth'.

One of the most lasting consequences of the Revolution was its irreverence, its rejection of the traditional deference of a hierarchical society. Irreverence was all-pervasive once censorship no longer prevented it. Caricatures of Archbishop Laud proliferated in 1641, showing him in all sorts of humiliating predicaments.[4] This was a novel and unforgettable shift in attitudes to authority, and to politics, from which the general public had hitherto been excluded. Mockery of public figures had been impossible in political discourse before 1640, except in illegal writings like those of Martin Marprelate or Thomas Scott, the latter bootlegged over from the Netherlands in the 1620s; or in the exceptional circumstances which in 1624 permitted Middleton's *A Game at Chess* to be put on the stage; or in a few rapidly suppressed plays at the popular theatres.[5] The personal savagery of Marvell's verse satires, and the more decorous irony of *The Rehearsal Transpros'd*, could not have got into print before 1640.

The supreme example of irreverence is Oliver Cromwell. His oft-repeated mots were very popular with the troops: they undercut centuries of tradition. The vulgar had of course long held irreverent views about their rulers and social superiors. In 1648 soldiers guarding his most sacred Majesty called him 'Stroker', in reference to his alleged gift of healing scrofula by the royal touch.[6] Cromwell and others like him broke the upper-class silence which had prevailed so long as the political nation remained united.

The Revolution had given many of its supporters a tremendous hope, a utopian optimism. Cromwell was 'the force of angry heaven's flame'. This hope often took the form of millenarianism, belief that Christ's kingdom would come on earth in the near future. It was essentially a political doctrine: the Quakers expected 'a new earth as well as a new heaven'.[7] Anne Bradstreet in New England foresaw a regenerated England whose 'armies brave' would 'sack proud

4. Cf. my *Writing and Revolution*, op. cit., pp. 86–7, and p. 52 above.
5. See pp. 210–11 above.
6. *Mercurius Elencticus*, 7 February, 1649.
7. Edward Burrough, *To the Parliament*, op. cit., p. 3.

Rome'.[8] Milton thought that Christ's 'shortly expected' coming would bring 'destruction to all tyrants'.[9] Like John Cook, John Canne and many others, Milton believed that the trial and condemnation of Charles I had been an anticipation of 'the great day of judgment, when the saints shall judge all worldly powers'.[10]

The failure of the millenarian hope led many to call in question the benevolence of an omnipotent God, and even his existence. Milton was not alone in feeling that God's ways to men needed justifying. The sense that God was on trial had its effect on restoration literature. We find it in Dryden and Traherne as well as in *Samson Agonistes*.[11] Here perhaps history can help literature. We must read *Samson Agonistes* in the light of the defeat of Milton's cause, and his belief that it was a religious *duty* to hate God's enemies. The moral of *Samson Agonistes* is that of the conclusion of *Paradise Lost* – hope in defeat. Samson is very carefully identified with the Good Old Cause of parliament, and with parliament's New Model Army. He too was executing divine judgment when he destroyed the Philistine aristocracy and priests, anticipating – as the elect were entitled to do – God's judgment on the aristocracy and clergy of England. 'The vulgar only 'scaped who stood without' – a phrase deliberately inserted with no biblical authority. At the end we see Samson's cause as an undying Phoenix.

I have said nothing about the period before 1660 that is not pretty familiar. But I think the consequences are not sufficiently reflected on, owing to our pestilential habit of periodization, which makes us draw a firm line between 1659 and 1660, and attach labels like 'Puritan' and 'reaction against Puritanism'. Some historians indeed try to obliterate the decades of the forties and fifties, suggesting that the sixties saw a return to 1640 rather than continuity with the fifties. Old-fashioned literary historians used to speak of French influences, and perhaps some *émigrés* did pick up some ideas in Paris. But I suspect that Rochester learnt at Wadham in the fifties everything he could have learnt in Paris, and more.

8. 'A Dialogue between Old England and New', in J. Hensley (ed.) *Works of Anne Bradstreet*, Harvard University Press, 1967, pp. 186–7; cf. George Fox, *To the Council of Officers*, 1659, p. 8.
9. Milton, *Complete Prose Works*, op. cit., III, p. 256.
10. John Cook, *King Charls his Case*, 1649, p. 40; Canne, *A Voice From the Temple*, op. cit., p. 14.
11. M.A Radzinowicz, *Toward Samson Agonistes: The Growth of Milton's Mind*, Princeton University Press, 1978, *passim*; my *Experience of Defeat*, op. cit., pp. 307–9.

I see the influence of the discussions of the revolutionary decades everywhere in restoration literature. As the editors of a recent volume put it, 'the literary scholar no less than the political historian cannot doubt that at the centre of all their histories stands the English civil war.'[12] How could it be otherwise? Men and women who had lived through that experience could not forget it, however much they might reject its politics. The clock could no more be set back in literature than in politics. Since censorship was restored in 1660, direct evidence of revolutionary ideas is of course minimal. But it can be traced.

Historians perhaps underestimate the generation gap. It is not always significant, but it appears in times of crisis – in the 1790s, after 1848, in the 1930s and 1960s. But especially after 1640-60. Aubrey and Clarendon are both specific about the generation gap. The restoration had been a compromise, sacrificing the extremists of either side: the younger generation on both sides tended to be sceptical of the heroics of their elders, *had* to accept the changes that had taken place. Prentices in the early forties were pro-parliamentarian; in 1659-60 their successors shouted for a king. The younger MPs in 1660 were the most enthusiastically royalist.[13] Samuel Butler was a royalist of the older generation. But he was as contemptuous of Charles II's courtiers as of sectaries. There are no 'good' royalists in *Hudibras* to set against the bad parliamentarians. Butler rejected 'honour' and the epic heroic virtues as firmly as Milton did – 'though no age ever abounded more with those images (as they call them) of moral and heroical virtues, there was never any so opposite to them all in the mode and custom of life'.[14] Worden suggests that the strong sense in the 1640s that Providence was on parliament's side had worn off in the 1650s – 'at least among younger men.'[15]

One reason why we take 1660 as a decisive turning point is that many influential contemporaries wanted to believe it was. Royalists saw it as a miraculous return to 'normality'. But historians, as Nicholas Jose rightly reminds us, should 'appreciate the uncertainty

12. Sharpe and Zwicker, Introduction to *Politics of Discourse*, op. cit., p. 10.
13. Hutton, *The Restoration*, op. cit., pp. 76, 80, 146.
14. I owe this point to Michael Wilding, *Dragon's Teeth*, op. cit., pp. 192, 199. The quotation is from Butler, *Characters and Passages*, op. cit., p. 278. See also my *Writing and Revolution*, op. cit., Ch. 13.
15. B. Worden, 'Providence and politics in Cromwell's England', *Past and Present*, 1985, 109, p. 98.

at the heart of the restoration'.[16] Steven Zwicker draws attention to 'the dislocation of language from meaning in this age', and politicians' 'long training in the arts of political dissimulation'. 'After civil war and political revolution, deception would enable men to approximate civic stability.' And not only politicians: Zwicker quotes Dryden's praise of London as having 'set a pattern to all others of true loyalty' – London, the main source of finance for the parliamentarian cause! But it was politically important to maintain this and other fictions.[17] The City had supported the restoration.

After 1660 former parliamentarians were trying to hush up their concessions to regicide and republicanism; they had been terrified by the social upheaval which followed the civil war, wanted 'normality', censorship and repression of the lower orders. The tinker Bunyan was silenced in jail, since he refused to silence himself. On the royalist side – to take only outstanding literary figures – Davenant had collaborated with Cromwell, Broghill had been the Protector's right-hand man in Scotland, the second Duke of Buckingham had recovered his confiscated estates by marrying poor Mary Fairfex, daughter of the parliamentarian general. Waller, Cowley, Sprat and Dryden wrote panegyrics to the Lord Protector, as Milton did not. Hobbes came back to England in 1651, Cowley in 1654. The latter in 1656, like Richard Lovelace in 1649, advocated ideological disarmament for the royalists. 'When the event of battle and the unaccountable will of God has determined the controversy, . . . we must lay down our pens as well as arms, we must march out of our cause itself, and dismantle . . . all the works and fortifications of wit and reason by which we defended it.'[18] Davenant, Broghill and Dryden invented the heroic tragedy of love and honour. Was it in order to forget the fifties, to create in fantasy the 'honour' which they – and so many in their audiences – had been unable to preserve in real life? To hush up the sordid compromises they had felt compelled to? Does this explain Butler's withering contempt for 'honour'? Such considerations affected parliamentarians who had abandoned their Good Old Cause no less than royalist supporters of the exiled Charles II.[19]

16. Jose, *Ideas of the Restoration*, op. cit., pp. 18, 29, 35.
17. Zwicker, *Politics and Language*, op. cit., pp. 31, 38, 206–7; cf. pp. 43, 50.
18. Cowley, Preface to *Poems*, 1656. Not reprinted in post-restoration editions, understandably; Gerald Hammond, 'Richard Lovelace and the uses of obscurity', *Proceedings of the British Academy*, 1985, LXXI, pp. 226–7, referring to *Aramantha*. Cf. Jose, *Ideas of the Restoration*, op. cit., pp. 74–96.
19. Neill, 'Heroic heads', op. cit., p. 116, cf. J. Sutherland, *English Literature of the Late Seventeenth Century*, Oxford University Press, 1969, p. 53.

> I served them, as many did;
> Laid by my conscience and took their money.

So said a character in *The Banished Shepherdess*, an unpublished play by Cosmo Manuche cited by Nancy Maguire.[20]

Real tragedy affecting kings and queens, it has been argued, was impossible after 1649.[21] 'It is not coincidental that the major serious genre of post-regicide England is tragicomedy', writes Nancy Maguire.[22] Or as Susan Staves put it, 'the preposterous complexity and wild exaggeration of the circumstances in which the heroic protagonist finds himself reflect an awareness of the heroic ideal as impossible'. 'One function of the heroic romance seems to have been to assuage the guilt of the post-war generation over its abandonment of the legitimate monarch.'[23] The society was 'purposefully retreating from serious political engagement', adds Martin Butler. 'There was much going on in the drama before 1640 which would find no place on the stage after 1660.'[24] The heroic was no longer plausible in the real world. The royalist gentry and aristocracy had come back, and they were very visible at court; but in comparison with the years before 1640 they had lost much of their automatic monopoly of positions of political importance. City money now talked.[25]

Restoration comedy attacks both bourgeois Puritan hypocrisy and traditional patriarchy, marriage for estates if not for money. The profound flippancy of this comedy relates to the irreverence of the revolutionary decades as well as to post-restoration cynicism. The literature is full of echoes of earlier irreligion and social subversion. The radical John Webster suggested that the Bible had been mistranslated in order to maintain belief in witchcraft.[26] Hobbes contributed to such attitudes; but they would have been unthinkable without the interregnum discussions. Whether the libertine ideas of restoration comedy come from the Ranters, from Hobbes, from

20. N. Maguire, 'The "whole truth" of restoration tragicomedy', in N. Maguire (ed.) *Renaissance Tragicomedy: Explorations in Genre and Politics*, New York, 1987, p. 222.
21. Catherine Belsey, 'Tragedy, justice and the subject', in P. Barker *et al.* (eds) *1642: Literature and Power in the Seventeenth Century*, Essex University, 1981, *passim*.
22. Maguire, 'Whole truth', op cit., p. 221 and *passim*.
23. Staves, *Players' Scepters*, op. cit., pp. 52, 110; cf. p. 60.
24. Butler, *Theatre and Crisis*, op. cit., pp. 160–2, 282.
25. Cf. C. Barber, *The Theme of Honour's Tongue: A Study of Social Attitudes in the English Drama from Shakespeare to Dryden*, Göteborg, 1985, p. 135 and *passim*.
26. Webster, *The Displaying of Supposed Witchcraft*, 1677, Ch. VI; cf. my *Writing and Revolution*, op. cit., p. 322; *Religion and Politics*, pp. 46–7.

'French influences' or from an older English tradition[27] – these are unanswerable questions. I am not trying to draw pedigrees: once ideas are about, especially in print, they are free for all to exploit. Libertine ideas were by no means limited to radicals.

The Duchess of Newcastle, for instance, expressed a deep religious scepticism, which was complemented but not cancelled out by her insistence that 'the chief pillar of religion is faith', not reason.[28] It was the Tory Thomas Otway who created the libertarian republican Pierre in *Venice Preserved*. Aphra Behn was a Tory too, but her play *The Widow Ranter* gave a not unsympathetic picture of a hard-drinking, smoking, hard-swearing Ranter lady; her novel, *Love Letters between a Nobleman and his Sister*, contained an attack on church marriage and a defence of romantic love, both of which recall Milton. Some of the best epigrams in her plays are aimed against mercenary marriage or against the clergy. ('Hymen and priest wait still upon portion and jointure'; 'Her reputation's ruined, and she'll need a double portion'; 'As uncharitable as a churchman'.) *The Town-Fop* (1676) is based on George Wilkins's *The Miseries of Inforst Marriage* of 1607.[29] In *Oroonoko* she contrasts the treachery and hypocrisy of Christians with the honour and honesty of the African prince Oroonoko. The Royal Slave 'would never be reconciled to our notions of the Trinity, of which he ever made a jest'. In Surinam 'religion would . . . but destroy that tranquillity they possess by ignorance; and laws would but teach 'em to know offences of which now they have no notion'.[30] Some at least of Oroonoko's jibes at Christianity were reproduced in Southerne's dramatized version of 1696.[31] Mrs Behn translated Fontenelle's *A Discovery of New Worlds*, accompanying

27. There appears to be no reference to Ranters in K.M. Lynch, *The Social Mode of Restoration Comedy*, New York, 1926, T.H. Fujimura, *The Restoration Comedy of Wit*, New York, 1952, Dale Underwood, *Etherege and the 17th Century Comedy of Manners*, Yale University Press, 1957, Earl Miner, *The Restoration Mode from Milton to Dryden*, Princeton University Press, 1974; nor even in McKeon, *Politics and Poetry*, op. cit., R.D. Hume, *The Development of English Drama in the late Seventeenth Century*, Oxford University Press, 1976. Honourable exceptions are Laura Brown (see p. 191 above) and Turner, *One Flesh*, op. cit.
28. Margaret Duchess of Newcastle, *CCXI Sociable Letters*, 1664, pp. 78, 353–8. See a forthcoming paper on the Duchess by Joanna Saxon, which she kindly allowed me to read.
29. Behn, *Works*, op. cit., I, pp. 81, 101, IV, p. 81; cf. pp. 40, 138, 151–2, 181, 192–3; II, pp. 255, 263–4, 379–80; IV, p. 323. For Wilkins see pp. 211–13 above.
30. Behn, *Oroonoko, or The Royal Slave*, in *Works*, op. cit., V, pp. 132, 160–6, 175, 196. The themes of a Golden Age and the Noble Savage recur in her poems (ibid., VI, pp. 138–44, 380). See pp. 191 above and 235–6 below.
31. T. Southerne, *Oroonoko: A Tragedy*, in *Works*, ed. R. Jordan and H. Love, Oxford University Press, 1988, II, p. 172.

it by some daring Biblical criticism.[32] Samuel Butler and Rochester echo many radical sentiments from earlier years. Mary Astell, Tory High Anglican feminist, asked 'If all men are born free, how is it that all women are born slaves?' But she was careful to say that she was not advocating insurrection.[33]

Restoration comedy attacked bad form rather than sin: dramatists assumed hostility to 'enthusiasm', to commitment. Social behaviour is becoming an elaborate game. The characters most mocked on the stage are not those who fail in the game but those who do not even know its name.[34] What matters now is fame, honour, reputation, whether in heroic drama or comedy; and honour has become a matter of petty personal punctilio. Hence the savagery of Samuel Butler's attacks on the concept. Why should female honour 'consist only in not being whores?', as if that sex was 'capable of no other morality but a mere negative continence?'[35] Hence Milton's disparagement of the epic virtues of courage in slaughter, echoed by Rochester in his *Satire on Mankind*. Robert Boyle, who early rejected traditional aristocratic moral codes, was nevertheless one of the architects of the restoration ideology of balance, moderation, as against the extremes of sectaries and atheists.[36] 'All who entered public debate,' as Zwicker put it, 'covered themselves with the garb of moderation', the mean. For Dryden in 1682 the Church of England represented the mean between papists and fanatics; after his conversion to Catholicism the Church of Rome became the mean between rapacious Anglicans and refractory dissenters. He was constant in his praise of a half-way position.[37]

I have discussed elsewhere the end of epic.[38] It would have been as difficult to write a traditional epic about the victorious New Model Army as Cowley found it to write one about the defeated royalists. The ethos of Cromwell and the New Model fitted better with Milton's

32. Duffy, *The Passionate Shepherdess*, op. cit., pp. 270–4.
33. Bridget Hill (ed.) *The First English Feminist: Reflections on Marriage and other Writings by Mary Astell*, 1986, pp. 76, 86.
34. I have benefited here from reading an unpublished paper by Glanville Heptonstall, recently of the Open University.
35. My *Writing and Revolution*, op. cit., pp. 280, 289–91, 324–6. See now Wilding, *Dragon's Teeth*, op. cit., Ch. 2.
36. Jacob, *Robert Boyle*, op cit., Ch. 2, *passim*.
37. Zwicker, *Politics and Language*, op. cit., pp. 54, 59–60, 88, and Ch. 4, *passim*; cf. pp. 35, 206–7.
38. See my *Writing and Revolution*, op. cit., pp. 324–5.

new standards of the heroic.[39] Joseph Wittreich's *Feminist Milton* makes out a case for seeing Eve as the hero of *Paradise Lost*. She plays a 'redemptive role' vis-à-vis Adam, and she is given the last speech in the epic. Milton and his readers well knew that this speech was always traditionally assigned to a god or to the hero. In *Paradise Lost* 'Adam heard/ But answered not':[40] he and Eve leave Paradise 'hand in hand'. In so far as it deals with Adam and Eve, *Paradise Lost* is well on the way to the novel; *Paradise Regained* perhaps even more so. Replacement of epic by the novel tells us something about the society, about its disbeliefs even more than about its beliefs.

In the 1630s popular drama had been censored and suppressed; in 1642 parliament closed the theatres, not least in order to free itself from radical criticism in the popular theatres.[41] Public theatres were reopened in 1660, but they too were very different from what they had been before 1640. Only two theatres were re-established, each very much under government control. The popular theatres were not reopened. As Martin Butler remarked, 1642 was 'a moment . . . of real, decisive discontinuity, for the stage that was restored after 1660 had been reorganized on a radically altered basis'.[42] Since the restoration had been made by an alliance against the radicals of conservative former Roundheads with former Cavaliers, both groups could feel satisfied.

Rationing by the purse was more effective than political censorship. 'The disappearance of the popular playhouses,' Butler adds, 'is the single most important difference between the Elizabethan theatre and the new theatre of the Restoration; it is an indication of the changes that had profoundly transformed the structure of Restoration politics and society.' The slow return of middle-class audiences, as Puritanism waned and dissenters prospered, no doubt contributed to the eighteenth-century decline of tragedies dealing with kings and generals. But even earlier, Hume suggests, most of the characters in restoration comedy are from the non-titled upper-middle class.[43]

Another innovation was the regular appearance of women on the stage. They first appeared in 1656, and after the restoration they were firmly established. This had far-reaching consequences for the relation

39. R.T. Fallon, *Captain or Colonel: The Soldier in Milton's Life and Art*, Missouri University Press, 1984, p. 95.
40. Wittreich, *Feminist Milton*, op. cit., pp. 99–109.
41. Heinemann, *Puritanism and Theatre*, op. cit., p. 34. See p. 214 above.
42. Butler, *Theatre and Crisis*, op. cit., p. 282.
43. ibid., p. 282; Hume, *Development of English Drama*, op. cit., pp. 162–3, 140. See my *Writing and Revolution*, op. cit., p. 328.

of the sexes. When Benedick and Beatrice or other 'gay couples' sparred on the Shakespearean stage, the edge was blunted by the fact that Beatrice was played by a boy. Boys were entitled to be pert, and women acted by boys could be given far greater freedom of expression in plays than in real life.[44] The sexual excitement aroused in male members of the audience was as likely to be homosexual as heterosexual. But with real women on the stage the case was different. Shakespeare and his contemporaries had explored the possibility of the equality of the sexes, denied by the conventional wisdom of the society, and by the Bible: so did Milton in *Comus* and in *Paradise Lost*. The fact that dangerous ideas could be tried out on the stage may have been taken into account by opponents of the theatre who had long denounced the players for acting a lie.

The post-restoration stage was different in another respect, as Catherine Belsey has pointed out: 'the introduction after 1660 of the proscenium theatre with its perspective backdrops radically changed the relationship between the audience and the stage'.[45] Restoration audiences, already much more exclusive than before 1640, were further removed from any sense of participation in the action on the stage. Theatres became more orderly and decorous, more remote from reality. These three changes seem to me symbolic for post-restoration culture as a whole.

The Revolution had lasting effects on religion. John Hales and Milton were not the only ones to bid good night to Calvinism, which lost the ascendancy over English thought which it had for so long enjoyed. Arminianism, with its emphasis on man's ability to work his own way to salvation, was one reaction to Calvinism. It led Milton first to *Areopagitica*, with its stress on the necessity of human freedom, and then to *Paradise Lost*, which is about the freedom of angels and men to stand or fall. The Presbyterian Blasphemy Ordinance of 1648 threatened imprisonment for anyone who said 'that man by nature hath free will to turn to God', or 'that man is bound to believe no more than by reason he can comprehend'. But by 1662 a bishop was saying 'nothing is by Scripture imposed upon us to be believed which is flatly contradictory to right reason and the suffrage of all our

44. Jean-Christophe Agnew, *Worlds Apart: The Market and the Theatre in Anglo-American Thought, 1550–1750*, Cambridge University Press, 1986, pp. 128–34.
45. C. Belsey, 'Shakespeare and film', *Literature/Film Quarterly*, 1983, XI, quoted by Graham Holderness, 'Radical potentiality and institutional closure: Shakespeare in film and television', in J. Dollimore and A. Sinfield (eds) *Political Shakespeare: New Essays in Cultural Materialism*, Massachusetts University Press, 1985, p. 184.

senses'.[46] We may speculate on the consequences of the intellectual shift away from Calvinism for the decline of tragedy and of the providential view of history. History as the working out of God's purposes for mankind yields place to secular history, to which Hobbist considerations of utility, pragmatic expediency, are more relevant than theology.[47]

The Calvinist assumption that the mass of mankind was predestined to everlasting torment may have ceased to weigh so heavily on men and women, though Bunyan still believed it. Perhaps most people had never taken it too seriously. Countless preachers in the early seventeenth century had deplored the ignorance and carelessness of the majority of the population: Dudley, Lord North, said in 1672 that lack of belief in life after death was common, 'especially among the vulgar'.[48] Perhaps Elizabethan and Jacobean dramatists were less obsessed with salvation and damnation than some critics have wishfully thought?[49] The dramatists' assumptions may have been more this-worldly than it was prudent to reveal. During the interregnum Gerrard Winstanley expressed very revolutionary ideas through use of the popular myths of the Norman Yoke, of Antichrist, and of biblical stories of Adam and Eve, Cain and Abel, Esau and Jacob. Did he believe them? It matters not much: it was a mode of expression which suited his poetic temperament and helped to get his message across. After 1660 the emphasis shifts decisively away from afterlife consolation. There is virtually none in Milton, surprisingly little in Bunyan. As the afterlife recedes from the centre of human attention, so in literature 'poetic justice' replaces divine retribution. Rymer and his like perhaps found justice on earth more satisfactory.

Millenarianism had spread the idea that salvation might come on earth, possibly in our time, not in the afterlife. Richard Coppin in 1649 – eighteen years before Milton – was looking for a Paradise within, happier far.[50] The Leveller Walwyn believed that a conviction of salvation would inflame men to fight against injustice.[51] For

---

46. John Gauden, Bishop of Exeter, quoted by Staves, *Players' Scepters*, op cit., pp. 13, xii.

47. McKeon, in Sharpe and Zwicker, *Politics of Discourse*, op. cit., pp. 48-9; cf. Jose, *Ideas of the Restoration*, op. cit., pp. 52, 172-4.

48. Quoted by Keith Thomas, *Religion and the Decline of Magic*, op. cit., p. 172.

49. This paper, I may perhaps remind the reader, was originally delivered at a conference devoted to 'Salvation and damnation in the religion and literature of the seventeenth century.'

50 Quoted in my *World Turned Upside Down*, op. cit., p. 221.

51. Walwyn, *The Power of Love*, 1643, pp. 38-41, in Haller, *Tracts on Liberty*, op. cit., II.

Winstanley, the Second Coming meant the power of Reason rising in all men and women, which would convince them of the desirability of establishing an egalitarian communist society: he expected no other Second Coming.[52] If God can be in each one of us, this is a potentially levelling doctrine. As Winstanley, Bunyan and many others insisted, truths are not found in books, but must come direct from divine inspiration. Nor are the elect necessarily bound by the Bible. 'The practice of the saints interprets the commandments', Milton insisted.[53] If each individual is in direct communication with God, he must follow his 'rousing motions', as Samson did, wherever they may lead. So salvation on earth leads to a this-worldly individualist morality. Mortalism, the belief that the soul dies with the body, was a heresy which Milton shared with the Leveller Richard Overton and with Thomas Hobbes, with the Muggletonians and with the Earl of Rochester. It could have a great liberating effect. Muggleton explained that he was ruled by 'the law written in my heart', not by the prospect of rewards or punishments in the afterlife.[54] This led him to be tolerant, some thought lax, in dealing with the moral peccadilloes of his followers. Everyone had to settle his own account with God, provided he had the basic faith. The Celestial City in *The Pilgrim's Progress* is very reminiscent of the future life on earth described by millenarians like Mary Cary in the 1640s. Marvell, like Milton, was concerned with how fallen man can live on earth. By the end of the century Dr John North, himself an Arminian by conviction, nevertheless thought Calvinism, 'with respect to ignorant men, to be more politic, and thereby, in some respects, fitter to maintain religion in them, because more suited to their capacity. But that is referred to art, and not to truth, and ought to be ranked with the *piae fraudes* or holy cheats.'[55] To such ends had Calvinism come. When Marlowe's *Faustus* was revived on the stage in 1688 it was rewritten to be played as farce.[56]

So far as the printed record tells us, active revolutionary millenarianism fades out after 1661; Christ's coming is put into the distant future. But the millenarian hope had given a new sense of historical time. History was not cyclical but linear, moving towards a

52. My *Religion and Politics*, op. cit., Ch. 12, *passim*.
53. Milton, *Complete Prose Works*, op. cit., VI, p. 368.
54. Muggleton, *Acts of the Witnesses*, op. cit., p. 140.
55. Roger North, *Lives of the Norths*, 1826, III, p. 344. First published 1740-2.
56. Hume, *Development of English Drama*, op. cit., p. 375; cf. my *Writing and Revolution*, op. cit., pp. 326-9.

culmination.[57] Traditionally reformers had looked back to the free Anglo-Saxons, to the primitive church, to the innocence of unfallen man; millenarians looked forward to a better future on earth. Winstanley made the point by calling one of his pamphlets *The New Law of Righteousness*; Levellers began to speak of the rights of man, not of the descendants of the free Anglo-Saxons.[58] The victory of the Moderns in their battle against the Ancients also helped to create a rudimentary theory of progress.

Millenarianism could easily be secularized. The author of a millenarian pamphlet in 1653 knew of 'nothing more important than matters of trade, as tending to strengthen the position against all eventualities'.[59] Marvell in *The First Anniversary* spoke in religious terms, but his vision of Oliver Cromwell forwarding God's purposes depended on a powerful English navy controlling the seas.[60] Harrington advocated a millenarian imperialism.[61] Dryden in 1666 dedicated *Annus Mirabilis* to the City of London, and depicted the English as God's chosen people; but his emphasis on national power and national trade was not related, as it had been in Marvell, to any idea of a Protestant crusade. This 'untroubled imperialism' was common among Dryden's contemporaries.[62] Acceptance in polite literary circles of the all-importance of trade and of the new foreign policy is one of the most remarkable ways in which the tone of English literature after 1660 differs from that before 1640. Davenant's *The Cruelty of the Spaniards in Peru* and *The History of Sir Francis Drake* were blatant propaganda, designed to impress Oliver Cromwell and his court. But after the restoration Dryden set the imaginary discussions in his *Essay of Dramatic Poesy* against the background of the great battle in which English and Dutch fleets 'disputed the command of the greater half of the globe, the commerce of nations and the riches of the universe'.[63] Dissenters dropped millenarianism in favour of pacifism and abstention from politics: secular imperialism took over.

57. L. Potter, 'The plays and the playwrights' in N. Sanders *et al.* (eds) *The Revels History of Drama in England*, II, *1500–1576*, 1980, p. 193. Cf. pp. 83–4 above.
58. Cf. Jose, *Ideas of the Restoration*, op. cit., pp. 172–4.
59. Anon., *The Coming of Christs Appearing in Glory and its Shortly Breaking Forth*, quoted by H.A. Glass, *The Barebone Parliament*, 1899, p. 52.
60. Margoliouth (ed.) Marvell, *Poems and Letters*, I, p. 112. For Marvell see M. Stocker, *Apocalyptic Marvell: The Second Coming in 17th Century Poetry*, Brighton, 1986, Ch. 5.
61. Harrington, *Political Works*, op. cit., pp. 329–33.
62. McKeon, *Politics and Poetry*, op. cit., *passim*; Zwicker, *Politics and Language*, op. cit., pp. 74, 82.
63. Dryden, *Of Dramatic Poesy and Other Critical Essays*, Everyman edn, I, p. 18. First published 1668.

So I want to insist that the restoration was not a return to 1640, but continued the tradition of the fifties. Here are some further examples from literature:

In the 1640s popular journalists created a new kind of prose, written in the conversational language of ordinary people. That was necessary if propaganda was to reach the man in the street, as in the forties for the first time it had to, since the man in the street was no longer being told that the mysteries of state were not his concern. Instead, he was being urged to fight, to pay taxes, to suffer billeting and free quarter: both sides wished to convince him that their cause justified his sacrifices. The royalist Berkenhead no less than the (ultimately) parliamentarian Marchamont Nedham played a part in this evolution of a simpler, more direct and forceful prose.[64] James Sutherland pointed out that shortage of space encouraged the restoration newswriter to express himself succinctly and fluently, often quoting the exact words of his correspondents.[65] And Defoe noted that English prose style had changed more in the fifty or sixty years before he wrote than in the preceding century.[66]

Plain conversational prose was not wholly novel, of course. We meet it in plays and Puritan sermons well before 1640. It has a long history in radical writings, going back through the pamphlets of Thomas Scott and Martin Marprelate to Tyndale and the Protestant propagandists of the reigns of Henry VIII and Edward VI. It had been an irreverent tradition. Scott's pamphlets supplied material for Middleton's *A Game at Chess*. Marprelate referred to his Grace the Archbishop of Canterbury as 'nuncle Canterbury', 'that Caiaphas of Cant', 'that miserable and desperate caitiff, . . . the Pope of Lambeth'; and to John Aylmer, Bishop of London as 'dumb dunsical John of good London'.[67] It has been argued that Richard Overton, who wrote some of the finest Leveller prose, had been an actor, and that his early satirical pamphlets in dialogue draw on his theatrical experience; they also consciously exploit the Marprelate tradition.

---

64. P.W. Thomas, *Sir John Berkenhead, 1617–1679: A Royalist Career in Politics and Polemics*, Oxford University Press, 1969, especially Chs. V and VI.
65. J. Sutherland, *The Restoration Newspaper and its Development*, Oxford University Press, 1986, p. 232.
66. Defoe, *The Compleat English Gentleman*, ed. K.D. Büllbring, 1890, p. 224. First published 1728.
67. Marprelate, *An Epitome* 1588, p. 20; *Hay Any Worke for Cooper*, op. cit., p. 43; *Theses Martinianae*, op. cit., Sig. C iiv; *The just censure and reproofe of Martin Junior* (1589), Sig. A ii: all in M. Marprelate, *The Marprelate Tracts*, Leeds, 1967.

Overton called himself 'Martin Marprelate Junior', 'Martin Marpriest' and 'Martin Claw-Clergy'.[68] His use of popular dialogue prepared for Bunyan, who, as we have seen, was also heir to a tradition of popular verse.[69]

Weekly newspapers, political pamphlets, chapbooks and almanacs, increased markedly in the fifties and sixties.[70] Spiritual biographies and autobiographies also boomed: as we all know now, they lead through Bunyan and Defoe to the novel. When Sprat said the Royal Society preferred 'the language of artisans, countrymen and merchants before that of wits or scholars', he was accepting the simplification of prose which journalists and pamphleteers had brought about during the Revolution.[71]

I can only list other apparent innovations of the interregnum. Diaries – Ralph Josselin and many other ministers, Evelyn. Pepys presciently started his diary on 1 January 1660. Freedom of the press in the 'Puritan' 1650s had included freedom to print bawdy literature. There are many examples of pamphlets and collections of poems which we would normally associate with post-restoration 'licence'.[72] *The Ladies Dispensatory* in 1651 was giving advice 'to cause abortion', 'to hinder conception'.[73] In 1655 Milton's nephew, John Philips, published a lewd satire on the state clergy, which I suspect his uncle enjoyed. The first translation of Aretino's *Dialogues* came out in 1658.

The masque, with its facile magical solutions to all problems, and the panegyrics to royalty which accompanied the divine right of kings, could no more survive the 1640s than could tragedy.[74] Emblems do not return in 1660 either. The genre descends to where it belongs – poems for children. Quarles and Wither, popular before 1640, sink out of polite literature after 1660: so did numerology. With them go

68. Marie Gimelfarb-Brack, *Liberté, Egalité, Fraternité, Justice: La vie et l'oeuvre de Richard Overton, Niveleur*, Berne, 1979, Part III, Chs. 2 and 3; Heinemann, *Puritanism and Theatre*, op. cit., Ch. 13.
69. See pp. 199–200 above.
70. M.Spufford, *Small Books and Pleasant Histories*, 1981, Ch. 4, *passim*.
71. Sprat, *History of the Royal Society*, op. cit., p. 113.
72. Martine Brant lists nine 'bawdy and erotic' pamphlets between 1650 and 1659 in her thesis 'The literature of the London underworld, 1660–1720', Newcastle-upon-Tyne Polytechnic, M.Phil., 1982, pp. 373–4. I am most grateful to her for permitting me to quote this thesis, and for much useful discussion. Cf. Frank, *Hobbled Pegasus*, op. cit., pp. 15–17.
73. George, *Women in the First Capitalist Society*, op. cit., p. 209. For works on midwifery and obstetrics published in the 1650s see Audrey Eccles, *Obstetrics and Gynaecology in Tudor and Stuart England*, 1982, p. 13. The novelty is that such advice was printed.
74. M.L. Donelly, 'Caroline royalist panegyric and the disintegration of a symbolic mode', in Summers and Pebworth, '*The Muses' Common-Weale*', op. cit., pp. 163–76.

funny-shaped poems, altars and wings, acrostics, rebuses and everything that Benlowes had enjoyed.

Satire, silenced at the beginning of the century, returned in the
favourable environment of civil war, and flourished after 1660 in the
hands of Butler, Marvell, Dryden, Rochester, Bunyan. The elevated
language which made heroic drama ridiculous was eminently suited
to the fierce political satire of Marvell and Dryden, and to Butler's
burlesque.

There was no real revival of metaphysical poetry, notwithstanding
Traherne, Norris and Edward Taylor. Violent juxtaposition of oppo-
sites is out of fashion: contradictions have been ironed out or pushed
under the carpet. Consensus is the word in politics: arguments are
neatly rounded off in a final rhymed couplet. The continuities in verse
run from Denham and Waller, each of them only just a royalist in
1642; Waller wrote *A Panegyric to my Lord Protector* (his cousin) in
1655.

During the revolutionary decades there had been so many conflicting
claims to divine authority, based on conflicting interpretations of the
Bible, that an exhausted scepticism had been the almost inevitable
result. Another consequence was a desperate attempt to find a new,
non-biblical basis for morality. Hobbes and Locke sought for a secular
theory of political obligation. Anxiety to itemize the laws of nature
written in every man's heart is widespread in the later seventeenth
century. How are we to distinguish between Winstanley's Reason
rising in all sons and daughters, the Quaker inner light, and Samson's
'rousing motions' – or indeed Milton's belief that God must exist
because it was intolerable and incredible that evil should triumph over
good?[75] A new intellectual consensus was needed. Primitivism
appeared with Almanzor in Dryden's *The Conquest of Granada* (1669):

> I am as free as nature first made man,
> Ere the base laws of servitude began
> When wild in woods the noble savage ran. (Act I, sc. i)

It was further developed by Aphra Behn:

> In that blest golden age, when man was young . . .
> When Nature did her wond'rous dictates give,
> And taught the Noble Savage how to live.

---

75. Milton, *Complete Prose Works*, op. cit., VI, p. 131; Staves, *Players' Scepters*, op. cit.,
pp. 257–8; cf. J. Beaumont, *Complete Poems*, ed. A.B. Grosart, 1880, I, pp. 183–4; II,
p. 107.

The *locus classicus* is her *Oroonoko*.[76]

Aubrey again and again emphasizes that decline of belief in divine or diabolical intervention in everyday human affairs dates from the Revolution.[77] Persecution of witches fades out from the later seventeenth century, despite the propaganda of clerical Fellows of the Royal Society who held that belief in witchcraft was necessary to belief in God. The decline of belief in hell, which D.P. Walker has so effectively traced, also came at this period; though here I would myself lay more emphasis on the scepticism generated in discussions during the interregnum than Mr Walker does.[78]

Anthony Low traces what he calls the 'Georgic revolution' from Spenser through Milton down to the eighteenth century. By this he appears to mean a recognition by poets of the dignity of labour, especially of agricultural labour. Labour had traditionally been despised by court poets; Low sees the revolutionary decades as a turning point both in this poetic tradition and in moral attitudes towards agricultural improvement, which became a *duty* for landowners. This of course was a consequence of the agricultural revolution of the later seventeenth century, itself a consequence of the transformation of land into absolute property by the abolition of feudal tenures and the defeat of copyholders' efforts to obtain equivalent security of tenure for themselves.[79] Locke had as little doubt about the duty of landowners to improve the value of their estates as he had about the duty of the lower classes to work for them.

In the 1650s some beleaguered royalists, unwilling to meet their conquerors half-way (as Cowley did), retreated into a classicism which emphasized that they were an intellectual élite even if they had (temporarily) lost their social superiority.[80] The Royal Society was to do something similar by emphasizing 'common sense', the common sense of the new élite. Whether consciously or unconsciously adopted, intellectual consensus was found by extending this 'common sense' to 'manners' and use of language as a means of dividing sheep from goats, the cultivated from the vulgar. 'Acceptance as a gentleman

76. Aphra Behn's *Miscellany* of 1685, in *Works*, op. cit., II. p. 380; cf. pp. 138–44. See also pp. 191 and 226–7 above.

77. Aubrey, *Remaines of Gentilisme and Judaisme*, 1881, *passim*; *Natural History of Wiltshire*, 1847, p. 5; *Brief Lives*, ed. A. Clark, Oxford University Press, 1898, I, p. 27, II, p. 318.

78. D.P. Walker, *The Decline of Hell: Seventeenth Century Discussions of Eternal Torment*, Chicago University Press, 1964, *passim*.

79. Low, *The Georgic Revolution*, op. cit., *passim*; my *Writing and Revolution*, op. cit., pp. 319–20; *People and Ideas*, op. cit., pp. 45–6, 100; cf. Chapter 2 above.

80. Thomas, *Sir John Berkenhead*, op. cit., Chs VI and VII; my *Writing and Revolution*, op. cit., pp. 96–104.

was probably becoming less a matter of birth and more a matter of breeding and manners', suggests Charles Barber.[81] The Royal Society's ideal of prose, although based on the language of artisans and merchants, was consciously directed against the enthusiastic style of the sectaries. (Recall Pepys's amused tolerance in 1663 of the old-fashioned language of Aunt Jane, one of his nonconformist relations.) Dryden in 1672–3 made the essential shift from 'plain' to 'correct' style, 'correct' style being that of the court. The new ruling-class solidarity was based on language, on education, rather than merely on birth: an opportunity society, in which the court was no longer isolated from the City of London.[82]

Alvarez put it well: 'restoration decorum is different from that of Elizabeth because it embodies a fixed principle of behaviour, almost of conformity, a determination to avoid . . . all emphatic gestures that might seem out of place in, to use Sprat's words, "the City and Court".' It was 'a new attitude to language and to the mode of argument'. Behind it was 'fear of [civil] war, chaos, instability and insecurity'. Behind the democracy of the mind, which the Royal Society preached, was a fear of argument as such. For 'hard indigestible arguments, or sharp contests' (Sprat, p. 152) 'are civil wars in miniature'.[83] Ordinary people can be inspired; inspiration is indeed more likely to come to them than to their social betters, or to scholars. But 'the rules' can only be learnt, preferably through a classical education at Oxford or Cambridge. 'The rules' led to denigration of Shakespeare vis-à-vis Jonson,[84] disparagement of Bunyan because he could not form a proper syllogism.

I am not suggesting that the ideology of classicism, opposition to fanaticism and claims to inspiration, which came to the rescue of deference after 1660 (or earlier) was planned, any more than the Revolution of 1640 had been planned. But some very clever men

81. Barber, *The Theme of Honour's Tongue*, op. cit., p. 22.
82. Dryden, *Of Dramatic Poesy*, op. cit., p. 181; cf. my *Writing and Revolution*, op. cit., pp. 323–4.
83. A. Alvarez, *The School of Donne*, 1961, pp. 166, 175–6; cf. T. Eagleton, *Literary Theory*, Oxford, 1983, p. 203: language is power. See also Sutherland, *English Literature*, op. cit., pp. 408, 414–15; Jose, *Ideas of the Restoration* op. cit., pp. 18–19: because language contains a culture within itself, 'when language changes a culture itself is also changing in important ways'. See Carolyn Merchant, *The Death of Nature: Women, Ecology and the Scientific Revolution*, San Francisco, 1980, p. 4; S. Shapin and S. Schaffer, *Leviathan and the Air-Pump: Hobbes, Boyle and the Experimental Life*, Princeton University Press, 1985, pp. 340–4 and *passim*.
84. Cf. Harriett Hawkins, *The Devil's Party: Critical Counter-Interpretations of Shakespearean Drama*, Oxford University Press, 1985, especially pp. 93–4.

contributed significantly to the new ideology – Berkenhead to the classical emphasis, Monck perceiving the political usefulness of the word 'fanatic', Charleton and Boyle grasping how essential it was to separate science from both atheism and radical sectarianism, which they believed (or said they did) led naturally on to atheism, Sprat with his artisans' prose, Dryden refining Sprat, Charles II becoming patron of the Royal Society as well as head of the Church of England, Charles touching for the King's evil, he and his brother licensing dissenting ministers and so bringing them indirectly under state control, Davenant taking over a theatre monopoly as well as denouncing inspiration in literature as in religion, Sir Roger L'Estrange taking over censorship in order to use it against 'the great masters of the popular style', Matthew Wren twisting Harringtonianism to the service of absolutism, Broghill writing heroic drama. Many of the cleverest, it will be noticed, are former parliamentarians, or at least former Cromwellians. Like Berkenhead and his group in the forties and fifties, they had learnt the hard way. When inspiration revived as a poetic creed with romanticism, it no longer had the same religio-political overtones as in the 1650s.

The seventeenth century marks a watershed in the history of patronage in England. Before 1640 aristocratic support was a virtual necessity if one was to devote oneself to the career of writing. This was true even for dramatists, much more so for an independent thinker like Hobbes. By the end of the century, thanks to the erosion of the censorship, it was possible for men, and even the exceptional woman like Aphra Behn, to live by their pens. Dryden complained bitterly when his salary as poet laureate was not regularly paid; but he could live without it, even if not at the standard to which he aspired. Bunyan marks the transition. He did not need to write for a patron, and his religious convictions made him despise social climbers. Yet he was not condemned to the drudgery of hack writing. His lower-middle-class readership enabled him to achieve fame without either aristocratic patronage or concessions to the money power. His unique talents permitted him to seize a unique opportunity. From Walton's *Polyglot Bible* (1654–7) publishing by subscription began to offer new opportunities of relative independence to authors, whilst some of the features of patronage were still retained.[85]

---

85. Sarah C. Clapp, 'The beginnings of subscription publishing in the seventeenth century', *Modern Philology*, 1931, 29; 'Subscription publishers prior to Jacob Tonson', *The Library*, 1933, 4th series, 14; R.M. Adams, 'In search of Baron Somers', in P. Zagorin (ed.) *Culture and Politics from Puritanism to the Early Enlightenment*, California University Press, 1986, p. 175; Susan Staves, 'Pope's refinement', *The 18th Century: Theory and Interpretation*, 1985, 29, p. 154.

In 1660 bishops were restored, together with the House of Lords and the monarchy. The state church survived, and so did tithes. Tithes maintained a clergyman in every parish, authorized to interpret the Scriptures whose meaning had been so controversial in the forties and fifties. The universities survived to train these interpreters. In 1672 nonconformist ministers had to be licensed – the next best thing to having them in a state church, very different from groups meeting for free-ranging discussion and electing a mechanic preacher as chairman. Hierarchy again, hegemony. On the other hand there could be no consistent revival of pre-1640 attempts to force nonconformists into the church, or to harry them out of the land. Instead they were made second-class citizens, excluded (in theory at least) from central and local government and from the universities. Their gentry supporters, of whom there had been many before 1640, naturally and necessarily abandoned them. The two nations became also two classes. Exclusion from the universities mattered less intellectually than socially. Dissenting academies gave a better education, but less polish.

Dissenters connived at their own subordination. They abandoned immediate millenarian expectations, and with them any significant involvement in politics. In 1661 the Quakers proclaimed the peace principle. But the necessity of defining a sect's belief, and of fitting it to survive in a hostile environment, led to internal splits and schisms, a preoccupation with the struggle to impose and preserve unity and purity, order and discipline. The congregations had no time or energy left for turning outwards to reform society – even if there had been the possibility.

The ending of the church's independence of parliament meant that there could be no reversion to Laudian social policies of the thirties – opposition to enclosures, attempts to control parish élites. The tyranny of the gentry was unchecked after 1660, with the game laws as its symbol. JPs took over from church courts control of moral behaviour, at least when its consequences were likely to cost the parish money. Compulsory church attendance every Sunday never recovered from its collapse in 1640 and its abolition between 1650 and 1657. Soon churchwardens were congratulating themselves if they could report that most parishioners did not absent themselves from worship.

In one respect at least the culture of the restoration period returned to that of Charles I's personal rule – censorship was restored. 'Tumultuous petitioning' (i.e. without the authorization of JPs) was prohibited and the Settlement Act of 1662 restricted the movements both of the unemployed seeking work and of itinerant preachers. Censorship was not always effective. One of the things historians need is a censorship chart, like the weather charts which we already have. Edward VI's reign would be the equivalent of a run of good harvest years. The 1640s would be years of liberty: so would 1659–60. 1672–3, after the Declaration of Indulgence, saw a relaxation: Marvell could publish *The Rehearsal Transpros'd*, even though anonymously. Between 1678 and 1681 the censorship was not (or could not be) enforced: there was a flood of pamphlets relating to the Popish Plot; new newspapers appeared after parliament failed to renew the Licensing Act in 1679. It is perhaps not a coincidence that some of Bunyan's greatest works appeared at this time – *The Pilgrim's Progress* in 1678, *Mr. Badman* in 1680, *The Holy War* in 1682. Rochester's *Poems* came out in 1680, Marvell's in 1681. Hobbes's *Behemoth* appeared in a pirated edition in 1679. 'A surprising number of new plays got produced' between 1679 and 1682, observed Professor Hume, 'including a fair proportion of really fine ones.' But this 'flood of political dramas' was followed by 'the virtual cessation of play writing' as control was re-established.[86]

In the new liberty after 1688 Selden's *Table Talk* could be published (1689), Locke's *Two Treatises of Government* in 1690, Milton's political sonnets and Fox's *Journal* in 1694. Failure to renew the Licensing Act in 1695 led to a whole series of manuscripts being printed which may hitherto have been thought too risky – Baxter's *Reliquiae* (1696), Toland's *Christianity Not Mysterious* (1696), Ludlow's *Memoirs* and Algernon Sidney's *Discourses Concerning Government* in 1698, Harrington's *Works* in 1700. Rushworth's *Historical Collections* (documents relating to the revolutionary period) which had started publication in 1659, and resumed in the liberty of 1680, was finally completed in 1692 and 1701, after Rushworth's death.

After 1695 literature was self-censored. Many of the works of Quakers reprinted in the later seventeenth century – including Fox's *Journal* – contained significant alterations and omissions, with disastrous results for historians' comprehension of early Quakerism. But after 1695 private enterprise did the censoring. Once the new consensus had been established, publishers did not want to risk disturbing it. There was no return to the licentious freedom of the 1640s, or even of 1678–81. Nothing too dangerously seditious got into print. Even a radical like Toland knew that certain things were better

86. Hume, *Development of English Drama*, op. cit., pp. 340–2; my *Writing and Revolution*, op. cit., pp. 51–4. 'Play writing' perhaps means 'staging or printing of plays'.

left unsaid in the nineties: he drastically blue-pencilled Ludlow's *Memoirs*, and possibly Sidney's *Discourses*. Works by Levellers were not reprinted. The press, which governments had never managed to control effectively, was brought to heel by free capitalist enterprise.

Slowly there evolved a new literary consensus to match the new political and religious consensus, a consensus for what Susan Staves has called 'the new class of the polite, . . . more inclusive than the old aristocracy'. 'On the one hand, refinement was a critique of older aristocratic styles of behaviour, including resort to physical violence. On the other hand, refinement, by definition not accessible to the vulgar, was the upwardly mobile virtue of the formerly vulgar bourgeoisie.'[87]

The new consensus had some deplorable effects on literature. Milton was sanitized by Toland and Addison: his radicalism was so effectively hushed up that even publication of the *De Doctrina Christiana* in 1825 failed to convince some critics. Bunyan was read mainly by the lower classes and by Americans until the middling sort revived appreciation of him in the nineteenth century, as they revived some aspects of radical politics, and when inspiration came in again.

Joseph Frank saw the London money power behind the drift towards secularization and deism.[88] Dr Laura Stevenson, taking a longer view, depicted middle-class authors under Elizabeth accepting the ideology of the gentry; but by the end of the seventeenth century their successors had worked out their own ideology, starting from repudiation of the traditional concept of honour.[89] Even writers like Oldham and Southerne could safely sneer at the idea of innate, inherited honour.[90] But it was a two-way process. The gentry were Janus-faced after 1660. Margaret Jacob has brilliantly demonstrated how the Royal Society involved gentlemen in *practical* science, first in the interests of agricultural improvement but leading on to a receptiveness of mechanical inventions and industrialization.[91] Nathaniel Fairfax in 1674 praised the Society's prose style as appropriate to set forth the things of a *working philosophy*, . . . the philosophy of our day

---

87. Staves, 'Pope's refinement', op. cit., p. 151; cf. her 'A few kind words for the fop', *Studies in English Literature*, 1982, 22. She quotes N. Rogers, 'Money, land and lineage: the big bourgeoisie of Hanoverian London', *Social History*, 1979, 4.
88. Frank, *Hobbled Pegasus*, op. cit., pp. 25–7.
89. L.C. Stevenson, *Praise and Paradox: Merchants and Craftsmen in Elizabethan Popular Literature*, Cambridge University Press, 1984, pp. 128–9, 157–8.
90. J. Oldham, 'A Satyr touching nobility'; T. Southerne, *Sir Anthony Love*, 1691, Act I, sc. i; Act II, sc. i.
91. Jacob, *Scientific Revolution*, op. cit., *passim*.

and land being so much workful as the world knows it to be'.[92]

I have argued that 1660 was not a return to 1640. When we ask how the myth arose, the answer is clear enough: conservative partisans on both sides wanted to hush up the revolutionary decades, to pretend that they had been an 'interregnum', that Charles II had succeeded his father on 30 January 1649, and that since no parliamentary legislation between 1641 and 1660 was valid without confirmation, those years had never existed. Winners write history;[93] it is very difficult to find out what early Christian heretics really taught, just as it would be difficult to know about dissent in eastern Europe until very recently were it not for the possibility of publishing elsewhere. The legend was fortified by the fact that nonconformity came to live up to it: in the two nations dissenters were good at making money and at science, but culture and civilization radiated from the laughing Cavaliers of the court. Upper-class standards of language reinforced what soon became to them a self-evident truth. But there is no need for us to perpetuate the myth.

So much was lost; some things were gained. T.S. Eliot may have given the wrong explanation by his 'dissociation of sensibility'; but something happened to English poetry in the seventeenth century, whose effects were not wholly beneficial. The new consensus – accepting the mechanical philosophy, individualism, utilitarianism and secular millenarianism, rational religion – took over many of the ideas of Puritanism but without its moral fervour and committed excitement. The greatest literature of the early eighteenth century is concerned to expose shams – Mary Astell, Swift, Defoe, Mandeville, Gay, Fielding.

There was no English Enlightenment, Professor Pocock rightly observed, though there was one in Scotland. In England the job had already been done. The ideas of the European Enlightenment are the ideas of the English Revolution,[94] and England was no longer a cultural backwater. But eighteenth-century Europe read not the Augustans who represented the compromises of 1660 and 1688, Dryden, Pope and Addison, so much as literature relating to England's pioneering role in overseas travel – *The Isle of Pines* by the

---

92. N. Fairfax, *A Treatise of the Bulk and Selvedge of the World*, 1674, To the Reader, in A.K. Crofton (ed.) *Two Seventeenth-Century Prefaces*, Liverpool University Press, 1949, p. 40. Italics in the original.

93. Staves, *Players' Scepters*, op. cit., p. 3.

94. J.G.A. Pocock, 'Post-Puritan England and the problem of the Enlightenment', in Zagorin, *Culture and Politics*, op. cit., pp. 92–108.

republican Henry Neville,[95] *Robinson Crusoe, Gulliver's Travels*. Seventeenth-century England invented not only political economy but also the novel, the bourgeois literary form. Richardson, Fielding, Sterne were read on the continent; Shakespeare had to wait for the romantic revival.

There was another heritage of the English Revolution of which we have only recently become aware. The book which was published in the largest numbers in nineteenth-century Russia, and so presumably read by the most people, was *Paradise Lost*. For a long time the world bestseller, after the Bible, was *The Pilgrim's Progress*, the book which helped to inspire the Taiping rebels who came very near to overthrowing the Emperor of China and seizing power in the mid-nineteenth century.[96] What did Russian peasants find in *Paradise Lost*? What did Bunyan's other Third-World readers get out of (or read into) *The Pilgrim's Progress*? Did they get nearer Bunyan's meaning than we do? We have still not yet properly evaluated the full historical significance of the English Revolution.

95. See Onofrio Nicastro, *Henry Neville e l'isola di Pines*, Pisa, 1988, *passim*.
96. For *Paradise Lost* see Valentine Boss's forthcoming book, *Milton in Russia*, which he very kindly allowed me to see before publication; for Bunyan, see Rudolph G. Wagner, *Reenacting the Heavenly Vision: The Role of Religion in the Taiping Rebellion*, California University Press, 1982, *passim*.

12

History and the present

[There is no] universal passport of a general historico-philosophical theory, the supreme virtue of which consists in being super-historical.

Karl Marx to the editor of a Russian newspaper, 1877, in Marx and Engels, *Correspondence, 1846–1895*, op. cit., p. 355

We have modern cloistered coxcombs who
Retire to think, 'cause they have nought to do.
But thoughts are given for action's government;
Where action ceases, thought's impertinent.

John Wilmot, Earl of Rochester, *A Satyr on Reason and Mankind*,
1679

History means two things: first the past as we believe it to have existed, and second the past as we attempt to reconstruct it in our writings. Cynics say that when historians claim to be describing the past they are really writing contemporary history – or autobiography. This is true to the extent that the new questions which each generation of historians asks inevitably reflect the interests of that generation. The women's movement drew the attention of historians to the fact that women were not an invention of the Industrial Revolution: the student revolution of the 1960s revived interest in the libertinism and scepticism of seventeenth-century Ranters. A kind reviewer even said that a book which I published in 1984 called *The Experience of Defeat* represented my reaction to Margaret Thatcher.

It is right and proper that historians should ask new questions of the past, and such questions may well be stimulated by happenings in our own society. I see no harm in this so long as our *answers* do not derive from the present. I remember having a rather unprofitable argument with a Chinese historian, who told me that what went wrong in seventeenth-century England was that the English revolutionaries lacked an organized and disciplined party with a clear ideology. He didn't say 'like the Chinese Communist Party', but that I fear is what he meant.

The most fruitful change in historical attitudes in my time, I think, has been the emergence of 'history from below' – the realization that ordinary people have a history, that they may have played a greater part in determining the shape of the historical process, whether for change or for continuity, than we have thought. This new emphasis, I suppose, must be related to the emergence of a more self-consciously democratic society. History no longer deals exclusively with kings and their mistresses, prime ministers and wars, statutes and debates in parliament. The work of Edward Thompson, George Rude and Keith Thomas has changed all that: and they, interestingly enough, are the historians who are best known outside Britain. A declining band of traditionalists continues to think that only political, constitutional and administrative history is real history: those who argue for history from below want to add a dimension to this narrower tradition. Recent TV programmes on events in Eastern Europe educated us.

Similarly with women's history, which as a serious subject dates from early in this century, and got going after the 1950s. I still remember the frisson of horror which went round Oxford historical circles when the *enfant terrible* Keith Thomas put on a series of lectures on 'Women in 17th-century England'. We have moved a long way since then. Women's history, I suppose, is the best advertisement for the beneficial result of asking of the past questions which arise from the present. As I suggested in Chapter 7, one of the things I am most ashamed of is that for decades I proudly illustrated the spread of democratic ideas in seventeenth-century England by quoting the ringing Leveller declarations, 'the poorest he that is in England hath a life to live as the greatest he', 'every man that is to live under a government ought first by his own consent to put himself under that government'.[1] The poorest he? Every man? What about the other 50 per cent of the population? I must have noticed the absence of woman from these statements; but I somehow assumed that that had to be taken for granted in seventeenth-century England. But if we are to understand that society we have to ask *why* it was taken for granted – not only by men, but even by Leveller women who canvassed, agitated, petitioned, leafleted and lobbied for the vote for

1. See pp. 118, 122–3.

their menfolk and apparently never even thought of asking for it for themselves. Once we ask the question, other questions are opened up – about the overwhelming influence of the Bible, about the law of property, about the prevalence of the household economy. We have to undertake a bigger rethink about the past than even feminist historians have yet realized.

Writing history from below is of course much more difficult than writing history from on top; and this raises problems about the training of professional historians. Today the potential D.Phil. student either finds for himself or herself or (more likely) is directed by his/her supervisor towards a cache of unpublished documents. He/she copies these out – or nowadays I suppose they are microfilmed for him/her – and spills them out into a thesis, whose acceptance is taken to qualify him or her for an academic job. But there are no caches of documents about the history of ordinary people, or of ordinary women as distinct from ladies. To study them, you have to read very widely in a vast number of published and unpublished sources, piecing together small bits of information, squeezing out indications of attitudes; you have to think about society and social relations in broad terms. You are unlikely to come up with significant results within the three or four years normally spent on a D.Phil. thesis.

Yet as a form of training, both for a teacher or further researcher, it is arguable that a wide range of study at an early stage of a man's or a woman's career is more valuable than the narrow groove of a thesis. That instils the important virtues of meticulous accuracy and inquisitiveness, but it may also lead to tunnel vision, to an inability to place the events of 1348–9 in Little Puddlecombe in any wider context and so give them real historical significance. 'Research is a means, not an end', wrote Tawney; 'it is less important to discover new material than to see the meaning of old'.[2] The historian's job is to understand society, social change, how we got from there to here.

So I think there may be something to be said for breaking the universal tyranny of the D.Phil. By all means let us retain it as *one form* of training: but let us try to evolve other ways less conducive to narrow specialization. A danger of the thesis approach is its encouragement of the classic historian's vice of continuing to learn more and more about less and less. Some never become interested in those wider aspects of society and its culture which seemed manifestly

2. R.H. Tawney, 'The study of economic history', 1933, in J.Winter (ed.) *History and Society: Essays by R.H. Tawney*, 1978, p. 58.

relevant to historians of the pre-D.Phil. generation, like Tawney, Trevor-Roper and Stone.

I should like to see some of those aspiring to enter the profession exempted from writing a thesis, provided they go through a course of wide reading in comparative world history and have ample opportunities of discussing it. Why, for instance, did the English peasantry in the seventeenth-century English Revolution fail to win the security of land tenure which French peasants won in the French Revolution? This led to the disappearance of an English peasantry, with lasting consequences for English history, comparable with the existence of a class of politically unprivileged nonconformists from the seventeenth to the nineteenth centuries. The two nations became two cultures, with two educational systems. Gentlemen educated at Oxford and Cambridge learnt to quote Horace and to despise science which dirtied your hands. Nonconformists were educated at dissenting academies, learnt modern subjects, and produced the inventors who created the Industrial Revolution. The split between cultivated amateurs who rule us and dirty-handed scientists who have the ideas still lingers in the English educational and political systems, with unfortunate results.

A similar split is likely to occur if the present government's latest proposal to separate university teaching from research, and to concentrate the latter in a few selected centres, is accepted. It would have disastrous consequences, at least so far as the arts are concerned. Research and teaching must be complementary activities. No amount of research will turn a bad teacher into a good one, but teaching is a necessary stimulant for researchers, because students are always making us rethink what we are saying, forcing us, however reluctantly, to make communicable sense of our ideas. Understanding history is a dialectical process, two-way. Teachers learn from pupils as well as pupils from teachers. To herd researchers into a ghetto of 'excellence', where they will only talk to each other, is a recipe for the production of erudite and incomprehensible abstract thinking.

Let me give an example of the sort of historical analogy which I find useful in giving new insights. I recently read a fascinating book by Dr Anne Hudson about fifteenth-century Lollards.[3] It is an authoritative and convincing book. One of the things she reveals is that while

3. Anne Hudson, *The Premature Reformation: Wycliffite Texts and Lollard History*, Oxford University Press, 1988.

Lollardy was primarily a lay movement, it also attracted many members of the clergy, who were able to articulate, in a more sophisticated manner, lay criticisms of the irresponsible wealth and greed of the church, and of its desire to prevent ordinary people from reading the Bible because they would learn from it to contrast the reality of the church with the Christianity of the Bible. At the same time I was reading in the press accounts of the political activities of Boris Yeltsin, the Soviet Communist Party member who had become a spokesman of non-party anti-party feeling. I don't want to press the analogy too far. But it did suggest reasons for the wild popularity among ordinary citizens of a leading party member who expressed in a well-informed and theoretical way grievances which non-party members had long felt on their pulses. Anne Hudson called her book *The Premature Reformation*. If the old guard in the Soviet Union succeed in silencing Yeltsin and his like, final achievement of the Soviet reformation may be delayed for as long as the century between Wyclif – Morning Star – and Luther's Reformation. But the analogy between the interests of the Soviet Communist Party and those of the late medieval church – vested interests in ideology as well as economics – seem to me helpful for understanding both societies. The common factor is the (normally) silent presence of ordinary people looking for the right answer, and its frustration by monopoly control of the agencies for opinion-forming. One hopes that a difference is that burning is out of fashion in the twentieth century.

One point emphasized in this volume is the desirability of historians studying the culture, and especially the literature, of their chosen period. I do not see how historians can really understand seventeenth-century England, which produced our greatest literature, unless they have steeped themselves in Shakespeare and the other great Elizabethan dramatists, in Donne and Herbert, Milton and Marvell, Bunyan and Dryden. Equally, I cannot see how literary critics who read merely the words on the page can properly understand what they read. Some words couldn't get on to the page, since for most of the period there was strict censorship. Of those I have mentioned, Milton, Marvell and Bunyan were politically notorious characters. They could not say in print exactly what they thought. It is essential to *literary* appreciation to remember that Milton only just escaped being hanged, disembowelled and quartered in 1660. In *Paradise Lost, Paradise Regained* and *Samson Agonistes* he is, among other things, trying to justify the ways of God to men, the ways of a God who (in the words of Milton's friend Major-General Fleetwood) had 'spat in the face' of those who had sacrificed years of their life working for what they believed to be His Cause. Bunyan spent one-third of his adult life in jail, because he refused to agree to abandon preaching – in his opinion the vocation to which God had called him. As soon as he was released he started breaking the law again. He was not primarily interested in politics, but government action forced political decisions upon him and his co-religionists. It is difficult properly to evaluate the writing of this, the most class-conscious author in English literature, if we are not aware of these constraints; and his writings help us to see the problems with which dissenters had to cope.

In Chapters 7, 8 and 9 I suggested that study of literature is relevant to arguments about history from on top or history from below. For political historians state papers and parliamentary debates are their primary source. Some historians dismiss 'literary sources' as insufficiently 'objective'. But state papers and parliamentary debates call for close reading and analysis of the same sophisticated kind as do 'literary sources'. When a civil servant drafts a memorandum he is not being 'objective'. He is recommending a course of action, to readers from a group who share assumptions and prejudices with him, assumptions and prejudices which we must analyse and take into account if we are to assess his paper properly. One very general assumption in the seventeenth century, rarely expressed, was that 'mysteries of state' should not be revealed to the common people. Some historians may share this assumption, and so are not on the lookout for its limiting effect. All governments lie to their peoples, we know from our own recent experience; but if ministers lie today, when there is considerable chance of exposure, how much more so in the seventeenth century, when this possibility hardly existed? So we should be sceptical of expressions of benevolent intentions.

In Chapter 3 I illustrated the point that speeches in seventeenth-century parliaments are subject to conventions of discourse which prevented men saying in public some of the things which they thought in private. They have to be interpreted. In printed material we should always be on the lookout for censorship and attempts to evade censorship. In short, official documents have to be subjected to literary analysis no less carefully than 'literary sources'.[4]

While historians have been busy reading parliamentary debates in which convention insisted that no one directly attacked the king, literary historians have become increasingly aware of strains and tensions in the society.[5] In Chapters 10 and 11 I have tried to take

4. See my *Writing and Revolution*, op. cit., and Chs 1 and 3 above.
5. See Ch. 10 above.

249

advantage of some of their insights. Like Choderlos de Laclos's *Les Liaisons Dangereuses*, like Beaumarchais's Figaro, like Chekhov's stories, Jacobean literature witnesses to a pre-revolutionary society. Men spoke of division within the 'double heart' of individuals, of 'self civil war', long before hostilities broke out between king and parliament. The collapse of traditional external standards led Protestants to turn inwards, to the conscience of believers rather than the institutions of the church. It led Sir Philip Sidney's Muse to tell him 'look in thy heart and write'. Sidney's friend Sir Fulke Greville contrasted traditionally accepted authority with the truth of the heart when his priests admitted

> Yet when each of us in his own heart looks,
> He finds the God there far unlike his books.

The individual conscience, or heart, was being forced to challenge accepted truisms even when it had no alternative ideology. And what the heart tells a man or woman is what the heart has learnt from a changing society.[6]

If space permitted, I should like to emphasize the use to historians of popular literature and songs. Hymns, generating congregational solidarity, are crucial to the rise of protestantism. Consider Luther's '*Ein feste Burg ist unser Gott*'. Christians today do not think of God primarily as a walled fortification, a defensive shield or an aggressive weapon. It takes us back to the world in which medieval craftsmen and merchants went in fear of plunder and murder at the hands of bold bad robber barons. Burghers *had* to join together in solidarity for self-defence behind the walls of their towns, preferably under the patronage of a greater prince who took his protection money in the form of taxes. Princes and towns were the strength of the German Reformation, we say: Luther's great battle-hymn expresses this *social* aspect of the Reformation, as well as the faith and mutual support of the congregations. Similarly, Cromwell's army, as it advanced into battle, sang metrical psalms set to popular ballad tunes, and fought the better for them.

Or – very different – take 'Lilliburlero', the song to which Englishmen marched to the final expulsion of James II. The tune is lively and cocksure, but the words are foreign and menacing, Irish words

---

6. Sidney, *Astrophel and Stella*, 1591, stanza I; cf. Winstanley's advice to 'read in your own book, your heart', in Sabine, *Works of Winstanley*, op. cit., p. 213; Greville, *Mustapha*, Act V, Chorus of Priests.

(or Irish words as heard by Englishmen). The reign of James II had raised a spectre which had haunted Protestant Englishmen for over a century: the possibility of Catholic and absolutist conquest via Ireland. Especially since the Irish revolt of 1641, and the mutual massacres and atrocities of the next twenty years, the Irish had been depicted in English propaganda as savage and barbarous. 'Lilliburlero' mocks the alleged barbarians, but now with the confidence of a united Protestant England the song finally dismissed the catholicizing Stuart monarchy. The song perfectly captures the brutal, exultant self-confidence of Englishmen who have established their liberty at home, and are marching to deprive the Irish of their liberty in England's first colony. Already we look forward to 'Rule Britannia', and to John Bull with his cudgel.

So when our present government calls for a standard national history curriculum for schools, it all depends what sort of history. I have no first-hand experience of teaching history in schools, which must be a task of formidable difficulty: schoolteachers, I am sure, can never be paid enough. But I have some ideas about the sort of history that should not be taught. History seen exclusively from on top might have been adequate for training a ruling élite – though I doubt it – but that is not what most schools are doing now. Ministers complain that England lacks a national tradition such as France enjoys. This is true. The French tradition of nationalism celebrates *popular* participation in the making of the nation. It centres on the French Revolution, on the public commemoration of Bastille Day, just as July 4 is celebrated in the USA, November 7 in the USSR. The memory of our national revolution has been suppressed.[7] Yet this revolution was the model followed by the Americans, the French and the Russians.

Neither Queen Elizabeth's Day nor Guy Fawkes' Day became a national festival approved by ruling persons; the former was forgotten, the latter now lacks high political seriousness. Patriotism ceased to be exclusively radical after the eighteenth century, when William Pitt and the radical Whigs still saw Frederick the Great as a Protestant hero and an ally against popish France. The wars against the French Revolution and Napoleon helped to end this legend.

Patriotic history tends to be sentimentally anecdotal – Alfred and the cakes, Drake and his bowls, Nelson's 'Kiss me, Hardy'. More serious patriotic history of the traditional sort was described by a

7. See pp. 3–4 above.

former Regius Professor of Modern History at Cambridge, Sir G.N. Clark, as 'lies about crimes'. I have tried to suggest in Chapter 6 that this history often tells us more about government PR than about the lives of ordinary people. It would be nice if a new national curriculum created a more truthful patriotic history. If we just go back to national self-glorification, to painting the map red, history will be in danger of becoming the plaything of party politics, to be changed with each change of government.

An example of national arrogance based on ignorance was Mrs Thatcher's notorious assertion (to the French people, whose guest she then was, celebrating the bicentenary of the French Revolution) that the rights of man were not invented by the French revolutionaries. The barons of Magna Carta, she said, had beaten them to it in 1215. (How the bold bad barons would have hated the idea of ordinary people having rights, if they had been capable of understanding it. A pity they were French-speakers.) A real seventeenth-century demo-crat, the Leveller William Walwyn, said in 1645–6 that Magna Carta was 'but a beggarly thing', whose importance had been hyped up by politicians who wanted to prevent the English people from enjoying real liberty.[8] Mrs Thatcher was equally wrong to claim that 'our calm revolution of 1688' had anything to do with democracy: it established the oligarchy which ruled Great Britain for the next 150 years until nineteenth-century democratic movements, not uninfluenced by the French Revolution, began significantly to modify it. Nor did the English 'manage things much more quietly' than the French revolu-tionaries. On the contrary: Mrs Thatcher might more justifiably have claimed that the French learnt about regicide and republicanism from seventeenth-century England. 1688 was peaceful because James II ran away prematurely, remembering that kings have a joint in their necks: his father, his father's first minister and his father's Arch-bishop of Canterbury had all been decapitated by English revolu-tionaries. The rights of men and women have never yet been proclaimed by a government of this country.[9] But we may legitimately boast that they were first put forward as political demands by the Levellers in the English Revolution. The first *government* to proclaim the rights of man was that of the American republic in its revolt against the tyranny of

8. McMichael and Taft, *Walwyn Writings*, op. cit., pp. 147–8, 226.
9. The Bill of Rights of 1689 was 'not . . . a serious limitation on the power of the crown', wrote Sir David Lindsay Keir in his standard *Constitutional History of Modern Britain*, op. cit., p. 271. One can see why Mrs Thatcher has no objection to rights which do not limit the power of the executive.

the English oligarchy: though unfortunately the word 'white' was tacitly understood before 'man'.

We should be no less critical of some attempts to construct new historical 'models', which all too often conceal unconscious (or conscious) twentieth-century prejudices. A whole ideology has been constructed around the concepts of 'modernization', 'take-off', and the assumption that modern capitalist civilization is 'natural', that all societies strive towards it, but some are still 'pre-industrial', 'pre-modern', therefore 'backward'. It is no more 'natural' for Asian and African countries to adopt 'western' economic norms than to adopt parliamentary constitutions – or indeed for East European countries.[10]

In my lifetime, there has been a re-evaluation of English history because England has ceased to be top nation. British freedom used to be seen as slowly broadening down from precedent to precedent until parliamentary government reached its perfection; and history, in the immortal words of Sellar and Yeatman's *1066 and All That*, came to a full stop. All that we had to do was to export the English constitution to lesser nations, and we should all live happily and peacefully ever after. Alas! But the emphasis continued to lie on constitutional history; on the history of 'freedom', as it was called, as it is still called in the USA. From the Angles and Saxons in the forests of Germany, there had been something specifically 'English' about liberty and constitutionalism, an idea which – against all rational probability – has recently been revived.[11]

What I could never understand is what happened to all those free peoples who remained in the forests of Germany. Did they become Prussian Junkers? The free Anglo-Saxons brought with them to England lower classes known as boors, villeins, clowns, rascals. The meanings which these words have acquired today suggest that perhaps some free Anglo-Saxons were less free than others. A historical study of our language might be useful for our national curriculum too. The idea that English history is uniquely different from that of the wicked 'continong' does not bear serious examination. To resort to national character as an explanation means that you have no explanation: national character changes with history.

---

10. Dockès and Rosier, *L'Histoire Ambiguë*, op. cit.; cf p. 3 above.
11. 'The end of history' has been proclaimed again, apparently seriously, this time by an American, Francis Fukuyama. *1066 and All That* should be compulsory reading for all teachers of history.

In the 1920s I had a political discussion with my bank-manager uncle, in which my views so shocked him that he protested, 'Surely you are patriotic enough to admit that the British Empire is the greatest force for good the world has ever known?' I replied, with teenage priggishness, that if it was true I hoped I should admit it whether patriotic or not; patriotism should not determine truth. There have been many worse institutions than the British Empire; but it is time we faced up to the fact that it was not an unqualified source of blessings for humanity.

Someone should write a book on slavery and the origins of the British Empire. In Chapter 2 I noted continuities from John Hawkins's attempt in Elizabeth's reign to corner the slave trade down to the asiento of 1713. How important were slavery and the slave trade in the formation of government policy at any given date? Was the seizure of this trade from the Netherlands and France a significant and conscious object of policy in the late seventeenth century? What part did the slave trade and slave labour play in the accumulation of capital which enabled England to become the country of the first Industrial Revolution? Was Davenant right when he said that the labour of a slave was 'worth six times as much as the labour of an Englishman at home'? ('Worth', of course, means 'worth to his owner or employer'.)[12]

That great historian Richard Pares, as he sat in the magnificent Codrington Library in Oxford, surrounded by a superb collection of books, used to reflect with shame that it had all been paid for by slavery. The human suffering had been even more enormous than the profits. We shudder when we read that 20 per cent of slaves shipped from Africa did not survive the middle passage: perhaps they were not the least fortunate. But capital was colour-blind: there was a similar rate of mortality among seamen of the ships which transported the slaves.[13] Comfortable profits were made even after these acceptable losses had been written off. What – if any – were the effects of slavery on attitudes towards free labour in Britain?

A state paper, just possibly drafted by Milton in 1655, proclaimed the principle that 'since God hath made of one blood all nations of men . . . on earth, . . . all great and extraordinary wrongs done to particular persons ought to be considered as in a manner done to all the rest of the human race'. A good principle, if we had lived up to it.

12. See p. 17 above.
13. Marcus Rediker, *Between the Devil and the Deep Blue Sea: Merchant Seamen, Pirates and the Anglo-American Maritime World, 1700–1750*, Cambridge University Press, 1987, pp. 43, 47–50, 259.

When we teach children about the wickedness of drug-trafficking, should we not remind them of the war which England fought in the mid-nineteenth century to force the opium trade on China?

Have we come to grips with these horrors in our past, as German historians are trying to come to grips with Nazism? The presence of descendants of slaves in our country today, in large numbers, poses social problems. They come here because the economies of the West Indies have not recovered from the concentration on slave-grown crops to the detriment of other forms of economic activity. For this we are mainly responsible. Is this not something that a new curriculum might encourage children in British schools to think about?

Even more obvious is England's historic responsibility for the present situation in Northern Ireland. Whether we blame the potato famine, or William III, or Oliver Cromwell – or go further back – the current war in Northern Ireland is England's historic responsibility. Cromwell prided himself on the cost-effectiveness of his massacres:[14] Ireland was conquered and subordinated on the cheap. We would hardly agree now that he was right.

Other chickens are coming home to roost more slowly. Scotland was bribed and swindled into union with England in 1707, and for two centuries, on balance, she did well out of it. But now? Scotland shares the depressed state of the north of England. We should clarify historically our view of and attitudes towards Scottish nationalism.

I may seem to have over-emphasized the dark side of English history. My intention was to redress the balance: the dangers of a nationally imposed curriculum are that it will tend to be jingoistically patriotic, to stress glorious victories like the Armada, Waterloo and the Falkland Islands. I end with things we can be proud of – our literature, for instance. This is related directly to our history.

Schoolchildren interested in racialism might do worse than to read Daniel Defoe's *The True-Born Englishman* of 1703, mocking those who turned up their noses at immigrants:

> Thus from a mixture of all kinds began
> That heterogeneous thing an Englishman . . .
> We have been Europe's sink, the jakes where she
> Voids all her offal outcast progeny . . .
> Fate jumbled them together, God knows how;
> Whate'er they were, they're true-born English now.[15]

14. See p. 146 above.
15. H.Morley (ed.) *The Earlier Life and the Chief Earlier Works of Daniel Defoe*, 1889, pp. 189–95.

We might recall, too, the struggles against censorship that made possible this greatest period of our literature – from Shakespeare's 'art made tongue-tied by authority' to Milton's *Areopagitica*, the classic defence of freedom to publish. Milton attacked censorship on patriotic grounds, as 'an undervaluing and vilifying of the whole nation'. 'If it come to prohibiting there is not aught more likely to be prohibited than truth itself.'[16] That might help schoolchildren to appreciate controversies over *Death on the Rock*; and might lead them on to reflect about the dangers of monopoly or oligopoly in the opinion-forming agencies.

When the late Ayatollah Khomenei condemned Salman Rushdie to death (*in absentia*) for his book *The Satanic Verses*, this gave rise to considerable discussion in England about limits on the right of freedom of expression, and on religious toleration generally. It reminded me that the Anglican church burnt its last heretic in 1612. The burning was in public; the favourable impression that the victim made on those present may have decided the authorities not to do it again. But Englishmen still had their ears cut off, were flogged, branded and sentenced to life imprisonment, for publishing ideas which the authorities in church and state did not like. In 1639 the Archbishop of York suggested reviving the burning of heretics: it had done the church much good, he remarked nostalgically. The Revolution of 1640 ended all that. By the end of the century ecclesiastical censorship had ceased to exist. Publication was freer in England and the republican Netherlands than anywhere else in Europe – something which Professor Eisenstein sees as vital for the survival of science in western Europe.[17] But it was not so long ago that ruling persons in England thought like the Ayatollah. It took a revolution and the continuing pressure of public opinion afterwards to change this.

If Mrs Thatcher's ideas of English history inform our national curriculum, our children may be in danger of becoming too self-satisfied about our liberties. They did not drop from heaven. Children should be taught respect for those in our past who resisted authoritarianism. They could learn from history how important the jury system and the right to silence have been in preserving common liberties against intrusive governments. And they should be taught about one especially English phenomenon – voluntary societies for promoting, reforming or abolishing this or that, which perhaps go

16. Milton, *Complete Prose Works*, op. cit., II, pp. 535-6, 565.
17. Eisenstein, *The Printing Press*, op. cit., II, pp. 678-82.

back to the Lollards,[18] which played a big part in the abolition of slavery, and which may become increasingly important as political parties ossify.

I have no big generalizations to offer about what history is or should be, and that is perhaps a properly sceptical conclusion. Let me try one from Nietzsche. He said that 'history keeps alive . . . the memory of the great fighters *against* history – the blind power of the actual'. The past is going to have power over us anyway, but we need not be totally blind. Within limits we can co-operate with or oppose what appear to be dominant trends. But that necessitates an understanding of history as a process, not just a bran-tub full of anecdotes. We shan't all reach the same conclusions if we study history – thank God. But historical understanding may give us a better chance of having clues about the present. My former tutor, the late A.D. Lindsay, used to tell the story of a Scottish Presbyterian minister who terrified his congregation with a vision of their future, roasting in hell. 'And ye will look up to heaven and say, "Lord, Lord, we didna ken". And the Lord in his infinite mercy and compassion will look down upon ye and say "Aweel, ye ken the noo".' The lesson of history is perhaps that it would be nice to ken a little before we find ourselves in hell: nicer still if knowledge led to action. We shall have to move quickly if we are to beat the greenhouse effect.

---

18. See J.W. Martin, *Religious Radicals in Tudor England*, 1989, pp. 13–14.

INDEX

Abbott, George, Archbishop of
  Canterbury 44, 46, 57, 60-2,
  65-8, 70n., 72, 79, 81, 106
Abbott, Robert 162, 182
Abingdon, Oxfordshire 170, 173
absolutism, absolute monarchy
  Chapter 2 *passim*, 55, 63-4,
  71-2, 80, 82, 84-5, 104, 110
Adam 119, 228, 230
Addison, Joseph 241-2
Africa 9, 12, 20, 135, 226, 253-4
African Company, the Royal 12,
  109
Agnew, Alexander 178
Agreement of the People, the 143
Agriculture, agricultural
  revolution, the 14-16, 236, 241
Aitzema, Lieuwe van 91
Albert, Prince Consort 113
ale-houses 52, 71
Alfred, King of England 251
Alva, Ferdinando Alvarez de
  Toledo, Duke of 134
Alvarez, A. 237
Amboyna, massacre of 21
America, Americans 7-8, 11-12,
  20, 126, 134, 147, 192-3, 202,
  209, 241
Ames, William 67n.
Anabaptists 51, 74, 92, 110, 171 *See
  also* Baptists
Andover, Hampshire 170, 172
Andrewes, Lancelot, Bishop of
  Winchester 46, 57, 68, 76
Anglo-Saxons 29, 49, 83, 116, 232,
  253
Anne, Queen of England 192
Anne of Denmark, Queen to
  James I 131, 205n.
Antichrist 46, 65, 74-5, 77, 83,
  104, 119, 134, 138, 140-1, 146,
  148, 150, 176, 183, 230
Antiquaries, Society of 49
Appleby, Joyce 99
Aquinas, Thomas 127n.
Aretino, Pietro 234
Armada, the Spanish 8, 105, 134,
  147, 255
Arminians 144, 153, 229 *See also*
  Laudians
Arminius, Jacobus 73
army, standing Chapter 2 *passim*,
  62, 72
Ascham, Anthony 89, 93, 96,
  130-2
Ash, Simeon 139n.
Asia 20, 253
Assarino, Luca 87
Astell, Mary 129, 227, 242
astrologers, astrology 82, 84, 89
astronomers, astronomy 82-3, 89
Attaway, Mrs 164
Aubrey, John 95, 223, 236
Austria 6, 133
Axtell, Colonel Daniel 142
Aylmer, John, Bishop of London
  45, 69, 233

Babylon 140; Whore of, the 176
Bacon, Sir Francis, Viscount St

Albans 7, 17, 33, 46, 48, 57, 70, 85, 135n., 150, 203–4, 209, 219
Bampton, Oxfordshire 161
Banbury, Oxfordshire 171
Bancroft, Richard, Archbishop of Canterbury 29n., 44, Chapter 4 *passim*
Baptists 148, 153–4, 158–9, 163, 166, 172, 191 *See also* Anabaptists
Barber, C.L. 99, 237
Barberini, Francesco, Cardinal 53
Barclay, Robert, Quaker 192
Barclay, Robert, historian 187
Barg, Academician M.A. 23
Bargrave, Isaac 63
Barker, Matthew 88
Barlow, William, Bishop of Lincoln 68
Baro, Peter 74, 76
Barrett, William 76
Barrington, Sir Thomas and family 34–6, 40, 43–4, 80
Bastwick, John 26, 79–80
Bauthumley, Jacob 155–6, 159, 169, 171, 177–8, 180, 187
Baxter, Richard 75, 138, 161, 163, 166, 173, 240
Beard, Thomas 48, 50–2
Beaumarchais, La Barre de Caron de 250
Bedford 172, 175, 177
Bedford, Francis Russell, Earl of 51
Bedfordshire 171, 175
Behmenists 163, 193
Behn, Mrs Aphra 191, 193, 226–7, 235–6, 238
Belsey, Catherine, 198, 229
Berg, Christine 198
Berkenhead, Sir John 233, 238
Berkshire 170, 172
Berry, Philippa 198
Bible, the 26, 57, 100, 155, 171, 175, 184, 208, 218, 220, 225, 229, 231, 235, 243, 246, 248; Geneva Bible, the 59n., 103; Lollard Bible, the 103; *Polyglot Bible, The* 238
Bidle, John 168
Birmingham 192

Bishop, George 93, 141
bishops, 8, 21, 27, 44–5, 49, Chapter 4 *passim*, 103, 109–10, 216, 218, 220, 239
Blake, Admiral Robert 11, 92
Blake, William 192, 196
Blasphemy Ordinance (May 1648) 157, 167, 229
Blasphemy Act (August 1650) 157, 189
Blount, Charles, 95, 191
Blount, Edward 87
Blount, Thomas 86, 99
Boate, Gerrard 147
Bohemia 29, 61, 65–6, 105
Bold, Henry 94
Bolton, Edward 87
Bolton, Samuel 139n.
Bombay 12
Book of Sports, the 69, 71
Bowden, Peter 115
Bowyer, Robert 37
Boyle, the Hon. Robert 18, 89–90, 97, 227, 238
Bradbrook, Muriel C. 197–8
Bradfield, Berkshire 172
Bradshaw, John, regicide 111
Bradshaw, William 69, 72
Bradstreet, Mrs Anne 221–2
Brailsford, H.N. 144, 146, 180
Braithwaite, William 187
Braudel, Fernand 82
Bridewell, 162–3
Bridge, William 139n.
Brightman, Thomas 43, 50
Brinkworth, Wiltshire 171
Bristol 144, 159
Broghill, Roger Boyle, Lord, later Earl of Orrery 97, 224, 238
Brome, Richard 214
Brooke, Christopher 85, 200, 202
Brooke, Humphrey 142
Brooke, Robert Greville, Lord 50, 69, 79
Brown, Laura 191, 198
Browne, Sir Thomas 97
Browne, William 40, 200–2, 211
Brownists 64
Buchanan, George 28–9

Buckhurst, Thomas Sackville, Lord, Earl of Dorset 37
Buckingham, Sir George Villiers, Duke of 28, 32–3, 35n., 37–9, 41, 44, 47, 53, 62, 66, 68, 77, 80, 202, 206, 210, 224
Buckeridge, John, Bishop of Ely 57
Bullinger, Heinrich 65
Bullokar, John 85
Bunyan, John 18, 53, 153, 161–3, 166, 170, 172–7, 181–3, 192, 199–200, 204, 218, 220, 224, 230–1, 235, 237–8, 240–1, 243, 248–9
Bunyan, Mrs 53–4
Bureaucracy Chapter 2 passim, 62, 72, 219
Burford 144, 146, 180
Burleigh, William Cecil, Lord 60, 200, 207
Burnet, Gilbert, Bishop of Salisbury 97
Burns, Norman T. 187, 193
Burns, Robert 192
Burrough, Edward 84, 141, 153, 158–9, 169, 218
Burton, Henry 26, 80
Burton, Robert 205
Butler, Martin 37, 106, 198, 213–15, 225, 228
Butler, Samuel 95, 191, 223–4, 227, 235
Byne, Marcus 168–9, 174
Byrne, Muriel St Clare 200

Calamy, Edmund 138
Calvert, Sir George, Secretary of State 210
Calvin, John, Calvinism 18, 28, 48, 57–8, 65–6, 70, 73–4, 78–9, 128, 144, 151, 163, 229–31
Cambridge, Cambridge University 26, 69, 76, 237, 247, 252
Cambridgeshire 171, 175
Canne, John 91, 222
Canny, Nicholas 134–6
Canons, the, of 1604, 62, 69, 72; abortive, of 1606, 49; of 1640, 76n.

Capp, B.S. 182
Carey, John 181
Carleton, George, Bishop of Chichester 68, 77
Carr, E.H. 1
Cartwright, William 214
Cary, Mary 231
Catherine of Aragon, Queen of England 103
Catherine of Braganza, Queen of England 12
Catholics, Roman, Catholicism 4, 8, 44, 61, 74, 76–8, 80, 96, 104, 110, Chapter 8 passim, 200, 210, 227, 251
Cavaliers see Royalists
Cawdrey, Robert 85
Cawdrey's Case 64n.
Cecil, Robert, later Earl of Salisbury 200
censorship 21, 24, 39–40, 64, 106, 110, 204–5, 210–14, 218–19, 223, 238–41, 248–9, 256
Chamberlain, John 36, 38
Chapman, George 41, 203
Charenton 66
Charleton, Walter 238
Charles I, King of England 4, 8–10, 21–2, 25, 27–9, 31–3, 35, 39, 42, 44–8, 51, 53, 55, 58, 61, 70n., 73, 77, 80, 84, 96–7, 103, 105–6, 115–16, 130, 137–40, 206–8, 210, 213–16, 220–2, 239, 242
Charles II, King of England 12, 16, 18, 21–2, 92–3, 95–6, 105, 107–8, 110, 113, 183, 219, 223–4, 238, 242
Chekhov, Anton 250
Chernaik, Warren 198
Cheshire 171
Chester 173–4
Cheynell, Francis 66
Child, Sir Josiah 16
Chillingworth, William 33
China, Chinese 20, 243–5, 255
Church of England, the, 21 Chapter 4 passim, 103, 105, 109, 227, 239

church courts 71, 78, 218
Civil War, the English, 15, 19, 25, 28-9, 34, 44, 105, 107-8, 197, 223-4; Second Civil War, the 139
Clare, John Holles, first Earl of 47
Clarendon, Edward Hyde, Earl of 71, 75, 117, 223
Clark, Sir G.N. 252
Clarkson, Lawrence 114-15, 156, 158, 165, 167, 171-3, 175-6, 178, 180, 188, 191, 194, 212
Cleveland, Yorkshire 169
cloth trade, clothiers 7, 9, 66, 114
Cobham, Surrey 116
Cockeram, Henry 85
Codrington Library, All Souls College, Oxford 254
Cogan, H. 86
Cohn, Norman 157-8, 187, 189-90
Coke, Sir Edward, Lord Chief Justice 30-3, 40-1, 46, 49, 65, 219
Coke, Sir John, Secretary of State 32
Colchester 172
Coles, Elisha 85-6
Collier, Thomas 156, 166, 170
Collinson, Patrick 56, 72, 77, 201
Colonies, colonization 8, 12, 16, Chapter 8 *passim*
Comenius, Jan Amos 66
Commons, House of, the 2, 7, 10, 16, 23, 27, 32-5, 40, 42, 47, 50-1, 53, 61-2, 64, 67, 76-7, 81, 100, 106-8, 110-11, 178
Commonwealth, the English 21, 108-10, 112, 117, 125, 144, 149, 209
Communism Chapter 7 *passim*, 142, 153-4, 163, 220
Cook, John 138, 222
Cooper, William 140
Coppe, Abiezer 156-8, 161, 165, 167-8, 171-3, 175-80, 188, 194, 207
Coppin, Richard, 156-7, 161, 163-4, 172-3, 176, 178, 180, 184, 230

Coppinists 192
Copyhold, copyholders 14-16, 236
Coriton, William 32
Cork, Richard Boyle, Earl of 135
Cornwall 170, 172
Cosin, John, later Bishop of Durham 65
Cotgrave, Randle 85
Cotton, Sir Robert 49, 53, 206
Counter-Reformation, the 78, 134-5
Covell, William 178
Coventry 159n., 170-1, 173, 177, 179
Cowderoy, Jeremy 181
Cowell, John 34, 63-4, 82
Cowley, Abraham 79, 224, 227, 236
Cranfield, Lionel, Earl of Middlesex 33
Crashaw, Richard 199
Crisp, Tobias 171
Crofton, Zachary 92
Cromwell, Oliver, Lord Protector 11-12, 16, 19, 23n., 48, 50-2, 55, 75, 90-2, 94, 96, 100, 109, 112, 124, 131-3, 139-41, 145-50, 153, 167-8, 178, 183, 203, 209, 221, 224, 227, 232, 238, 250, 255
Cromwell, Richard, Lord Protector 92
Cromwell, Thomas, later Earl of Essex 51, 103
Crowley, Robert 199-200
Culloden, battle of 150
Culpeper, Nicholas 161
Cumberland 192
Curtis, Tim *ix-x*, 19
Cust, Richard 36, 38-9

Daly, J. 84
Daniel, Samuel 199-201, 205n.
Davenant, Charles 17, 254
Davenant, Sir William 214, 224, 232, 238
Davies, John, of Hereford 199
Davies, Sir John 136, 145, 147

D'Avila, H.C. 29
Davis, J.C. 120, Chapter 9 *passim*
Davis, Julian 57
Defoe, Daniel 18, 75, 233–4,
242–3, 255
Dell, William 162, 173
Denham, Sir John 214, 235
Denne, Henry 172, 175, 180
Dent, Arthur 181
Derbyshire 170
Dering, Sir Edward 47
Descartes René, 18
Devonshire, Charles Blount, Earl
of 213n.
D'Ewes, Sir Simonds 25–6, 40, 46,
50n., 74, 78, 85, 206
dictionaries 82–7
Diggers, the 45, Chapter 7 *passim*,
141, 154, 160–1, 184–5, 190,
204, 220
Digges, Sir Dudley 47
Digges, Dudley, son of the above 75
dissent, dissenters 106–7, 109–10,
219, 228, 232, 239, 247
Dissenting Brethren, the Five 88,
91
divorce 164, 174, 220
Dollimore, Jonathan 37, 98, 106,
198, 202, 205–6, 208
Donne, John 248
Dorset 170–1
Dort, Synod of 66
Downame, George, Bishop of
Derry 68
Drake, Sir Francis 42, 251
Drayton, Michael 40, 200n.
Drogheda, massacre of 146, 168
Drummond, William, of
Hawthornden 26
Dryden John 55, 93–4, 113, 205,
222, 224, 227, 232, 235, 237–8,
242, 248
Dublin 192
Dumfries 178
Dunkirk 22n.
Dury, John 66, 89n., 179–80
Dutch *see* The Netherlands

East Anglia 139, 171

East India Company, English 20–1,
109; Dutch 20–1
Eastcourt, Sir Giles 32
Ecclesiastical Commission, Court of
see High Commission
Eccleshall, E. 128
Edgeworth, Maria 150
Edinburgh 171
Edward VI, King of England 57,
104, 119, 201, 233, 240
Edwards, Thomas 142, 144, 163,
171, 181–2, 188
Eisenstein, Elizabeth 18, 256
Eliot, Sir John 30, 32, 42, 51, 76
Eliot, T.S. 242
Elton, Sir Geoffrey 31–2
Elizabeth I, Queen of England 4,
8, 12, 17, 19–20, 27, 30, 40, 42,
48, 53, 57, 59–60, 65–6, 72, 77,
84, 103–6, 135, 140, 147, 198,
201, 206–11, 216, 230, 237, 241,
251, 254
Elizabeth, Princess, Queen of
Bohemia 41, 46, 105
Ellesmere, Sir Thomas Egerton,
Earl of, Lord Chancellor 35–6, 42
Elstow, Bedfordshire 175
Ely, Isle of 172
Emmison, F.G. 45
enclosure 15, 19, 71, 126–7
English Channel, the 9, 11
Enlightenment, the European 18,
204, 242
epic 227–8
Erbery, William 84, 148, 167–9,
182
Essex 45, 65, 98–9, 170–1
Essex, Robert Devereux, second
Earl of 60, 62, 84, 208
Europe 1, 7–8, 11, 17–18, 20, 48,
72, 87, 101, 104, 108, 112, 149,
255–6
Europe, Eastern 245, 253
Evans, Arise 90, 208
Eve 176, 228, 230
Evelyn, John 96, 234
Everard, John 162, 194

Fairfax, Nathaniel 241

Fairfax, Sir Thomas, Lord 224
Falkland, Lucius Cary, Viscount 32, 78
Fall of Man, the 119, 127
Familists, Family of Love, the 64, 158, 163, 166, 179, 193-4, 218
Farnsworth, Richard 159
fasting, fasts, 40; Fast Sermons 88
Fawkes, Guy 4, 251
Feake, Christopher 91, 96, 141
Fell, Margaret 169
Felton, John 28, 47
Fenstanton, Huntingdonshire, 161, 172
Ferne, Henry 75
Ferrar, Nicholas 46
feudal tenures, abolition of Chapter 2 *passim*, 211, 236
Fielding, Henry 242-3
Fifth Monarchy, Fifth Monarchists 141, 153-4, 185
Filmer, Sir Robert 129-31
Finch, Sir John, Lord, Lord Keeper 33, 47
Firth, Sir C.H. 187
Fisher, Samuel 159, 162-3, 165, 220
Fitz-Brian, R. 93
Five Members, the 33
Flanders 22
Fleetwood, Major-General Charles 248-9
Fleetwood, Sir Miles 35
Fletcher, Giles 200, 202n.
Fletcher, John 74
Fletcher, Phineas 200
Florence 87
Fontenelle, Bernard de 226-7
Foster, George 156, 183, 188
Fowler, Christopher 162
Fox, George 153, 158-9, 165, 169, 180, 187, 192, 240
Foxe, John 51-2, 77-8, 103-4, 111, 133-4
France, French, Frenchmen 1, 3, 6, 8, 12, 15-18, 27, 29, 39, 41, 46, 58, 61, 64-5, 72, 85, 100, 107, 120, 133, 140, 144, 222, 226, 251-2, 254
Frank, Joseph 241

Franklin, William 170, 172, 178-9, 186
Freeman, Captain Francis 178
'French Prophets', the 192
Friedman, Jerome 156-7, 172, 176, 188-9
Fronde, the 88n.
Fuller, Nicholas 30-1
Fuller, Thomas, 76n., 98, 163, 173
Fullwood, Francis, 194

Gadbury, John 161, 170
Gadbury, Mary 170, 176, 186
Galileo Galilei 18
Gardiner, S.R. 37, 66n., 75, 186-7
Garland, Edward 157-8, 163-4, 173, 185
Garment, Joshua 156, 171
Gauden, John, later Bishop of Worcester 108, 111-12
Gay, John 242
Gell, Robert 161, 170, 173
Geneva 65
gentry, the 7, 9, 14, 18-19, 24, 39, 67, 71
George I, King of England 113
George II, King of England 113
Germany 4, 9, 140, 253, 255
Geyl, P. 74
Gil, Alexander 28
Gilbert, Claudius 167, 173, 185, 192
Gillespie, George 88
Giraffi, A. 87
Glamorgan, Edward Somerset, Earl of 138
Glanville, John 39
Gloucestershire 140-1
Goldberg, Dena 2, 198, 213
Gondomar, Diego Sarmiento de Acuña, Count of 210
Good Old Cause, the 93, 110, 222, 224
Goodgroom, Richard 131
Goodman, Christopher 103
Goodwin, John 74, 191
Gookin, Vincent 147, 150
Gorges, Sir Arthur 200, 205, 208
Gorton, Samuel 114

Grand Remonstrance, the (1641) 33, 44, 47
Greaves, R.L. 196n.
Greenblatt, Stephen 198
Greene, John 75
Greville, Sir Fulke, Lord Brooke 27, 37n., 40, 46, 84–5, 105, 200, 202n., 205, 208–9, 211, 250
Grindal, Edmund, Archbishop of Canterbury 44, 48, Chapter 4 passim, 106
Grotius, Hugo 145
Guiccardini, Francisco 87
Guizot, François 101
Gunpowder Plot (1605) 134
Gura, Philip 188
Gutch, J.A. 92

Hakewill, George 203
Hales, John 229
Halifax, George Savile, Marquis of 96
Hall, Joseph, Bishop of Norwich 61n., 68, 70
Haller, William 70
Hampden, John 29, 39, 43, 51
Hampshire 170, 172
Hardwick, Humphrey 88
Hardwicke's Marriage Act (1753) 174
Hare, John 116
Harford, Rapha 162, 194
Harington, John 28, 48
Harrington, James; Harringtonians 18, 22, 38, 93, 96, 98n., 113, 131–2, 199, 204, 220–1, 234, 238
Harsnett, Samuel, Bishop of Chichester, later Archbishop of York 57, 63–4, 69, 78
Hartlib, Samuel 66, 147
Haslerig, Sir Arthur 87
Hatto, J. 87
Hawkins, Harriett 198
Hawkins, John 17, 254
Heath, Sir Robert, Attorney-General 30
Heath, Robert 89
Hedley, Thomas 31, 35, 126
Heinemann, Margot 37, 106, 198,
200, 210, 214
Henri II, King of France 41
Henri IV, King of France 104
Henrietta Maria, Queen of England 53, 105, 137, 213
Henry IV, King of England 206
Henry V, King of England 41, 206
Henry VI, King of England 41, 201
Henry VII, King of England 7–8, 89, 134, 206
Henry VIII, King of England 7–8, 27, 41, 56–8, 76, 103–4, 110, 112, 133, 200, 233
Henry, Prince of Wales 42, 105, 109, 201, 205
Herbert, Lord Edward of Cherbury 108
Herbert, George 111, 199, 202n., 216–17, 248
Herbert, Sir William 27
Herrick, Robert 199
Hertford, Edward Seymour, Earl of 59
Hexter, J.H. 195
Hibbard, Caroline 44, 80
Hicock, Robert 172
Hide, Edward 173
Higginson, Francis 166, 173
High Commission, Court of 8, 21, 60, 62, 64–5, 71
Hirst, Derek 10n., 52
Historians' Group of the Communist Party of Great Britain 189–90
Hobbes, Thomas; Hobbism 18, 40, 48–9, 95–6, 100, 109, 127–8, 130–2, 179, 198, 203–4, 207n., 220, 225–6, 230–1, 235, 238, 240
Holinshed, Ralph 103
Holland see Netherlands, the
Hooker, Richard 46, 69, 84
Hookes, Nicholas 162–3
Hopkins, John 199
Hopton, Andrew 158, 180
Horne, George, later Bishop of Norwich 192
Horsham, Sussex 170
Horton, Thomas 139n.

Hoskins, John 41
Hotham, Durant 170
household, the 129-30, 246
Howard, Edward 96-7
Howard, William 92
Howard family, the 66
Howell, James 11-12, 85, 87
Howgil, Francis 141, 158
Hubert, Sir Francis 206-7
Hudson, Anne 247-8
Hughes, Ann 42-3, 56-7, 108
Huguenots, French 29, 39, 65-6, 72
Hull, John 90
Hume, Robert D. 228, 240
Hunt, William 52, 71-2
Huntingdon 52
Huntingdonshire 43, 171-2
Hutchinson, Mrs Anne 80
Hutchinson, Mrs Lucy 53, 94
Hyde, Sir Edward see Clarendon, Earl of
hymns 250

Ilford, Essex 170
impropriations; impropriated tithes 67, 78
Independents, the 58, 159, 181, 183
India 12, 135
Indians, American 134-6, 144
Indulgence, Declarations of 21, 109, 240
Inquisition, the Spanish 60
Inverness 192
Ireland 3-4, 7-8, 10, 12, 20, 80, 126, Chapter 8 passim, 167, 171, 250-1, 255
Ireton, Commissary-General Henry 118-19, 126, 141
irreverence 52, 210-11, 221, 225, 233-4
Italy, Italians 17-18, 134, 199, 203, 211

Jacob, J.R. 95
Jacob, M.R. 17-18, 241
Jamaica 11n., 148
James I, King of England;

Jacobean 9, 20-1, 25-9, 34-5, 45-6, 48-9, 57-9, 64, 66, 69-70, 72-4, 76-7, 85, 87, 104-6, 108, 136-7, 140, 147, 201, 206-8, 210-12, 216, 230
James II, King of England 21-2, 109, 134, 183, 219, 238, 250-2
Jerusalem 159-60
Jesuits 74
Jewell, John, Bishop of Salisbury 104
Joachim of Fiore 83
'Jock of Broad Scotland' 178
Johnson, Dr Samuel 174
Jones, Inigo 70n., 102
Jones, Colonel John 152
Jones, Rufus 187
Jonson, Ben 2, 86, 203, 205, 213, 237
Jose, Nicholas 233-4
Josselin, Ralph 91, 234
Jubbes, Lieut.-Colonel John 143
Justices of the Peace 196, 206, 239
Juxon, William, Bishop of London, Lord Treasurer 56

Kendal 166
Kent 62, 66, 139, 157, 171
Kentish, Richard 139n.
Kenyon, J.P. 96
Kersey, John 85-6
Keynes, John Maynard 10n.
Khomeini, the Ayatollah 256
Kiernan, Victor 212, 215
King, J.N. 198-201
King's Lynn, Norfolk 170
Kirby Stephen, 166
Kirton, Edward 32
Knollys, Sir Francis 60, 68
Knox, John 103
Koran, the 219-20

Laclos, Choderlos de 250
Lancashire 114, 176
Lasky, Melvin, 83
Laslett, Peter 82, 95, 97n., 197
Latin 84, 86, 89, 112, 127
Laud, William, Archbishop of Canterbury; Laudians 8, 21, 27,

34, 40, 43–4, Chapter 4 *passim*, 104, 137, 185, 213–14, 216, 219, 221, 239, 252
Laurence, Anne 188
Legate, Bartholomew 110
Le Goff, Jacques 97
Leicester 169
Leicester, Robert Dudley, Earl of 19, 60, 62, 202
Leicestershire 170
Lenin, Vladimir Ilyich 52
L'Estrange, Sir Roger 113, 238
Levellers, 14, 18, 45, 55, 92, 112, 115, 118, 122–3, 125–7, 139, 141–8, 151, 153–4, 158, 160, 167, 180, 183–5, 190, 200–1, 204, 207, 211–13, 215, 220, 230–3, 240–1, 245, 252
Levine, David 72
Levy, Leonard W. 177
Lewalski, Barbara 198
lexicographers 84–6, 96
Libertines; libertinism Chapter 9 *passim*, 215, 225–6
Lilburne, John 118, 122, 143, 146, 153–4, 185
Lilliburlero 250–1
Lilly, William 89, 161, 163
Limerick 167
Literature and History 196
Little Gidding 68
Locke, John 18, 82, 95, 97, 100, 126–31, 235, 240
Lockier, Lionel 161, 163, 182
Lockyer, Nicholas 88
Lollards, the 103–4, 173–4, 218, 247–8, 257
London, City of 22, 35, 43, 49, 114–15, 117–18, 137–40, 149, 169, 172, 192, 201, 215, 224–5, 232–3, 237, 241
Long Island, New York 192–3
Lords, House of 21, 37, 47, 50–1, 64, 104, 106, 113, 115, 139, 148, 182, 218, 239
Lorraine, Charles, Duke of 140, 146
Louis XIV, King of France 22
Louis XVI, King of France 96

Lovejoy, D.S. 192–3
Low, Anthony 236
Ludlow, Edmund 240–1
Luther, Martin 103–4, 248, 250
Lyly, John 200

MacCaffrey, William 48
McGregor, J.F. 165, 188–9
McKeon, Michael 93, 198
Macpherson, C.B. 188
Madrid 131
Magna Carta 32n., 51–2, 252
Maguire, Nancy 225
Mahomet 95
Manchester 114
Manchester, Edward Montagu, Earl of 51
Mandeville, Bernard de 242
Manning, Brian 45, 52, 75
Manton, Thomas 205
Manuche, Cosmo 225
Manwaring, Roger 29, 31, Chapter 4 *passim*
Marlowe, Christopher 38, 203, 205, 231
Marprelate, Martin; Marprelate Tracts, the 34, 45, 52, 58–9, 65, 70, 79, 104, 200, 221, 233–4
marriage 136, 164, 174, 203, 211–14, 226
Marshall, Stephen 46
Marten, Sir Henry 41, 47
Marten, Henry 25, 90, 106
Martin, Mr, MP 62–3
Martines, Lauro 195
Marvell, Andrew 55, 81, 92, 95–6, 105, 112–13, 149–50, 162, 205, 215, 221, 231–2, 235, 240, 248
Marx, Karl; Marxism 24, 101, 123, 148, 150, 166
Mary I, Queen of England 58, 76, 110, 134, 137; Marian exiles, 58, 65; Marian martyrs 104, 110
Masham, Sir William and Lady Elizabeth 44, 50
Masques, court 105, 215, 234
Massachusetts Bay, Massachusetts Bay Company 8, 44, 50
Massinger, Philip 74, 205n.,

209-11
Masson, David 26, 186-7
Maynard, Sir John 92
Mazarin, Jules, Cardinal 22-3
Mede, Joseph 37, 40, 50, 219
Mediterranean, the 9, 11-12, 148, 210
Melville, Andrew 66
Mencken, H.L. 197
Merchants 7-10, Chapter 2 *passim*, 48-9, 66n.
Mercurius Politicus 90, 186
metaphysical poetry 235
Mexico 103
Middlesex 170
Middleton, Thomas 106, 203, 210-11, 213, 221, 233
Midlands Revolt (1607) 15n.
millenarianism, millenarians, 43-4, 49-50, 83-4, 91, 109, 113, 115, 148, 182, 221-2, 230, 232, 239
Milton, John 15, 17-18, 28, 49, 53, 58-9, 68, 74, 79-80, 84-5, 89, 98n., 108, 111-13, 123, 132, 138, 148-50, 155, 164, 174, 183, 192, 200, 202, 204, 213, 215-16, 219-20, 222-4, 226-31, 235-6, 240-1, 248, 254, 256
Moderate Intelligencer, The 144-5
Monck, General George, later Duke of Albemarle 51, 87, 228
Montagu, Richard 61n., 63, 65, 70, 73-4, 77, 81
Montaigne, Michel de 87
Mooney, James 187
More, Sir Thomas 17, 115
Morison, Fynes 86
Morley, George, later Bishop of Winchester 76
Morrill, John 1
mortalism 155, 181, 187, 219, 231
Morton, A.L. Chapter 9 *passim*
Moyle, Walter 97
Muggleton, Lodowick; Muggletonians, 154, 156, 163-5, 167, 172, 181, 185, 191, 231

Nalson, John 75
Naples 87

Naseby, battle of 51, 138
Nashe, Thomas 49, 59, 200
Naunton, Sir Robert 70n.
Navigation Act, the (1651) Chapter 2 *passim*, 148-9, 209
navy, the 7-8, 12-13, 19
Nayler, James 153, 156, 159, 167, 169-70, 186, 196
Nedham, Marchamont 23, 75, 92n., 112, 179, 233
Neile, Richard, Bishop of Durham, later Archbishop of York 63, 73, 256
Netherlands, the; Revolt of the; The United Provinces; the Dutch 8, 10-11, 13, 18-22, 27, 29, 38, 41, 45, 48-9, 58, 61, 65-6, 73-4, 76, 78, 91, 94, 107, 134, 144, 147, 203, 209, 221, 232, 254, 256
Neville, Henry 22-3, 95, 242-3
New England 43, 50, 67, 91, 136, 192, 221
New Model Army, the 53, 100, 139, 141, 148, 219, 222, 227
Newcastle, Margaret Cavendish, Duchess of 226
Newcastle, William Cavendish, Duke of 75
Newcome, Henry 90
Newcomen, Matthew 139n.
newsletters 38-9
Newton, Sir Isaac 17-18
Nietzsche, Friedrich Wilhelm 257
nonconformists *see* dissenters
Norbrook, David 37, 106, 198, 200, 202
Norfolk 170
Normans, the; Norman Conquest 30, 87, 116
Norman Yoke, the 18, 30, 49, 83, 116, 119, 230
Norris, John 235
North, Dudley, Lord 230
North, Dr John 231
Northamptonshire 171
Norwich 66, 169-70
Norwood, Robert 172
Notestein, Wallace 37

Nottingham 192
Nottinghamshire 169–70
novel, the 228, 234, 242–3

Oates, Titus 96
O'Day, Rosemary 56–7
Oldham, John 241
Osborne, Francis 220
Osborne, John 161, 173
Otway, Thomas 226
Overall, John, Bishop of Norwich 57, 76
Overton, Richard 45, 112, 143, 146, 180, 212, 231, 233–4
Owen, John 88, 145–6
Owen, Sir Roger 32n., 63
Oxford English Dictionary (OED) 84–7, 99
Oxford University 69, 78, 192, 212, 237, 245, 247, 254
Oxfordshire 161, 171
Oxinden, Henry 50

Pagitt, Ephraim 166
Palatinate, the 61, 66
Panzani, Gregorio, Papal Agent 77
Pares, Richard 254
Paris 66, 104, 222
parish élites 52, 71, 78, 108–9, 239
parish registers 174
Parker, Matthew, Archbishop of Canterbury 59–60, 62
Parliament 4, 7, 9–10, 12–13, 15, 22, 63, 73, 75, 81, 93, 110, 125
   of 1586, the 106
   of 1601, the 105
   of 1610, the 35, 126
   of 1621–2, the 25, 46
   of 1624, the 40
   of 1640, the Short 41, 73
   of 1640, the Long 10, 15, 18, 50, 52, 55, 66, 87, 100, 103
   the Rump of the Long 87, 90
   Barebones 90, 174
   of 1657, 220
   of 1659, 92
Parnell, James 159
patronage 238
Patterson, Annabel 198, 213n.

Pavlova, Tatiana 154
Pearson, Anthony 159, 169, 182
Peele, George 201
Pembroke, William Herbert, Earl of 61, 202, 211, 216
Penington, Isaac 169
Penn, William 13
Penry, John 65
Pepys, Samuel 13, 94, 96, 129, 234, 237
Perkin, H.J. 14
Perkins, William 181–2
Perrot, John 170, 194
Peter, Hugh 136
Petition and Advice, the Humble 92
Petition of Right, the 4, 31, 34, 42, 46, 64, 108
Phelips, Sir Robert 30, 32–5, 41–2
Philip IV, King of Spain 22–3
Philips, Edward 85–6
Philips, John 234
Philips, Katherine 94–5
Pilgrim Fathers, the 44, 202
piracy, pirates 7–9, 11, 13
Pitt, William, later Earl of Chatham 251
Pocklington, John 77–8
Pocock, J.G.A. 97, 242
Poole 170–1, 178
Pope, Alexander 242
Pope, the 44, 74–5, 77, 104, 134, 137–8
Popery *see* Catholicism
Popish Plot (1678) 240
Pordage, John 162–3, 172, 191
Pordage, Samuel 191
Porter, John Holland 187
Portugal 6, 8, 10–12
Pory, John 31, 38
Povey, Thomas 94
Powell, Vavasor 141
prerogative, the royal 30–1, 36, 62–3, 81, 106–7
Presbyterians, Presbyterianism 58–9, 70, 72, 78, 81, 158–9, 181, 228–9, 257
Preston 114
Preston, John 7n., 19n., 26, 80

primitivism 49, 130, 191, 235–6
Prince, Thomas 143, 146
Prior, Mary 67
Privy Council, Privy Councillors
  21, 35, 37, 60, 64, 71
property 30–1, 54, 62–3, 69, 93,
  100, 107, 110, Chapter 7 *passim*,
  136, 155, 184, 220–1, 236, 246
prophesyings, the 60
prose Chapter 10 *passim*
Protestantism, Protestants 4, 8–10,
  Chapter 4 *passim*, 83, 103, 137,
  138, 140, 142, 151, 159, 167,
  173, 198, 200, 201, 209, 218,
  232, 233, 251
Providence Island, Providence
  Island Company, the 8, 12, 19
Prynne, William 26, 43, 75, 79–80,
  215
Psalms, metrical 199
Puritans; Puritanism; 'the Puritan
  Revolution' 7–8, 26, 37, 44–5,
  52, 55, Chapter 4 *passim*, 114,
  139, 153, 167, 173, 181–2, 185,
  188, 201, 210, 218, 222, 225,
  228, 234, 242
Putney; Putney Debates, the 109,
  118, 126, 203
Puttenham, George 199–200
Pym, John 19, 29, 31, 33, 41–2,
  51, 63–4, 70, 73, 76, 141
Pyne, Hugh 27–8

Quakers 45, 74, 84, 129, 131, 148,
  Chapter 9 *passim*, 220–1, 235,
  239–40
Quarles, Francis 199, 214, 234

Rainborough, Colonel Thomas
  118, 122, 126, 178
Rainborough, Major William
  171–2, 178
Ralegh, Sir Walter 9, 19, 30, 38,
  48, 50, 209, 211
Randall, Giles 43
Ranelagh, Katherine Boyle, Lady
  97
Ranters, the 45, 74, 85, 90, 114,
  117, 141, Chapter 9 *passim*, 213,

220, 225–6, 246
Read, Lieut.-Col. Thomas 178
Reading 169
Rees, Joan 199
Reeve, John 84, 154, 156, 163–5,
  168, 171, 187
Reeve, Thomas 164
Reformation, the 57, 65, 67, 69,
  76, 78, 83, 102–3, 133, 216, 250
Restoration, the (1660) 16, 21,
  53–4, 93–4, 108–9, Chapter 11
  passim
Revolution, the American 112,
  251–3
Revolution, the English 1–3,
  Chapters 2 and 3 *passim*, 56, 58,
  79, Chapters 5 and 7 *passim*, 133,
  139, 141, 148, 197, 204–5,
  208–9, 211, 216–17, 220–3, 229,
  236–7, 242–3, 245, 247, 252, 256
Revolution, the French 1, 3, 15,
  19, 37, 101, 112, 139, 247,
  251–2
Revolution, the Russian 1, 3, 19,
  139, 251
Revolution, the 'Glorious' of 1688
  21–2, 82–3, 96, 100–1, 110, 113
Revolution, the Industrial 1,
  16–18, 20, 23, 247, 256
Revolution, the Scientific 17–18
Rhode Island 192
Rich, Sir Nathaniel 32, 47
Rich, Lady Penelope 213n.
Richard II, King of England 25,
  206–7
Richard III, King of England 206
Richardson, Samuel 243
Rinuccini, Archbishop 138, 146
Robins, John 156, 164, 166, 171–2,
  179, 187–8
Robinson, Henry 75
Rochester 184
Rochester, John Wilmot, Second
  Earl of 95, 110, 191, 205, 222,
  227, 231, 235, 240
Romania, Romanians 43
Rome 140, 153, 207
Roses, Wars of the 89, 107, 206
Ross, Alexander 163, 185

Rous, Francis 76, 157
Rous, John 39, 46
Royal Society of London, the
17–18, 109, 234, 236–8, 241
Royalists 80, 84, 108, 112, 139–40,
143, 162–3, 185, 223
Rudé, George 245
Rudyerd, Sir Benjamin 27, 74
Rushdie, Salman 256
Rushworth, John 93, 240
Russell, the Hon. Conrad, later
Earl 1, 34, 42, 73, 198, 203
Russia, Russians 3, 20, 243
Rymer, Thomas 230

St Bartholomew's Day 134
St George's Hill, Surrey, 116
Salmon, Joseph, Ranter (or
near-Ranter) 85, 90, 156, 159n.,
169n., 172, 176–9, 187, 194
Salmon, Joseph, Swedenborgian
192
Salmonet, Robert Mentet de 87–8
Sandwich, Edward Montagu, Earl
of 94
Sandys, Sir Edwin 32n., 49, 202,
216
satire 205, 235
Sawyer, Sir Edmund 33
Saye and Sele, William Fiennes,
Viscount 50
Scotland, Scots 8–9, 13, 22, 28–9,
65–8, 80–1, 88, 134, 137–9,
149–50, 171, 214, 224, 242, 255,
257
Scott, Thomas 26, 38, 44–5, 80,
104, 200, 210, 221, 233
sea-dogs 7–9, 19
Second Coming, the 121, 123,
230–1
sectaries 140, 182
Sedgwick, William 93, 148, 168–9
Seekers 159, 166, 193
Selden, John 28, 31, 40, 63, 75,
240
Selden, Raman 198
Sellar, W.C. 253
Settlement Act, 1662, the, 239–40
Seymour, Sir Francis 30

Shakespeare, William, 2, 38, 86,
106, 163, Chapter 10 *passim*,
229, 237, 243, 248
Sharpe, Kevin 105
Sharrock, Roger 176
Shelford, Robert 74–5
Shelley, Percy Bysshe 202
Shepherd, Simon 37, 106, 198
Sheppard, Samuel 162–3
Sheppard, William 163
Sherland, Christopher 41
ship money 10, 43
Shirley, James 214–15
Sibbes, Richard 182n., 202n.
Sibthorp, Robert 61, 63–4
Sicily 209
Sidney, Algernon 100, 240–1
Sidney, Sir Henry 17, 140, 147
Sidney, Sir Philip 27, 40, 105,
208–9, 250
Simnel, Lambert 134
Sinfield, Alan 198
Skinner, Quentin 99
slavery, slave trade 4, 9, 12, 17,
254–5, 257
Smith, H.F. Russell 131
Smith, Nigel 158, 180, 193–4
Smith, W. 178
Snow, V.F. 82–3, 87
Society for the Propagation of the
Gospel, the 17
Somerset 171
Sommerville, Johann 54, 63, 75n.
Southampton 170
Southerne, Thomas 226, 231, 241
Southwark 161
Spain 4, 6, 8–12, 16–17, 19, 21–2,
25, 35, 41, 44–6, 49, 61, 65–6,
74, 76–7, 87, 133–5, 137, 140,
144, 206, 209–10, 213
Spelman, Sir Henry 40
Spenser, Edmund 40, 60n., 135–6,
145, 147, 150, 200–1, 211, 236
Spenserian poets, the 200–2, 211
Sprat, Thomas 94, 98, 224, 234,
237–8
Staffordshire 171–2
Staithes, Yorkshire 169
Stalin, Josef 189–90

Star Chamber, Court of 21, 64–5
Stavely, Keith 198
Staves, Susan 55n., 198, 214, 225, 241
Sterne, Laurence 4, 243
Sternhold, Thomas 199
Sterry, Peter 168, 192
Stevenson, Laura 241
Stockholder, Katherine 199
Story-Wilkinson separation, the 170
Strafford, Earl of see Wentworth, Sir Thomas
Strangeways, Sir John 30
Stone, Lawrence 52, 247
Strasbourg 65
Stratford-upon-Avon 163
Strode, William 33
Stubbe, Henry 95
Suckling, Sir John 215
Suffolk 43, 46, 171
Suffolk, John de la Pole, Duke of 41
Surinam 226
Surrey 115
Sussex 169–70
Sutherland, James 233
Sweden 66
Swift, Jonathan 18, 242–3
Switzerland 65
Sydenham, Colonel William 167
Sylvester, Joshua 200

Taiping rebels, the 243
Tangier 12
Tany, Thomas (Theauraujohn) 155–6, 160n., 163–4, 166, 172, 178, 189
Tawney, R.H. 37, 246–7
taxation Chapters 2 and 3 passim, 62–3, 68, 107
Taylor, Barbara 98
Taylor, Edward 193, 235
Taylor, Thomas 181
Temple, Sir William 94
Thatcher, Mrs Margaret 244, 252
Thirty Years War, the 8–11, 72, 80, 137, 140
Thomas, Sir Keith 46, 98, 195, 197, 245
Thomas, Peter 216
Thomason, George 219
Thompson, Edward 15, 196, 245
Throgmorton, Francis 65
Tickell, John 173, 185
Tilbury 105
tithes 78, 173, 239
Tobago 9
Toland, John 97, 240–1
Torr, Dona 188
Tourneur, Cyril 86
Traherne, Thomas 191, 222, 235
Trapnel, Anna 162–3
Trapp, John 163, 173
Trevor-Roper, H.R., now Lord Dacre 247
Tricomi, A.H. 205n.
Trinidad 9
Turkey, Turks 83, 120, 208
Turner, James 198
Turner, Thomas 199
Turner, Timothy 42n.
Tyacke, Nicholas 56, 58, 76
Tyndale, William 200, 233
Tyranipocrit Discovered 144

Udall, John 65
Ulster 151
Underdown, David 188
USSR, the 4, 100, 248, 251
United Provinces, the see Netherlands, the
USA 3, 100, 102, 251, 253
Usher, R.G. 67, 70
Ussher, James, Archbishop of Armagh 46
Uxbridge 170

vagabondage, vagabonds 16, 136, 140, 174
Vane, Sir Henry 163
Vaughan, Henry 111, 199, 202n.
Venice; Venetian Ambassador, the 9, 22–3, 27, 35–7, 46, 48, 70
Victoria, Queen of England 113
Villiers, George see Buckingham, Duke of
Virginia; Virginia Company 8, 202

Voltaire (François Marie Arouet)
101
Vossius, Isaac 17

Wadham College, Oxford 222
Waldensians the 144
Wales 134, 139
Walker, D.P. 236
Wall, Moses 15–16
Wallace, William 214
Waller, Edmund 224, 235
Walsingham, Sir Francis 19, 60
Walton, Brian 238
Walton-on-Thames 160
Walwyn, William 118, 142–4, 146,
148, 151, 154, 160, 180, 230, 252
Warbeck, Perkin 134
Warboys, Huntingdonshire 161
Wards, Court of 21, 211
wardship 14, 205
Warwickshire 93, 170–1
Waterhouse, Edward 96
Waterloo, battle of 255
Weald, the 66
Webbe, Thomas 156, 171–2, 178–9
Webster, Charles 17
Webster, John 2, 167, 198, 201,
205, 213, 224
Wellingborough 171
Wells 171
Wentworth, Sir Thomas, Earl of
Strafford 33, 41, 65, 70–1, 137,
206
Wesley, John 192
West Indies, the 9, 12, 17, 91, 147,
192, 255
Western Design, Cromwell's 11,
209
Westphalia, Treaty of 140
Wexford 168
Weymouth 27–8, 169–70
Wharton, Philip, Lord 97
White, Peter 57
Whitehead, John 169
Whitgift, John, Archbishop of
Canterbury 44–5, Chapter 4
passim
Whiting, C.B. 187, 192
Wigan 114–15, 118

Wilding, Michael 100, 198, 216
Wildman, John 96, 220
Wilkins, George 205n., 211–13, 226
Wilkinson, Robert 194
William of Orange, William III,
King of England 12–13, 96, 113,
255
Williams, C.M. 90n.
Williams, John, Bishop of Lincoln,
Archbishop of York 75
Williams, Roger 91, 143
Wilson, Arthur 36
Wiltshire 25, 36, 164, 171
Winchester 170
Winstanley, Gerrard 83, 100, 113,
Chapter 7 passim, 154, 160, 163,
167, 174, 180, 185, 189–90,
193–4, 200, 204, 207, 230–2,
235, 250n.
Winthrop, John 80
Winwood, Sir Ralph 31, 36, 61n.,
210
witchcraft, witches 236
Wither, George 40, 90–1, 143n.,
200–1, 234
Wittreich, Joseph 198, 226
women 53–4, 155, 160, 176, 213,
228–9, 244–6
women preachers 158
Wootton, Sir Henry 102
Worden, Blair 223
Wren, Matthew, Bishop of Ely 63,
91–2
Wren, Matthew, son of the above
238
Wrightson, Keith 52, 72, 110
Writer, Clement 220
Wyclif, John 248
Wyke, Andrew 172–3, 175n.

Yeatman, R.J. 253
Yeltsin, Boris 248
Yonge, Walter 39, 50
York 169, 178, 256
Yorkshire 169–71
Young Thomas, 88

Zurich 65
Zwicker, S.N. 54–5, 198, 224, 227